NO PROVEN SCHEME

A Culture of Mendacity

Anthony Falls Jr.

After painstaking work and innumerable hours, the author wishes to acknowledge his many mentors having given support, advice and invaluable insight into the characters and meaning the novel portrays–based on the tragic and true story of the once, and nearly forgotten world's largest farmer – AFJr.

CHAPTER 1

A number of rather sinister actions were connived at with the same view in mind; for instance, people who should have been put on trial and sent to Siberia, were recommended for promotion.

–Fyodor D

Robert Walsh was born into what was commonly known, in the days of a declining agrarian way of life on the plains, as a relatively-speaking "dirt poor" dust bowl farm family, more typical than not perhaps in 1928. Their homestead was located twelve miles from the nearest town, Nundas, South Dakota, on a gravel road that was albeit impassible in winter because of blizzards, and in spring because of mud.

One of Robert's mementos of the country to city transition was the familiar image he and the family observed as they traveled the narrow gravel road of the family's journey to church and toil–a cycle of countless seasons he would experience throughout his life in a split second–the snow covered, then barren fields turning to green sprouts under the sun becoming stiff stalks before turning yellow as he stared out the window on the driver's side. In his mind the same countless views appeared again and again, as over time the experience united into one image. It was as if the unconscious was reincarnating his memories that appeared like motion picture previews flashing across his mind in an instant before the main features; and, not unlike a *petit mal* those incursions occurred at the gateways of consciousness, the borderlines of experience, when he felt stress, or euphoria, merging the events of past and present in his life into a single unit not unlike a microfiche under the viewing apparatus. As time passed the narrative oddly became shorter and even more compressed. Nonetheless, it was always similar: the vision ended at the weather-beaten Barbasol sign, and only extended a few hundred feet further west into the city limits of

Nundas. The daydream was just as he recalled the scene on the east side of town, on the south side of the road–the lone signal of life in a dying community, planted fifty feet away from a faded and long-neglected speed limit post. Over time, the color of the subconscious flow changed from black and white to gray. It would fade away and recur again unpredictably.

The town survived precariously on the edge of the gaunt prairie that stretched west to the Summit hills. For agricultural commerce reasons, the county maintained the one tar road of Nundas with curb and gutter that ran straight down main street between several old wood framed, tar paper, brick facade buildings on either side of the street, including a general store at the east end, and a US Post Office on the north side attached to a small café with a closed sign in the window. Nundas lays on a diagonal about 50 miles either way NE to SE between Watertown and Sioux Falls, SD as the crow flies. The lone speed limit sign–15 mph strictly enforced–leans slightly to the road twenty feet from another sign that read: "City of Nundas" Population 650. The sign was not updated after 1945, the year Robert graduated from high school.

The Walsh farm, along with few others in the area, had barely survived the Great Depression living on the edge of the dust bowl raising corn, wheat, barley and oats, along with a few milk cows, and pigs in the annex of the barn. A ramshackle coop close to the thick boxelder grove, that broke the fierce winter gales, housed a few laying hens that produced limited income for Robert's mother who did laundry, and housekeeping for the elderly folk that remained in town. She depended on that trickle of petty cash to maintain a scant weekly budget selling her produce at 20 cents a dozen to her "customers in the city" as she referred to them. To cut corners, she mended her sons' school clothing though her crippled legs and frail fingers were shriveling, ravaged by a mysterious disease, until the weakness and fatigue that put her in a wheelchair limited her involvement in supporting the household.

In Robert's memory, no woman could have done more for him than Agnes did. She had contributed a great share of the

ANTHONY FALLS JR.

labors of a small farming business, while maintaining the two-bedroom Walsh home and caring for her two boys. Harold became increasingly irascible as his small farm slowly faded into ineffectiveness the way the town itself that is no longer featured in the *Rand McNally* did. The rural economy was shrinking along with its population and those few folks and families that scraped out a living within the city limits of a residential area not much larger than the modern sports and university complex of SDSU, home of the Jackrabbits, the growing State college within miles of the farm which was becoming the showcase of the athletic talent of eastern South Dakota and Western Minnesota at War's end. From that time on, Brookings continued to evolve as the prime university of South Dakota, thriving and expanding as the weeds were choking out the Walsh homestead, and Harold was renting 80 acres to his neighbors.

Father Harold Walsh was oldest son of the original homesteader Abner Walsh. His father's brother died of an untreated appendix when the doctor from Madison could not reach the farm during a snowstorm in the brutal winter of 1915. Thereafter, Harold Walsh was the only son of German immigrants who arrived in St Paul about 1870. He had two sisters Edna and Alberta. The family rode the Milwaukee Road to Milbank fifty miles north of Nundas, which was as close as they could ride the train to the tiny community they intended to settle in.

According to Agnes, in order to reach their new home, the settlers rode a freight lorry that resembled a prairie schooner pulled by four mules, that held all their worldly possessions, south to Madison where they stayed over a few days before moving on to the 80-acre parcel of land Father Harold had purchased at $5.00 an acre that amounted to his $400 life savings. The Walshs arrived at their homestead with no fanfare, claiming land Father Abner had allocated at a discount from the government on contract arrangements to own and buy land and transportation from the JJ Hill railroad trail, in the aftermath of the Black Hills gold rush.

Robert was informed often of the epic Walsh journey from the old country to a homestead in the new land by his mother as if some nobility was attached to it; the description changed from time to time as though it may have been more fiction than fact. Robert never really knew if his parents had a choice to live anywhere but in a rundown clapboard shack his folks owned as he grew to manhood. The drafty two-bedroom house, its walls stuffed with newspaper insulation, the red-hot potbelly wood burner, a kettle of water steaming on top of it—remained an indelible image of the experience of his impoverished youth forever stamped in his mind.

Years later, Robert would recall the bitter cold prairie wind shaking and rattling their home about in the howling blizzards of January that raced across the South Dakota prairie those terribly harsh winters. As a kid it hadn't bothered him. In his later years he wondered how his ancestors had survived. It is not surprising young Robbie had learned to live with a latent resentment to his legacy; he carried a chip, sometimes a boulder, on his shoulder until his dying day toward those farmers more fortunate than he.

Born a year before the Wall Street crash, Robert attended country school and began high school in Madison as the wars on both sides of the ocean were winding down. In the early grades, he wore one pair of blue jeans washed every Saturday; his school trousers were supposed to last the entire school year, which was more than some of the other boys had. Besides his work overalls and two flannel shirts his mom bought for him at Woolworths in Watertown, when she visited her sister and husband, young Bob wore a pair of work boots to school except when there was a dance. In the closet he shared with his brother hung one suit his size for special occasions; to those events he wore shiny black bluchers bought from the Sears Roebuck catalog. Father Harold made sure his sons polished their shoes before church on Sunday at St. Lawrence Catholic Church of Madison, SD.

Until he outgrew them, his worn out clothes were replaced by another of the same style until he tapped out at a size 10 shoe in eighth grade. His brother Ansel was three years older so most of young Robbie's hand-me-downs were either worn out or two sizes too large for Robert to fit well in. From his early experiences, frugality was one of the first traits the young Mr.

ANTHONY FALLS JR.

Walsh acquired. In those early days Robert had not yet learned to resent poverty. To their credit his parents never mentioned the subject of resentment toward thy neighbor's good as it was preached in the sermons of Father McDonald. The Walshs appeared to live and have just like everybody in the Catholic Church; Robbie owned as much as the rest of the kids in his class of 31, 14 boys and 17 girls. In those days none of the farm kids had more clothes and goods than he did, and that's what he kept track of.

His earliest measurement of class status compared to others was that of Johnny Vernon, the barber's son, his best friend in town. John had a bicycle but you didn't need one on the farm according to his mom. The barber's kid had a comic book collection he shared with Robbie; he loved to stay over at John's house because his mom was a lively healthy woman who treated him like one of the family. He looked forward to those overnights and sometimes a weekend in town when he was invited into the Vernon home once in a while.

In contrast to the urgency of his younger sibling, Ansel was a reserved, scholarly boy who spent most of his time with his father in the fields. Robert's older brother seemed to have little interest in the life of the town although at six feet and one hundred seventy pounds Ansel was recruited to played tackle on the Madison football team. Ansel enlisted in the Navy as soon as he graduated from high school. He was stationed at Subic Bay in the Philippine Islands in 1944 and '45, carrying on his assigned duties as a first mate in ordnance loading shells on the fleet of battleships and destroyers that floated in the Manila harbor as the war in the Pacific theater ended.

After the war, Ansel went on to college at Iowa State under the G.I. bill; while there he earned a research fellowship in behavioral psychology. Ansel Walsh became an assistant professor who eventually achieved tenure at Indiana State University. He married and had two daughters. Robert and Ansel remained in close contact over the years. As his business expanded Robert relied on the counsel of his brother, and on his insight into abnormal psychology and personality disorders caused by financial stress.

Isolated Nundas folks didn't think about poverty during the foreign war or for several years after. As Robert reflected later, in those days the country was celebrating a spectacular event that had no relevance to the community whatsoever. But those who could read were excited about the headlines of the bomb and the remarkable re-election of Harry Truman, the highly successful farm boy from Missouri. Ansel and Robert admired men like the President who had shucked their "shit-kickers" for wingtips.

The reality on small farms and small towns in the middle of the country was not affected by the global turmoil. These communities remained roughly a generation or maybe two behind the cities of the East, including the rapidly growing metropolitan area two hundred miles east known as "Mill City", as Harold referred to the Twin Cities, with its cluster of grain elevators dwarfing the other buildings and surrounded by parking lots.

In tiny isolated rural communities, bygone and forgotten places like Nundas that are no longer listed, a certain sense of resentment is bound to happen when its name is de-listed on the road atlas while its tiny neighbor Rutland appears on the Sinclair Oil map. The general perception was that nobody was better off than anybody else. There was solace in commiseration of the congregation; under Christ they shouldered their resignation–at least they were not as bad off as the "poor and needy who shall hope on the Name of the Lord" spoken of in *Sophonias 3*: "We are not as poor as them God help them," his mother affirmed more than once.

The few folks who were exempt–the doctors, dentists, lawyers, and business owners spared the load–were scarcely seen at Mass, rumored to be in Phoenix in February or vacationing at Lake Okoboji or the Black Hills in August. Unlike booming New York, the fading towns of the prairie were still suffering side effects like a delayed moonshine hangover from the dust bowl days. What young men there were planned to be

ANTHONY FALLS JR.

moving along to the cities where there was work; or those in the military re-enlisted. The country folk accepted the harsh reality the giants of the earth had imposed upon the people of the plains. Though there were fireworks displays on the 4th of July, a sense of unseen oppression existed virtually at the unconscious kernel of community thought.

Nothing more than the Sunday collections, gathering at the bottom of the hand to hand passed basket, reflected that state in the church. Young Rob was well aware the priest was shaking his finger at his father for "holding back his tithe from the church"–when he could barely afford gas for the tractor and truck let alone drive 15 miles in treacherous cold to attend 8 o'clock Mass. Robert dreaded those sermons, as Father McDonald *railed* upon the miserly offerings of his impoverished parish each Sunday, as if that particular message lay at the core of every Gospel reading, "and he will strike down those who oppose his will; and you will know I am the Lord when I lay my hand upon you," keeping his parish informed they were the *skinflints* of eastern South Dakota–letting the congregation know their small sacrifices were not enough to please Bishop Schladweiler of the Diocese of Sioux Falls, who would be coming for an audit and to preach at their church on the Feast of the Blessed Virgin Mary.

Everybody knew the only people in town with any money were the Mallory family, who owned the Farmers Bank of Rutland-Nundas branch that doubled as the post office–closed on Saturdays. Rumor had it that John Dillinger himself, or one of his gang, had deposited $15000 cash in the Rutland branch under an assumed name after he robbed the Northfield Bank in Minnesota. Hearsay was that Mr. Mallory had asked no questions at the time because the well dressed, heavy-set depositor had parked his sedan outside the front door of the bank, carried in a suitcase obviously packing heat under an expensive overcoat, and the mysterious depositor was doing the Rutland bank a *favor–doubling* its deposits–by harboring their loot in a remote location; and in the process, laundering gangster money. This was just a rumor of course.

The Mallorys appeared on Sundays and holidays spilling out of their sparkling new Chrysler with their three children, two girls and a boy a year younger than Robert. After church the prospering and proliferating family would routinely appear at the Pheasant Feather restaurant of Rutland for coffee, fresh baked rolls, ice cream and sodas for the children in the summer–for a brief moment joining the community conversation, laughing and joking with everybody else about the good Father McDonald's redundant sermons.

There was one doctor available to the community associated with the Madison general hospital. Doc Hanson made house calls; he appeared at an improvised clinic attached to the part-time police station in Rutland. The clinic was open on Tuesday through Thursday. Mr. Hanson drove a black Ford with skirts and a front window visor on it; the doctor's car reminded young Robert of a mobster car he had seen in a Cagney movie, looking ever so much like the one Bugsy Malone rode around in while he was creating the Flamingo he imagined. Doc Hanson had a son who was a decorated pilot in the air war going on in Europe. Mason Hanson had at one time played guard for the Jackrabbit basketball team before graduating in 1942 with a degree in engineering. According to the *Watertown Herald Tribune*, Mason, who flew a Thunderbolt over France, visited his parents in Madison in March 1944 while he was on leave from his station in Europe.

And there was Mr. Stralen whose partner in the lumber yard, if rumor was correct, absconded with half his fortune. Stralen managed to salvage enough of his money from the Redfield Federal S&L to set up a Coast to Coast franchise in Madison. He had two handsome sons, one older and one in Robert's class. As youngsters, the Stralen boys rode brand new Monarch bikes around town and always wore the best clothes at school. They were the boys who every girl in high school longed to sit beside, especially Donald Stralen with his blonde crew cut, wearing blue denims with a comb sticking out of the back pocket, looking a lot like James Dean as Robbie recalled. No wonder the girls flocked to him–he could still see the image of Donny proudly wheeling

ANTHONY FALLS JR.

up and down main street in his father's green polished Packard. The fortunate son would be seen "dragging main" with a new girl every week hanging on his shoulder before the Friday night movie at the Orpheum Theater next to the Oldsmobile dealership that had gone out of business.

Only the first six grades were taught in Nundas elementary that was closed in the 60's; after that the young kids were loaded on a bus and hauled to Madison. Until he entered high school, the only vehicle on the Walsh farm was his dad's ancient Dodge grain truck that he, his mom, and Ansel would squeeze into for the Sunday drive to church. Naturally, one of Robert's primary goals was buying a new Buick. In his youth the only folks that owned fancy cars were business owners; the few teachers who were tenured and drawing a salary drove old Fords and Dodges.

Most new teachers stayed only that first year, closely monitored as they were by parents and the school board that audited poor student performance and lack of discipline. Education graduates from Brookings could not help but perceive the shades were drawn early–activities of Nundas came to a standstill at 4:30 p.m. The town itself seemed to withdraw into a hibernate state as the six months of winter descended upon the community after All Souls Day until eight weeks after woodchuck's day.

Young Mr. Walsh was obviously intelligent. Robbie was encouraged by his mother to follow the scholarly path his brother Ansel had pursued; his parents were proud of the academic record of their oldest son. Ansel was always on the honor roll of Madison High School. On the other hand, Robert was seldom honored for his academic work. He regretted his reticence for study later when SDSU would not accept his application because he had not passed algebra in high school. Robbie's elementary teachers seemed disinterested in him for some reason; and he resented that. It seemed like the teachers only cared about the smartest or richest kids in school. His educators appeared bored with the curriculum, unable or unwilling to inspire Robert to achieve as his brother had. The only subjects that interested him were arithmetic and shop.

In particular, Robert was uninterested in the subjects of history, reading and writing, and his grades reflected his indifference. He suffered for lack of knowledge and related skills later in life. Yet Robert scored well in math and science compared to the less motivated farm kids he competed with who were looking forward to the day they took over dad's farm, an alternative much more attractive than the drudgery of going to class beyond middle school. In those days, kids could drop out after sixth grade if they were needed to work on the farm. Students that showed academic promise, as Ansel had, were bussed to Madison for junior and senior high school classes. At the same time, the quality of education in Nundas elementary declined as newly graduated SDSU teachers found it a cup of coffee whistle stop on the career path, before moving on to bigger schools in Watertown, Huron or Aberdeen.

Unlike his brother, Robert was bored with sports. It didn't seem practical. Nonetheless, the maturing young man was becoming increasingly aware of the pretty girls hanging out in the halls of Madison High, especially the high school principal's daughter Molly Raymond who he imagined dressed and acted like Marlene Dietrich in *Blue Angel*. Robbie lacked self confidence in dealing with sexuality issues, believing from an early age he had no chance whatsoever of ever attracting a girl as attractive as Molly who was out of reach in his estimation because of his stature as a poor farm boy. Molly was a year older than Robert and he never spoke a single word to her in four years at Nundas High. Molly was the first girl he actually desired so much it hurt. He often imagined what it would be like being in bed with her, and masturbated about acting upon that urgency.

As the impulses of puberty increased in intensity, the young man found himself dreading those church confessions that entitled him to communion, more and more each Saturday. Robbie started to rationalize his fantasies, and by the time he was a junior he no longer made any mention of the "lust for women" to Father McDonald who seemed to be as interested as he was in the taboo; it was McDonald who always brought up the subject in the booth that drove a spike between Robert and the

ANTHONY FALLS JR.

holy sacrament. He detested discussing a subject that was never mentioned in his home.

"Chastity" as if she were the Blessed Virgin herself, was the topic of religious instruction during release-time catechism classes. Along with the rest of the Catholics in elementary school, Robert had to attend afternoon classes Wednesday during the school year and for two more weeks during summer; that "dirty feeling" toward women he was attracted to increased during those sessions being taught by Sister Monica, who resided in the nunnery next to the church.

The same desire that plagued him was intensified in sessions discussing the catechism in depth. At the same time, the Catholic girls were encouraged to suppress their anxieties about sexual sin and never bring up the subject. By the time he was fourteen, Robert had discovered his expanding desire was not just for the girls in high school, but at Mass where he was attracted to the wives of the parish principals, being enamored by the trophy women of the rich and privileged in the church, as though the only reason he was there was to observe *them*–made him feel even more guilty. Robert could only look forward to the day, to the time he would be married and finally released from the curse; the burden that fantasy, as well as real sex before marriage was a mortal sin.

Such thoughts about religion constantly harassed young Robbie. By that time, he had started having the mysterious nocturnal emissions Father McDonald was so concerned about, their frequency and so on; he seemed to know all about them beforehand. More than any spiritual factor, confession was driving him away from the church he was strangely attracted to for its power to attract and assemble so many people for a purpose that was unknown to him. He could live with the guilt of anything, admitting it to someone else was a different animal completely. Since he had started to confess his more serious sins like lying, stealing and cussing, occasionally smoking cigarettes, he had developed a method of deflecting the grand inquisition to the more banal aspects of sinning. Over time, to escape detection, Robbie learned a technique to avoid confessing his dirty thoughts to Father McDonald when they were alone together in the confessional booth at St. Lawrence Catholic Saturday afternoon, so he could receive communion on Sunday.

By that time, about 7th grade, young Walsh knew Father McDonald recognized his voice and that he was admitting his irreverent desires to a perverted priest, like some kids were telling him about in their experiences with the reverend. Soon after Confirmation, Robert, who was proving to be a resourceful lad, had found a solution; he began tagging his hidden sins vaguely at the end of his list of legitimate venial sins like swearing, lying, stealing various items like candy, or -smoking, forgetting to send his mother a birthday card and so on, to deflect McDonald away from the normal question,

"Did you have any sexual thoughts about girls R–(oops)?"

"No Sir Father," he was prepared to respond. It was so much easier that way when all of our sins are viewed as mere omissions beseeching God, "forgive me Father for these and *other sins I can't remember.*"

After that experience, Robbie relied on and was comforted that he had developed a strategy of denial similar to that used by the Sicilian mafia; that strategy would serve him for the rest of his life. After seventh grade, knowing Father Mac knew his voice in the dark confessional, he conveniently relegated his reflections on Molly and an expanding roster of imaginary conquests as subjects he had forgotten to confess to the cabinet of abstractions from truthfulness, that replace reason and ethics from an early age to compensate for some perceived weakness– that must be overcome by cunning and deceit. From the age of twelve on, Robert developed a sophisticated but hidden personality that depended on denial of normal ethical and moral bases in dealing with authority. Using this method of deflecting blame upon more innocuous items served him well; from his youth through adulthood, Robert would receive the "Body of Christ" just as righteously as the rest of the congregation at Mass every Sunday.

Although he remained a Catholic all his life, Robert found it necessary to develop a philosophy to rationalize that if he just

ANTHONY FALLS JR.

happened to conveniently forget about his sins, add on a few good Samaritan acts for his inner circle, just fudge a little on the details of his sparse love for his neighbor; by going through the ritual, he would be forgiven by Christ and God–if in fact they actually did exist–more than figuratively within the dogma of prayers. By maturity, Robert had perfected an adjustment and adaptation to various congregations based on the Catholic catechism and specific religious ceremonies such as performing the "sign of the cross" and genuflecting; as well as speaking "In the name of the Father, the Son and the Holy Ghost. Amen." The authorities, principalities, and powers whoever they were would know he had at least made a symbolic effort and that's what the Catholic religion was based on–symbols, figures and property–thirty *trillion* dollars worth of real estate in the mid-19th century. To please his parents, Robert learned that all he really needed to do was to be there participating in the blessed sacraments, and learning the catechism. His minor shortcomings could always be forgiven eventually by plenary indulgences, mentioned in his parents' Douay Bible under Pope Pius the Twelfth–tithing; and, then there was always purgatory or "limbo" as alternatives to heaven other parishioners looked forward to.

Because religion was important to him, the possibility of détente or deferred, and hence *negotiable* judgment was appealing to Robert. It served as a cushion against inevitable condemnation that might be postponed for Catholics who avoided it with estate and will planning; that included those who were pious enough to pray and prepare for an alternative to eternal damnation in lieu of a plenary indulgence they could afford–*that* required intervention of the papacy.

Robert reviewed the principles of salvation he would someday be able to fall back on in case, for some reason, he couldn't make it to that last confession; dreading the loss of heaven and the pains of hell along with the privileges that went with it. His conscientiousness trait dovetailed neatly with religiosity, inherited from his mother, and was fully developed in those formative years. By the time he was eighteen, Robert's adult personality was emerging from its shell.

From that time on, Robert's unique hybrid of religious belief and customized moral and ethical code were all the assurances any Catholic desired. If he could make it to extreme unction he could not be denied his reward. Because of this strategy Robert was convinced he would be spared the fires of hell. No matter what he did one more sin would not matter; in case he had to commit them he assumed he would always have a chance to repent of any mortal sins at the last hour. Robert was reinforced by the blessings of his mother. As a child Robbie loved Agnes as Christ loved the Blessed Virgin. It was the saddest part of his life to have to watch his mother's once vibrant personality and health decline after his tenth year, when his mother was forty.

He would never forget the daily image of the grandfather clock ticking, its pendulum swinging as it sat in the background, off slightly to the left of Father Harold's recliner. There Robbie read the funnies, lying on the rug in front of the kerosene stove. His father dozed off after supper, Sunday paper on his chest open, where he had been reading the want ads looking for used farm machinery, in the cozy living room of the Nundas farmhouse. But then the hands on that clock forever stopped moving at 10:20 a.m. The scene in his mind never changed since the day the family had discussed the problem of putting mom in the nursing home, if it came to that; and it became fixed as an icon in Robert's mind–as clear as the image of the Mother of Christ had been on first Holy Communion day–and the family's last dinner together before his mom went into the nursing home.

Robert linked the two events; there was no need to start the antique clock purchased at his neighbor's farm auction after Harold's best friend, who helped every year at harvest, became tangled in the power take-off of the tractor when they were working together baling in 1940. As the grim tale spent, there wasn't much left of him when Harold found him after the tragic event; and how afterward unopposed Harold bought the clock on a single bid at the auction.

Like no other object, the image of the grandfather clock remained locked deep in his memory forever, with always another imagined-spin around the dial reminding him of those

ANTHONY FALLS JR.

awful days his mother had been diagnosed with some strange disease that put her in the hospital first, and thereafter kept her in bed for days at a time; until, finally a specialist from the Madison hospital announced that his mother's sickness was something the medical profession was just learning about during and after the War called *muscular atrophy*, an incurable disease not unlike Lou Gehrig's but different in terms of mortality. The young doctor, fresh out of medical school, informed the Walsh family Agnes might live in this state many years. Robert knew his beloved mother Agnes–probably the only woman he ever truly loved–would never be the same. Robert's father, as well as his mother, had never actually recovered after the grave diagnosis.

The stopped clock in the living room often reappeared to him as a memento of past failings, whenever one of his decisions had been compromised doing business as usual, with boundaries that may have appeared as unethical and immoral to some. It was the many acts of past contrition related to his boyhood experiences in Nundas, and Madison days, that were the security Robert needed to believe his spirit would ride forever above the frozen stubble of eastern South Dakota. He was the man who would return someday, wealthy. If he had been rich, he might have been able to save the farm and his mother as she slipped away. Instead, he and his father could do nothing for Agnes except place her in a hospice in Sioux Falls, which was better than wasting away in Madison. It was as if poverty itself created the hopeless situation Robert was determined to prevent from ever happening again.

Robbie, as he was known to his few friends, was a shy young man, uncoordinated and skinny, with little motivation in calisthenics and physical education, and even less interest in being on the Nundas Warriors football or basketball team as his brother had been. Athletics didn't interest him, which mirrored the attitude his father had that sports was a waste of time. However, Harold did attend all Ansel's football games, home and away, most of which were losses. And yet Harold relished those hours he spent on the sidelines with the other fathers who were proud of their boys. Those Friday nights under dim pole lights of the athletic field were the only involvement Harold had with the community. At those rare events he appeared to enjoy himself in the company of his peers sharing in a common interest with the other hopeful fathers on the sidelines. Despite their differences, it was apparent that Harold favored his oldest boy over Robert.

Though he was slim, Robert appeared as if he could have been an athlete: raw-boned, potentially muscular and one of the tallest boys in class at 5' 11", but he was not available. Tackling and shooting baskets didn't attract him. It would mean time away from chores his folks depended on him for. That was the excuse he used with Coach Raymond, the science teacher, who tried to persuade him to try out for the B-squad as one of the only boys his size in the freshman class.

"We don't have enough players your size Robbie. You won't have to dribble much. You're strong. All you have to do is stand under the basket. I can teach you how to rebound. One more chance, you could start right away."

"No thank you," Robert apologized, fall of his sophomore year.

Robbie was surprisingly an excellent swimmer, having learned to swim at his cousin's farm in a creek near Bellingham, Minnesota. He assured Mr. Raymond that if they had a swimming team at Madison he would have joined right away. Robert claimed his father needed him on the farm, so he never got into sports like his brother. There were times he regretted it because he knew that decision also kept him away from of the weekend social life of the school, as little excitement as there was; on Friday nights during harvest time, the high school football team was the only interest in the city. The town people sparked to life for those events on a crisp fall evening especially if one of their kids, or relative's kids was playing for the Dragons. The decision would keep Robbie even farther away from the prize cheerleaders he desired.

Robbie was not a bad looking young man. But he didn't fix himself up either, like the Hanson brothers who he secretly admired and yet despised for their sharp clothes. He had not seen such vanity (he recalled Jerry combing his gleaming

Brylcreemed locks in the lavatory between classes)–those brothers were the guys with the looks–the style the guys and the girls all desired obviously, he imagined. That and money. He envied *that* more than anything–that he was not like the town boys. *I'll have money someday*, he thought; the charisma would be there then, that he attached to Garfield and Gable puffing a cigarette. In those days, Sinatra was nothing more than a punk leering into the camera. But then again, sinister Frank looked something like his dad looked like when he was younger, before his hair turned gray and then white–before his farm accident– when the tractor came out of gear and backed up unexpectedly pinning him to the side of the barn, where Ansel found him screaming for help, with a broken rib cage, and lucky to be alive. Father Harold had spent three weeks in the Madison Hospital, barely surviving one of the most painful injuries a man could have according to the doctors and nurses. The elder Walsh was never the same after his farm accident.

Robert admired the way his Father appeared in the wedding picture on the mantle above the antique clock in the living room of the Walsh farmhouse. His dad was very handsome when he was young, before the Depression and his wife's illness changed his cheerful disposition. Robert often wondered what Harold's personality might have been had he not been saddled by the farm. Unlike his father, Robert would achieve the image he desired. To accomplish his goal, he would have to become the head of a commune–a conglomerate that resembled the Farmer's Union of Madison the Walshs bought fertilizer and fuel from. He would own it, while expanding one farm to many under a brand like Peavey, Continental and Cargill, where the names of the farms and farmer organizations that had replaced him, would be owned by him. It was an obvious assumption but not a practical thought under the circumstances, so he didn't dwell on it. Robert would need to start at the bottom and he knew it. In order to accomplish something in life his parents never had, he would have to come up with a design for a farm monopoly like the game he and his brother played monotonously as his parents listened to the radio.

The young man had his initial opportunity to join society he had felt no part of, in high school as an 11th grader, when one of the neighbors who rented 20 then 40 acres of alfalfa pasture with an eye toward eventually buying the farm, stepped in. Ansel was overseas. Since Harold had been crippled by his farm accident, Emil Johnson, who already owned a section in Grant-Duehl, volunteered to help his dad with milking in the afternoon. This neighborly act allowed Robert to join the Madison High School annual staff his junior and senior year. Robert knew, at a comparatively young age, he would not shoehorn into the business as a few of the other farm boys he grew up with had, and go directly from school into owning the family farm. There would be no farm to own by war's end the way it was going with the Walsh 80 acres. By the time he was ready to pull up stakes in Nundas, he knew Emil Johnson would be renting to own the Walsh homestead. For practical reasons, like increasing wealth through farming the land, young Walsh had basically retreated and begun his own vision of success; it was not so much title to the land that attracted Robbie to the profession, it was rather the more feudal aspects of managing a coop that appealed to him.

His first taste of society and the media whetted Robert's appetite for life in the fast lane as he perceived it, and after the hysteria of the war had cooled down. He learned that composing little stories and vignettes of his classmates was exciting but his language use was poor as a writer. His basic job was to sort and arrange photographs for different sections of the annual. From that experience, Robert learned he could become very good at organizing and arranging other people's work.

The youthful Robbie took a liking to the recognition and exposure he had to the intellectual side of life, and he relished his new experience in an office. His first exposure to media and what the city kids were doing gave him a glimpse of what his future might become. His annual staff position would lead the way to opening doors of a career in cities like Sioux Falls and Iowa City; these were the big towns as he pictured them when visiting by truck with Harold and Ansel and a load of corn ready for the scales and better prices than the Madison Farmer's elevator offered. Gas was cheap; some stations were selling for 15 cents a gallon, and the trip was worth it to each Walsh just to see those places where Robert imagined all the opportunities he had been missing on the farm existed.

"You will find your place Robert; that's what this life is all about," he recalled his mom saying. "If you don't give up, someday you will make it."

The experience on the Madison annual staff was the initial step in his profession. Before that, Robert had been an average student with no pretensions, expectation, or desire to go to college; and, he had never taken the intellectual side of his personality seriously. As his brother before him, Robert throughout high school had thoughts of joining the Navy after graduation, but with Japan's surrender the drama of the A-bomb altered his career plans.

With no actual goal in mind, Robert applied for a job at the Skelly station in Madison, pumping gas, cleaning windshields and changing tires. He felt obligated to his family since it was through his dad's influence with his longtime friend Elmer Raymond, who delivered bulk fuel to the farm, that he was offered employment, when there were so few jobs available with all the veterans returning to town.

His father had his own motives. Robert's dad needed help on the farm and didn't want his available son leaving town so soon or being too far away from home after he graduated. Harold could barely lift his left arm and needed him for chores around the farm by then. He had quarreled with Johnson, the renter, about the prices he was offering for his land, which would barely cover Agnes's bills once they moved her to a better nursing home.

Though he denied it, Robert's father had never recovered his strength after the farm accident crushed his arm and broke several ribs; that all happened the year before his brother Ansel left town for good to join the Navy. As he approached 60, father Harold's physical and mental health had deteriorated to the point that he was physically unable to lift Agnes around the house, when they had celebrated their "silver wedding anniversary" at the Madison Legion only a few years before.

By that time, Agnes could barely roll out of bed with his help into a wheelchair. Mr. Walsh was faced with the reality he could not do it himself, or afford nursing home care for his wife. Robert was thinking of finding an apartment in Madison, but he felt he owed his parents. He could not leave while they were both still living on the farm. If he stayed at home, he could help out on the farm driving tractor, and baling hay, because Robert's father had developed severe arthritis as the doctors called it, that disabled his arm after the accident that nearly took his life at harvest time 1942. All he could do was sit in his recliner next to the grandfather clock, listening to the farm market reports on KWAT. But Robert was restless. At one time he had plans to take over the 80 acres and expand to at least 160 renting, adding sections here and there as market prices increased; he would be buying up land as the surrounding farms went down, just as Emil Johnson had. But by graduation his plans of buying the homestead had vanished.

He realized that even if his father retired, he would not be satisfied–he wanted so much more to life than Nundas could ever offer. Every time a shining Buick with chrome hood vents or a flashy Studebaker drove through the Skelly station, he envied the driver, the passengers, the car itself as he washed the windshield, checked the oil and pumped gasoline. But the only business he knew was farming and it seemed like a handicap. Robert was resigned to slug it out in the trenches until something better came along: he had no other choice. He was resigned to his fate in 1948.

But Robert's life was about to change. He was taken by surprise one day when the county agent George Tate, a regular customer at the station, asked him if he would be interested in doing some weed inspection for the county in the spring of 1949. It would only be a seasonal job, but it could lead to opportunities with the government in the future.

Robbie jumped at the opportunity. That first spring of 1949, he began what he considered his first career. For the first time in his life, he felt a sense of professional pride like nothing he had known on the farm. He was now driving out of the county garage every morning in an ancient orange Dodge pick-up truck with a fifty-gallon tank welded to the box. Faded text read "Grant County Weed Inspection" on the door. With a sense of pride Robert believed he was performing a necessary, and in that sense, professional function like a physician or surgeon eradicating disease. He enjoyed recounting the progress he made while chatting with farmers about their pesky insurgent weeds. At that stage of his life Robbie relished being paid for driving insouciantly from farm to farm, in a fog as it were; and, odd as it seemed in his line of work, a man adjusted to the vapors of DDT, 2-4D and other chemicals suspended in an oily vapor he sprayed daily several summers he lost track of–for lack of a social life–while he remained indirectly attached to society through public service.

Robbie would remember the chemical scent and the strange attraction he felt toward the source of his first tangible power. He would never forget the stench that penetrated his clothes– and his nightmares–as well as his nose tissues. It's not "Old Spice" but it's not that bad he told himself. I won't be doing this forever.

Despite its limitations, the job had benefits. Robert loved the sense of being on his own, doing something important, extirpating different genres of noxious weeds; at his higher moments of the trade, he believed that the science of eradication would ultimately benefit through his research. The thought of being a scientist in his own realm of power excited him. For the time being, he was doing the job he was destined for: out of sight, out of mind, strangely alone. He would nod off at times after lunch or after coffee break in the afternoon thinking about the few available girls his age left in Madison; then he would snap out of it in a quarter, sometimes half an hour, and wake up with a start–as if he had passed out in the cab of his truck. At those moments he would be refreshed, anxious to be back on the path of his dreadful mission against the cockleburs and bitter nightshade.

He was free for the first time in his life from the care and cares of his parents; mowing down decadent weeds with his tank and chemicals he thought of as his weapons, eradicating the annoying invasive weeds that soaked up moisture and hindered production: hemp, thistle, mustard, dandelions, milkweed, and unwanted dogwood in ditches. Robert learned to recognize all the invader species his first summer on the job. In the evening returning to the farm, he could barely wash the chemical scent off his hands, and his clothes reeked of it. There were times he avoided his favorite hangout, the Legion Club on a Friday night, because he imagined that even a shower, shave and clean clothes wouldn't wash away the skin deep stench.

As a favor, his southern neighbor who farmed a half section, Fred Anderson said that Robert didn't have to drive all the way back to Madison Friday after servicing the hind end of the county. Fred would allow Robert to rinse and empty his herbicide tanks spraying the remaining chemicals around Fred's barn, as the weeds, crab grass, and dandelions of the manure field shifted from year to year. The impression of chemical odor he had adjusted to in his youth, reminded Robert throughout his life–like every time he drove into Super America–of his boyhood chores back on the farm, filling up the tractor from the hundred-gallon fuel tank standing on four legs and filled with *"petrol"* –as father, who could speak German, used to call it. It had always been his particular job to fuel up the ancient Allis his dad depended on back in the day on the farm. Robbie found the work experience of his youth helpful as he moved up the career ladder.

"Now don't you be lightin' up any of them damn Lucky Strikes around my farm neither Ansel, I mean Bobby. I seen that pack you're always carrying around in your shirt pocket; that habit could kill ya'll someday. It's no good for nothin' what you learn't from them young fellers in town, that got you into a bad habit," Anderson warned. "I don't know how you can stand the smell of that tobacco puffin' out your nose and ears all the time anyhow?"

Harry Walsh had admonished his son Robert about the same vice he had picked up at age fourteen. But he had every reason

ANTHONY FALLS JR.

to keep him on the farm as his arthritis worsened, so he let Robbie smoke, "but not in your mother's house." Years later he quit the habit but it may have been too late to prevent damage to his heart, lungs and brain cells. In fact, a particular reason Robert enjoyed his solitary work was the ample time he had for smoking cigarettes in the cab of his weed inspector's truck.

For several years in his early twenties, the young man was content performing a job that lasted from March into the harvest season. Another benefit of seasonal work was he had the winters off; he could lounge around the farm helping his aging parents. Later in life, as the ditches narrowed, he often made unconscious comparisons noticing that fields widened sometimes another twenty percent as swamps were drained and natural watershed ditches shrunk, adding more tillable acreage to farms where once native prairie grasses, stands of red dogwood, sumac, and sage brush served as wild life habitat.

Robert was of a generation that had the privilege of observing a natural state of the prairie in the post war pre-DDT years when red wing blackbirds roamed as rare as sparrows; flocks of pheasants thick as smoke rose from golden cornfields that surrounded Redfield. It was at once a spectacular view of mallards, redheads, bluebills, pintails and canvasbacks circling the abundant sloughs before descending on mirror-like surfaces as the fiery sun rose in the East on a frosty fall landscape; and, witnessing the same spectacle, repeating the cycle in another magnificent purple and gold sunset.

He had a rare opportunity, like a wildlife photographer, to observe and preserve the absolute beauty of nature without the distractions of school and a persistent desire for venal pleasure. All cares receded as he drove about the plains amidst tall Dakota blue grasses, that seemed to engulf the gravel and dirt paths he traveled upon performing the work that had been granted him, weaving his truck between clumps of willow, hedge growths of boxelder and buckthorn. He unconsciously calculated that the ditches were twice as wide in his youth as they had become a generation or two later. Robert noted he had been a part of that conversion to a more comprehensive and productive agricultural base, and he was proud of his contributions.

In his unconscious, Robert never lost sight of the hundreds of miles of ditches and solitude they offered the younger man. He would dream of traveling the old roads of his youth searching for the experience that once invigorated him but no longer; subconsciously, reviving his daily work in nightly nightmares– extending the dreadful labor for all time.

Somebody had to do a job nobody else wanted and he was the chosen one. It was he who had eradicated an immense population of alien invaders without regard for his own health. Strange as it seemed–and he never questioned the thought of it– that for some unexplained reason it was the sight of the wilted weeds, in retrospect, that he had killed and reported in his log in the line of duty, that gave him as much if not more satisfaction than the sacred portraits of nature, preserved in the recesses of his mind, like statues of saints in the church.

The little publicized dangers of chemical poisoning and its health consequences in later life, hinted at on label warnings, never crossed Robert's mind in those days. The hazardous material had been redistributed from the original containers by county employees before his usage, so he paid little attention to vague warnings. He was careful enough with the dangerous chemicals he handled. He wore bulky rubber gloves to avoid direct contact with the liquid and a mask to prevent inhaling the vapor on windy days. His protective actions were minimal in the thirty or so years before the MSDS was strictly enforced as the regulations manual warned it should be. He knew enough of the basics–to never piss or spray DDT directly into the wind. The job eliminating weeds of all species suited his personality well for the time being, while he carried on in his first real job. As he penned to his brother Ansel, "It's a hell of a lot better than fighting the North Koreans isn't it?"

After a few seasons eradicating weeds, he was looking forward to a promotion, if and when his supervisor retired. Robert was in no hurry; a few more lazy years working for the county until he figured out his real life mission would be soon enough. He read over the posted jobs on the bulletin board in the county garage every week; most of those positions required a college degree, as did most positions that were open with the South Dakota Department of Agriculture. But he could bypass some of the requirements because he had two years working experience with the county. Robert was determined to get ahead. His brother Ansel had received a research and teaching graduate assistantship in the psychology department of Iowa State University. The promotions Robert desired would have to wait until he finished the extension course out of Dakota State College. He enrolled in winter quarter 1950, on a probationary basis, as his high school grades had been prohibitive until his experience opened the door a crack.

With time on his hands and no distractions, Robert was about to begin developing his learning skills, sharpening the focus of training that began back in his two-year stint sorting and filing for the Madison High School annual. In his last assignment for his first *Agriculture Technology 101* course, Robert aced the final paper with, "Loss of production acres due to drainage problems in the Missouri River Watershed Basin" that would bring him an A- for content and organization, and a C- for style, grammar, mechanics and spelling. That piece of writing, once it was corrected by his instructor Mr. Ready and the research that supported it was codified correctly, caught the attention of the Agricultural Engineering faculty at Dakota State College. Robert eventually achieved an associate's degree in plant and soil science. From that time on, document writing became an irreplaceable skill in Robert Walsh's career development.

One morning in the garage, before heading off to a selection of sloughs in Otrey Township, while Robert was inspecting his tanks of 2-4D armed with weapons to stop the unwanted intruders dead, Eddie Rausch, who had replaced Raymond, slipped up quietly next to him. Rausch, with little time remaining before his pension, informed Robert he would be ready to retire by 1954–reminding him that was only two and a half years away–the blink of an eye in a career.

Rausch informed Robert the commissioners liked his work ethic. He kept to himself, didn't interfere with other employees, and did his job effectively showing signs of initiative whenever it was possible on a job nobody else wanted, or held, for more than several years. His boss encouraged young Walsh that if he made a career of it with the department of agriculture, he would be drawing a decent pension from the government or with the county, if he was thinking of lifetime security for him and the family, if he thought of having one, and how this job could work for him in terms of stability in the community–you will come to know what I mean– "*when the bullet hits the bone*" echoed in his memory.

"You're probably too young for that now, but think about your future Bob."

Like Rausch, Walsh thought about retiring in his forties and going back to farming with a pension to bolster the uncertainties of a potential bust a farmer faced every year. Rausch informed young Robert that if he was willing to take a two-year extension course in grain marketing, offered out of Brookings night school, his supervisor promised he would recommend Robert to the county board for a position as full-fledged county agent when he retired.

For the ambitious but frustrated young man he had become, this opportunity was something he should think about; he might be able work out of Sioux Falls or Yankton in the future. It might even be the break he needed to move into politics. At that age Robert wasn't sure he was cut out for the career commitment without the higher education degree–some novice, wet behind the ears with a sheepskin, could always bump him in a heartbeat.

These were the dialogues he carried on in his mind. Robert had never been an honor student who thought of going to college. He believed he was as bright as his brother Ansel; he might even have been smarter than his brother. He had learned it was the detail, layers and extensions he could add to his papers based on his own experience, that had proved to himself and faculty he could do college level work; but, long hours in the classroom, and constant reading and writing like his brother enjoyed, never appealed to Robert.

* * * * *

Robert's mother passed away in 1952. Harold Walsh's health declined rapidly after the death of his beloved wife, soon after they celebrated their silver anniversary. Robert saw his once iron strong idol becoming weaker by the day struggling with memory loss and depression. He became even less able and interested in doing farm work after Agnes passed on. In the future such signs of mental and physical issues became known as Alzheimer's syndrome.

Another neighbor Albert Larson seized the opportunity, asking Ansel at the funeral if he could rent to buy the north forty; he would be willing to do the chores to boot if Robert needed to take some time off or wanted to move to town. At their mother's internment, Robbie and Ansel spent their time together discussing Harold's condition, the alarming memory loss, and sharing the costs of placing their father in a nursing home. They shared the inevitability and grief their Father Harold would live only a few more years.

Robert had decided to rent the farm to Larson, who had begun helping with chores after the Johnson negotiations for its sale fell apart, canceling arrangements between neighbors lasting nearly ten years, as an agreement once had been that allowed Robbie to spend time after school his junior and senior year. In those tenuous times dealing with the farm accident, while at the same time his father's favorite son Ansel was leaving the farm behind to join the Navy, and after that heading off to the university on the GI bill, Robert needed a place to live until he could buy a home in Madison. Larson's son-in-law Brent Nelson and his family of five would want the house to themselves if he bought the farm.

Until he decided what to do, the Larson cash rent helped Robert defray nursing home expenses before his dad passed away around Thanksgiving time 1954. Crop and land prices were low in the early 50's. Young Walsh had lost interest in the mundane aspects of farming after trying to farm 80 acres plus 80 rented alone part-time by 1953, so he put the land up for sale at $70 an acre along with the house and barn for $8000. The homestead was sold at auction in 1954, with Albert Larson getting the bid.

After paying the bills, taxes and deferred internment expenses, Robert had enough money for a down payment as foundation to arrange a loan with the county credit union to buy himself a spanking clean demonstrator with 1700 miles on the odometer from the auto dealership in Redfield. The first car he owned was a gray Plymouth sedan with a protruding sun visor on the windshield. He stayed in the farm house a year as part of the deal with Larson who had a daughter whose husband worked for him. The neighbor, who had started out renting land south of the Walsh's as Robert grew up, was becoming known for buying up foreclosed farmland all over the county.

Approaching his twenty fifth year, Robert was bored with living miles from nowhere in the old Walsh farmhouse. With his parents both gone, he didn't feel lonely; instead, his sense of hollowness, where life had been that no longer existed, became overpowering. To compensate for the void in his life, Robert purchased a two-bedroom rambler with garage, on a contract for deed, at the outskirts of Madison, SD. The experience of turning over the farm was nostalgic, when as far as he knew the heritage of the Walsh family and Agnes's, the Krause family, had been rooted in German agriculture for centuries; their land was now part of the Prussian dynasty that financed National Socialism in Germany. The transition to existence in a parochial community was an unexpectedly traumatic experience for him; he had never experienced alienation to such a degree since he transferred from Nundas elementary to Madison middle school.

The legend was that Harold's grandfather had purchased pasture land from a Junker prince early in the 19th Century, but the land was repossessed under suspicious circumstances, before Kaiser Wilhelm became emperor. The sale of that farm near the Polish border had financed the emigration of the Walsh family first to Indiana, and later to St. Paul, where Harold's father made arrangements with the Hill Railroad to transport his son and family to land purchased from the train company in the Dakotas. Axel Walsh planned to follow the tracks west later but died of pneumonia on the East Coast.

The loss of his roots, and resulting alienation at his core, left an empty and incomplete state of mind upon Robert. As he approached the third decade of his life, it was as if he had been missing something other folks had; he compensated for the void by imagining he might buy the farm back someday in the future. Someday, he would re-establish the Walsh line in America as it had been in the legends of the old country.

At one time he thought about joining the National Guard, but he had pressed his luck and a deferment, remaining at home working on the farm helping his parents. When the Korean War broke out he was glad for the decisions–working on the farm he had no fear of being drafted. He recalled stories about the Guard being called up and the atrocities North Koreans committed against the Americans; he barely dodged the draft as the only son helping out on the farm. There were moments of appreciation for the "gifts God had given him." He felt good stopping at the on-sale liquor after work Friday and a hard day mowing down the adversary–a few whiskey charges later, Robbie believed for a moment or two he was leading a *charmed* life–in not just any other lonely little town on the prairie.

The original Walshs had no roots in Madison as first generation settlers. Robert was isolated in another tiny town with few friends after graduation–not by choice–but because most of the kids his age he grew up with had moved out of town as soon as they graduated. A few had gone off to college, but not any he was close to. Robert's high school buddies found jobs in factories, garages and banks in Sioux Falls, Huron, and Watertown. His brother Ansel was an exception. He had achieved a higher education bought and paid for by the government after the war, and took full advantage of it. He was going to teach college someday.

Robert was satisfied with seasonal inspection work for the county. He made more than his father could afford to pay him and stashed what he could save working for other farmers during baling and harvest. Robert was proud of the Plymouth he was paying the bank fifty bucks a month on, after a down payment of 300 bills. He could celebrate frugally now that he had a chance to make something of a career as a county agent, once his boss retired.

* * * * *

And life in small town America suddenly became a lot more interesting, as Robert found himself instantly attracted to the new waitress at the Four Seasons Café on main street Madison. He learned through the grapevine her husband had deserted her for some hussy, and they ran off to Montana. The rumor was that Shirley was starting over after a messy breakup and divorce. Shirley had a small child from a previous marriage–the little girl lived with her grandmother in Watertown. She was renting a small one bedroom on the west side of town.

To make a positive impression on Shirley, Robbie began to dress in creased khaki slacks and a dark denim barn coat his father had worn to town. He visited the barber every two weeks instead of once a month. He made sure his fingernails were scrubbed and his hands were clean of the grease and dirt they accumulated, and that his clothes were absent the stench of 2-4D he dipped into at the county garage.

An important thing his mother had stressed upon her boys was the importance of cleanliness. He kept his hair short and trimmed his nails regularly. He began to hang around the restaurant a bit longer, after the farmers cleared out–leaving the gossip and coffee of the café behind before they mounted their tractors and combines. Robert felt he had moved beyond that stage. The coast was clear; no other young bucks were rutting for Shirley when the coffee rush from six to eight a.m. was over.

Shirley Larson Bauer, as he learned her name through gossip at the garage where every available woman was discussed, didn't wear makeup or eye shadow. She was not an unattractive woman, far from it. Especially in view of how few single women worked in downtown Madison. Shirley didn't seem to mind that Robbie lingered a little later on the mornings he dropped in Four Seasons for eggs, hash browns and unlimited coffee refills. Robbie was good company in the small town with few available men. He didn't get fresh with her like the other men did.

There were times Robert felt guilty loitering, being tardy at the county garage just to be around Shirley, as he sipped refills while the café emptied. She was good with that. Shirley had noticed Robert was a handsome lad with light brown hair and a cowlick smoothed down with Vaseline hair tonic. But she wouldn't want him losing his job; they would need that income if they got serious about each other.

Shirley had a vague sense of control as she knew the boy evolving into a man was falling for her, and not without reason. She was a little older than Robbie, approaching thirty and was hungry for another man to erase the shame she felt when her husband left her for a younger woman. Shirley depended on tips to make ends meet; with that small change added to her wages she could send along a little money to her mother and baby in Watertown. Robbie sensed her need and consequently always left her at least a fifty cent tip that was generous for those days. Shirley had another mouth to feed and could use the money for groceries.

As his career blossomed, Robert stood out among men of the community; he became known as one of the home boys who had stuck around town. He smoked too much, but he didn't drink regularly at the Legion and VFW. Before that time, he had always felt alone in an isolated small town where there were few opportunities; there was no way out, no way to escape his fate. Then he had a stroke of luck, when the county agency job materialized.

Robbie could be charming when he wanted to be. Once in a while, Shirley caught a whiff of his Old Spice. One morning as he paid his guest check, when the cook was in the kitchen and the last of the farmers had cleared out, he asked her if she wanted to accompany him to the dance at the Madison American Legion club on Memorial Day weekend. Lawrence Welk had played there once. On a Saturday night in June 1955, Bob and Shirley rocked out to Bill Haley and the Comets, and Elvis Presley, this new hotshot young singer from Memphis the world was in a rage about, on the jukebox. Later that night they kissed goodnight before Bob drove the babysitter home.

Robert and Shirley dated for almost two years until Robert saved enough to finance the two-bedroom rambler on the east side of Madison. In 1956, Robert and Shirley became engaged and were married the next year in the St. Lawrence Catholic Church. Within a year they had a son, Robert Jr. to grow up with Shirley's daughter Louise. The first years of their marriage were happy ones. Shirley compiled three albums of snapshots of the Walsh family as they visited the Black Hills, gazed at Mt. Rushmore, and visited the gulches of Little Big Horn where Custer tangled with Crazy Horse and his braves. On the way home they stopped and bought souvenirs of their trip at the Wall Drug.

Before long it was 1961, John F. Kennedy was president; Robert had been working as county agent with a government job and money in the bank. Shirley no longer needed to waitress. She quit her job at the café to raise the kids. During the 50's, Walshs were one of the first families in Madison to convert from radio to television. They had a 14" Dumont black and white attached to an antenna on the roof that looked like the rack of a 32-point buck. Robert liked to be home for the Friday night fights sponsored by Grain Belt beer. Little Louise Bauer Walsh loved the TV and never missed *Fury*, who reminded her of *Black Beauty* on the cover of the book that sat next to her on the couch. The Walsh children were hypnotized by the television. Shirley sat quietly reading pulp fiction and romance novels, sipping coffee in the kitchen, keeping an eye on the TV screen in case anything happened. "Deuce", as Robert referred to his son, watched Dave Dedrick, *Captain 11* on KELO faithfully. Together on Sunday evening, the family would be watching the night Elvis Presley sang "Blue Suede Shoes" on *The Ed Sullivan Show*.

ANTHONY FALLS JR.

The Walshs were content in a relationship that was destined to last another forty years. Robert liked it that Shirley was concerned with raising a family like his mother had been. His wife didn't question him about what he did for a living. Shirley had the security every woman needed; a good man with a steady job was more than she could hope for after the "no good bum Eddie" she was married to, for a very short time, before Robert came into her life. Evelyn claimed her one-time son-in-law had never paid a dime of child support for Louise either, so he would never get to see his daughter if she had anything to say about it.

To kill time on what would have otherwise been a boring job, Robert, who was never what you would call a Sergeant York, would regularly stop at the gravel pit a few miles north of town. There he enjoyed honing his marksmanship plinking on tin cans and bottles using the .22 rifle he carried with him in the cab of his truck; and after he was promoted, in a leather case in the backseat of his agency car. Robbie normally used shorts, because they just popped, there was no loud crack when he shot out the window; he kept a clip of long rifle hollow points in the glove box in the event he might see a chicken hawk on a fence post or a ring-neck popping its head out of the weeds.

During hunting season Robert carried his prized possession, inherited from his father Harold, loaded in the back seat with him as he traveled between farms. Ansel had received an expensive Waltham watch as a memento of his Father's favor before he left for the Navy boot camp, but the second son of Father Walsh was pleased to retain the antique shotgun his dad had treasured, by default.

As county agent, one step below game warden, Robert knew it was illegal, even for him as a public official, to shoot out the window. He knew the game warden was checking the city hunter ids and limits because there were so many, and obvious versus the locals he knew for years, there was no need to check them for licenses and limits around the soil bank and federal reserve. They would never check the trunk either. So with practice, Robbie rarely missed a rooster in the ditch–if it dared to poke its heads up out of the underbrush. He would slow down, back up, and *bang* the Walshs had pheasant for dinner.

Pheasant hunting season was the happiest time of the year for Robbie. He knew where birds were because of his job inspecting the ditches. He had a license in his billfold, but he really didn't need one. He had known Leon Randle ever since high school; they were friends who had chatted in Shirley's restaurant–ten years later Leon was the game warden. As county agent, Robert was under the radar basically, immune to inspection. He would bring home a couple of roosters every week in season and a few times after the season closed, handing the dead birds over to Shirley who had an excellent recipe for wild rice and pheasant.

* * * * *

In the fall of 1959, fate continued to be on his side; Grant-Duehl County agent Robert Walsh got an unexpected opportunity to advance his career when the political connection he had hoped for finally materialized at a banquet for supporters of the Dakota Sportsman's Association. At that event Robert met Joe Foss, former South Dakota State representative and Governor from 1954 to 1958 who would later become the Secretary of the US Department of Agriculture during the Kennedy administration. The night Walsh met him, Foss was guest of honor and main speaker, attending the event sponsored by *Ducks Unlimited* along with his wife DiDi, held at the Corn Palace in Mitchell, SD.

Every male in the State of South Dakota had heard of and admired the legend of Joe Foss, a true to life American folk hero– the rare Midwestern star universally revered along the lines of George Washington and Sergeant York. By war's end, the former Marine pilot had become a role model for the youth of America. Ironically, Foss himself had once been a small town farm boy whose father had died in a tragic accident when Joe was still a teenager. Despite great obstacles, Joe went on to live the American dream. For Walsh, the meeting with Governor Foss would become a life changing event. Robert walked up to Foss and asked him to sign the Mitchell program. They chatted a moment, shook hands; both men recalled the meeting in the years that followed.

Colonel Foss took an interest in the reticent, but determined county agent from Madison, SD. Perhaps Mr. Foss, a very popular and warm Christian, sensed a certain spiritual need in the man who was so obviously and intensely interested in his program that night in Mitchell. What Foss sensed was what he felt among his squadron of flyboys in the Pacific–the subdued emotion of his brave platoon of lost lonely boys thousands of miles from home and family–and not a few who would never see the States again.

This sense of unspoken loss was an experience the two strangers shared as they shook hands for the first time. By the time Walsh met him, handsome, dashing and still dark-haired Joe Foss was the most recognized face in South Dakota–a nationally recognized celebrity and WWII flying ace as a member of United States Marine air corps in the Pacific theater. Foss had become one of the most decorated of WWII heroes, shooting down 26 enemy planes–the first pilot to do so since Eddie Rickenbacker had knocked down 17 kraut aircraft during WWI.

Only PT 109 hero Jack Kennedy had done more for his country during the war, and that was doubtful; there were those who said the legend of the sinking PT boat, and JFK swimming ten miles with a wounded comrade in tow, was invented for political reasons. But there were no doubts about Colonel Foss's records–as if chiseled in granite like Rushmore itself–his feats would stand forever.

The Ducks Unlimited fundraiser was an opportunity Robert was looking for to meet the legend in person. Walsh knew instinctively he needed political allies if he was to expand his career beyond the boundaries of Madison. After the 1963 assassination, Governor Foss would be considered for a position in the Johnson administration. The famed aviator turned the offer down preferring to spend his post Kennedy years in service to his native South Dakota.

Walsh was well aware of the stature and power and what a political connection with an established media star, who would one day host a syndicated hunter's show *The Outdoorsman* and a few years later the ABC series *The American Sportsman*, could mean to his career. Probably the most famous Dakotan since Sitting Bull and Crazy Horse, Joe Foss became a legend, eventually becoming the first Commissioner of the fledgling American Football League from 1959 to 1966.

Robert had growing ambitions; his ten-year friendship with county agent Rausch had been the spring board to a career in government. After the sportsman's show in Mitchell, Walsh believed he finally had a chance to hitch his wagon to a pulsar; as if the dormant grandfather clock logged in his memory had been wound again and started ticking.

At the Ducks Unlimited banquet, Joe Foss delighted the audience crediting his experience shooting pheasants and ducks as a boy on the South Dakota prairie for his success in combat. Joe claimed that he learned the technique from hunting ducks and ringnecks out on the farm near Sturgis–"deflection shooting" Foss called it. You had to lead those whistling blue bills, flying 60 miles an hour downwind, at least seven body lengths to knock them down. When you had Jap zeroes that were diving out of the sun at 300 mph at you, the same principle applied.

"Just make sure you teach your kids to aim their .410 loaded with number four shot, one length for each mile per hour the wind is–shoot that far ahead of the birds, depending on which kind of duck it is." Mallards were his favorite; the best tasting birds were a bit slower on the wing flying at about 45-mph. Pheasants on the other hand were slower yet; you could put the *bead* right on them when they jumped up from the corn row in front of you.

Foss claimed he applied the same technique he had learned from his father. He hesitated a moment as if reflecting on that experience, and wiped his brow with a white kerchief. Basically, he had applied his gun training when knocking down what he believed were closer to *fifty* Jap Zeroes; then he laughed. The crowd in the palace erupted in cheers, stood up and applauded as their smiling personable hero finished his wonderful program waving the flag, answering questions about his war record.

"No," Joe told the audience, he wasn't proud of his accomplishments shooting down all those Japanese pilots. They were brave young men, the very best Hirohito had to offer. He could have been sitting behind a desk. He was a college graduate going into the Marines; that was why he was a commissioned officer. Joe claimed he wanted to teach agricultural engineering, but they needed his skill in the Pacific.

Like the rest of the men of his battalion command, the Marines were just doing their job for the country. They had wives, children and families like he had. But with all the Jap Zero diving out of the clouds, flying at you at 200-mph you didn't think about those things. The adrenaline was pumping. An hour in a fire fight flashed by in ten seconds; you had to use all your strength just to maneuver the P-40 Mustang. The Thunderbolts won the war in the sky over Okinawa he claimed–before they entered the war the Zero was a faster plane. The hair stood up on your neck. He didn't have time to keep a head count every mission. He didn't keep track as the flaming planes plummeted into the ocean below, the jungle, or sometimes crashed into allied ships. Many pilots who witnessed his shooting skill never made it back to the Marine base airfield the Army engineers had carved out of the jungle, or to the rolling decks of the aircraft carriers.

As he made his run for Governor, thousands of sportsmen and war vets from all over South Dakota and western Minnesota flocked to hear Joe speak, at Sioux Falls, Watertown and other auditoriums around the state. They were spellbound, sitting silent as Colonel Foss spoke of his heroics–just doing his duty, he claimed. The one time Private who rose to Colonel from the 47th Field Artillery, Sioux Falls, SD National Guard 1937-1940, wiped tears in his eyes, and sweat from his forehead as he recounted the harrowing tales of his war experience. As he ended his many speeches, a number of which Robert Walsh attended after he first met him, Joe lightened up from war and politics as he recounted his days in duck blinds or trudging through cornfields around Brookings, Mitchell and Redfield, South Dakota with favorite black lab retriever "Buddy" he sometimes brought with him.

Joe had been a regular guest in the White House, charming the politicians with his down to earth brand of humor, telling the same stories over and over. Foss would become a great asset to the national Democratic party apparatus in the Kennedy and the soon-to-be Johnson administration. But Joe chose to retire from politics and returned to the state he loved after one term as Secretary of Agriculture.

Foss was an evident artist, someone Robert could model his future after. The Colonel was a gifted speaker capable of projecting the drama he had experienced. Robert knew he could never do that in another lifetime–he knew his limitations. For the audience of rabid hunters, his stories of war reminded them of opening day of hunting season on a Flandreau slough with Zeros,

"I mean, the *Redheads* diving out of the clouds (*the crowd of avid hunters roared with laughter*) flying at you from all different angles and directions. It was a common sight to see a flock of pheasants rise thick as a cloud of smoke out of the Redfield cornfields." Some of the veterans stood and clapped at the Governor's reference to the sacred hunting rituals of the plains handed down from father to son.

After a Rod and Gun Club show in Aberdeen, Robert stood around chatting until a line of avid hunters, mostly farmers, and sporting goods store owners from all over the Dakotas, respectfully marched before the most famous man in South Dakota. Robert was reminded of his strength by the iron grip of Foss's handclasp. He was surprised and honored that Joe remembered him from their brief meeting in the Corn Palace. There was little time to reacquaint, but Joe signed a program for Robert before quickly shaking hands with the next man in line, like he was in a hurry. It was midnight before the crowd finally dispersed. The important thing was that Walsh had made an impression on the United States Secretary of Agriculture.

Perhaps he had found the connection he needed to move into the more important role he yearned for after his years as an

ANTHONY FALLS JR.

obscure weed inspector from Madison, SD, who had barely risen to a county agent by the time he was looking at forty. That day Governor Foss shook Walsh's hand, he sensed the professional intensity of the low government man as he met the eyes of the county agent from Madison. He would remember him at their next meeting. Perhaps Mr. Foss felt the pulse of killer instinct a test pilot needed; you never could tell how much risk a man would take. It was hard to decipher the mixed traits he had observed in Robert Walsh, not unlike the personality of his ordnance staff sergeant in the Solomon Islands.

After their first meeting, Robert became an avid follower of Governor Foss's campaigns for the Democrats. In the year before the election Robert attended a dozen fundraisers in three states. In their brief moments of light conversation, exchanging hunting vignettes, Foss sensed that Robert was not as serious about hunting as he was, but that he was a supporter nonetheless. He had some other purpose on this earth. As a onetime Marine colonel, he understood the distinct personalities of his men–he knew for an instant the strange man from the South Dakota had some of the character a man needed to survive the unspoken cold war.

This small-town boy seemed to the WWII ace to have the raw-boned toughness of the infantry, along with the determination to succeed in a mission at all costs, like the men in his squadron of twenty Thunderbolt pilots, college graduates, not a one of them over 25 years old. More than a hunter, Foss sensed Robert had become a mercenary without a purpose–like a veteran who couldn't leave the trauma behind him.

At a Yankton fundraiser for the South Dakota Democratic Party, Governor Foss thanked Robert for coming. As he signed his autograph on the program menu, Joe's hand was steady as a rock. Foss shook Robert's hand indicating he appreciated his support. The Secretary wrote his office number on a business card looking him in the eye saying,

"In one of our conversations I recall you mentioned the B.O.T. Robert. I do have some friends, I should say *connections*, on the Missouri Valley Board of Trade. They are always looking for bright, energetic people in agricultural marketing services. I have heard they need specialists familiar with layout of the land in eastern South Dakota. It is possible those folks can use your experience. You grew up there; you know the people. If you need a reference just give me a call at my office. My home phone is listed. I'm very seldom there. My wife DiDi will always take a message."

That Christmas he received a card from Governor Foss with a picture of him hugging his wife and children. The family portrait was taken standing in front of a tall, decorated tree with the lights on outside the White House. In Joe Foss, Robert Walsh believed he had found himself an ally in his conflict with the increasingly present archetype that appeared at unpredictable moments–it was some shadowy image he didn't recognize that had begun peering and disappearing before him in the filthy bathroom mirror at the county garage–and happening more frequently as he washed his hands in unfamiliar restrooms using commercial hand cleaner that smelled worse than the kerosene stench of 2-4D.

CHAPTER 2

"Comprising 45,000 acres spread across Minnesota and half of South Dakota, David Zehlen's farming operation could be the ultimate nightmare of the sustainable agriculture movement."

–*Farm Futures Magazine*, June 1992

David Zehlen was born in October 1954; had he been born a month or so earlier he would have been a member of the graduating class of 1972. He was the son of a second generation farmer, Jacob Zehlen, who was born in 1930. He had identical twin sisters two years older than he was. Slow to recover after his birth, David's mother was diagnosed with multiple sclerosis several months after he was born. Because he was born in the fall, while his father was harvesting soybeans and corn, David was one of the older members of the 1973 graduating class of Rockland High School.

David was born with a silver spoon in his mouth. As the only son of the most progressive and prosperous farmer in Granite County, he was destined to takeover a multimillion dollar farming operation. Although he was not an above average student, David excelled in drama and agriculture. He was a favorite in class with Jolly "Rolly" Hobart, the agriculture teacher. Always joking with arguably his best student, Hobart gave Dave straight A's. He excelled in industrial arts as well. He was a solid B student in Algebra, which compensated for his lack of interest, and getting good grades, in the rest of the curriculum.

Of course, David was the undisputed champion of the *Future Farmers of America*, Granite County chapter. Elected President his senior year by his classmates, on homecoming day he drove and parked his dad's new yellow Case diesel at the high school. That afternoon following the high school band, waving to the crowd, wearing a cowboy hat and his Trojan football jersey,

David pulled the senior float in the parade down main street on the tractor. On most occasions, David chose to wear his orange and black leather Rockland High School letterman's jacket, with his letters in football sewn on the sleeve, rather than his royal blue FFA jacket with gold piping, during the 1973 football season. With his teammates, David wore it with pride until the winds of November forced a parka on his broad shoulders. He was especially pleased to wear that jacket with a sense of honor after the Trojans won their only game of the season, his senior year, the last game of the season against their greatest rivals outside the Little Sioux Conference, whipping the Milbank Bulldogs 7-0 on the Rockland home field. Rockland hadn't beaten the mutts from South Dakota since the late 1940's, according to Dave's father. The Trojans carted their coach Boyd Lefkowski off the field on the team's shoulders after that historic victory.

As the town expanded, the Zehlens found themselves living and raising crops on the very north edge of Rockland city limits, with Mound cemetery to the south and the municipal 9-hole golf course on the west side. David could see the water tower in town from their farmyard. Jacob Zehlen had hit a lucky streak in the grain marketing business while Dave was finishing high school. Jack as everybody knew him was the first and only farmer to explore alternatives to traditional crops that had sustained the industry in Granite County in favor of higher market value crops. In the conservative community, he was reviled and envied for his deviations from the norm–and Jack Zehlen prospered as no one believed he could.

Tired of growing soybeans corn, wheat, oats and barley at $3 per bushel while being at the mercy of the Chicago grain exchange and local elevators, he was fed up with how the industry ran its business; and, along with it the constant arbitrage of grain prices so that it was impossible to make a profit with an income controlled by market fluctuations thousands of miles away. Jacob, "Jack" to his friends, Zehlen took a chance and began growing sunflowers that he could sell as high as 25 cents a pound. At up to 2000 pounds per acre, he nearly tripled his income within 5 years in the late 1960's and early '70's. Jack expanded his 160-acre homestead, buying and leasing land; gradually, increasing the size of his farm until he owned 3500 acres in Granite, Stevens, and Swift, while he leased land in other surrounding counties including several sections in South Dakota, near Corona.

Jack and Marie arranged financing for their twin daughters to buy a duplex in the Phillips district just off Franklin Avenue in Minneapolis. He paid for his daughter Kristine's education at the Minneapolis College of Art and Design where she met and dated Stephen Rivkin, film editor of Cameron's *Avatar*, Disney's *Pirates*, and other motion pictures under star-studded directorships. Kristine studied painting, which was a talent she had inherited from her mother who had been crippled by MS and was confined to a wheel chair on the farm. Steve Rivkin later became one of David's best friends, serving as best man at his wedding in 1975.

By 1975, David's father was grossing over two million dollars a year growing at that time experimental flowers, for profit. Jack upheld tradition as well, farming several hundred acres of soybeans and wheat on the homestead. But it was the brilliant sunflowers with their heavy yellow seed heads nodding in the breeze, a whole field in rippling motion, each plant in unison pursuing the wheel in the sky as it circled to the South Dakota hills; such an unusual spectacle, visible an entire growing season one mile north on Hwy 75, in a display of brilliant color that could not help becoming a main attraction—gathering the attention of the little town on the prairie for a brief moment—before it went on vacation as soon as school let out the middle of June.

As it was, this colorful phenomenon, observable from the cemetery and golf course along a stretch of pavement just north of Rockland, captured the heat and headlines of summer on the front page of *The Independent* when color printing became available, focusing the small hamlet's attention on a feature article about agriculture, and specifically one pioneer taking a risk on sunflowers, a crop that had become a notable economic force of the community. The special issue generated increased readership, at least for a week or two each summer, among those readers interested in the royalty parade and details on the

August Corn Festival. The summer special issue arrived annually whenever the publisher of the paper, former USAF pilot, lieutenant JD Kaercher who graduated with Jack as one of his best of friends from an early age, could make a profit devoting an entire section of the weekly to progressive agriculture, sponsored by local advertisers–out of an issue the locals took for granted.

In the mid 1970's as the price of soybeans was in recess, after a boom period, young David was stepping into an extremely profitable business at 18 years of age. For then and many years after–until the farm went under in 1992–the Zehlen farm operation was the most dynamic four-star business in western Minnesota.

Upon graduation, David's dad bought his only son a bright yellow Volkswagen that he shared with his sisters, while Jack drove around in a set of golden tan, harvest-colored GM pickups; one was just a shade darker than the other. On Sunday he drove his two tone green Ford LTD II to the Methodist Church in Rockland. With money to spend after the frugal years of his youth, Jack enjoyed spending the hot summer weekends in his cabin on Lake Minnewaska near Glenwood MN, trusting his son could run the show back on the ranch in Granite County.

By 1980, Jack himself was unable to care for his wife whose progressive MS condition continued to worsen. Home care resources were scarce in Rockland, and the nursing home cost a fortune. To be fair to his wife and leverage health care expenses with a separation and divorce, Jack moved David's mother into a house in Rockland to better avail her of community health services. He provided Marie as generous a settlement as he could afford.

Under the circumstances, Jack had calculated it was cheaper to divorce his wife, buy her a home in town and pay for a live-in nurse, rather than place his wife of thirty years in a nursing care facility. He did not have the patience or training to manage her care. Jack believed he had done the right thing, as much as humanly possible under the grim circumstances of his wife's progressing health issues. In 1981 Jack divorced his first wife and married a younger woman, Phyllis Connelly who he had originally hired as his secretary. In the same year, Jack purchased the old Rockland Hospital where his identical twins Kathy and Kristine were born. With money to invest based on multiple crop production, he remodeled the historic brick building into an office complex in downtown Rockland later to be named the Anothene building.

* * * * *

In 1975, David married his high school sweetheart Nancy Hoven, the oldest daughter of William Hoven, who was a practicing pharmacist at the Larson Drug and variety store in Rockland. The Hovens owned a spacious home on the shores of Big Stone Lake, the 10th largest lake in Minnesota, many of the town folk claimed was the true source of the Mississippi River. Nancy was an excellent water skier, and could have been a cheerleader if she had chosen to be. Bill Hoven was a double bogey golfer and member of the Rockland Country Club. Nancy's mom was a dedicated jogger, but athletics did not appeal to Nancy; her younger sister Kris aspired to be a writer, and her younger brother Bob was a photographer.

The Hoven family preferred artistic pursuits, and did not encourage their children to be involved in high school sports. Nancy played guitar and sang in the Methodist Church as an alternative to being involved in school extra-curricular activities. Nancy's dad used his influence as a pharmacist to arrange an apprenticeship for his daughter, as a dental assistant after her sophomore year at Rockland High, through Bill's friend DDS Peter Hanson whose son Pete Jr. was the most prolific scorer in Rockland history. Unfortunately, PJJ, at 6'6", became designated point man in the jungle, one of three casualties former stars of Rockland sports teams suffered in the Viet Nam War.

In contrast to the agricultural focus, local media followed the post war tradition of not exactly suppressing, rather, scarcely mentioning such tragic incidents that might impact local recruitment and enlistment in the country's armed forces or the local guard unit. In that grim atmosphere, according to David privately speaking Nancy hated her job, even if there was an abundance of work and a potential lifelong career ahead. Her prospective lifelong partner promised his future bride he would be her knight in shining armor, and after a few years she could quit her job. David looked at her enrollment in a University certification program as an investment that he would eventually pay for regardless.

The pragmatist father Bill Hoven presented his daughter with an Alvarez guitar Christmas Eve of her freshman year of high school. Nancy was delighted and practiced religiously, becoming a performer in a matter of months. By the time she was 15 years old, Nancy had a repertoire of "Just a closer walk with Thee" and ten secular songs featuring "If I had a hammer" by Peter, Paul and Mary and "Desperado" by the Eagles. She played and sang "Kum ba yah" on a weekly basis at Bible studies and fall hayrides. Nancy had an excellent alto voice and participated in the high school chorus; she performed in a small choral group with her sister Kris and some friends at church events. It was at one of these events she first came to know David who played the part of Joseph in the Christmas pageant.

David was an agreeable extrovert known for his publicly well dressed, handsome appearance. Nancy was a stunning blonde girl who appeared more mature than her 15 years, which she was when she started going with Dave Zehlen. His future bride resembled the young Madonna in appearance and in performance. She acted the lead role in *Little Women* her junior year, in what Dave claimed should be broadcast on public TV out of Appleton, as was one of the best performances he had ever seen in his life!

In their youth, the two lovers seemed like they belonged together. Dave was persistent. He looked forward to seeing Nancy at school, and on Wednesday night's bible studies at the Methodist Church. The religious setting seemed perfectly harmless as a natural way of getting together, with parents on both sides insisting their children must attend. Dave flirted with

ANTHONY FALLS JR.

Nancy, and charmed her into going out to coffee with him at the Cashtown Cafe after bible study. The two of them made a natural pair, attracted to each other physically and emotionally. At that stage, they were necking and petting as one thing led to another. Dave later revealed that pushing the limits inevitably led to going the distance, but Nancy never became pregnant. Her father, Bill the pharmacist, was providing his daughter birth control pills to ensure there was not a problem.

Everybody in Rockland High and in the church knew the young couple was going steady, as dating practice was referred to in those days. Virtually the whole town knew the outcome of the relationship from the year Dave graduated, after Nancy's sophomore year in high school, that the couple would eventually be married. So what was the difference? Her birth control pills and advice from her father the pharmacist about how to use them so she wouldn't become pregnant in high school out of wedlock was reassuring to both sides of the family who assumed the promising couple would be married the summer after Nancy graduated.

In a strange coincidence that hinted at some future psychological event perhaps, Dave's best man at the Rockland wedding in July 1975 was Stephen Rivkin, his sister Kris's boyfriend, who she had met while she was attending the Minneapolis Institute of Art. Kris had met Rivkin in one of her classes while Rivkin was studying film production. He became David's close friend. Rivkin entertained the wedding guests the day of the wedding sitting on a stool playing acoustic guitar in the lobby of First English Church. Steve went on to become technical director of more than a score of films including David's favorite, *Behind Enemy Lines* with Gene Hackman, and *Avatar*, working beside James Cameron, the internationally renowned Hollywood film producer. To this day, Mr. Rivkin visits Dave's sisters in Minneapolis occasionally, always encouraging Kris to market her unique paintings on the internet.

Throughout the 1970's and 80's the Zehlens appeared to have an ideal marriage. With a good income the couple lived comfortably in Jack's Uncle Martin Zummach's remodeled farm house a quarter mile north of Jack's place. Dave started farming full time for his dad, learning the ropes and expanding the business in the late 1970's, gradually taking over as Jack considered early retirement–his fortuitous interest in sunflowers had made him a fortune by the time he was fifty.

Nancy received her degree as dental technician from the University and was drawing a second income working forty hours a week, occasional Saturdays, and emergencies. She had a steady job cleaning teeth and assisting Dr. Hanson in dental surgery, always looking forward to the day she could quit her job. The couple and their growing family spent a few weekends each summer at her father in-law's cottage on Lake Minnewaska that reminded her of her dad's home on Big Stone Lake. Being a stay-at-home mom would have to wait for a while; but with Dave's work ethic, and the farm prospering the way it was–at least 15 percent a year growth David claimed–that day didn't seem to be too far off.

In 1983, Dave and Nancy had their first child, a son Noah, who David doted on as his father had on him. As a first time father, he was already planning ahead what the fourth generation Zehlen farm might look like on a spreadsheet at the rate it was growing in 1983. Two years after Noah, a daughter, Hannah was born; however, there were problems with delivery eight weeks prematurely. Weighing slightly more than two pounds at birth, Hannah was diagnosed with cerebral palsy, and challenged with a severe handicap from birth. In 1989 a pair of twins, Aaron and Jordan, joined the family. The two strong, handsome identical sons grew to be 6' 5", eventually becoming stars on the Trojan basketball squad, and co-captains of the golf team their senior year.

David Zehlen was among the first generation of American farmers to innovate using modern computer technology in his farming operations. By the mid 1980's, he and his father were operating a 15,000-acre production that included leasing land in northern Minnesota and North Dakota. At that time personage payments, that could be allocated to family members, became available to farmers if they were able to navigate through a complex system of requirements to qualify for what amounted to millions of dollars in government subsidies. The Zehlens had their detractors. There were a number of farmers in the area who had either failed before the system was in place, or because they did not qualify. Those farmers, who did not benefit from government subsidies, resented that the Zehlens were entitled to large sums of USDA money to grow what many considered a non-essential food-oil bearing crop of sunflowers.

Regulations varied from state to state. Personage program requirements, documentation, and counseling services were available from local Agricultural Stabilization and Conservation Services (ASCS) offices that offered sessions designed to help farmers understand government farm policy, and an increasingly complex system of rules and regulations the local offices monitored and administered. The overarching plan of the US Department of Agriculture was designed to assist in creating a sound economic environment for American agricultural producers, whereby they may receive a fair price for their production; as a result, American consumers would be assured of an abundant and continuous supply of food. By the mid 1980's, Congress had empowered the USDA to work toward these goals by enacting a number of legislative programs which provided for price supports, acreage or production controls, grain reserves and related programs. The Zehlens took full advantage of the government programs in their growing farm empire in Granite County.

There were few individuals in the community who owned, or had ever operated a computer. David had always been fascinated by technology. His interests in hanging around the adults in the machine shed were encouraged by his dad and Uncle Martin, although they constantly warned him to be careful, especially when the power take-off was running, to stay away– always pay attention–it's dangerous in the barnyard.

Continuing his technical education, David began working with an instructor from the high school, his former math teacher JD Rosen, who introduced him to a computer programming template for agricultural operations. Based on that learning,

David developed a farm management program that he sold to Control Data for a quarter million dollars in 1983. A version of that program 3.0 was still in use in 2012. With proceeds of the sale, David paid off his dad $50,000 for the Martin Zummach farm home a half mile north of Jack's place on US 75, and title to the five acres it sat upon.

David invested the remainder of the profits, from the sale of his first outside business project, in the joint Zehlen farming operations. By harvest 1984, the Zehlens owned six sections in Granite and Traverse County and were lease/optioning 12,000 more acres, including some land across the border in Grant County South Dakota. With his operations stretching across two states in the middle of the decade, David spent half his time on the road driving between farms. It had been his plan to allow himself as little time away from his growing family as possible, and especially from his son Noah.

David was working an average sixteen hour day, nine months of the year, either in the office managing accounts payable and receivable or managing billing using the program he created. If he wasn't on the road or in the office, David was working in the fields himself, monitoring the work of his seasonal employees.

By the mid 1980's, farm land values had dipped in half, roared back again, and then flat-lined at about $1000 an acre in Minnesota. After that fluctuation, prices held for ten years maintaining similar levels until 1998, while lending rates soared as high as 21%, and big business was deregulated by a Republican Congress to create tax and investment incentives with low taxes on corporate dividends. Federal Savings & Loan banks were converted to commercial banks to allow free flow of capital to progressive land developers, creating bubble pricing in high end real estate markets in the Southwest, coastal properties and luxury developments.

The boom of the late 1970's-early 1980's was followed by a bust; the reasons for the collapse few farmers understood, while many suffered for it. A crash in the crop and land market was initially caused by surplus grain, increased foreign imports and weather-related disasters. Soaring interest rates followed with bank failures and government bailouts. Mass foreclosures and repossession of devalued properties, by the same commercial banks originating questionable investments in large-scale development projects and real estate trusts, were now being repossessed at *dimes* on the dollar. The exaggerated crises of the "boom and bust" farm economy that followed, produced shock waves in capital markets of central and regional banks out of which a new era of corporate law and finance evolved.

By 1986 the Zehlen operations were enveloped in the crisis: crops in northern Minnesota were not meeting yield expectations, under-performing because of unusually cool average temperatures and higher than normal precipitation. The Zehlens' credit line with major lender Midwest Federal S&L was frozen; the bank was placed in receivership for Federal takeover as the nationwide S&L crises created a serious cash flow problem, impacting the farm production and leasing arrangements. The Zehlens began searching for another loan provider.

To protect their capital and property investments in the local community in 1987, Jack and David decided to withdraw from their expansive leasing venture, ratcheting back operations 60%, dropping their remote production leases and concentrating on their six local sections until the situation improved. Riding the storm out, in the meantime they were planting traditional crops: soybeans, corn and wheat, along with continuing sunflowers along highway 75 north. The Zehlens had taken a conservative stance, choosing to maintain their 1980 owned acreage, while at the same time taking advantage of ASCS and LDP programs that were expanding in response to the shortage of farm loan sponsorship by banks and S&Ls.

In an unprecedented and unexpected move–to the skeptical community–the Zehlens invested in, and opened up a drug and alcohol rehabilitation center in the building that was once the hospital, where Jacob Zehlen and his two twins were born. They invested hundreds of thousands of dollars from the reserved profits Jack and David had accumulated during their booming expansion into sunflowers and land lease income. As a service to the community and a liberal investment in health care services, in 1986 the Zehlens opened the Anothene Drug and Alcohol Treatment Center, visible from the ASCS office. The modern 3-story office tower stood out for its original grandeur restored and improved upon by the Zehlens, as one of the three largest buildings in downtown Rockland. In following years, both the Carnegie library built in 1919 and the old Rockland Hospital were given historical status as two of three genuine landmark edifices in the community.

Bill Goodwell, a licensed counselor, member of the Methodist Church and the Christian Men's Fellowship group, was named acting director of the rehabilitation center. Bill was an AA member with twelve years' sobriety under his belt. David Zehlen was given an honorary position as a religious counselor; he maintained an office in the building and filled in as a part time drug and alcohol counselor. He stressed a holistic faith-based psychology, using his experience as a highly successful model farmer, at the bottom line of his philosophy stressing the 12-steps of Alcoholics Incognito; and that hard work, sobriety and faith in Jesus Christ leads to recovery. The Anothene building, worth at least $500,000, was one of the spoils of war Robert Walsh allocated in the fire sale liquidation of the Zehlen farm property that he, as power of attorney for the Zehlen family, administrated in the demise of David and Jack's farm a decade later.

CHAPTER 3

In 1978, Robert Walsh's career hit a speed bump–he was convicted of cattle theft in Grant County South Dakota. At that time, his acquaintance with Joe Foss paid him an important dividend; the ex-Governor who was no longer practicing law, referred Walsh to one of his former associates who was himself trying to resurrect his career after an unfortunate experience. Foss referred Walsh to Bill Janklow who was on the road to becoming first officer of the State of South Dakota. As Robert Walsh explained years later, in a letter to his business partner at that time,

> *"Whatever you do, please don't think there is any kind of strong arm motive behind my intentions with you or any kind of threat, and if it sounds this way I apologize because it is not meant that way. I ask that you accept this letter in a way that I was trying to help everyone that is involved. Please remember that I was charged as a felon in a business deal that I had no idea was going on behind my back. It took my family's way of life away from us: my wife, my step daughter and my young son Robert Jr. The case cost us $86,000 in legal fees and 3 years of my life in jail, in prison and in courts throughout the state, to finally absolve myself of guilt for another man's crimes.*

> *As I told you, once we finally got all of the facts, the case was dropped without prejudice. It was dropped when I was able to prove that when certain documents were signed I was not even in America; and the fact that the collateral– the cattle I was charged with stealing–was specifically moved to a location for the benefit of the contractor and bank involved in the deal. The instructions of my counsel meant absolutely nothing because there were agents involved that did things that I had no knowledge of what so ever. Even so, the jury issued an indictment against me. I was never allowed to tell my side of the story to the Grand Jury, which no suspect ever is. I can assure you once you are in the commodities business and you are a convicted felon, your life is over here in America."*

Like his mentor Colonel Foss, Bill Janklow knew the legal and political ropes. He was probably the most skilled attorney practicing criminal law in the State of South Dakota by 1980. Despite some setbacks, Janklow made progress through the mainstream South Dakota legal system during the decade after he was accused of sexual assault of his baby sitter, on a Lakota Indian reservation. "Wild bill" as he became known in the press was able to put the accusations behind him by resigning his position, and some skillful legal maneuvering. Putting his shady past behind him, Janklow eventually achieved status as the state's Deputy Attorney General by the time of the 1973 American Indian Movement (AIM) occupation of Wounded Knee.

Opting to run for Attorney General the following year, he undertook a campaign of hard line prosecution of AIM members designed to win him the advantage of local headlines and support of South Dakota's virulently anti-Native American white citizenry. At the time Walsh met him, Bill Janklow conducted a private practice mainly through his associate staff, maintaining an office in Sioux Falls. Walsh's case was an aberration. Janklow wouldn't ordinarily touch a case like Walsh's except with a referral; but, for a friend of the stature of Joe Foss, Janklow would crawl through barbed wire with machine gun bullets zipping over his head, or navigate through enemy flack. Foss supported him during his tribulations with the Sioux. Janklow realized Walsh would need an expungement of his felony theft conviction, which was rare as a white buffalo on the plains, in the South Dakota justice system.

There were actually two legal strategies that could be applied in Walsh's case: if he were granted an expungement of records motion for the man, he could seal his criminal records. If the Governor had faith in Walsh, he must be worth the effort. As long as the man didn't commit another felony the record could be withheld from the public. The expunged records could only be opened in a trial under a judge's order; which would only happen if Walsh was involved in another felony case upon the request of a presiding judge, as part of the investigation. Robert Walsh's future in commodities, in the government grain or livestock trade depended on whether or not he had learned a lesson from his criminal experience; and if Walsh was determined, he would never be brought to trial as a criminal defendant after the events of his fall from grace. Beyond the implications of his own brush with tribal law, which he finessed his way out of by exiting the reservation on the night train, Janklow indicated he was no legal expert in the area of expungement, a little used process in South Dakota. But Bill understood and explained to Robert the success of the motion depended on presenting an argument the convicted felon was rehabilitated, and had paid the penalty to the people. The petition had to convince the judge that the stigma of being a convicted felon would impede any chance even a rehabilitated man had of attaining employment in the future.

Walsh needed another chance; both Foss and Janklow were fully in tune with that concept. His brother Ansel, who held an assistant professorship in psychology at Indiana State, wrote to Janklow pleading that his brother had been set-up and had gotten a raw deal–that Robert deserved another chance. It was evident that release of Walsh's criminal record to the public would prevent a once promising, but no longer, young man from fulfilling the potential he had shown in the workforce. The record reflected that Robert Walsh was not a violent man; sealing this criminal record wouldn't prevent him from at least semi-professional employment with the passage of time. If any employer ever did a criminal background check, only local police files were never completely sealed. So he had nothing to worry about in his line of work located on the back roads of the country. Walsh would be working in remote locations with his customers– he had that part already planned.

Walsh hadn't done much prison time. He spent six weeks in jail after his conviction. It was his first offense; probation followed the maximum six year sentence for theft of over $50,000. It was clear he didn't have the money in any of his accounts. He had been more of an accessory. As his brother Ansel pointed out, Robert was only the middle man on a three party swindle; he took the fall while his partner and girlfriend drove off with the money their partnership accumulated through illegal sales of "other people's cows" as he put it, at a series of sales auctions near Redfield and Flandreau.

Janklow requested that Walsh do as much as possible in terms of a discovery of relevant cites and legal cases which could be used as precedents in the petition he was preparing, because his staff was limited and he could cut him a deal for half the price of his usual fee on such an undertaking that would normally cost about $5000. Walsh himself discovered that a deal could be made with the presiding judge in his case; only a motion would be needed. A preliminary hearing might not even be necessary with Janklow pulling the strings and finding the right judge.

Walsh had served his sentence two years before the time he assembled the petition; he realized post-conviction relief was rarely granted in South Dakota–a conservative law and order state. Only in special cases where the influence of a Governor was involved were they ever granted. The memorandum Walsh forwarded Janklow cited the statutes relative to sealing his criminal records, noting the process looked complicated; what was necessary was the "Motion for Expungement" signed by a reputable attorney like Janklow, with the underlying argument basically, that the motion was necessary so Walsh could remain employed, or find another job if necessary.

His attorney kept assuring Walsh the situation was complex, but not completely hopeless. He had survived much worse situations with accusers and with his clients. Sensing Walsh might be an asset in his future campaigns for office, Janklow, like Foss, would stand up for the man agreeing with the idea that Walsh deserved to someday re-enter society as a rehabilitated man.

There was another plus to what could have been a complete disaster; Robert found he had an aptitude for legal matters at that time. He had spent many hours in the Madison library and had learned a skill that combined his fledgling writing skills with practical legal matters. He was reinforced in the fact that it was his work providing the relevant cites, and the basic language Janklow and his staff needed to construct the motion for an appeal. Walsh's case tweaked a bit of angst and the bitter memories of past battles in the attorney general, who always retained some anxiety about matters involving tribal members that had been *buried* at Wounded-Knee and might be resurrected by his political rivals. His concerns were needless as the case went unpublished; the motion to seal Robert Walsh's records forever was granted in Sioux Falls District Court by Judge Clarence Alderson.

He had paid his dues, his fines, and court ordered restitution of $5000 (since it was determined Walsh did not have the money or property) on a loan arranged by his brother he was bound and determined to repay. Robert recalled that the day John Lennon was shot, December 8, '80, he received word his records had been sealed. Attached to the notice of expungement there was a note from Bill. *"Dear Robert, Keep a low profile a while, and stay out of trouble. Merry X-Mas 1980! Wm. J. Esq."*

After the events of those days of infamy were redacted from his history, even the government jobs he still retained slim hopes for, involving investigation of agricultural matters where he could apply his expertise to jobs–those that did not require a high security clearance–were not out of reach once his conviction was hidden by time and by law. After the first of the year 1981, "Bob" as no one but Janklow called him, received an unexpected letter in the mail,

"Dear Robert, It appears you are just about out of the woods on this legal matter. Frankly, I was impressed by your diligence and the discovery work you did on the case. I know you have done some work up in the Grant County district. I would like you to get in contact with one of my friends up in that area, former State Representative Ray Clark who works with USDA conservation and stabilization programs. Ray has a tree farm, and raises a lot of Siberian elm, willow, and box elder for the farms around that area. I would like you to get in touch with him. He knows nothing about the case. Mention you know me and so on. He is a fine man, and I'm proud to call him a friend. You might be working with him someday up in that part of the country. Best, Bill"

Robert paid one final visit to the Janklow offices in March 1981, to put down the last $500 dollars he owed on his legal bill. Yet another governor of South Dakota shook hands with Walsh assuring him his legal problems were behind him; he had no worries about his future, and that he was welcome to write or call him any time. Walsh left the office of the once and future first-political officer of the State like a renewed man, leaving prison behind for the first time in three years, rejuvenated by the feeling and thought, he would once again be able to enjoy freedom, fresh air and blue skies without a cloud in the sky, like a normal person.

* * * * *

With his legal successes and consultations with both Freeman and Janklow behind him, Walsh was more convinced than ever that if he studied the law and practiced his writing craft he could be like them. There would be no charismatic experience in war or politics on his resume; but he knew he had the brains and ability to succeed in any field he chose. Despite the setbacks in the swindle, agriculture was still his best bet to make a name for himself, and hope of a future for his family.

No, he would never be the incredible sky-warrior that Joe Foss was; neither had he the warm personality that would make men follow him into combat, following Joe's Mustang as it streaked through enemy flack–the type of experience he could not control frightened him. He was not a violent man, he was a passive aggressive, and had weathered a criminal experience he was none-the-worse for. He was confident that he could deal with any farmer on earth.

Robert Walsh was not interested in high political office. He had a fear of flying over fifty feet above the ground. The natural fright so absent in a guy like Joe Foss, was his constant companion. From those days forward he lived in the state of awareness, or danger of discovery of his felony "alias" which bolstered his ability for stealth; in his profession you had no desire to attract attention. Clinging to his seat in a Piper Cub

ANTHONY FALLS JR.

skimming low over the corn in Grant County, he shuddered as Civil Air Patrol Captain Rep. Ray Clark flew around his 80 acres of bluegrass seed crop, and ten different varieties of trees, including the exotic Nanking Cherry, "great for jelly," he raved about, airborne over Milbank on a pristine morning in spring 1981.

Clark had at one time moderate political aspirations as State Representative for the county, but he told Robert Walsh he had found political life stifling and boring. He had observed and admired the careers of Janklow and Foss, realizing he had traits in common with them both, but he had dropped out of NDSU after two semesters on the GI bill. Ray Clark was content as Walsh never had been, settling for an 80-acre tree and bluegrass seed farm five miles west of Milbank. He was satisfied as owner of a modern 3-bedroom yellow rambler, with a barn and tool shed out back.

The man who Janklow had referred him to in Milbank, thrived on a custom growing operation supported by a government contract to produce 30,000 seedlings a year at $1.50 to $2.00 a unit. In addition, Clark produced ten acres of blue grass seed at $3.50 pound which suited him "just dandy" he told Walsh.

"I haven't seen Bill for several years. What can I do for you Mr. Walsh?" Clark got to his point in their first meeting, over coffee served in the new house 100 feet north of Hwy 12, on the eastern edge of the Yellow Stone Trail where he raised Acer Negundo, Lombardy Poplar, Siberian Elm, Ash and seedless cherry bushes, row on row, like other folks raised corn. He would then sell the products, the one and two-year-old seedlings and grass seed by the pound from 'Clark's Nursery' to the ASCS department of the USDA. As a government employee, Ray then distributed the trees and bushes as windbreak and soil erosion prevention products, through county agents to local farmers, at a reduced cost.

To Robert Walsh entering his forties, it seemed like he was the only man on the block without a career. He was determined to change that. If he had not been moonlighting in the farm auction business, he would still have his county agent's job; he was beyond that now. On the other hand, there was the life of Clark as another example of what a small community could offer. He owned a modern home that had replaced the traditional farmhouse built in 1920 that he and his wife had lived in for a year before he built his new house. The family could have lived in the old house he said, but he built the new one for the comfort of his wife and daughters, where the original homestead of the Jurgens family had been, just a driveway off the edge of Hwy 12 that stretched west to the Rocky Mountains.

"You can call me Ray. A friend of Bill's is a friend of mine," he urged Robert in no certain direction, letting the discontented, but still ambitious man Robert had become know he was perfectly happy living within view of the fast lane in an unusual and alternative agricultural existence. Ray was from Rapid City originally, like a tourist destination on the edge of the Black Hills. He liked living deeper in the country along with his attractive wife who ran the office in their home. Clark had two vivacious and popular daughters; the youngest Sue, was a cheerleader for the Bulldogs. Ray's girls attended school in the city of 3500. Walsh recalled the experience later as a job interview that would have placed him ten years farther behind the eight ball—if he had asked Clark for a job.

Clark had his stories telling Walsh that if he had been a good writer, and had the legal mind for it, he would have gone to law school like Janklow had, but the political side of it never appealed or interested him that much. He was a horticultural specialist, with a unique agricultural vocation, and Clark liked having one foot in the community. He appreciated the advantages of churches and schools in a low crime non-violent environment for a family, having the benefits of safety and security. There would always be an open market for his products which were distributed free by the USDA. He delivered the goods and was paid a nice salary at the same time many farms were collapsing in the sagging farm economy.

It was also apparent Walsh had more ambitions than the normal farmer he was used to dealing with in Grant and the surrounding counties; he sensed Walsh had latent political ambitions, those desires for grandeur always a fatal sign unless, well, he didn't want to think about that. For some reason Clark didn't ask the obvious question, "Are you looking for work Robert?"

It could be his doubts were spurs of ambition that would fling Robert past the streak of misfortune that plagued him–those brilliant, black spontaneous flashes like the luster of a shining Buick fender in the morning sun–when he barely noticed the shadow that grazed the side of his right eye coming from within, projected ahead slicing to the right like an errant drive, escaping at times with a *snap* before vanishing. He was not consciously aware as this flash erupted, originating from the right side of his brain then exiting through the eye, followed by a quick pulse of white light that left a dull glow–he imagined a tiny neutron bomb had exploded somewhere in his head.

Yes, once as a youth he had a "spell" in class while taking a math test, followed by terrible migraine pain and an outburst of incoherence when some incomprehensible sounds came out of his mouth the school nurse could not understand. Because of such experiences, similar to a walking *petit mal* after which he could function, but barely, Walsh was never ready to put such doubts away and never actually came to terms with, or told anyone except Shirley–he had no proof but he was "pretty sure"–as sure as a person could be after watching *Twilight Zone* and *Outer Limits*: there actually *was* something "out there" shadowing him. Haunting was too strong a word; it was just there, like another being hanging around–lurking. Walsh's more discreet personality projected alienation as he toyed with his customers, almost as if the experience of the Nundas farm slowly disintegrating, permeated into his ever evolving personal transactions.

The fear somebody would uncover the felony slowly receded, nonetheless the dread of discovery placed him immediately on the far side of the negotiating table in business and society; existing in denial of the regrettable events of his life became his preferred psychological method, connected with erasing his roots in Nundas–especially as he witnessed other men his age prospering while he had failed to accomplish even meager success. The cattle theft swindle was always in the back of his mind, and the first thing to be denied as he tried to maintain a normal conscious relationship with his peers. Walsh had always considered himself smarter than average; the thoughts and feelings that accompanied being swindled by a partner who he considered an intellectual inferior made the telling an even more unpalatable introject in his conversations with professionals. Clark was among the first men that made Walsh keenly aware of what he believed he had missed out on in his life. The very first had been his brother Ansel, his father's favorite son, with a place and reputation he believed he could never live up to.

* * * * *

The felony years persisted as like a cancer in Robert's memory. How could he be so gullible to trust Ritter, the man who robbed him? It may not have been the actual event that tormented him; it was the consciousness of failure, a consequence of his actions. It was the blown opportunities caused by other people; he had been set up and took a fall when he could have worked his way out of the cattle theft charges–if he'd had the money and a decent attorney. Sure they had him dead to rights on the plea agreement for less time; but he had not been allowed, as he was entitled to under law, to tell his side of the story. Because of that one mistake, he could never be too ambitious, and would always have to be cautious of his background. But it occurred to him often, that he might someday be able to become a private investigator using his experiences; that way he might be able to maintain and take advantage of his connections with politicians.

Robert was fascinated by the Johnny Rivers song "Secret Agent Man"–always had been. That song and "Memphis" was played all day long at the top of the hour on the KWAT and KFGO those days when Rivers was number one in the country. Both he and his wife Shirley never missed a Sean Connery *James Bond* movie on a crowded Saturday night at the Madison Rialto Theater.

There's a man that leads an exciting life, a life of danger; he lives on the *shady* side, or he wouldn't need to be secret. *I like that*, he thought. The idea of being a good bad guy was fascinating to Robert who was anxious to project himself out of the strait jacket of emotions, resentment and fear of another failure that drove, and yet stopped him in his tracks. How he admired tough-talking Broderick Crawford in a beat up '49 Ford highway patrol car in his youth. Coburn and later Mel Gibson became equally as fascinating, for reasons that appeared later in his life, Robert was charmed with those skills–that type of character appealed to Robert. His father Harold was a great fan of Edward G. Robinson and Jimmy Cagney; but Hollywood glamorization treatment of films custom-made for the box office stars did not teach moral and ethical values to Robert. Even in his youth those values had no meaning, as his conscience seemed to have vanished between the lines of his inventory of venial sins. He read through a hidden stack of *True Detective* magazines stored in the crawlspace when he graduated from comic books. With the end of his existence staring him in the face, the movies–the fantasy–made it appear that infamy, crime and mayhem had an impact on the wallet, and major bearing on business outcome in general.

"Sure," he spoke silently; he loved to see DeNiro as Capone dispensing justice at the banquet with a baseball bat–he got caught, but not before stashing millions. There were thousands more just like him who succeeded in covering up their crimes, their families living in luxury–the roots of the corrupt fortune never revealed–for that reason, the people never know about it. Sometimes the feds are in on it. His action, like few others, would be designed to capitalize on both sides of his steadily dividing personality.

By the time he met Ray Clark, he was thinking along those lines. He recalled the shining faces of Foss and Clark as they gave advice on hunting, farming and politics; those men, the political leaders of the Dakotas, were confident and positive. To them,

Walsh appeared like a man with a still undiscovered mission, a strange man with no particular goal in life, who never seemed sure of what he was doing. The high priests of the plains caught glimpses of the bright ambitious character Walsh would appear to be in brief flashes of light, like a powerful genie straining to be released from its bonds.

As they sat in Trevett's Cafe on the west side of Milbank, Clark, like Foss offered some free advice,

"All I know Robbie is that if you want to be involved in politics you have to be a reader and more than that a writer. That was not me," he continued, "When I come home after a day in the field, or distributing trees, or flying around my property, I like to sit down to the news, and watch Jim Burke talk sports on KDLO. By the time supper is over and the dishes are done, I'm ready to take a nap, walk the dog, and maybe watch Johnny Carson. The last thing I do is pick up a book, or want to type out some report; my wife does that for me. I think that's what kept me away from law. I knew I couldn't write those damn memoranda all the time for the court. Yeah I checked into it. A lot of service men in my unit, pilots too, were like Joe Foss. You say you met him; I *knew* the man, could never be that kind of man. Maybe I never had the brains for it. I could never pass the bar exam or argue in court. Sure enough you had to understand and write memoranda, you know–intent, causation, evidence. That was not my line of work."

Clark told Walsh that he wasn't old enough to enlist in the Marines during WWII; he graduated from high school in 1945. He had joined the civil air patrol out of Huron South Dakota after the war. Clark was married with two kids when Korea broke out, so he wasn't drafted. He bought the Piper Cub at an army surplus auction, and flying it was his only hobby to speak of. He had to keep that engine in tip top condition, especially if he expected to take up a passenger now and then like Walsh. Parts were getting scarce, but he loved that old scout plane. His prized possession it was. The tools that kept it in the air were mechanical skills he had learned from his father in the garage back in Rapid City.

"She's an old war horse, but the only action she saw was here on my farm. I have to keep her tuned to get her off the ground, and keep her in the air once I get up there. Don't worry Bob. I never take the 'Alona Gay' more than 500 feet off the ground. You're one of those *white knucklers* we call 'em. I could tell that as soon as we took off from the pasture." Clark was amused that day flying in the piper cub; it took Walsh a while to loosen up after the ride, and a bumpy landing in the field.

"If you want me to, I'll introduce you to some farmers from around here. I have to pick up my daughter after play practice. You drive. I'll take my pickup. You know where it is, right on the highway west side of town on 12. Meet you there in fifteen minutes." In Trevett's Café they resumed their conversation.

"Now you speak of Joe Foss on the one hand, I met him at the Democratic caucus back in the sixties. He told me he learned to like that legal writing stuff. He said he looked at those memoranda like stories about crime–maybe it was from his days in the Marines. He was a Colonel you know; he always had to be reading reports from headquarters. He told me he wrote hundreds of letters back home to parents of the boys on his squadron who had been killed in action. That's how he learned to type he said. He didn't want to pawn that job off on his staff sergeant."

"Nope, writing those letters he dreaded was the worst of any job in his life; but it was his job to write to the parents. Politics was gravy after that. Those chores, Joe said, are what made him an attorney first, and then a politician. He would always mention that, and his faith in the Lord; he probably told you that he imagined Jesus in the cockpit with him. It got me thinking, I don't know about you Robert. I'm a member of St. Charles Catholic, and my daughters went to parochial school there before they went to public after eighth grade. You said you Walshs were Catholic as we flew over my boxelder hedges. By the way, from the horticulturalists point of view, that's the only tree I know of used both as a hedge and a windbreak. We were only fifty feet off the ground most of the ride Rob. I wasn't trying to scare you to death," Clark said chuckling, picking up the check and rising from the booth. "I pick up my daughter after cheerleader practice because she misses the bus. Other one's off to college in Fargo. Meanwhile back at the ranch, you know, I've got a few chores myself", said Clark as he offered Walsh his hand before they parted company in the parking lot.

"If you are working in this area Robert, someday I would like you to meet my son in law Miles Shannon," Clark added as he handed Walsh a business card. "I taught my future son in-law how to fly in my scout plane before he became engaged to my oldest daughter. Miles runs a flying service now out near Ft. Pierre; he does crop spraying and that type of thing. We had our agreements and disagreements–he does spraying for me from time to time. We will leave that discussion for another conversation."

"I'm kind of rattled you might say," Walsh stammered, reliving his lifelong fear of crashing, as they parted ways shaking hands in the parking lot. "It scares me to death. I always had that phobia of heights. You couldn't pay me enough to be flying all over the country and overseas, like you pilots. I leave that to you people. I hope to chat with you again Ray."

He had a strange feeling, and it was all Walsh could think about to block out his fright of flying, as he drove back to Madison in the dusk with poor headlights on his faded blue '73 Dodge Coronado sedan. *God* he thought–it made him tremble all over to think of that horrible ride–the plane trip to hell he couldn't refuse. And yet somehow he couldn't turn the guy down, revealing he was the coward of the county who would *resign* rather than be fired straight-up for being drunk in an agency car–it was just bad luck–he had fallen asleep at a stop sign in Volga, drunk with an empty fifth of lemon vodka on the floor– a consequence of chasing it all night long. You don't tell a story like that to a Foss, Janklow, Clark, or any other government official. He had to fudge his credentials if he couldn't avoid discussing them at all. But yet again, Walsh was more convinced of his future mission, kindled by the strange anecdote on Foss's writing that Ray Clark related to him. It's old school, hard to learn; it takes practice to write with the power of an attorney.

ANTHONY FALLS JR.

For many years later, Walsh would dwell on the insult from a Nebraska judge that his petitions were incomprehensible. He would learn to be more clever about exposing his attitude and purpose; obviously these particular individuals as a group didn't grasp his intellectual point of view–that alone could be a problem unless personal transactions with legal authorities were involved and informed. His brother Ansel was an excellent writer who had published his thesis "Emerging behaviorist practices in clinical psychology" on the way to his PhD. Walsh was determined he could improve his writing and proceed with a personalized, what they called "pro se" approach to creating memoranda. Although he had never heard of a case in South Dakota, he was aware the State gave you ten years for impersonating an attorney–he would never make that mistake. He looked upon his early errors as benchmarks of the territory, useful if he put together the marketing business he was considering, writing marketing agreements with farmers around the area. After all, it was his improved writing that had interested Janklow; that was the specific skill that gave him immediate relief from the depressing weight of a felony theft conviction always on his mind.

Robert Walsh never had been one of those fellows usually in bed by eight or nine o'clock, sitting in a recliner like his Father Harold, chilling over a cup of tea like Ray Clark–or God forbid–like his wife Shirley, who sat around all day long in her nightgown, suffering the depression caused by her first husband's desertion for all her husband knew. Robbie was up and about his business night and day, sometimes pacing the kitchen floor until 3 o'clock in the morning. It seemed like whenever he was out on the road a while, the wife's restlessness returned as it often did with Robert's increasing business absences from home. Like any normal woman whose husband had grown cold and distant, Shirley suspected *Robby baby*, her husband's alter ego she seldom observed, was having affairs on the side–though she had no proof of it.

After the Janklow intervention, his faith renewed, Walsh believed he could pull himself up by the bootstraps, putting his reservoir of unsatisfied ambition to work reading and studying cases in agricultural law, learning to write better; eventually, he would be putting his studies and practice to work in a new profession that had not yet materialized for him. In the meantime, he considered applying for a job as a used car salesman in the Brookings GM dealership that appeared in the *Watertown Herald Tribune* want ads.

CHAPTER 4

The Zehlens had a way of attracting unusual charismatic people, some of them with money, to their cache of friends. They thanked Providence regularly in the Methodist Church for their position in the community. At the same church David and Nancy attended bible studies together, the Zehlen clan witnessed the advent of former Canadian football league star who had just committed his life to Christ. The newest member of the New Testament study group was Bill Gilbertson who played tight end ten years for the Calgary Rough Riders, before a neck injury sidelined him permanently in the '70's.

By a strange coincidence, Jack Zehlen and Gilbertson owned side by side lots at the edge of the lake. What had been native grassland became farmland, before the pioneers plowed as close to the beach as possible, cultivating every square inch of rich alluvial soil that had never felt the gash of the plow before 1900. Now that rich topsoil had become more valuable as perimeter real estate up for sale; choice lots evolved into model homes, in a showcase development of what was once "Julia's Point" and rumored to be a battleground and burial site for the Lakota. Next to the football star's lake shore property, Jack Zehlen was laying the footings of his dream retirement home. Two stars in their own realm–men who had pursued entirely different paths to success and wealth–were living one door down from each other.

An eagle nested in a grove of burr oak along the shore of sand and gravel. Pan-sized bluegills could be seen at sundown going airborne to snatch a dragonfly six inches above the water. The majestic bird was a spectacle–skimming the lake for its prey–snatching a walleye fingerling in its yellow beak, before making a meal of one of the ten thousands of little fingerlings hatched out of the Meadowbrook fishery managed by the DNR.

Jack, the historian of the family, would claim to his visitors that they were witnessing the same stunning sunsets Sioux and

Chippewa had observed 10,000 years before, as Lake Agassiz slowly shrank and divided the continent near Browns Valley. Both Zehlen and Gilbertson were building their spectacular homes of brick, cedar and glass as tributes to their successes on different and diverse fields; they were neighbors–and not a more incongruous pair existed on earth as these two–alongside the ancient footpaths of thousands of tribesmen and their kin, trekking along the shores of Big Stone and Lake Traverse. One of the local historians, Sally V–– donated hundreds of aboriginal artifacts and arrowheads, discovered on her father's farmland adjacent to the end of Zehlen's property, to the Granite County Museum.

Jack was fifteen years his neighbor's senior. Gilbertson was a recovering alcoholic with a limp from first knee, and then hip replacement. He and his wife Kitty became familiar with the Zehlens in the Methodist Church, where they became close friends in Jesus at these meetings. The ecumenical revivals resurrected during summers were a version of fundamentalism, related to a naturalism of the old Chautauqua generation that attended outdoor religious rallies in the thirties as a festive gathering barely recalled by the eldest of the parishioners. Such ritual was becoming a part of the new ecumenical movement evolving out of the Hal Lindsey *New World Coming* era–merging the new religion with the tradition of open worship that swept the area, some said *"like spirit wind"* in the late 19th Century.

Dominating the scene was the new age Christian rock sound of muscular Vern Bullock, the bi-sexual minstrel, who took worship to the burlesque level, pitching his work on vinyl and eight-track for sale at every church event as another memento of the fading Christian minstrel role in religion. Occasionally, Vern's most compelling work, "Walking and talking with Jesus," a catchy tune that resembled "Imagine" by Lennon, would filter into the Saturday afternoon rock rotation on KDIO wedged between covers by Fleetwood Mac and the Grateful Dead–there were *that* many requests pouring in from Vern's Christian rock friends. Vern charged no royalties for his original album title of the hit cover song. Nancy Zehlen's parents were enchanted by

Vern's power of words, and karma, as much as his music. The charismatic Christian leader stayed at their lake home while he was on an evangelical mission in Rockland.

In the late 1970's, David and Bill Hoven often attended Daystar Christian fellowship gatherings in Fargo. That nucleus of friendship, led by Bill Gilbertson and his wife Kitty, began to germinate as soon as they became members of the select group of bible study veterans, and their unified prayer circle of the community that included the Methodist, First English Lutheran and Zion Lutheran churches of Rockland. The wealthy couple became immediate candidates for the Board of Directors in any church they chose.

In those days, the younger brethren were encouraged to listen to, and be inspired by the intense charisma of Lowell Lundstrom, the *picker* from Peever who could be heard preaching his fiery sermons on KDIO on Sunday mornings before church. After attending a number of Christian conferences, David maintained a cautious respect for the community heads of religion who dared to speak out against agnosticism when few people understood the concept.

"I warn you, do not look at my eyes when I give the call to be saved!" David recalled Lowell's admonishment as the pious preacher thundered another warning against apostasy to his followers, while his blazing eyes scanned the crowd gathered at the Sisseton High School for any signs of rebellion from his decree. True believers sat enthralled at video cassettes of rising super-minister Kenneth Copeland's sermons on Christian TV; they rose, inspired into action by Andre Crouch and his music for God as he uttered his dire warnings the world was on the eve of destruction. "Keep the collection plates moving please, will you? Life as we know it could be suspended at any moment. Christ could crush out an H-bomb like a lady finger. We are always on the lookout for a *leader*, the new rising firebrand to pass the baton of global Christianization that is now sweeping through Sierra Leone and Liberia."

"Do we have any true believers in the audience?" Vern the youth minister challenged. "Then show yourselves. *Commit* to

Christ!" His eyes projected dark fire, daring some sheepish agnostic soul to step forward. Not a soul budged as Vern's deep tenor voice crackled like lightning over Julia's Point, as the sun set highlighted dark purple clouds to the northwest.

"I might ask this if you are agnostic. Did anybody out there see *Left Behind* on the religion channel? You do not want to be among those unfortunates, locked out of the wedding feast, when Satan is alive and well on earth as it is; you saw that electric pulse-like shock from the tiny stun gun implanted in the anti-Christ's hand didn't you? Once it hits you, watch out! I know it was hard to visualize in a flash of 30 frames per second black and white—but new technology will fix that highly symbolic scene once Hollywood gets a hold of it. It's an image to live by. Destruction is a handshake away," Bullock warned those who were listening at bible studies as he interpreted the gospel for a handful of high school students including Nancy Hoven.

It is no wonder the religious media, the daily bible verse—just the thought of religion—was of no interest or relevance to David Zehlen. He actually thought more about reincarnation than the standard dogma. Minus any mystery, the message was more boring pabulum from the adults trying to control their kids by sending them to church. His mother approved; he would take advantage of it. He liked being around his little woman. He felt comfortable with the Robert Plant generation hanging out among younger kids making their way as best they could amidst the vague notion of church supremacy over all matters—attendance alone was as good as it gets in the Rockland religious community.

Involvement in the new Christian media only made it more boring for David. The men's fellowship group that included the Zehlens, Gilbertson, Nels Paulson and Dick Rafferty, former star quarterback for the Milbank Bulldogs, and Bud Robertson, WWII war hero with a purple heart, would gather in homes and in the Methodist Church basement, intently listening as Nancy, stunning as usual, strummed along on the Martin guitar David presented her after the birth of his twin sons Aaron and Jordan.

ANTHONY FALLS JR.

Early in town, these same men spread the gospel of Paul, the wanderer, for Christ; the CMC (Christian Men's Club) gathered in small prayer groups, centered on their morning coffee, in the banquet room of the Cashtown Café, where they would roll the dice to see who picked up the tab. The exclusive Christian's men group thanked Jesus and the grace of God every day for keeping the peace, for sobriety, and the smooth serenity to meet life's challenges whatever they might be in the secluded hamlet of Rockland.

These men were firm believers in the return of Christ; but each man had his own interpretation of when that might be. Talking about what those interpretations were was strictly forbidden, unless some intruder tried a different spin on religion, like Bullock obviously had: it was the Christian men's job to run him out of town as a heretic–though that particular "mission" was never clearly defined or revealed in the church. When it became obvious the charlatan has introduced *entertainment* to religion, the ultimate sacrilege–at the very least the CMC knows *that can't be happening* in Rockland. These men were neither professionals, nor intellectuals, few as there were in Rockland (teachers being exempt), and represented what they believed was the elite, upper echelon of successful businessmen in the community–they were thankful for their blessings, and they wanted to *keep* it that way.

It was David's and his mother's firm belief that the arrival of men such as Gilbertson, who could make a *lot* of things happen in a short time because of their wealth and the power it brought, was a sign of God's blessing. It fit her notion that Stephen Rivkin would someday make a movie about Pleasant Valley to rival *Paradise* with Don Johnson and Melanie Griffith. You could tell they were not a real farm couple anyway, according to Marie–"no matter what *Siskel and Ebert* said."

With the help of Gilbertson, who held a license in drug rehabilitation counseling, and the co-investment he made in their alcohol and drug treatment program in 1985, the clinic emerged like a phoenix from social rubble, providing the cushion Zehlen production operations needed, staving off problems because of a fortuitous event. The advent of the faded football all-star, and his investment of close to two hundred thousand dollars in the community, much of that money invested in restoring the old hospital was paid in a union contract, at local pipefitter's scale in a package that amounted to $50K with benefits in salary David took advantage of, using his homegrown skills to completely renovate the boiler system and replace an old HVAC installation. After working as a pipefitter for six months, David directed the sandblasting and tuck-pointing operations as foreman of the exterior restoration of the old Rockland Hospital.

At least fifty prominent people from the community attended the groundbreaking ceremony in March 1986. Rockland *Independent* publisher Jim Kaercher wrote up an article about the legacy of the Zehlen family, and what their contributions meant to the town, honoring Jack as a classmate and dear friend of Jim's until the day he died. JDK praised the Zehlens for their contributions to the community and undying support of the arts and religion as well. The unusually long article described the services provided in the Anothene counseling business in the old, newly-restored Anothene drug and alcohol treatment center.

Few but the Zehlens themselves understood how they had managed to survive the '80's farm crisis, by the skin of their teeth, adapting to the shrinking farm economy by making the clutch switch from major flower gardening to rehabbing the few drug and alcohol addicts the teetotaling community would cycle through the door. By changing hats, the Zehlens were able to take a brief quietus from the staggering agriculture fast track, narrowly avoiding the 1986-87 farm lending crisis that took down thousands of farms in the Midwest. The family managed the gambit with a guaranteed subsidy from the government for two years with an option on the third depending on County patient admissions for services—if the program met certain standards *nobody* was monitoring. In a largely experimental venture, there would be little or no enforcement of vague regulations during a standard three-year window of opportunity the rehabilitation grant provided. The homespun Zehlen administrative staff would have a business to run for the next three years. Under new arrangements, the Zehlens would be able to ratchet back into farming once the S&L crisis had passed.

From the onset, the major problems facing the Anothene systems long-term plan was a relatively low amount of alcoholic and drug addicts in a small community of two towns, Rockland and Odessa, with a combined population of less than three thousand people, walking through the door when there was a program in place for the same services in the Graceville Hospital. To cut costs, David, who had no license to counsel, gave his free time to sit in at the treatment center as a volunteer, babysitting at the detox unit. It was inevitable after six months of operation, unless the administrators figured out a way to treat more patients, Anothene would have a hard time meeting the two-year volume necessary to qualify for another extension.

Nonetheless, this brief chapter in David's life–when he was a "counselor"–remains as anecdotal material; in terms of what happened to the promise of Pleasant Valley, this experience was invaluable ethnographic material for the study of the many records David would leave in his wake. As he revealed in future sessions, the Anothene experience was probably among the *last* pleasant and successful enterprises Jack and David shared on this earth. David would never relinquish his experience as a therapist in rehashing his past.

Combined with the private financing of Gilbertson, Phyllis Zehlen, Jack's second wife, used her talents as official grant writer for the farm; she had written the many successful Zehlen applications for USDA funding in the 1980's. For the first two years, the Anothene project was able to receive grants and subsidies from the government, underwritten by the credibility and a healthy investment by a former professional athlete in the Tri-County State Bank of Rockland, providing a basis for several operations loans the bank sponsored. The church group sang in barbershop harmony when the grant received final approval from the State Board of Mental Health and the Bank Board of Directors in the same week: "Drop kick me Jesus through the goalposts of life, straight through the middle not left or not right," to the tune of Nancy Zehlen's guitar in the victory celebration held at the Lantern Inn in Milbank, SD.

The counseling boom of the seventies created many jobs in the field, but most of them were in the cities where the bars and nightclubs flourished. There was only one watering hole in Rockland and it was visible from the sheriff's office, and court house. The Cove was open till ten most nights and for Vikings games on Sunday, serving as home to thirsty voyagers, alcoholics and designated drivers. The only bar in town was located kitty-corner across the street, and it was rumored, closely monitored during high traffic weekends and holidays, by the Rockland Police Department.

In hindsight, the home economic specialists of Rockland concluded "the program was not far sighted" enough in designing a program to serve a teetotalist-leaning population in a small conservative town on the edge of the frontier. It might still be open at 42nd and Broadway in Robbinsdale in the cities. For the insiders who knew the truth of the matter, the real business of Anothene was administrating the rehab center support loan legitimately, while riding the storm out was the main objective.

* * * * *

The Zehlens did not escape from the bank S&L loan crisis of the 1980's unscathed. Along with thousands of other farmers in the Midwest, the Zehlens found themselves in default on a frozen three quarter million dollar operations loan for which their property collateral was vulnerable; however, because the crisis had evolved out of low production linked to drought conditions at that time, it was business as usual. Farmers normally had special protection in bankruptcies; however, in the midst of crisis the bank collapsed, taking the Zehlen line of credit with it. In order to sustain operations, David and Jack restructured ownership of the farm with their wives, re-organizing their equipment and employee base into a custom farming operation.

ANTHONY FALLS JR.

The Midwest Federal S&L default and associated mortgages on thousands of farm properties were placed in receivership of The Resolution Trust Corp., a government-sponsored asset management program for failed S&Ls. Real estate and farms were cherry-picked into a Land Fund while banks were offered incentives to refinance new terms for owners or find new buyers. Under an arrangement with First National Bank of Omaha, the Zehlens were able to establish a cash-flow again in the nineties. They resumed farming operations on large parcels of land after arranging a deal to custom farm 16,000 acres of safflowers and sunflowers for Hector Sexton, a grower for SigCo Seeds and Ceres. With the crises of the late 80's under control, the Zehlens were able to continue their agribusiness operations as an expanded custom farming operation.

To increase efficiency of his operation and qualify for ASCS personage payments, David created a new entity as an affiliate of the Zehlen farm that was co-owned by his wife and step-mother, Phyllis. That evolved into a separate corporate partnership associated with the custom farming operation David named MinGo. Confident their problems were behind them, David and his father were able to ratchet up the farming operations again in 1990. The custom farming company resumed the Zehlen land leasing policies of the eighties; within a year the father son team was running a 45,000-acre enterprise that was as challenging a task as any CEO's job in America. David's dream of becoming America's largest farmer appeared to be a realistic objective in the sustainable agriculture movement.

In those days, David's employees showed up for work with the latest technology at their disposal. At sunrise in late March and April 1991, a half dozen flatbed semis arrived at leased-acre sites ready to download a cargo of 4-wheel drive Case IH tractors, cultivators, air planters and fertilizers. A crew of up to 20 men was prepared to spend a day or two in the field planting several thousand acres of sunflowers, safflowers, soybeans, and wheat before moving to one of the other eight counties the Zehlens custom farmed across Minnesota, North and South Dakota. A few members of the crew brought their families along, living a couple months in their RV's and campers or checked in at a local motel. David paid per diem and picked up the tab, sometimes personally delivering pizza to his crews after the day's work was done. A few of the men camped out in sleeping bags, rising early to fuel the tractors from the 5000-gallon fuel tanker truck that accompanied the fleet.

Before the men signed on to his crew, they were informed of their assignments in the job interview process conducted in February at the Anothene office in Rockland. Employees understood they were at will; no confidentiality agreement was required. Each member of the team David assembled knew going in that the plan required coordination, teamwork, and planning so that tens of 1000's of acres of planting could be accomplished under the best of conditions; which meant, weather allowing, the men could be working up to 16 hours a day to get the crop in the ground.

His crews worked 16/6 with Sundays off from April to the end of May depending on the soil conditions. There was little time off for rainy days, that were rare in the mid 1980's and early '90's in the drought-stricken Midwest. If rain canceled work, employees were paid half a day's wages and were guaranteed per diem and room at the nearest motel in remote locations. It was a good deal in those days when work was scarce in Rockland. The Zehlens paid ten dollars an hour and time and a half for overtime. His foremen received $15.00 an hour; crew percentage bonuses, up to 10 percent, were paid if the work was finished in less than the estimated time frame.

In his spare time, David was interviewed as part of the live farm news broadcast on a local radio station that served farmers in the Ulen, Minnesota northwest region. On one such occasion, Zehlen responded to falsehoods spreading relative to the phenomena of "low input sustainable agriculture"–which stated that its impact on communities in Northwest Minnesota was detrimental. One of the crew, of then-out-of-work farmers working for Pleasant Valley, stopped to fill his thermos after delivering mail at the post office in town for the boss, and heard this opinion among the gossip in Charlie's Cafe, "You big shot farmers come out of nowhere into our little town and take over what little we have without giving us anything in return." When Zehlen heard of this mild altercation with one of the locals he responded in a congenial fashion,

"Well, from now on I guess I'll have to deliver and pick up the mail personally rather than pay somebody to do it. That kind of remark is hogwash. Some people just don't get it yet; the crops MinGo plants add value to the property for the landowners. We lease land at the highest bid in the area, otherwise we wouldn't be here. Those farmers pay income and property taxes based on our work in the fields. That money is pumped into the real estate value of the community, and keeps the schools and hospitals open." As if he had to apologize for the size of his farming operations to the townsfolk he believed he was serving, Zehlen continued his defense of his method of operations,

"Believe it or not we are not the predators some of you folks believe we are; in fact, MinGo is legally a partnership. I am not the corporate bully I am mistaken for, and labeled as–far from it. When has farming ever been more than seasonal work? Think about it, while normal farmers do not collect unemployment benefits, our employees are entitled to unemployment insurance benefits if their duration of employment meets the program guidelines; we match their social security taxes. My father's wife Phyllis is the bookkeeper; with 20 years secretarial experience, she manages the office back home. I can assure you my men are paid very well for their services; probably twice what your employers are paying locally. The success of my operations dispels the idea that corporate farming is necessary for communities and resources just to make a profit; rather, that view of a business is irrational prejudice, with a certain amount of resentment at my success factored into my rival's opinions. I make my payments on time; the bank owns these Case tractors and combines–some of them worth more than a farm in this area. My truck belongs to my father who is back tending the homestead; he prefers driving his camouflage colored GM around Rockland so as not to raise the ire of the locals at *his* fortunes. We live well but not *ostentatiously*. I just learned that word from my sister."

A sense of humor was a valuable trait in dealing with parochial attitudes he encountered along the path of success. David believed it was radical attitudes of people who envied his accomplishments, that had kept progressive operations like his under a cloud of suspicion; those attitudes kept low input sustainable agriculture out of the mainstream of mid-western farming operations. LISA, as he called his post-modern farming philosophy, was legitimate. The Zehlens, by one method or another, had been practicing progressive farming since the 1960's–before it was labeled as radical, and with derogatory connotations. David admitted the Zehlens narrowed the ditches, but they increased cropland 5% in the process. Increased land meant greater production, more taxable income and increased capitalization. In their lifetimes, both David and Jack had seen wildlife conservation areas, habitat, and waterfowl production wetland expand 10% as many more farmers contracted their land to the government. The Zehlens went the other direction and suffered contumely and opprobrium for their innovation as their fortunes grew.

Zehlen, who was 36 years old in 1992, believed that the size of his farming operations was irrelevant. He had farmed 3200 acres in the 1980's and had been in minimum tillage since the 1970's. His operations defied the common belief that large scale farming, such as he was practicing in 1992, was environmentally unsound. Zehlen disagreed with his critics, stating his LISA technology was the most ecologically safe method of farming on the planet. Though his father was considerably more conservative than he was, David believed the environmental backlash was just another spin on the general prejudice he had experienced from the onset of his and his father's progressive farming philosophy.

"All this negativity is ridiculous," he stated on the radio. "Our detractors first resented our sunflowers. We could have planted sugar beets like the Harvey brother's operation, but we chose not to for appearances sake–the sunflowers had more aesthetic

ANTHONY FALLS JR.

appeal to the community than ugly stacks of vegetables lined up along US 75. That farm is located three miles north of Odessa on county road 29 where nobody sees the dreary production spectacle. We spared our community the grotesque, and some still resent us; we might have made more money with a commodity, but we chose not to. The spring markets were stalled, according to my dad we were losing money on standard crops alone. We would have been out of the business in five years if he hadn't decided to change the farming operations in the late sixties, he told me. That decision put me in front of the microphone today. From the start, many of the locals claimed we were doomed with the flowers. We proved our critics were wrong," he argued.

"Now those same people begrudge us our success. I intend to be the most successful farmer in the Midwest, and I plan to retire and turn my operations over to my three sons by the time I'm 50. All this resentment creates a vacuum; it's just a narrow-minded view about success in business and prosperity that falsely relates farm size to environmental damage when there is not a connection–that beef is a red herring. The same people who use that argument object to any ASCS or Soil Conservation program allocations I take advantage of. The method we use for distributing the $550K of government funds, is adjusted at harvest time based on each partner's contribution to production; the percent is then calculated relative to PVC eighty-percent ownership of the equipment, and settling MinGo accounts after marketing in 1992. Keep in mind, we set aside another 1000 acres in wetlands and soil bank just east of the homestead in Akron township. We had to take 3000 acres in all out of production, much of it adjacent to wildlife management areas, to qualify for that money. You won't find our local hunters complaining about lack of ducks and pheasants after walking the cornfields and sloughs on Zehlen land. There are plenty of whitetail deer also; we let people hunt there with permission, and don't lease any of it." Zehlen defended his position and off the record stated,

"We lease land from retirees, and 3rd generation farmer's sons who don't accept the concept of LISA, which has been in circulation and discussed in farm literature since the dust bowl days. I could explain it to them until I'm blue in the face, but I don't have the time to argue it. My dad went through it for years. It changed his personality; he is a quieter man because of it."

"Those people that are against it can learn about LISA like I did. We use the latest advances in technology on Pleasant Valley Farms. The same techniques I learned of in extension bulletins the government sent my dad on the farm. I read them, and learned what they meant. Those methods were preached in my agronomy classes at school. I studied the ways to increase production and prevent soil erosion on our farm, and practiced them for a profit," he responded to his vocal critics.

"Farming isn't rocket science. Anybody with a lot of land and money can learn it. Just look at Archer Daniels, Peavey, and Cargill: Do you imagine those companies don't know what they are doing? I'm competing with giants of the earth not just your local farmers whose land has been foreclosed by the small town banks, and then sold to the highest bidder, maybe a couple times already. We still own the original Zehlen homestead, purchased with Swiss bank notes and coin my great grandfather carried with him from the old country. Most of the original homesteads in these parts were bought up after the Depression. The owner, more than likely, is not another farmer like me. Born with a silver spoon some say. It was probably one of the entrepreneurial groups I am competing with. Ours is a method of survival against the predators that are stealing the land from the farmers. Have you ever read Faulkner lately?"

"This reaction to agriculture is what sounding a warning to the country is about–selling the south eighty for a year in Harvard, or the section in Otrey Township for a guarantee of a lifetime extended in the nursing home for my mother with MS– they say the board of directors will manage services, when there are several other customers, I should say patients in on that arrangement; and what does that amount to in today's economy where healthcare and treatment in a facility is greater than a farmer's average yearly income? My family was living through the national health care reform crisis before we changed our

ANTHONY FALLS JR.

providers; but that's another subject I don't want to get into on this program. My dad had to switch to sunflowers to make money in a shrinking farm economy, competing with increasing foreign control over the domestic markets in the seventies. Witness soybeans at triple the price we had ever seen in 1973, the year I graduated from high school."

"Maybe we would be out of farming, and I wouldn't be defending myself today, if he hadn't converted some of his production to sunflowers. I would probably be selling shoes in the city like my friend Allen Folkens. They had a half section but it was not enough to support him, his growing family, and his father in a nursing home with early Alzheimer's. Harold, I remember baling hay with him out on my uncle's farm before his stroke; he was always joking despite the never ending chores, but that is another story."

With those words he concluded the interview. If he had an attitude, it was probably attributable to his mother who reminded David often, among other religious instructions, he too would be defending himself like King David against the Philistines, always with the same message for his critics,

"Like the song says, 'before you accuse me, take a look' at your own erosion problem. Terracing with minimum tillage methods increased production of our corn 30 percent on some of our leases over the last twenty years. I can print the records from my computer program. Before you get all riled up, compare the percentage increase of your income and production over the same time frame. You will see I know what I'm doing. I'm as devoted to the land I farm as any farmer in the Midwest," he argues. "My statistics prove it."

In 1991, David planned to offer bonuses and retirement benefits as other corporations did, linking incentives and bonuses to employee performance, encouraging his workers to explore creative solutions that increased the efficiency of his production program. Property taxes increased and the cost of farming operations rose while market prices for standard grain crops remained steady and slowly crept lower. From his youth, Zehlen was always aware of the shifting farm economy and gradually gained an understanding of the competition his dad was always talking about, integrating bits and pieces of information with the farm market reports his dad never missed. By the time he graduated, David understood why the Zehlens were not milking a herd of twenty Holsteins and Jerseys like his dad's fishing buddy Clarence Johnson. It just wasn't worth the effort and investment. The farm markets affected every aspect of business in hundreds of small communities in the Midwest.

Approaching twenty years in the field together, the Zehlens had seen a number of farms and other businesses related to shipping cattle and grain to Chicago, Sioux Falls and South St. Paul go under as the farm expanded. David's managing driver, Niles Paulson once owned a fleet of 18-wheelers that hauled freight across the grain belt before rising fuel costs, and increased capital debt, forced him to sell the business that had been handed down to him by his father. Paulson in his gray Ford pick-up, now led the flotilla of Zehlen equipment on flatbeds, paving the way from field to field with beacon lights flashing, and a "WIDE LOAD" sign atop his vehicle, fronting a column of big Mack trucks, hauling massive farm machinery from farm to farm. While Dave surveyed his leased properties, his mechanic and supervisors rode along with him in the club cab, listening to the farm market reports on the mighty 790–each man, calculating what his share of the profits will be if the market improves even as much as a cent per bushel.

Most of the work done on his leased land was performed by men selected from the local communities. Some of his employees at one time owned the ground leased to Zehlen. A few of his men farmed for generations before being forced off the land during the financial crisis of the 1980's–the same crisis that the Zehlens avoided because they had converted crops, and received higher prices on sunflowers than on the standard grain crops most farmers had stayed with. They saved some of their money in the process, investing in real estate, IRAs and Keogh accounts. That was before the Zehlens primary lending institution Midwest Federal S&L failed in 1991; these events occurred at a time David Zehlen was managing his way out of the

Warner Elevator collapse that cast a dark shadow over the South Dakota farming operations–an issue that was becoming the subject of far greater scrutiny than the fortunate son ever imagined.

During the recession of the 1980's, the Zehlens farmed only the homestead and sections in Otrey and Akron Township. There was a profit to be made on traditional crops, but they were grossing 60 percent less without the volume mark-up of large sunflower crops, the stream of income the Zehlens had capitalized on during the boom years. The 3500-acre homestead, local leases in Swift and Lac Qui Parle, in addition to the Granite county operations, paid their taxes and produced slim profits.

Thanks to the Anothene grant, federal medical program subsidies helped to support and sustain operations on a minor scale. Through the tough years, the Anothene alcohol and drug rehab program was a life saver for not only their clients–it was a strategic move that sustained the farm until farm financing became available after the savings and loan collapses of the 1980's. The investment in a subsidized medical business gave the farm itself a boost with added income and tax shelter until the S&L crisis passed over, and a new lender materialized.

At that time, it appeared as though by a strategic business investment, and an amazing coincidence, the Zehlens were able to sidestep disaster, weathering the financial storm while many small farms in the Midwest were unable to. Using tax credits, cash reserves and real estate such as the converted hospital in Rockland for a facility, the Zehlens had successfully "red shirted" the farm, as Gilbertson, who would a few years later campaign for State representative in Meeker County, used to say.

* * * * *

One of David Zehlen's managers was Rodney Oberg, who had been one of the many victims of the pervasive financial crisis of the 1980's. His father was unable to locate a buyer for their Ulen farm before it was foreclosed by Farm Credit Savings and Loan of Fargo, ND. Oberg was a benefactor of Zehlen's philosophy. He didn't expand his farming operations by driving people off the land, unlike the corporations his was compared to. In view of the farming crisis, he would have never survived on the half-section farm his dad started out with. In his opinion, without the expansive, progressive operations Pleasant Valley farms represented–that had to be managed effectively in an extremely competitive industry–farm managers like Rodney would be working elsewhere.

Few if any of his employees he depended on, the foreclosed or already unemployed farmers, had advanced education or preparation for another profession besides farming. Without a job with Pleasant Valley, most of his men would be competing for scarce jobs in the small towns in the surrounding communities; or pulling up stakes, and abandoning centuries old careers, and family histories before moving to the cities looking for factory work in Fargo, Minot, St. Cloud, or hunting for labor and manufacturing jobs in the Twin Cities minus the high tech skills needed to survive in a highly competitive job market of more than enough at-will and seasonal employment, low wages and high rent.

In an effort to derail his critics who accused him of exploiting the communities, and the resentment that follows growth and success while others are traumatized by loss of their occupation and the only career they have been prepared for, Zehlen at times sounded apologetic for his success. As a man of agrarian principles, he did what he could to deflect criticism: he bought fuel, fertilizer, clothing and supplies from dealers and businesses in the communities his farms surrounded.

Whenever possible he dealt with local banks. He could have purchased the ten new Case four-wheel drive tractors he bought in 1991 direct from the factory and saved tens of thousands of dollars–instead he made a deal with a farm implement dealer in Milbank, South Dakota, 14 miles from his hometown farm base. The Zehlens had been doing business in the communities they served, buying millions of dollars of farm equipment: tractors, combines, cultivators from Whetstone Valley Implement since the 1950s, when Jack began farming the homestead with his father after graduating from Rockland high school in 1948. Jack had tried to enlist in the Korean War but discovered one of his legs was an inch shorter than the other; still, the National Guard artillery and ordnance unit from Rockland, that was called up in WWII, let him join despite his handicap.

By 1979, David and his father had expanded the original homestead to 3600 acres, adding another 13,000 lease-hold acres in the next ten years. Before Jack struck it rich with sunflowers, the Zehlens had a long history of crop rotations planting spring wheat, soybeans, oats, buckwheat, barley and rye. They had several decades of experience in conservation tillage and terracing, in an effort to preserve moisture that was scarce in the '70's. In 1975, July daytime temperatures averaged 89 degrees, with a stiff wind from the west fanning the heat. Outside of the sparse morning dew that evaporated within fifteen minutes of a warm sunrise, there was no precipitation from June 10th until the end of July. At night the temperatures dipped to 80.

That summer the first recorded earthquake in Rockland seismographic history rocked the town. A 3.5 event at 11:30 a.m. July 17th, 1975, rattled the china in his mother Marie Zehlen's cabinet. The quake did little damage other than leaving a few folks trembling, wondering what happened. David recalled that he had been rather disappointed he missed the once in a lifetime event, as if some kind of amulet of security was protecting him. He didn't feel a thing because that particularly muggy morning he was riding a tractor, mowing weeds west of the farm along the railroad tracks that stretched north to Moorhead. When he arrived for lunch, radio KDIO was buzzing about the historic phenomenon that had rattled the plates in his mom's cupboard. Marie Johnson Zehlen had felt the quake in her wheel chair, and was genuinely "all shook up" about it for the rest of the day.

CHAPTER 5

According to David, the low input sustainable agriculture business didn't really start booming–and that was for a relatively short time as it turned out–until Pleasant Valley enlisted a managing consultant in 1989. Tom Adelman and David met for the first time at a seminar on innovations in technology and machinery involved in emerging global applications, becoming acquainted the winter of 1989 at the former agriculture school that became the University of Minnesota Morris in the late 1950's. Tom and Dave immediately struck up a friendship that lasted over twenty years.

Adelman was a Jewish business man from the Twin Cities with a Master's degree in Business Administration, and a double major in Organizational Development. His professional development included adjunct faculty lecturer and mentoring at the Carlson School of Business branch of the University of Minnesota in Minneapolis. His specialty was international marketing; he had been a consultant for Cargill and ADM and had designed contracts in India, China and Saudi Arabia. To David it appeared attending the seminar and meeting a key individual was another milestone, and fortuitous event in his evolving career; and it was no coincidence he believed, as he had been searching for a marketing manager for his specialty crops. Obviously Adelman had the expertise he needed to administer his planned expansion into international organic production.

Adelman recognized immediately that David Zehlen was the exception to the rule, who seemed to be a very intelligent and progressive farmer with mixed traits of assurgency and agreeableness. To the professional trained in psychology, David projected a mix of religiosity, risk taking, and a sense of humor. Adelman could understand how such an extraverted personality as Dave's could serve his international marketing strategies. To Adelman, who was one of the first true professionals the Zehlens had encountered, David was someone who could serve him well within the international grain marketing industry–not as conservative as some of the sons of corporate farmers he had been familiar with at the St. Paul campus; in the multicultural educational agenda of the University, prejudice against other races or nations had no place in the curriculum. Adelman recognized David as a farmer with a global perspective, like himself–willing to expand and experiment. It was Adelman that set up an interview that eventually led to the *Farm Futures* feature article in the summer of 1992.

Mr. Adelman agreed to tour the farm in July 1991, and signed a consultancy agreement with David soon after. At the time Adelman agreed to marketing services for Pleasant Valley, he had an office on the 4th floor of the Grain Exchange building, located at 3rd and Washington overlooking downtown Minneapolis; in the years that followed he would be operating out of his home in the Seward neighborhood. Business was booming for him, as he lined up customers including foreign buyers in Europe and Asia for a number of clients, few with as much potential as the Zehlen enterprise appeared to offer.

As they toured the farm Adelman lectured Dave, as he was accustomed to at the University, on his general assessment of collateral damage experiences with other farmers during the S&L collapse, adding that he admired the strategy the Zehlens had used to preserve their production organization virtually intact through the rough years when hundreds of Minnesota farms had been foreclosed. Adelman advised him that he knew how to arrange financing, and find investors–exactly the skills David knew he needed.

Adelman had been a keen of observer of the greenhouses, and experimental fields of the St. Paul campus. He was fascinated with the "boy wonder" as he called David, who had never attended formal college, but appeared to be way ahead of the curve the conservative farm boys of AGR and Farm House fraternity were on. On the other hand, David recognized what working with a bold entrepreneur, willing to experiment with specialty crops that he grew, meant to his organization. David explained that he was among the first farmers in the Midwest to plant test plots of saskatoon, raspberry and nitrogen-fixing buckthorn, suggesting any one of those crops would make ideal showcase crops, growing along Cleveland and Larpenteur.

Smaller farming operations could not afford to take the risk of finding buyers for small acreages of specialty crops; finding those markets was Adelman's special skill. While many farmers had given up on non-standard varieties after failures to discover markets for their production–growing large quantities David was able to depend on Adelman's shrewd marketing skills, and connections in the international market. Under Adelman's marketing strategy, Pleasant Valley was able to forward market 100% of its harvests. The unusual size of his operations that required a fleet of semis and flatbed trailers hauling equipment with specially designed features such as custom machined air seed-planting nozzles, requiring adjustment from field to field, were modifications of equipment and operations few farmers in the Midwest could afford. Low input sustainable farming depended on application of the latest production technology across the entire operation. Coming out of a recession in the latter 1980's, few farmers in the Midwest had the resources or were willing to take such a risk or hire a consultant like Adelman who charged $50.00 an hour on a strict contract basis; but he was well worth it according to Zehlen.

In 1990 Pleasant Valley partnered with the University in employing a graduate assistant from the St. Paul campus; the male student from Bolivia was working toward a PhD in plant pathology, staying in Jack's old house, compiling data, and gaining experience in the field to supplement his research findings while developing a thesis on the effect of drought on seed insertion technology in the upper Minnesota River Valley.

David Zehlen's proprietary software, the Control Data custom program, was aided by USDA soil maps he used in conjunction with the sustainable input technology, allowing for more precise applications than had ever been possible in the Midwest before computer innovation. Relying on "micro-management" utilities programs that were unheard of before their time, the Zehlens incorporated and invested in advanced techniques and experimental technologies borrowed from the progressive agriculture movement to increase the efficiency of their farming operations; as a result of applied technology, the Zehlens were able to apply pre-emergence products at 25% to 75% lower rates than their competitors–while any pesticides being used were applied on a spot only basis.

* * * * *

If David Zehlen's dream had come to fruition, he might have revolutionized the sustainable agricultural movement in the 1990's with Pleasant Valley showing single owner profits of a customized farming operation unimaginable a generation earlier. Unfortunately, his banner–the idea that a farm has to be small to be sustainable is false–was used against him by one of his hired hands.

Instead, the eerie report of one of his foremen began to make some sense, about the time David's trusted Dakota manager from Ulen, Rodney Oberg, left a message to call him back, like he very rarely did; informing the boss something *weird* happened while he was overseeing the combining operations on a lease near Clear Lake, SD. He was just mentioning it, wondering who that man was he observed on a Saturday morning in October, examining the machinery with a notepad in hand. The strange event that lingered in his memory, like a bad dream, became relevant because Walsh had begun tracking equipment purchases for the bank about that time. That conversation came back to haunt him a few years later,

"I saw this guy I had never seen before snooping around the equipment. He had this air of authority about him like he was some kind of official, like a county agent, or a sheriff out of uniform. It was strange; the man was sneaking around in plain sight as though he had every right to do so. As far as I know nobody knew who he was. I may have been the only person who noticed him, because the rest of the men were in the field. I first noticed this stranger taking photographs of the tractors and combines; and later I saw him copying down the serial numbers of the tractors. I should have run him off, but I didn't want any trouble, and paid him no mind at the time. You know how it is. I thought he might be part of the lease owner's business. I didn't need the hassle. He was walking around like he owned the place examining the equipment, at least a half hour or so. It took a while but I became curious what he was doing there. I walked up to him and asked him who he was. He scowled at me and said, 'None of your business.' He had this irascible nature I could tell. After that, he must have had enough information. It was like he disappeared into thin air. I never saw the man drive up, and I never did see him leave the place."

David retained the impression whoever it was, was an ornery cuss; he knew Rodney was a peaceful man, never wanting to cause trouble, much like he was. That conversation with Rodney Oberg had always haunted David Zehlen until he discovered several years later: the man taking pictures and copying down serial numbers in South Dakota was later identified as his nemesis, Robert Walsh.

Robert Walsh would testify in a 1993 FBI affidavit that he had been a part of a federal inquiry that began in '89, about possible illegal dealings involving Zehlen, in which he claimed to have informed Zehlen that his name was being used in an international grain swindle being run through Woods Elevator in an agricultural marketing partnership with a community co-op. Walsh stated that he had learned through one of his associates that Zehlen had been having problems with Woods Elevator in North Dakota and had learned that their PMS personal marketing services, owned by Pete Werner his partner in the elevator, was involved in a lawsuit which included some Zehlen entities. Woods elevator had declared bankruptcy. According to Walsh, Zehlen had been liable for the elevator losses so Woods had pursued a civil suit against Zehlen that had yet to be settled.

Soon after his arrival, Walsh convinced Zehlen that as helm manager of his 15,000 South Dakota acres, it would be possible to eclipse the record-breaking profits of 1991. The odd fact was– that the Zehlen's home folk "naivety" rendered them vulnerable to being buffaloed by the rude Walsh spin–almost as if David and

Nancy had been trained to obey the harsh, rather than the kind master.

As a wealthy man, David was an attractive target for the predatory scheme Walsh had developed with other failing farmers. Using his best traits against his opponent–Robert's latent aggressive personality along with extroversive shock treatment connected to his inherent ability to launch a paralyzing sting into a rival's flesh–an unusual *trait* evolved from *pychopomp* ancestry, Walsh used his personality to deadly effect as he grew more adept at manipulating the victims he chose. The good-natured gullibility he observed when attached to natural agreeableness and hospitality of farm folks and their families, offered all the reinforcement Walsh needed to install his predatory nature into domestic affairs.

After ten years of polishing his methods to perfection, Robert had developed the necessary skills to affect the transfer of large sections of agricultural property, and laundered government money into the ledgers of Marketing International.

* * * * *

In late December 1991, an advertisement appeared in the Clear Lake *Valley Shopper* announcing a job opportunity in eastern South Dakota. Walsh noticed the new ad as he was posting used-cars ads for his employer's Brookings Dealership and Automotive Services:

> Help Wanted: South Dakota operations manager with large acreage management experience. If you have the credentials contact the Pleasant Valley Farms office in Rockland, MN

On a cold day in the middle of January 1992, Robert Walsh appeared at the headquarters of Pleasant Valley Farms located in the former Anothene building in Rockland. KDIO announced the morning temperature was seven below, and with a stiff breeze from the northwest off the lake the wind chill index was dangerously low, hovering at minus 23 degrees according to the weather reports on the radio.

Old glory was snapping briskly in the wind in front of the government offices, at the bottom of the hill where Washington intersected with 2nd. Like everyone else in town did, Walsh was ready to complain about the cold and now he had the occasion to do so with the very attractive secretary of Pleasant Valley Farms, Phyllis Zehlen, using the weather topic as an icebreaker with Jack Zehlen's wife of the last several years who at 42 looked just a few years older than Nancy, David's wife.

Wishing he had brought a bouquet of roses, Walsh introduced himself at the front desk before presenting himself to David Zehlen in the President's office; he was well prepared to win this interview and charm the seasoned and successful farm owner and operator, David Zehlen. The young man he was dealing with had considerable experience in managing farm operations, as well as functioning as financial manager of a business that grossed around ten million dollars in 1991.

He had run a successful business that made a profit despite the failures of partners in the past. Unfortunately, David had little knowledge and ability in litigation matters that Walsh claimed to be experienced in; he was impressed by Walsh's pitch. He stated that if Pleasant Valley needed references, as if his resume wasn't enough, he put David on the defensive immediately urging him to contact Bill Janklow, former governor of the State of South Dakota.

"You've heard of *him* haven't you David?" as if to imply he was some kind of rube who never read the news. And that was a fatal flaw Walsh was ready to capitalize on, to make a fool of him over trifles; as it was intended, the shocking coldness of the Walsh reply stunned David a moment.

"Yes I heard that name many years ago," his voice trailed off. "But that doesn't really matter. My secretary told me you had some information for sale. I'll look it over and make my decision in a week on both deals. I'll let you know by phone." He was thinking to himself, *this guy has me paying him 10 thousand bucks before he's done a day's work.* In his subconscious desperation, at the thought of losing someone who could manage an insurmountable task, he was willing to dismiss his vague suspicions.

"That information is what you need: the annual weather, average rainfall, soil conditions, and yield per acre. The details you need to succeed. All for $10,500–the information is worth ten times that."

As it rarely happened in his line of work, traveling from farm to farm, Robert met a woman with so much beauty, charm and power as Phyllis. His urge to have her was spurred on by a related irresistible force that united in his true being with religious *frenzy*–Walsh's hidden nature–the lecherous daemon delivered a low- frequency spark into the palm of his adversary.

"Okay Robert as you say, let me and my experts review the information," David stood up and reached out his hand, immediately feeling a strange sensation as if a tiny electrical shock jumped up his right arm; the weird feeling he had at that instant left an indelible imprint on his psyche as well as his conscious life. He was introduced–or perhaps inoculated into the psychic world Walsh had tapped into following the irresistible urge to have authority–over a situation destined to be out of control from the moment he arrived on the scene.

"I will look forward to your call in a week David!" For a second it seemed as if commandant "Klink" of *Hogan's Heroes* was barking an order to his subordinate. He felt oddly bound to obey some sequence of orders as Walsh executed an imperfect about face, and marched out of David's office.

* * * * *

Successfully married nearly a score of years, David could not have been happier at the peak of his career. He was about to embark on the next LISA based phase of his industry, featured as the *Farm Futures* man of the summer on the cover of the June 1992 issue. He was content to hang on to what he had at home and expand the farm. There were no other women in David's life; he had all he wanted and needed in his wife and children.

Prepared for their first meeting, Walsh mustered all the charm he could put together, for one brief presentation representing himself as a devout believer capable of doing almost any job. As the situation required, he was willing to do "whatever it takes to get the job done" in an efficient and organized fashion. Before he accepted the offer, Walsh said he would like to look over the farm and whatever information David could offer him on the condition of the farm, maybe take a look at the books if David was willing. Walsh indicated they could have a phone discussion on the nature of the job he would be doing after he looked over the job description; there was some mention of contracts to be clarified before signing on with Pleasant Valley Farms.

Walsh indicated he would confer with some of his associates in Marketing International before making his decision. But by the end of the month Walsh had accepted the offer and position as a registered agent and manager to work in tandem with Tom Adelman, David's consultant on the Minneapolis Grain Exchange, who arranged customers for organic crops including foreign buyers in Japan and Europe. From the outset that was one arrangement that failed to materialize. Although he gave lip service to the idea in the initial interview,

"He's Jewish isn't he?" Walsh inquired, "Never heard of him."

He was being mendacious. He already knew the details of Adelman's professional and academic career; and that he had a reputation as an honest business man and shrewd consultant who had become wealthy as an advisor in continental and international grain deals. He built his reputation as an advisor to the Cargill family foundation legacy.

Although David did not know it at the time, his new manager had absolutely no intention of working with his business model or existing market consultant. Walsh had learned such points of disagreement and controversy, in the early stages of a takeover, could be quickly deflected by ignoring the matter and by changing the topic whenever David brought up the subject of teamwork and cooperation, blowing off the inquiry realizing it will all be over in a flash–no one will understand what's happening. From the onset, Walsh would rely upon such methods as uncertainty, ambiguity and ambivalence as tools to mask his intentions, until outright threats were more effective.

Adelman would never guess what he was doing. David had in fact been shocked by the tone, voice and purpose of Walsh's strange allusion to Adelman's race–a cold flash of what he would experience in their business–but Walsh's remarks made an indelible impression consciously and unconsciously on David that he would not forget in twenty years. In one of his invaluable consultations with David in February 1991, Walsh claimed that he had received a call from one of his marketing connections in the Far East requesting information, intending to learn if David Zehlen had the ability to produce large quantities of corn and soybeans. Walsh said he believed the Bank of Asia was forming a loan package and might be using a letter of credit or warehouse receipts involving Pleasant Valley Farms and David Zehlen. Walsh claimed to have completed an investigation and determined that Zehlen did not have the capability the foreign bank required; that year they had only raised 300 acres of corn.

In an unrelated incident, although he wasn't aware of it at the time, in 1988 David Zehlen outbid Robert Walsh on a sealed-bid land auction contract to lease cropland for growing soybeans in Carthage, South Dakota. Subsequently, Walsh held a grudge against Zehlen. According to David, after that event Walsh was looking for a way to get even, when the ad for an operations manager with experience in low-input sustainable agriculture technology for large applications in eastern South Dakota appeared in the Missouri Valley shopper.

By January of 1991, Walsh knew all about the vast Zehlen farming operations having learned of the various leases the Zehlens were buying up around the county from farmers he knew. It was big news when suddenly 13,000 acres of leases were being sold in what had been recognized as unproductive land. Walsh recognized it as the window of opportunity he had been waiting for to gain a measure of revenge against an adversary, to affect the rise and fall perhaps of another mid-western farmer–and earn some cash in a hurry.

In the immortal subconscious conflict of the races, the eternal Walsh *demon* of revenge (at alienation) was there to oppose, punish, correct and remediate the corruption. What he viewed as the unjust transfer of generations of wealth accumulated by the landed aristocrats of Europe as they embarked upon America, he was carrying the sword of destiny for–as far as that approach could take a Teutonic warrior, whose aspirations to world supremacy had adjusted to relocation in America.

As much as anything, Walsh resented that Zehlens had a modern office in the City of Rockland, when the population had soared to 3000 during the construction of the 100,000 megawatt Ottertail Power Plant on the Big Stone side of the lake. Walsh begrudged that Jack was popular with the men of the town and the church as he had been since high school. Jack was known for his years of charity and many unspoken and generous acts in the community. Walsh could never be that open and popular; he had to always be aware to conceal his background and his purposes.

He complained to Phyllis privately that he thought Jack and David, in his estimation, spent much more time in town and in the bank than on the farm. Yeah he was picking up spare parts alright, at NAPA, which just happens to be right next to the Cashtown Café. Walsh pretended he was joking around with Phyllis; sure, there was a new young waitress–a pretty girl that has a young child–you know the type. She needs the money, working the cafe isn't much competition for the leisure crowd, Walsh continued smiling crookedly.

"Anything with money looks good to her. I'm not saying Jack's looking her over or anything similar to that, but the fact remains I know what these other lechers around town are looking for. That's all I'm saying. It's not something you should worry about. I'm just telling you this is Jack's crowd. I just hope he is a better man than them."

"You know as well as I, those two always are leaving the real work of running the farming to these downtrodden farmers they hired. And they don't really know what's going on in the market or in the field. Again, I'm not trying to cause trouble. I'm just telling you for your own good. Do you hear what I'm saying Phyllis?"

"Yes Robbie I hear you," said Phyllis. She later informed Nancy she was repulsed by the heavy *stench* as she recalled Walsh's Avon "Clint" cologne; she claimed later in a civil case deposition for a Zehlen creditor against Jack's estate, "I wanted to scream more times than not at Robbie when he was hanging around flirting–it was disgusting. I felt like saying, 'Are you getting fresh with me you old goat?' but I chose not to say it. I always respected Jack too much to even think about a man like Robbie. I knew he was a fraud the minute he walked in the office. It seems so weird now, but 'Clint' was one of my most popular fragrances when I sold Avon for a while after my divorce."

"I'm a city girl Robbie, I can take care of myself. Now if you don't mind, I have work to do. We need to finish this billing information for one of our customers. So excuse me. We can talk another time."

Robert's attitude was probably a reaction to growing up within earshot of his father's resentment, and the endless stories of gloom and doom tales of one farm after another by the time he was ten. He had heard of those less fortunate transient renters, who had lost their farms to various "shysters in cahoots" around Nundas from the time he was born it seemed. That training continued until he was old enough to understand, and by then his father was too exhausted and distracted by infirmities of various kinds to continue the narrative. What once had been innocent childhood desires to exact revenge against his father's opponents, had adapted to more practical goals of business acquisition, taking a more proactive approach to prevent that from ever happening again.

Though he did not consciously acknowledge it, Robert believed his father's experience proved that even in the new country the curse persisted; as he relived the farm drama of his father struggling, powerless to resist such anarchy in the market as had prevailed against the Walsh family heritage in the fatherland. In many ways Robert learned to believe the Walshs lost their farm because of entrepreneurs like the Zehlens.

Walsh was not bashful about his feelings. He commented to Zehlen about how he had felt slighted by the Carthage incident. Zehlen thought of it as a joke; if you can't raise the bet, fold your cards was the name of the game in high stake LISA farming. David never voiced opposition when that voice of rage and ruin rumbled as a threat to any contrary opinion; after all, Robbie was proud his brother was an assistant professor–he came from intelligent stock. David believed in freedom of speech. He was used to voiced opposition to his ideas and will around Pleasant Valley. Jack was always critical of his son's expansionist philosophy believing they had enough–managing 3500 acres close to home was a huge task. But David acted upon his ideas, while other farmers felt the same way as he did about expansion, none of them dreamed at the scale and scope David Zehlen had in mind. The Zehlens could afford to win or lose in the lease game like few other farmers could, a primary advantage of having a large operation and credit to boot. David had no clue–until it was too late–just how much his new trail boss resented that idea.

Walsh was being well-compensated by Pleasant Valley. He received a $10,000-dollar retainer–calling it a deposit for services rendered when, and if they ever were–for the use of his report on growing conditions in Eastern South Dakota. Walsh would accept the check as a down payment and a contract for a 5% share of the net plus up to a 5% bonus depending on the profits of the farming operations he was supposed to manage. It was their policy, Pleasant Valley operations made their margin on volume. They had done it many times to be in the position they were in on the verge of farming over 40,000 acres the year Walsh went to work for them.

After his criminal incident, Walsh was very careful. He was practical enough to realize he wouldn't be making a career in regular law enforcement or politics. Law was a challenge, if he passed the bar exam, as a felon he could never practice law; someone would find out when they reviewed his application and did a background check. His ex-partner on the cow caper would blow the whistle on him if he saw his name in the paper. If he were to run for office that blip on the radar would most certainly be uncovered. His hopes for a complete expungement faded. It would be a short lived run with the Board of Trade–it was not his fault he fell asleep in his B.O.T vehicle with the lights on after a night of heavy drinking and bar hopping in Huron. There would be no background check if he remained grade 4 grain sampler, but if he ever tried for a promotion it would involve a *criminal* background check.

There had been no resume check when he interviewed for the job as a car salesman in Clear Lake. The dealership needed a fast talker–a shyster really–who could move the used cars piling up in the lot before the new year models arrived. Making his ten percent commission was his only concern. At home Robert faced the prospect of Shirley on the verge of a nervous breakdown, raising two kids in elementary school on an economy budget, addicted to *The Price is Right* with Bill Cullen, curlers in her hair, smoking Pall Mall non-filters–rarely changing out of her nightgown and bathrobe until the kids came home from school. Until then, in her pink nightgown, she sat glued to the "Matinee Movie" every weekday afternoon at 2 p.m. on channel 9, with the coffee table in front of her laden with cups and saucers, stacks of *TV Guide*, *Reader's Digest*, *Life* magazines and the local shopper. After 15 years of marriage, Shirley was becoming increasingly dissatisfied and bored with life in small town South Dakota. Haunted by the ghosts of the prairie, she threatened to move back to Mobridge and live with her mother. A report from a home health care worker revealed that at the time, Shirley was becoming dependent on "mother's little helpers," prescription drugs to relieve the stress involved in raising two small children. Robert accepted his wife's treatment program, believing the drugs made her calm and easy to deal with. He assured his wife he had a plan that would take them out of poverty. He just needed a little more time.

Shirley was the only woman Robert had ever felt close to after his mother died young. If she was even the *shadow* of herself, Robert didn't want to lose her. He worked hard, nights, weekends, and on Sundays he drove a late-model with a "For Sale" sign in its window to St. Francis of Assisi Catholic, parking in front of the church. He became an award-winning car and truck salesman for Honest John's Chevrolet and Cadillac, rising to sales manager in two years, commuting to Brookings where he eventually relocated from Madison.

Despite his success in the automobile sales, Robert was moonlighting. He never lost sight of his lifelong goals in farming and farm affairs; that was where the land was, that was where the agriculture money was to be had through his contacts he made selling new cars to wealthy farmers. The great fortunes of the Cargill, Continental and Ceres organizations were founded on the buying, selling and transportation of grain, and ultimately, property. While his professional journeys led in other directions, Robert had for many years worked two jobs, talking the grain market quotations with his customers at Honest John's, and establishing contacts with some of the successful farmers in the Clear Lake and Brookings area. He sparked enthusiasm for his products at the Crystal Springs Rodeo as its part owner in the early '80's.

By the middle of the decade, Walsh had put the cattle theft incident in the rear view mirror; by then he was taking advantage of the reference of Governor Bill Janklow in his briefcase. Walsh had set up a grain marketing business to service the connections he had established with farmers in Grant and Duehl counties of South Dakota in Brookings, S.D called Marketing International. He stayed clear of the declining livestock business altogether. The resume he handed to David Zehlen stated Robert had done a three-year study of the State of South Dakota for Continental Grain Company; the study generally identified the productivity of various agricultural acreages in eastern South Dakota and western Minnesota. It was during those days that he met Hector Sexton at a marketing convention at the Corn Palace in Mitchell South Dakota.

"You've heard of Governor Janklow before haven't you?" uttered as if it were some kind of threat to his intellect, indirectly connected to the dreaded thought of being beheld as a rube, by a stranger. That happened spontaneously under tense conditions, as if the pitch and subtle threatening tone of Walsh's order, eliminating any doubt of his credentials–in a cunning fashion inferred David had to be ignorant if he hadn't heard of Bill Janklow–adding the specter of doubt immediately to the conversation over who's the boss of space and time under the umbrella the Walsh proposal consisted of. At those instants, David recalled his wife making the same form of innuendo, the vague sense his wife was implying, he was *naïve* about important matters, when she inquired too deeply of him about issues that didn't include him.

* * * * *

"Haven't you ever heard of John Cage David?"

"Wasn't he the leader of the Zombies honey?" Dave answered in his usual dismissive fashion relative to the fine arts.

"Oh you insult me with your stupid spins. You insist on being an authority on my performances, and every subject that way, when you know absolutely nothing about art. That is the trait I hate most about the man I chose," she moaned as her voice faded. Nancy was disgusted with her husband's lack of interest in conforming to her social register. If he wasn't acting dumb, he was being dumb; proving how ignorant he was time and again. Like the time he bought ten pairs of Levi's the same size so he wouldn't always have to be washing dirty jeans while he was in traveling mode.

For Nancy knew David cared little for the culture occasions his wife of ten years thrived upon as opportunities to perform. She had grown up being a part of society--in the center of it– always the main attraction. Her parents taught her to act like a star as if it was her moral responsibility in the church as well, where it all started: the seat of religious fervor, *absent* the spirit. If Walsh was 25 years younger, he had an extroverted trait that was attractive to her. Walsh could promote the talent; her beauty and power over men she knew she had. Getting involved with an older man who looked and acted like Nick Nolte was ridiculous–that situation was out of the question.

"I never had another man besides David; sure I've thought about adultery many times, but I never committed the physical sin. You don't mind me watching my program do you?" Nancy, unembarrassed, was tempted to say, '*Do you want to hear the details old man?*' As Robbie's face contorted into an odd grimace, Nancy turned to the afternoon soaps for entertainment on her day off, continuing his probe into the private lives of the Zehlens as the TV echoed in the living room, "*like Days of our Lives, the sands of the hourglass,*" turned to what's going on, behind closed doors. As usual inane lyrics created the mood, amidst the sound of the kitchen radio echoing in the hall next to where Walsh had taken a chair. As the mid afternoon sun filtered through the trees on the west side of the house, further in the background the sound of the Thursday afternoon country classic rotation, was muffled, but well managed by local disc jockey Paul Zahrbock.

"One thing we have is an active sex life Robbie," Nancy confessed as he *cringed* at the thought. "But I never dwell on other men. The thought of it is too creepy. I really don't like to talk about it; you keep bringing it up like you're a priest or something, trying to convict me of shame, guilt and sin."

"You believe in Christ don't you?" he inquired. "That's good enough; you're free of sin." Robert desperately wanted to ask, *Did you have sex before marriage? And at what age was that? So we know you two were having underage sex, and that is a felony in my book. Yes, you have avoided the details*, he thought. *That is until now, you now know I know what was going on after religious instructions your junior year, and after play practice. Who instigated that contact is what I'm concerned with? That knowledge gives me power over your marriage.* Walsh conceived his ideas over many hours, but did not use the leverage at that time, as Nancy went about her housekeeping chores before the kids came home from school; all the time Walsh was passively assuming the director's chair in the homespun drama that someday might rival *Our Town* in his imagination. Any man in

Rockland would crawl through hot coals for that woman. His leading lady was headed for prime time.

Young Ms. Zehlen, at 27, had the looks and charm of a rising Madonna. Yet there was something oddly incongruous about the sexy star quality of a girl brought up in the heart of the church. But being a wife with four kids in rural America, one disabled with handicap, living at the edge of a little podunk visible from the city limits–she was forever a town girl with one foot in the country. David was satisfied with his trophy wife, definitely one of the most beautiful women in the county, like his maternal ancestor Zeus (one of David's email handles) he once had Aphrodite to wife, and to bed. Like any husband confident of his wife's love, honor and obedience, it took a while before David realized how a somewhat uncouth, aging man with seemingly nothing to gain could completely destabilize his marriage.

While David appeared to be rather unconcerned over government funding issues he believed were under control though Walsh routinely seemed like he wanted to argue about; in discussions, he would begin in an agreeable fashion and quickly become annoying to David who had no idea how dead serious Walsh was. He found himself thinking often of how intimidating the initial interview had been.

"We are entitled to the USDA money because of our capital investment period," Dave stated.

"But the rules state that custom farming operations are not entitled to government funding," Walsh riposted.

"We handle that issue because Pleasant Valley is an invested partner in MN Go."

"Then why would you want a third party getting the money?" Walsh inquired.

"That's the way we do business at Pleasant Valley. We trust our partner's intentions. Now if you don't mind. I have my other leases to attend to at this moment."

David could not imagine such resentment against him–the scope of damage that trivial grudge over the failed Carthage bid, had fostered–or what the success of his farming operations would amount to as a result. He could not help thinking that

Walsh was joking with him, because if he was serious why would he have taken the job in the first place? He pondered without resolving the unimaginable obvious. "What had he gotten himself into this time?" David thought. He had dodged a bullet in the Werner elevator swindle that had cost him $250K hard; he couldn't afford another fiasco like that one just as he was getting his new partnership off the ground.

In the course of his life, he had met his share of skeptics and dissenters in Rockland, but never a man with such an overwhelming personality as Walsh projected–who had taken it upon himself to appropriate what he was unable to pursue politically–because of the ever present issue of his criminal background. His philosophy amounted to a personal crusade against government funding of small farms. He had support in his belief from the conservative financial institutions that had rebounded from the collapse of the eighties–reactionary forces Walsh aligned his policy with agreed–that drastic measures needed to be taken against government programs that allowed farms like the Zehlens to expand beyond the original 400-acre homestead.

And although there is no evidence other than the fact that Walsh stated to the FBI that he had numerous contacts in government, that he was a private investigator with easy, if not immediate access to bureau officers in March 1993, and that he was "working for the government"–Walsh went as far as stating the Feds were actively engaged in eliminating subsidies to small farmers that allowed them to expand their operations beyond one section adjacent to the original homestead–farms which would have never survived without arranging funding from private banks that were now in jeopardy with government-guaranteed loans. A form of panic had set in among banks and farmers alike in fear of losing their livelihood, as government programs began shrinking under stricter regulation.

Although they had broached the subject in conversations in the office and at Cashtown Cafe, David did not recognize the implied threat having anything to do with his farming operations. And in maintaining such denial, David Zehlen remained unaware

ANTHONY FALLS JR.

that Walsh had other intentions on his mind. As he shook his hand that day in Walsh's office in Brookings, David felt what he vaguely described later as a slight electric shock to the palm of his hand that traveled up the wrist into his right arm. The little spark reminded him of an image from the religious film *Left Behind* he had seen at the Methodist church, the thesis of which he had dismissed as superstition. He forgot the memory completely until he heard his dad referring to Walsh as a "snake in the grass" during the desperate hours of the takeover.

From David, Walsh had learned more details of his business relationship with Hector Sexton; and that in January1991, Zehlen was approached by Sexton to custom grow sunflowers under contract for his company, Ceres, funded by Specialty Vegetable Oils, SVO, a wholly owned subsidiary of Lubrizol. Just as he was coming on board Pleasant Valley in February 1992, the "Growers Agreement" contract was being reviewed by Sexton's attorney. As Zehlen understood it, the contract conditions remained the same as they had for the 1991 growing season; Zehlen was clearly defined as the manager for Sexton's crops, with a production bonus of 25% net for a profitable year.

According to Zehlen's interpretation, Sexton was also required by the contract provisions to provide equity loans, equivalent to the personage payments utilized in production, to fulfill equity requirements for each of the 11.5 MN Go partners, that amounted to half a million dollars or more, to be distributed to the MinGo crew and associate enterprises David was working with–that provided all the labor for operations. As it was with the custom farming assumptions, Walsh was highly skeptical of Zehlen's beliefs in his entitlement under federal programs.

A partnership was set up under guidance of Counsel Ray Rylance of Rapid City, South Dakota to meet the government's farm subsidy standards and enroll the sunflowers and safflowers under contract that amounted to 16,000 acres, in the farm program. There was a very successful sunflower crop in 1991, and for that reason the 1991 contract with Sexton and the bank was extended by all parties for the 1992 growing season. The agreement was expanded to include the original sunflowers, adding experimental safflowers. Under the contract, these crops were to be financed by Ceres/SVO/ Lubrizol as owner; and also by a third party to the deal–First National Omaha held the equipment lease on the ten new tractors, and upon providing additional capital to the Zehlen Sexton grower's arrangement, they took a 1st lien on the crops.

Fall 1991, David informed his partners in MinGo that he was a bit concerned, even though he had made a profit on volume, because Sexton had suddenly cut the production payments they had originally agreed on from $28 to $18 dollars per acre citing declining markets and increased costs as the reasons. He explained he was withholding distribution of the personage because Sexton was seriously in arrears, anywhere from $300,000 to $500,000 dollars, relative to the ASCS funds that had been allocated in July; but, he assured his men Sexton agreed to make up any differences when the 1991 harvest was marketed spring and summer 1992.

Sexton was well connected with a number of years experience dealing in the Chicago grain market as a representative of one of the largest agribusinesses in the country. As field representative of Ceres-Lubrizol-Sigco, an agricultural marketing giant out of Toronto, Canada that was seeking growers for their company's specialty crops, Sexton was looking for large farming operations he could offer marketing services to, operations big enough to produce large volumes of grain at harvest, and in storage, to interest foreign buyers in Asia and Europe.

In particular, Sexton was looking for growers who had enough of a margin, enough cash reserves to invest in specialty crops, some of them experimental. He offered his package based on Zehlen, the government's and the bank's willingness to invest millions in an experimental crop, high oleic safflowers. It was Robert Walsh who knew in intricate detail the risk involved in large scale testing operations which were uninsurable in many cases. In Pleasant Valley's case, premiums were very high based on potential losses on 13000 acres of safflowers.

"Eventually," Sexton stated. "I would like you to meet my brother-in-law Jeffrey Provo some time; he owns an insurance business in Fargo. Jeffrey handles all my accounts out of his office with my sister as his bookkeeper. He offers discount rates on specialty crops when the bank won't approve loans without insurance," Sexton assured. "I don't know where he finds his underwriters; but he never failed me yet." Hector patted his shoulder. Walsh knew the risks as he handed him his business card.

"You know what these rural people are like, friendly, trusting–not like your East coast kind," Walsh continued. "In general, easy to work with, nice down home folks."

"I've heard of the Zehlens around these parts," the heavy-set Jamaican stated.

At the time he signed on with Zehlen, Walsh was fully aware of the nature of Hector Sexton, who in 1989 had been involved as a government witness in an arbitration case involving ASCS eligibility requirements that included hours of expert testimony concerning governmental agency rules on commodities fraud. In that case the agreed on rate was affirmed. Sexton's lawyers demanded that he share half the forfeited $20/acre expense of common costs as "finder's fee" entitlement, explaining to Walsh, that because of a pending divorce and bankruptcy he did not want to receive the money he was due from arbitration directly from Farmland once a settlement was reached.

Sexton planned on extracting the same fee from current production contracts. In the DeKalb fraud case, he arranged for his stepbrother John Donovan to be the receiver through a dormant off-shore corporation, JEX International. In the proceedings, Farmland insisted that the payments were secret bribery, and that the fees were nothing more than payment for consulting services rendered to a client of Sexton.

Like his partner, Walsh had already witnessed and testified in a number of cases, as he stated to the FBI in 1993, in the Pleasant Valley case. He was a regular as witness for the state, in numerous farm foreclosures across the Midwest, and a frequent attendee at property auctions, especially in eastern South

Dakota, hard hit by lack of precipitation and cool weather at harvest in the late 1980's, usually after blistering summer heat had fatally stressed the crops reducing yields sometimes in half to nothing. Walsh was well aware of the marginal soil quality, below contract specifications, at the Sully crop site Zehlen and Sexton were considering as suitable land for safflower production.

Under the right conditions, high-oleic safflowers could be a gold mine, but the seeds turned to fluff if pollination conditions weren't absolutely perfect. SVO was in fact testing eastern South Dakota to determine if there was any potential for successful safflower production. In his study for Continental, Walsh claimed he had not found land or conditions suitable for that particular crop: it might be right for certain hillsides in Turkey, perhaps North Dakota or Canada, but not for planting on the South Dakota farmland prairie where there was always the greatest possibility of drought. Walsh factored nature's threats, the thousands of acres of delicate stemmed safflowers that probably would be deluged by heavy rains and tornadic winds, into the business equation–when 16,000 acres he managed, and an investment of close to $2.5 million was involved. They had been fortunate in 1991 making a substantial profit. Walsh, Sexton and David Zehlen all knew they were pushing their luck in 1992.

Walsh was cunning where Sexton was shrewdly relying on leveraging obscure government program regulations against his customers for his own benefit; in his system the legal system reinforced *his* business. Before these two men converged on Pleasant Valley Farms, they had seen the rise and fall of unfortunate farmers on small farms, with low cash reserves, who expectantly took out a few leases, over-extended themselves, perhaps gambling on buying a $150K combine, when they were counting on a good crop. The success of the small farming industry depended perilously on an uptick in the Chicago futures grain market, a major sale of hard red wheat to Premier Gorbachev negotiated by his boyhood idol Ronald Reagan, or perhaps a drought in South America. Walsh had seen and been there, as far as the port of New Orleans working out of the

Peavey and public elevator for the board of trade, inspecting barges from Sioux City that had gone sample grade after three months cooking in the green Mississippi.

From the Board of Trade, Walsh learned the trade of sampling and grading (corn, wheat, beans and rice) for weight, moisture, and foreign material; for example, determining through a microscopic inspection when too much sample grade bean, with a tainted dose of three percent foreign matter, is mixed into the grade "A" beans some of his customers shipped from Iowa. Crops fail because of drought, hail, poor seed quality and sometimes because of poor mixing and drying at the elevator. If one of his customer's insurance didn't cover the margin in crop failure as loss of revenue, he had barely enough to pay the production costs. Sometimes an elevator would explode in the middle of the night from over-accumulations of heat, dust, gas–one match lit in the dark–the explosion could be heard all the way to Baton Rouge, like what happened at Continental in August 1977, while Walsh was inspecting corn at the Reserve terminal.

In the system as he viewed it, the small farmer is completely out of luck, one bad crop from being unable to make payments on the new feed lot, combine, or pole barn financed by a high-interest farm loan. And he would be first witness to the collapse when the bank forecloses suddenly without notice, citing some hidden feature in the contract structure violated as cause; the farm and the machinery are lost. A thousand farmers a year were losing their properties in the mid to late 1980's.

CHAPTER 6

Hector Sexton had been employed by the Ceres organization in various capacities over the course of two decades. He was a descendant of an 18th-century marriage partnership between Jewish and Spanish immigrants who settled along the east coast of the United States. His father was a native Jamaican of mixed blood and underworld connections. Sexton studied agronomy at Georgia Tech. With a bachelor of science and graduate courses in plant genetics, Sexton received a fellowship through the Norman Borlaug Institute for continuing research, developing environmentally adapted varieties of triticale for food grains, working alongside farmers in the western mountain regions of Mexico. Sexton and scientists from Argentina and Latin America developed low moisture, heat resistant strains of corn and wheat for growth in mountainous soil.

He became an account executive for Fraser-Perrone Commodities, working as departmental head under Christopher Perrone in 1985. In his role, Sexton made consulting agreements with Ceres, SVO (Specialty Vegetable Oils) and Lubrizol. He had established an office and a partnership with his brother-in-law Jeff Provo, a licensed insurance agent in Fargo, during the hay days of high commodity prices, and the trading bonanza of the mid 1970's.

As a bi-lingual executive, Sexton represented Ceres in negotiations with Argentina that netted the parent company millions before the price of soybeans plummeted, when a surplus developed as thousands of farmers switched from growing wheat and corn, to soybeans for higher market value, creating a commodity surplus that eventually slashed profits.

Hector Sexton was known and respected among the grain traders and middle men running the gulf port elevators from Houston to New Orleans, where most of the samplers along the coast and river were Mexican. To his associates, he predicted a market collapse was inevitable. In Cassandra-like fashion Sexton was ignored, but he was well remembered in the trades; his language skill allowed him to become a consultant in negotiating longshoreman contracts for loading his customer's grain onto foreign ships. His career was always a step ahead of failure. While the national farm crisis widened, Sexton continued to build a resume and his career in agribusiness, rolling like a machine– while the crash cost fortunes as the bottom fell out of the futures market in soybeans, a few years before Ceres offered him a research position in Argentina in 1975.

In the following years, Sexton would be accused of fraud in a 1983 lawsuit against Farmland. At the trial, Farmland attorneys contended that, with respect to the charges that were the basis of Sexton appeals, the district court had erred in excluding expert testimony concerning agency rules on commodities fraud in affirming the judgment of the lower court. The case was settled out of court while no criminal charges were ever filed against Sexton. Walsh was of the opinion that if it had not been for the backing of the legal staff of Sigco and Lubrizol attorneys interpreting the contract liability issues in his favor, Sexton would have done time for securities fraud and money laundering.

* * * * *

In January 1991, David Zehlen was approached by Sexton to custom farm safflowers and sunflowers under contract for his company Ceres that was affiliated with Specialty Vegetable Oils; SVO was a wholly owned subsidiary of Lubrizol Inc. In February, the "Growers Agreement" contract for the 1991 growing season was drawn up by Sexton's attorney John Freeman.

In that agreement, Zehlen was clearly defined as the manager for Sexton's crops, with a production bonus of 25% net profit. According to David, Sexton was also required by the contract guarantee to provide equity loans to each of seven partners in MN Go Farms (MinGo), as custom growers, in exchange for personage payments which would eventually flow into production as payoffs to the lending relationship for in-kind labor and operations management. A partnership was set up under the guidance of agricultural attorney Ray Rylance of Rapid City to meet the government's farm program eligibility, in order to enroll the 16,000 acres and producers under the contract; the same set of standards included enrollment in federal programs for hybrid soybeans, and safflowers, genetically engineered by SigCo for growth on his Sully County leases.

By the time an arrangement between Sexton and Zehlen was affirmed a second year, Walsh had already begun his covert operations to *secure the beachheads* for a takeover of Pleasant Valley by the middle of the summer. In the previous year, Sexton had expanded services to grain producers, with pre-production contract sales of specialty grains ready to reach experimental stage, using test plots larger than the parent had previously attempted. That being to establish whether or not the crop could be produced profitably, and at what percentage of yield, on much larger tracts of land than could be produced on SVO test plots. He was looking for leases of 10,000 acres or more. Consequently, when Robert Walsh contacted his former associate in the grain marketing business to discuss and compare notes on the man he was now working for, David Zehlen, his response was,

"Oh yeah I heard of them, the big shots from Rockland expanding into my territory. Some of my leases used to work for them," Sexton added. "Others say they bit off more than they can chew. They dodged the Werner swindle through some fancy lawyer work is what I heard."

"That's why they hired me to straighten things out Hector." Both Sexton and Walsh realized an ideal situation was in the making. It was Zehlen that encouraged Walsh to work with his marketing consultant Tom Adelman searching for buyers and expanding markets in India, Japan and Europe while finding customers for their organic crops. That would be out of the question in dealings with Walsh; the challenge would be working around Adelman, or he would be sourcing information to Zehlen that didn't fit the pogrom's needs.

Walsh was well aware of the potential Zehlen had for success or failure in a joint venture, having witnessed the demise of many farmers in eastern South Dakota as they failed to develop profitable markets for their production. He and Zehlen agreed that was one of the main reasons why he was hired, to avoid such situations that had ruined smaller farms, even those of some men who worked for him like his operations manager Rodney Oberg. The potential of having much larger quantities than the average sized farms had helped Zehlen clear that obstacle with his resident advisor Adelman. With Walsh on board, he could double his foreign sales, well worth the price for expertise Zehlen had paid him $10,000 in advance for–with his Team USA assembled–it was Zehlen's belief they could contract and farm forward 100% of production on the global market, and then manage price fluctuation into profits.

Like his idol John Lennon, David was a dreamer, believing the world could live at peace and be one. He ran a legitimate small business; he paid his men, he paid his bills. He depended on credit and the profit margin he could assume he was entitled to under government programs. Unlike Lennon, he did not have a $130M fortune to fall back on, every cent he had was invested in production with no credit left, and very little margin to live on. Considering David had personal income over eighty-thousand dollars a year for a decade, there were no frivolous expenses or luxuries under the tree at Christmas in the Zehlen household with four kids to feed.

Above all, David wanted people to know he did not support un-American activities. He had mixed thoughts about the condition of the economy. Traditional farming had never been like what it could be. A farmer's occupation was always a crap shoot. Along with other secure professions, with the market and growth ensured for them–when the security of our nation's food supply depended on him taking that risk every spring–in his dealings with banks and the USDA, Dave assumed that gamble, the personal risk involved deserved to be completely credit worthy in the late twentieth century.

With such a massive operation production cost, in the neighborhood of $250,000 a week during peak operations, Zehlen was always on the lookout for financing options to augment accumulated cash reserves and revenue that trickled in from stored grain sold for cash to local elevators, and through marketing agent Tom Adelman, before the arrival of Robert Walsh. He was beginning to feel like there was something going on behind the scenes; that was why his farm manager was always needling him about something that really irritated him, the sources of the narrow warnings he forgot immediately. He had to forget so he could concentrate on controlling MinGo, amid explaining constantly to his wife what he did not understand, and this confusion was happening as he was working 16 hour days just to keep the fuel lines open and the machines running? David expected his men to work with the same dedication he had. The specialist he hired was always in his thoughts. He had a sense Walsh was working diligently at something within his marketing business, but the man was constantly arguing with him about his judgment. Nonetheless, the crops looked good–there was nothing to worry about–according to Walsh the South Dakota operations were in good hands.

"Time off will do you some good David. I heard the walleyes are biting at Foster Lodge. Phyllis and I can run the office for a few days," Walsh urged him as seasonal work volumes increased.

Up until harvest in 1991 there were no visible issues, or serious problems with the production contract. Sexton had indicated no intention to withhold fulfillment on the contract. In spite of the modification he found necessary on the distribution of the ASCS funds, Zehlen believed he had faithfully fulfilled his end of the bargain; and despite the unexpected shortage, both Sexton and Zehlen made money in 1991. There was no reason for Sexton not to cover all billed production costs, labor, fuel, fertilizer, pesticides, machinery, while Sigco furnished the seed.

Walsh was aware of every detail of the contract. He insisted there be no misunderstanding between him and Sexton; there could be no doubt he was doing what he did for the sake of Zehlen's best interests. At the same time, he was giving Sexton a few clues of how he intended to implement the takeover of Pleasant Valley operations. In the first place as representative of the Zehlen family, he would expect Sexton to make good on his debts to the farm. Unless they came up with some other private arrangements between themselves, that is.

It was written in the language of the contract that Zehlen would arrange the leases and could expect above average returns on a crop that had never failed–in Sigco research test plots where growth conditions were carefully controlled–the average yield was determined in pounds per acre; with an expected yield of 1200 pounds average seed per acre at a price up to $.30 cents per pound, depending on oil content. Sexton was offering a standard compensation agreement: 25% of the net income received from sales.

Sexton estimated a $133 per acre cost to the producer on the sale of seed with 10% moisture and estimated 40% oil content to the Ceres Williston North Dakota elevator, a new facility specially fitted out with a custom drying operation to condition the high oleic seeds as an initial step in producing insulin–he could recite the Toronto script in his sleep;

"We need more sources of medicine because children are dying from diabetes in Africa. Just imagine the global demand for insulin Robbie–it's amazing what they can do with genetic engineering these days." Sexton quoted him more information about the Williston, ND elevator that had been designated as the exclusive point of sale for raw product with a state of the art system owned by SVO that served Montana, North and South Dakota.

"A BNSF rail yard runs through the complex of elevators and silos; it's amazing: you should visit there someday Robbie." Relevant facts and figures rolled off Sexton's tongue like a Spanish flamenco sonata. Walsh's mind wandered as it had during the Borlaug lectures; he was partial to Wagner waltz's and John Phillip Sousa marches his mother used to play over and over on the phonograph in the parlor of their Nundas home–on one of her good days. That image flashed through his mind, but he understood the marketing landscape in North Dakota as well as he needed to bring the news of the deal to David Zehlen in future discussions.

"I'll see what I can do," Walsh commented.

"Don't worry amigo, we're in this together. I will take care of you." You bet you will; Walsh assured himself silently. "Make your client an offer he can't refuse, I'll take it from there," Hector urged as if he took the cliché more seriously than the offer.

What Sexton was not being completely forthcoming about was the hidden risk factors; as a scientist he knew high oleic safflowers were an annual, native to a mountainous climate with a consistently long dry season and a limited rainy season. The best seeds were produced for their compatibility to those conditions. The leggy plant's defenses were very poor against numerous fungal diseases in rainy conditions after the seedling was in the ground.

Sexton and Walsh had to be aware of the risk of planting 16,000 acres of an uninsurable crop when farmers were losing their farms helter shelter coming out of the depressed 1980's. If Sexton was going to interest Zehlen in risking 40% of his total acreage–on non-insurable specialty seed under federal crop insurance–it was going to take all the persuasive techniques he had managed to perfect in the twenty odd years he had been in sales and test marketing for Sigco, his major employer before contracting with Lubrizol, a global lubricant manufacturer in the 1980's.

Walsh advised Sexton he would need to sweeten the pot, offering a guarantee clause on the contract, along with a healthy deal on the sale of the safflowers. Sexton assured him he would work up a generous contract; and that ultimately working together they could convince Zehlen the risk was worth the gamble. After all his own relative Provo, a trusted associate was providing the insurance policy; and Lubrizol had become one of the most powerful and wealthiest agricultural organizations on the planet. Surely such a great company under the auspices of Sexton, one of its best and brightest, could swing a production deal with the rising star of the Midwest farming industry, the small town farmer David Zehlen from Granite County Minnesota,

ANTHONY FALLS JR.

"No problema." he chuckled.

"Don't be so sure of that," Walsh admonished. "His father is old school, and he is no fool. He gambled once on sunflowers and hit the jackpot. Jack took the risk when everybody in the county thought he was a damn fool for trying something besides corn, wheat, oats, and barley. He planted soybeans too, but he was a smart conservative guy, just a few years older than me, probably not willing to press his luck. These are safflowers Hector; they resemble sunflowers–we know the difference. They are by no means a hearty crop. No banks will insure them. There is a reason for that, much less resistant to insects, the weather, and a fragile plant with stalk weakness. Storm wind can take down a whole crop. I don't even know why you mess with the damn things."

"That's what my bosses pay me for Robbie. There is money in drugs like insulin. You are dealing with the Jamaican gambler remember? Black Jack is my game. I like craps too. I fly to Reno once a year out of Fargo. But, I am a conservative kind of guy, who doesn't trust Vegas." *You will see all the risk is on David if I have my way with him like the others–because I do this for a living,* he was thinking.

"Rockland is a microcosm compared to Kingston where I learned the ropes of this commodity trading business. It's not the best fit; we were late to the party and had to take the leftover leases. Sully is one of them. The insurance issue is covered in the contract that features product liability with a minimum combined single limit of two million." Sexton was dreaming of how he couldn't lose with his bets covered at both ends. David has all the investment. SVO Ceres is my hedge he assured himself. Nobody can touch the green giants once they plant their foot in the valley.

"I'm talking crop insurance Hector not personal injury." Walsh argued. "I will make my money on the reduced contract margin because I take the risk on the marketing. I deserve the extra percent."

"That's all covered by my independent broker, brother in-law Jeffrey Provo. I believe you have met Jeff; he was at the Corn Palace with me when we spoke. He was a younger man, thick black hair then, now it is streaked with gray. Jeff is a good looking honest man married to my sister Tonya. The premium is high, but the bank will accept his coverage; we probably won't need it–this is 100% safe seed. I give you my word if you find the right land and the weather holds out like it has been the last two years dry, no rain late July and August, we might get as high as $30 dollars a hundred weight with 45% oil content at Williston."

"The elevator boss knows me personally at Williston. They call the flowers *chimichanga* south of the border! I can hear the change jingling in my pocket already," he joked.

In imagination, his budget expanded to include a pair of $300 dollar designer jeans–under black leather chaps would be ideal–worn with Mexican tooled Tony Lama rattlers, showing off a rich image at Cinquo de Maio in St. Paul with his new girlfriend. Such ideas flashed among his layered thoughts, of what he would do with his share of harvest commissions on the deals he authored, while he listened to another Walsh lecture.

"You and Zehlen should have stayed with beans. These flowers you are so dedicated to are next to impossible to grow where I live, and we are talking marginal top soil in South Dakota, not rich Turkey mountain hillsides with exactly the same climate conditions every year. Zehlen read my report on the productivity of various agricultural lands. He knows how to select land in Minnesota not South Dakota where your 16,000 acres on a contract with Zehlen are going in the ground. He hired me for my survey, but I see only marginal land available at best," Robert cautioned.

"Believe you me, my friend, I'm depending on you. You have a history, that's why we're talking. I know you can find the right soil to accomplish our purpose. You mailed my company your resume, and they forwarded it to me remember? You have a reputation with the bank we mutually depend upon in our business. Back In the days we were friends, when we started talking deals in the 80's, if you recall."

"Yeah and a lot of things have happened since then in your legal matters that have altered my opinion, as I recall reading about your trials in the *Argus Leader*."

"I agree. We've been together a long time. Just recently I reviewed your report on 'the productivity of various agricultural lands.' Based on that I think we can work together again. Frankly, I was impressed with the research, what do you want me to say? I haven't written like that since my Borlaug days. You quote your study all the time. Right now it makes all the sense in the world to me. So I'm counting on your scholarly research to make us both some cash. All I ask is you do your job, I will do mine," Hector was serious. "You know what to do better than me compadre. Call me as soon as you have the deal set up Robbie. Adios amigo."

CHAPTER 7

In his negotiations, Robert Walsh represented himself to David Zehlen as an experienced and successful farm manager and financial manager with exclusive funding sources and ability in litigation matters. In the original job interview, Walsh came across as an honest, professional, Christian man capable of doing whatever it takes to get the job done.

At the end of January, Walsh accepted the position to be a registered agent and South Dakota operations manager, supposedly to work in tandem marketing with Tom Adelman, David's consultant, who was doing business out of the Minneapolis Grain Exchange in the years prior to the umbrella of Ceres contract arrangements. Before the arrival of Walsh, it was Adelman who arranged customers for anticipated PVC organic crops. A positive marketing forecast, a solid long-term lending relationship, the generous ASCS allocation, on top of expected Sexton contribution elements, became loosely integrated into the time-honored Zehlen formula of successful farming. David–overwhelmed with production details–depended on his market advisors who inferred he would soon be fending off a boatload of grain buyers in Japan and Europe. Sexton claimed he was specifically searching for markets for the thousands of acres of SVO hybrid seed growing at Walsh's doorstep in South Dakota.

Walsh knew from the onset that Sexton was in arrears from the previous harvest, but it was during spring planting in 1992 Pleasant Valley began experiencing serious cash flow problems, as the reserves had been exhausted in the previous year's attrition on contract payout–down forty percent, while the spring 1992 futures marketing deal with Sexton was in limbo. At that time, the "full nelson" stranglehold was being applied as Hector, who was the actual owner of the 16,000 acres of high oleic safflowers and specialty leases near Canton, SD, balked at his promises, continuing to withhold his share on Zehlen's production contract. Walsh had counted on the developing crisis

ANTHONY FALLS JR.

with plans in place to take advantage of it. Eventually, he would request a series of meetings with local and federal authorities to tip them off on the *dire straits* of Mr. Zehlen.

In his various interviews, as he had informed David himself, Walsh reported to the FBI, "he was a private investigator who specialized in all areas related to agriculture." On the resume of litigation Walsh fostered, he appeared to be little different than a normal plaintiff in a civil case; he accomplished his purposes by avoiding any indication he was behind the downfall of his customers–he could not be held liable for any judgments against his clients–he would always be listed as a defendant, as though in court to help his customers out of a *jam*.

Although Robert never achieved professional or semi-professional status in law, by his *methods* and particular skills, gathering evidence, providing witness testaments of the supposed criminal acts of his victims–he achieved his purposes before darkening David's door. Walsh fulfilled the profile of an attorney in other respects; citing his vague credentials, Walsh proceeded to inform local and federal authorities as soon as he had observed and recorded, and perhaps manufactured the *"dirty deeds"* of his clients in excruciating detail.

Because he had connections with the feds and local sheriff, he had numerous contacts at intermediate levels of government. In an FBI affidavit, he reported that he had received a telephone call from an associate of one of his contacts with the Bank of Asia, in December 1989, mentioning Zehlen's name in connection with an ongoing investigation of an international grain scam being run through the Woods elevator, owned by Zehlen's partner at the time–a career shyster named Werner. Walsh stated he was certain that Pete Werner, who was selling commodities in Sioux City, Iowa, "would be instrumental in putting the same scheme together again," –insinuating the partners in a shrouded past would be reuniting with Zehlen at an uncertain time in the *future* with their marketing strategies.

Walsh furnished no further information for the bureau about his background or his employment arrangement with David Zehlen. Walsh was of an unusual *nature* described in the Melvillelegacy as "confidence men"; over the course of time off a normal resume as a salesman, he reported IRS income from other 1099 sources–he had become a paid informer for at least two financial institutions, First Omaha and Resolution Trust. It was true, that while he did interpret various agricultural land surveys for productivity values, he actually relied and depended on USDA and Board of Trade reports that were public information for his sources, data that anybody with an interest had access to. Walsh had been using information in those reports as he evaluated "customers" doing his job fast-tracking candidates for the informal reclamation program connected with his sponsors and their RTC affiliate over the years. Walsh had become First Omaha's special agent, useful to them in situations where farmer's domestic organization needed to be penetrated physically, to substantiate cash and property on applications seeking credit for agricultural loans and financing expansion, livestock, farmland and machinery, when their credit rating was below par (and the people still had some property left) –such unobtrusive observation required understanding of accounting, coupled with a substantial ability in the manipulation of women, and dramatic monologue delivery.

Before the '80's recession, Zehlen was a prime customer of farm lenders for over a decade; now there were suspicions afloat that the bank industry was investigating the Zehlen accounts based on their knowledge of the MWFSL default. The firm of Meyer and Wilber was enlisted by the Omaha institutions involved to restructure the contract between Zehlen, Sexton and the bank–to fit the needs of a pre-arranged foreclosure plan the bank had perfected on other customers numerous times–at $200 per hour.

Eventually, Walsh planned to inform the County Attorney as he had in other cases, that he suspected the man he was working for, David Zehlen, was involved in a fraud scheme involving a large financial loss by a Federal Reserve institution that had tipped him off. Walsh urged Watkins that by the next time David appeared in his office, a team of FBI investigators should be within strike-force distance of the interview; drastic measures were necessary because the crimes were becoming more serious. He was prepared to submit evidence a prime suspect, someone he knew well–a prominent citizen in the community– had stolen over a million dollars from his partner in a business deal that went *south* in Granite County; that same person was involved in the loss of half a million dollars of government money.

Walsh stated matter-of-factly that because the victims were nearly bankrupt as a result of the swindle he was reporting, he was willing to offer Watkins five thousand dollars as a retainer just to review the merits of the case. He informed the county prosecutor a discovery was already in progress. He was willing to turn evidence over to the county attorney if it was necessary.

"I've made you an offer Bill to represent us in litigation for Pleasant Valley. I know this comes as a shock to all of us. This is what someone we all trusted has been doing behind the scenes, swindling his partners first and then his family that I now represent as power of attorney, and the future owner of the farm. I don't expect you to accept my client's offer, but I would write you a check from Marketing International Company."

"So you are working for the FBI I take it?" Watkins inquired. "It would certainly take that kind of bureau resources and effort to uncover a swindle of this nature in this community, as we have very limited investigative funds. I have the Minneapolis number on my Rolodex in case something happens. They can have their men out here in a matter of hours. We thank you Mr. Walsh. I will get back to you as soon as I read some of your ideas."

In real time in his gumshoe role, Robert Walsh had been tracking David Zehlen long before the job interview–ever since his rival shut him out on a land bid in Carthage, South Dakota in 1989. The job opening was a fortuitous event–word was that Zehlen was a cautious man. He usually hired known-only-locally people from the community he lived in. There were exceptions. In special cases, he let the farmers whose land he purchased farm their land. If that worked out, they might be able to move up the ladder like his lead foreman Rodney Oberg had. He was going against his better judgment to hire an outsider.

What Walsh had been doing behind the scenes that David Zehlen, Sheriff Bernard and the bureau were unaware of, was a carefully guarded secret as to what the actual "bait" of the scheme was. It just so happened, that part of agent Walsh's job was to advertise the availability of low-interest loans from his bank and affiliates, for individuals growing crops that would not normally be considered for credit. Those selected must meet conditions that included a fair to good credit rating, a guarantee to make an investment in crops grown on leases financed by the bank, a record of keeping track of expense, and being able to procure independent risk insurance providers. The chosen farmer would estimate bumper-crop yields that specific bankers and appraisers would be willing to confirm using deflated land values as the collateral required for surety on the loan.

Hector himself made good on the insurance stipulation of the bargain. His brother-in-law Provo provided carriers of high-risk premiums for Sexton's customers. Once the foundation of the predatory lending swindle was established, the tolling process kicked in. Usually the bank or financial institution would cancel the contract within four to six months after the recipient of the loan had invested in leases, improvements, machinery, labor and whatnot. The bank or lending institution would then commence a lawsuit claiming the farmer had been fraudulent in his loan application for some reason that varied from lawsuit to lawsuit, leading toward law firms of contract attorneys claiming the collateral: the crop, the machinery and the farm. Usually, it was all accomplished in remote rural courtrooms, through supposedly legitimate court judgments.

In the David Zehlen organization, Walsh had found the perfect candidate for his *procrustean* treatment script. In a coordinated effort with the bank and with Sexton, it was the insider Walsh who made the behind-the-scenes complaint to investigators with the FDIC, Secret Service and FBI that the original loan application was fraudulent–because a Resolution Trust Corporation debt in receivership was not disclosed. According to David, there was a catch-22 clause relative to government "grace" as he described it: farm debt resulting from weather-related losses could not be used against him in the loan-resolution process; nor he believed, could it damage his credit in securing another loan from First Omaha. David thought he was off the hook, and that he would be able to pay the RTC off within a year under the Sexton contract. All this time, Zehlen assumed any farm losses could be attributable to weather-related factors under most interpretations; with those ideas in mind, when combined with the yet-unresolved Midwest Federal bank insolvency and RTC negotiations, it was the *lull* before the storm hit. David's first assumption was that under any circumstances the drought or disaster stipulations of farm bankruptcy law automatically postponed any attempts to foreclose on his property. According to David, at that time Father Jack stepped up to the empty plate and made an offer to settle the farm debt at principal; *that* was not accepted.

In a routine disclosure, Zehlen notified and negotiated the situation with bank loan-officer Jeff West like any other farmer would. The bank authorized the loan despite the S&L default situation that was redeemable under farm bankruptcy rules; but a year later, (as in the Zehlen's and other farmers in the same situation) the bank suddenly changed its decision–charging loan fraud against the unsuspecting customer; who was in this case a once-upon-a-time prime lending client, David Zehlen, and had invested every cent of the loan in farming operations, plunging deeper into the black hole debt structure that promissory fraud of his partner Hector Sexton had created.

Robert Walsh boasted to the FBI, in March 1993, that he had participated in a number of similar lawsuits–presumably as "pro se" petitioner and power-of-attorney for the selected farmers. In each case, Walsh emphasized the importance of his agency role in the decline of a particular farmer–it was important to Robbie that he receive credit for his interventions. He relished describing each discovery as unique, as he learned the various methods farmers used to commit loan fraud against the participating bank or lender. He believed it was his duty to inform enforcement of the illegal activities he had ferreted out.

In the Zehlen case, bank directorship named Walsh a finalist for a position of manager in the First Omaha Trust Department based on his achievements. Outside of the actual feeling of accomplishment, Walsh achieved the status of full-fledged "whistle blower" among a cohort of specialists who brought about the various demises of unsuspecting farmers *he* had accomplished by informing for the loan provider exactly when to foreclose–*at the most vulnerable moment.* It was his job to act like a seismograph recording the exact instant the earthquake hit.

By 1991 Walsh had not accumulated great wealth himself. He projected the Zehlen fortune to be the biggest prize he had ever netted; he intended to profit from the Pleasant Valley liquidation process as an administrator of the estate the bank had taken on foreclosure. He rejoiced as he reviewed the perfect scheme he had created in his solitary moments–not to be shared with anyone.

In dealings with law enforcement and apprehension, Walsh maintained a low profile. He visited with prosecution and defense attorneys projecting his role as defendant's power of attorney. He made an appearance or two in criminal and civil court. Once the criminal complaint was initiated and thoroughly developed behind the scenes, attorneys for the state, the bank and the defendants took over. Professional FBI agents despised him and his dirty job; participating counsel appreciated his work creating crime, where there was profit to be made in litigation. Outside of collecting his fee on original contracts, and whatever was left over after liquidation once his customers were scuttled, Walsh had profited little from his extended pro se writing.

With the Pleasant Valley case involving property worth upwards to ten million dollars, Walsh planned to retrofit himself into the business as power of attorney once the corporation was dismantled–this time it would be a different story altogether–Walsh would get *his* share of the booty. In the memorandum he was putting together for Granite County Attorney William Watkins, he would be writing for the "big money" this time, *all* the marbles would be at stake once he completely took over

Pleasant Valley Farms Corporation. His hours of study in the law library at Brookings and practice on other cases involving the demise of mid-western farmers–learning the language of corruption, authoring legitimate-appearing documentation to mask his intentions–would finally be paying him the dividends that rich corporate lawyers were reaping across the country.

The vulnerable Zehlen situation represented an opportunity Walsh had imagined might some day arrive. The corporation was small enough that family members were involved in the records management; and they were far from professional. David's wife Nancy was a dental technician bored with cleaning teeth, but knowing little of farm operations, and caring less. She and David needed the money with four kids, a farm mortgage, and a lease on ten new tractors to fulfill.

Jack's second wife held a diploma from the Minnesota School of Business. With a decade of experience in real estate, Phyllis ran the books with little if any corporate bookkeeping background. Jack was the county's most distinguished farmer, soon to retire and hand the business over to his son. In the August heat, he preferred to spend his time at the cabin on Lake Minnewaska near Glenwood with Phyllis, who Walsh told David reminded him of Helen Mirren in *The Cook, the Thief, his Wife and Her Lover*. Walsh the teetotaler, after swearing off liquor, accused David's father of drinking too much. For those reasons, among many involving envy of wealth and prestige, Walsh was probably more determined to crush Jack than he was to unseat David.

David ran his own set of books religiously, jotting the progress of each field upon his infrequent office visits during planting season. He had complete faith in his automated system; at any time, he could fill in the blanks, write short reports, add remarks and comments on the word processor feature of each indexed field, describing as much as a month of operating expense in shorthand generalization, using the proprietary Control Data agricultural management program he had lifetime rights and access to as author.

Spring and fall he was seldom around the homestead as he patrolled his massive farming operations that spanned three states. The four Zehlens, plus a few key employees including Tom Adelman the consultant, and Rodney Oberg, operations manager, received salaries and personage payments. Through phone calls and letters, an occasional meeting with those key individuals, David ran the corporation from the cab of his truck for all practical purposes.

Through his bank intermediaries, and working a month in the office, Walsh became tangibly aware of the vulnerabilities in a small corporation that was grossing millions, with upwards to twenty leases and 30 employees scattered across three states at peak operations. He recognized what he considered critical weaknesses in the organization, structure and management of Pleasant Valley Farms, with the boss secluded in remote locations handling the landscape of operations in the Dakotas and northern Minnesota.

CHAPTER 8

Hector Sexton was mild mannered, not unlike many foreigners are who from introduction to the dominant culture, to reach perfection within it, must have a certain awareness they are outsiders needing to rely on a sixth sense and cunning if they hope to achieve success in a competitive alien environment. He preferred to keep a low profile, having grown rich following orders from a succession of superiors beginning with his father.

By 1980, Sexton had accumulated a small fortune and a reputation in personalized marketing in the Dakotas. He was bilingual which gave him an advantage in the international agribusiness conglomerate that was sponsoring him. As a senior account executive, he had access to unlimited financial and legal resources that allowed him to take risks that only corporate officers could afford to take.

Before he went into a partnership arrangement with David Zehlen, Sexton had been involved in a grain marketing incident that resulted in fraud litigation with the Dekalb Seed Company. In late 1990, Zehlen was approached by Sexton to custom grow sunflowers under contract for his company, Ceres, on a joint venture sponsored by Specialty Vegetable Oils, SVO a wholly owned subsidiary of Lubrizol Inc.

Under the agreement he interpreted very liberally, David believed Sexton was also required by the contract provisions to provide equity loans for ASCS "personage" funds used in production costs, to be distributed to David Zehlen's business partners in MinGo. The partnership was set up, under the guidance of Counsel Rylance of Rapid City which was designed to meet the government's farm program standards. The corporate structure of Pleasant Valley LLC and partnership with MinGo would allow the Zehlen operations to enroll the 16,000 acres of contracted sunflowers and safflowers in the current government ASCS program–a tidy sum of close to half a million dollars, that under the Rylance "partnership" agreement his operation were entitled to funding under government farm programs in the form of personage payments, in lieu of LDP or price-support subsidies.

At the surface level, it appeared the first year of the contract was very successful; informal discussions about minor adjustments to the contract did not indicate suspicious intentions, meaning the contract would be renewed by Sexton and Zehlen for a second season. The initial contract was expanded, to be included with the original grower's agreement, to produce sunflowers, safflowers and soybeans. When Zehlen complained that he had suffered the loss of over thirty percent on production the last contract, Sexton claimed he would make up for the losses in spring 1992 marketing profits. Under the contract, these crops were financed by Ceres/SVO/Lubrizol as owner; and also by First Omaha, the primary lender and first lienholder on all crops produced under the Zehlen Sexton contract they were financing on a $1.2M loan the grower was liable for.

It was Robert Walsh who first informed David of his partner's background, that he was the offspring of a vague British Jewish marriage. Sexton's father was of Jamaican African origin; as he matured his personality evolved in a Kingston dynasty of some wealth and prestige. The Sexton patriarch had established his career brokering grain deals for Strachan Shipping Enterprises out of the port of New Orleans.

According to Walsh, the senior Sexton had accumulated a fortune before retiring in the Caribbean, having land holdings in the Carolinas after two generations of dealing in commodities along the East coast contracting on commodity exchanges with African and European customers. Walsh also was aware, but did not inform David Zehlen, that five years before Sexton worked with Pleasant Valley Corporation, Farmland Industries brought suit against Sexton's marketing apparatus, claiming that several brokerage houses and their agents, including Sexton, had conspired in fraud through insider trading in crude oil futures contracts without Farmland's authorization. Farmland appealed the verdict granted to Hanover Commodities, Inc., a licensed commodities futures broker, and to Gulf Coast Research Inc., Hammond's parent corporation, arguing that evidence Farmland presented at trial supported its theory that both Hanover and Gulf Coast had actively participated in a scheme to defraud Farmland.

> "The defendant appealed, based on judgment entered upon a jury verdict for Fraser-Perrone Commodities, Inc., Fraser-Perrone president Calvin Perrone, Fraser-Perrone account executive Hector Sexton, and Sexton's cousin in Kingston, Phillip Ortega. Farmland contended that with respect to these appellant claims, the district court had erred in excluding certain expert testimony concerning agency rules and specifications that were neglected in framing various jury instructions on commodities fraud.
>
> In the attendant confusion, Sexton managed to negotiate a commission of 20 percent based on performance of futures–his firm was offering an amount substantially lower than the rate Farmland paid their other brokers..."

Walsh continued the narrative as if he was reading a book,

> "judgment of the district court was confirmed in Farmland's petroleum futures trading."
>
> "*This* is the type of character you are dealing with."

* * * * *

The partnership with Zehlen was attractive to the plant and soil scientist background in Sexton, allowing him to exercise his latent reductionist ideas about western culture that he regarded as a curiosity cabinet of outmoded theories alongside theosophy and transcendental idealism. Philosophies were just "other methods of knowledge" he had detected and, over the course of his formal education, rejected in his undergraduate programs at NC State. As his aspirations to excel in the graduate school culture faded, his expectations became more practical; his father was ill, soon to be turning over a fortune–unfortunately he would be battling the old man's third wife, rumored to be a prostitute, for a share.

In the meantime, Sexton turned to applied scientific theory in general, working among the vine-dressers as an occupation, depending on experimentation, and political methods in discussions of modification of genes with senior executives on what was emerging as the primary objective of agricultural research–finding a global solution to hunger, at the same time making a living among the various profit making businesses attached to food production, a noble cause to attach his ambitions to. His practical approach to economics suited him well in an environment where volume of production concerns reign supreme.

In general, he regarded the scientific culture as just another way of knowing, a *contrived* mental posture maintained by American and European males, and held exclusively by college professors that he was opposed to in philosophy–if not in motivational psychology. He had evolved under the mentorship and discipline of his father who was as successful as any businessman on the island. He saw the opportunity in his previous business dealings with other Midwestern agricultural corporations, as he had in the Farmland lawsuit, that he could take advantage of what he perceived as an error in practical thinking, caused by a tendency to be reckless and get away with it, and character flaw he believed was well-disguised by the extroversion and agreeableness visible in his naïve partner. Beyond those attributes, he saw some severe deficiencies that hindered David Zehlen in plains trading and dealing with the locals–the aboriginals, and blacks like he was. Sexton viewed progressive LISA farming technology as more dependent on physics and logistics, less cost-effective per plant than the science, when genetic solutions to production were outpacing and overtaking all competition. In his opinion, the third partner was transparent in normal conversation, revealing himself as less intelligent than his attitude and tone of voice would lead one to believe. As an amateur psychologist, Sexton observed those traits that rendered the junior partner vulnerable to the envy, enmity, and spite of the people–making him *fair game* for the planned anarchy of outsiders.

Both Walsh and Sexton shared the same deconstructionist views as confidence men indirectly working for the government. In their respective roles, employed simultaneously by the USDA, the FDIC and the FBI, Walsh was an undercover saboteur, and Sexton was an agent of a nationalized producer fulfilling government contracts. Of course, these two parties had a vested interest in keeping things the way they were–when only the government officials and handmaidens, the rich, got richer–the successful conspiracy paid its taxes ahead of time, supporting increased ownership of the state as a *partner* in an expanding global agricultural enterprise.

In many ways, Walsh and Sexton shared the elitist views of the *illuminati*, as each man sought to increase central control instead of support to subsidize individual farmers who took advantage of government programs, to enrich themselves at the taxpayer's expense. Reforming state sponsorship of financial programs, along with eliminating loopholes, and the undeserved advantages personage payments brought to reckless expansionists like David Zehlen and other farmers like him, was Walsh's secret mission, along with elimination of the advantage subsidization offered certain, careless individuals like David Zehlen–while Sexton's objective was to allocate the subsidies into his production.

One of the companies Sexton represented, Special Vegetable Oils (SVO) was experimenting with varieties of safflowers that were showing great promise in research for the treatment of diabetes. In addition to its use in food products and cosmetics, medicinal uses of safflowers products were recognized as an unexplored market with potential for global applications, as the problem of diabetes among young children was becoming epidemic in the 1990's. Sexton had acquired a company-wide reputation for success in the sales of seeds for large-scale operations. He had made his reputation marketing, but he relished the hands-on genetic experimentation in the field. He was proud to be a part of the core of plant and soil scientists, and agronomist who developed environmentally-adapted crops such as the Mexican cross-bred varieties of corn, modified for hardy mountain conditions, and soybeans developed in Argentina, genetically adapted for dry plains climate.

To increase his credentials and introduce Hector Sexton as their premier salesman in the Dakotas, the corporation sent him to a symposium on the medicinal use of safflower extracts, held at the University of Toronto Hilton. At the seminar Sexton learned it was in Canada that the drug was first isolated in the laboratory, and specifically, why its production was so important to the parent organization Ceres, with its corporate offices in Toronto.

Insulin experimentation was a new subject to Sexton who had a long resume and background in agricultural research. After daily seminars and workshops, Hector reviewed the VHS tape in his hotel room; feeling like his old self in graduate school, he poured over the brochure. The third day of the conference attendees explored the menagerie of plants in the agronomy greenhouse. He loved that fresh feeling and smell of the greenhouse; he would be back in research alongside scientists in the lab that recent clinical trials of safflowers had indicated its oil would become a major source of insulin; alas, he was in sales—there was more commission in the field.

As it turned out, the early diabetes researchers didn't know how lucky they were to have Hector on task. He could understand what Professor Glass had been ranting about in organic chemistry better after twenty years of application of the essentially abstract theory of biochemistry in the field like few people could; he knew how to take the pro's word for it and make a profit at the same time. Soon the world would benefit knowing the amino-acid sequence of insulin in humans is almost exactly the same in certain animal species, such as pigs; theoretically, with more funding fueling research, that information would lead to life saving medicine for the human race. According to one article on animal science, insulin's basic structure, two peptide chains with three disulfide bridges, is conserved in all the nearly 100 different species investigated in the past half century of research, with associated tables to prove it. Hector realized he would have to figure out a way to condense the information into a convincing presentation to his partners.

At the week-long conference, Sexton learned that the new product was the bio-equivalent to recombinant human insulin with the expected and required safety profile the pharmaceutical industry required. The insulin protocol was equivalent to the industry leader Sanofi's insulin, the competitor's brand that was to become the most widely-used human insulin in North America. Laboratory and field tests indicated the final product of the SVO partnership with BioSynth International, when processed in humans, showed pharmaco-kinetics/pharmaco-dynamics as indistinguishable from the competitor. In intensive lab experimentation, tests proved the new variety of high oleic safflower oil was well tolerated at pharmacologically active stages. Canada was a leading producer of synthetic drugs for the US; it was bound to be a quantum producer of generic insulin for the international market before licensing the Ceres protocol to domestic drug companies like Pfizer.

Charts projected on a screen in front of the small auditorium at company headquarter were reviewed in the brochure; the seminar indicated that full results from the Phase I clinical trial at the American Diabetes Association Scientific Sessions in June 1989 were not yet available, but would be as soon as more field trials were accomplished. In addition to traditional insulin, Sexton learned that research and development was in progress on insulin analogues for fast-acting or slow-release options, improving disease control.

The companies Sexton represented, Ceres, SVO and Lubrizol were seeking well-positioned manufacturing commercialization partners to co-develop plant-derived insulin across the industrialized world and beyond its shores. Sexton recognized that if David Zehlen, with his well-publicized interest in "LISA" technologies, and the potential of genetic engineering were combined—the progressive idea alone would be easily sold based on the idea of the humanitarian interests, producing safflowers for the benefit of world health, and specifically, afflicted children in Africa–not to mention the profits to be made in global health products. Sexton left the conference briefcase in hand. Inside was a video tape of the program that he handed to David Zehlen in January 1991 and offering this advice,

"Look this information over David. Ceres is planning to become the world's largest producer of insulin. I am gathering information for them on the type of farmers–entrepreneurs like themselves that are looking to expand into a global health care network. Are you with me on this or not? This could be a life changing event for your career. You will know the answer after you watch this video. You have kids and the money to buy insurance and health services, and know how expensive that is– children worldwide don't have that benefit."

In the final presentation, the corporate sponsors made a compelling if not altogether accurate analysis entitled, "Diabetes & The Need for Insulin:"

> Diabetes is growing at the alarming rate of one new diagnosis every five seconds: the incidence of diabetes is expected to increase to over 380 million cases world-wide, according to the International Diabetes Foundation. Approximately 50% of diabetics requiring insulin therapy have limited or no access to treatment. With a worldwide perspective in mind the combined corporate interest of Ceres, Lubrizol, SVO are expected to partner with the pharmaceutical industries under their banner: BioSynth International believes that lack of access to economical insulin–now being offered in greater supply with safflower oil production by the corporation–is the leading cause of death in children with diabetes worldwide.

As Sexton read over the literature on his return flight from Toronto, he realized how important planning his sales pitch to David Zehlen on the safflower contract was to his own career; and ultimately, what it might mean to his eventual retirement in the Cayman Islands that he was planning in foreseeable future. In his mind, he believed he had contributed as much to the Borlaug triticale invention as any scientist, yet he never received credit and fame like Norman. Genetically-adapted safflowers could have as much impact on the health industry as Borlaug's had on nutrition.

Nonetheless this was a step ahead in his career—he could feel it coming on like a Jamaican rumba. Just as David's father had, Hector planned on retiring by age 50. That speculation was as unpredictable as the Chicago grain markets unless he had a guarantee. The corporations he represented depended on his knowledge and the considerable skills in litigation he had demonstrated in the Farmland case, though it had not turned out favorably. A settlement was reached. There was no bloodshed; nobody went to prison. The Ceres plan for global expansion was something that grabbed his interest immediately.

Genetic modification had saved millions of people in India from famine through his triticale. If he could convince his financiers to produce his safflowers with LISA technology, together they would introduce a revolutionary new product. As a scientist, he recognized safflower seed was a different species that was not native and hardy in the Dakotas. Pheasants imported from China had survived and thrived. He had witnessed the spectacle of exotic bird hunting on the Zehlen farm—let us hope and pray in solidarity, in the name of the Christian religion the Zehlens swear by—Turkish flowers will fare as well as pheasants.

Ceres and SVO corporate management had determined it was worth the risk, if the right situation evolved, in which they invested in a contract with a farmer, with a personality like David Zehlen, willing to gamble on a large planting. The only guarantee would be terms of a production contract, an easy arrangement to manipulate as he had in the past. He could manage the documentation, not whether the plants grow well or otherwise. Testing of the safflowers was in the nascent stage with Ceres. They needed a test subject. If the crop failed, there would be a way out with a fall guy to pin the blame on.

Sexton would be able to use his experience as middle man, the organization associate able to convince a "client" there was no risk, and the participant could only make a profit on the deal.

Meanwhile he would find the corporation what it needed for the experiment, a large tract of land to conduct a field test upon. It might take a decade to modify the safflower seed to Midwestern conditions. They had to start the trials somewhere; a dead field was as good as a live one for experimental purposes–if the deal didn't work out with Zehlen there would be other farmers willing to climb on board, as there had been in the past.

He dozed off in the adjustable bark-o-lounger in his Fargo office thinking how he would present the safflower project to David Zehlen. Foremost, the project would be represented as a philanthropic venture with global medicinal benefits to mankind. Consequently, there was no ostensible purpose to increase the food supply in the safflower projections whatsoever, unlike the Triticale project, the cross breed of wheat and barley that was designed to increase the food supply for third world nations– that fed the business billions, and the taco industry ever since. Sexton had witnessed the remarkable emergence of Triticale, as it was introduced south of the border and in the Indian peninsula, as a food crop; this venture was not about hunger other than greed. The trick would be to overpower David with an avalanche of confusing information.

Sexton had visions of developing a universal bean-seed variety capable of automatically adapting to climate conditions, encouraging the early buds with a derivative of colchicum–in effect cross breeding hardy disease-resistant sunflowers with Turkish safflowers. As the ultimate international challenge R&D was facing, someday he would bring that idea to the governors, with a patent number held to thwart all competition: for now, he had his orders from corporate headquarters, post-convention.

Sexton knew the flowers were susceptible to frost. Growing them on the test plots a couple hundred acres at time was the risk the research department, DNA-modification division was insured to take. In previous protocols, research had determined that selected land must have no history of potatoes or edible beans. Suitable land should have no sunflowers grown within the last three years, because test results had shown reduced productivity of up to forty percent under those conditions.

ANTHONY FALLS JR.

Assured his company could accept that risk, it was no skin off his neck. His patrons had backed him before in a half dozen failed crop lawsuits.

Hector recalled his father referring to his experience in the commodities business, "*corporate attorneys are hired to make and break contracts.*" In other words, you can pay them to do *anything* you want; his son realized that some years later when the avuncular words of wisdom affected his actions in various lawsuits.

"So as long as the big shots pay me to be a fall guy, and then pay my attorneys to argue in their lawsuits to defend their money, yes I should say Robbie, as long as they back me with their wall street law firm I have no other choice," he joked, chatting with his crony Walsh on a land line in his Brookings office, a cold January morning with wind chill of -30, a northwest wind steady at 20 mph.

Glancing out upon the frozen tundra from the frost framed picture window Walsh stated,

"I heard that. Just remember Hector, what a farmer's business is now days–to calculate risking their necks every spring. Take advantage of the incentives we have been discussing; that will sway Zehlen from being cautionary to visionary," Walsh continued. "The Zehlens have the potential to grow 20,000 acres of sunflowers, corn and soybeans in South Dakota, that's what I'm looking for; that's the volume your company is looking for. By then I plan to be in control. I doubt either Jack or Dave has any interest in safflowers unless you have some kind of incentive for that risk," Walsh repeated his caveat.

"I'm not telling you how to run your business Hector. I'm just reminding you. The Zehlens have about $11 million equity as of 1991. They own about 7500 acres and have lease-options on the rest. But I don't see where they have the cash reserves to expand operations to 42,000 acres David is planning on in 1992."

"The Zehlens are going to need some major cash, more than the USDA has available to them, the rest from an outside source, be it their bank or what I have in mind with my sources. That is not accounting for what you might have to offer. They have the credit, some debt to MWFSB to deal with, then again if you factor in what they can pick up from the government ASCS programs?" Walsh had a sudden coughing spell as he thought, *my job is to convince David, as owner, you deserve a share of those funds when you are not entitled to them officially.*

"Pardon me Hector. Over-the-counter drugs just aren't working for me these days. You know the drill well enough. What has worked for you in the past will work again. All we need is that dummy corporation of partners to claim as personage. We have Rylance working that angle," Walsh cleared his throat.

"He needs a title of some kind, managing the men he has working under him, and that would be under your sponsorship because you own the crop. That might be enough for the government to send David the money a second time, or the application itself might be suspect. But then the question arises, why would you get government money for marketing you are not legally entitled to? Beyond that issue I have been consulting with him on, as far as I can tell, he is not entitled to government funds as a *custom* farmer."

"If the government remains unaware that the office wives transferring contract ownership to MinGo is not completely legit, he might be able to slip the ASCS application by them based on past history. Then you and Zehlen can work out some kind of deal. I don't personally care. I have no stake in that matter presently. With what I have now, I could retire and live comfortably on the French Riviera–you've heard of Queen Latifa Borbon Borbon, heir to the Spanish throne, haven't you Hector?"

"I don't believe I have Robbie," Hector replied. "Why don't you inform me more on that topic, a current event is it?"

"She lives on the Mediterranean coast near the Italian border. Though I have not visited her castle, we have partnered on European deals before; we think of her as an overseas investor, involved in the international branch of Marketing International. But I don't want to go too deeply into the subject of overseas investment at the moment."

"How old is this princess Robbie? I would love to meet her sometime," Hector was willing to play along with the joker.

"Maybe you will sometime Hector, because I have separate and connected interests with both you and David Zehlen, but it is he whose interests I have in mind as my first cause; what you do is your business. And I will tell you right now, it is risky business dealing with the government on that level when a judge might figure out it was some kind of scheme. You don't want that–and neither do I. And we don't want to talk about it until I learn exactly what David plans to do with his share of the personage payments–other than invest them in your crops..." (click, click) "Wait a minute. Damn phone buttons. Hold on. This is David on the other line. I'll put you on hold. I've got another call coming in I expect any minute. I will talk about my thoughts on ASCS when I learn Pleasant Valley's plans. I'm looking at 13,000 acres five miles south of Clear Lake; same lease, two parcels ten miles west of Hwy 29 where I can keep an eye on it. But the Zehlens haven't decided what to plant yet. Keep in touch with me Hector, will you?"

"Ok Robbie. Just remember to tap into Zehlen's concerns for humanity on the medicinal benefits for mankind of an improved strain of insulin. That should seal the deal. The world needs more medicine with more than enough beans already. Adios partner." Sexton heard the click of the line disconnect, as Walsh took the other call. He looked at the information Walsh turned over as a tip. No one would ever know it was illegal insider information that would benefit both him and Robbie exclusively.

Sexton's bosses were looking at what a large crop of safflowers, well beyond the standard field test range and size control of crop conditions would amount to. With his reputation for sales in the Dakotas, Sexton was the obvious choice of a salesman in such a large enterprise. He would receive his guaranteed commissions on the grain brokerage services he and his "brother" Jeff Provo, married to his sister Tonya, were entitled to under his consulting contract with Ceres Lubrizol. The Provos could expect a large bonus plus insurance brokerage fees. In the first year, they would be hoping for at least a 250% return on their investment. If the flowers came in at 40 to 45% oil content, the experiment would be considered a successful field test for a first-time operation.

His managers assured Zehlen he would not be responsible for the insurance payment. That would be deductible to offset forecasted imaginary profits for the 1992 spring marketing as part of the overall reduced margin he would squeeze out of the first harvest production. Sexton would be able to operate in his usual capacity, as an independent sales manager and grain broker, with the option to market through his own consultant agencies or marketing contacts out of the Chicago grain exchange. He could depend on capitalizing at his usual margin and commission of 12%, which was where he had made his fortune over the years. It was all set up, 90% of the flowers would flow through the Williston, North Dakota elevator, and the only elevator in the upper Midwest now equipped to handle raw safflowers with no appreciable loss of oil during drying and processing. The towers and storage silos were rigged with a modified mixing apparatus, blowers with centrifugal dryers and ventilation systems designed to handle the delicate safflower seeds.

If his plan worked, by late 1991 the remainder of the crop would be shipped through various outlets in the Midwest for cash, and as a sample product for evaluation and research. After attending the convention in Toronto, Sexton was sold on the idea he could put the safflower patch in the Dakotas to work for him–in the same fashion as he had on no-risk contracts with *other* farmers in the Midwest.

CHAPTER 9

After celebrating a mixed bag British Jamaican New Years, Hector Sexton, who was half British and half African American could not restrain himself any longer from phoning Robert Walsh about the prospect of their increasing fortune. Walsh had described his new customer as naïve, who would be a "cupcake" as he put it. A spoiled rich farmer's kid with no leadership ability, it just appeared the huge farm had fallen into his lap as his father aged. It was frustrating to Walsh, who had tired of the caring for his wife, discussing her depression and what new drug she was taking. He was distracted from his marriage by much younger women in general, though it was quite obvious to Sexton what Walsh coveted out of the deal besides money–Jack was aging, older than he was. Sooner or later Phyllis was going to be available.

Visions of the expansion of the safflower industry in North America, and millions of dollars rolling in on his commissions, danced in his head as he sipped his Old Jamaica Rum on the rocks to the soothing sounds of Andres Segovia, the Spanish encores cassette collection his mother had sent him for a Christmas present. Sexton played that tape over and over in his office, and on the tape deck of his buffed out black and gold Lincoln TownCar, that best represented his polished image, the one he depended on in performance to impress his customers, particularly the Omaha bankers, of the value of the dry stretch of land along the Eastern South Dakota border.

"Gentlemen, if you look to the west, it is overcast today; but on a clear day you can make out the first hills of the ridge at Summit. This landscape resembles the topography the Turkish grower prefers for safflowers. As much as possible, we select land that will ensure your investment is secured, as well, in soil and growing conditions our hybrids will flourish upon. This land resembles that of Turkey in one significant way. You can see if you look to the far northwest, from this angle we are looking at the gray, very low foothills of the last plateau of the mountains out west. The land slowly slants down from the foothills of the Rockies off its eastern plateaus which we believe will be open to leasing; for now, it is cattle range for 400 miles west of the rise at Summit as you see the sun setting behind it. It requires a little imagination, but I know you visualize what I'm saying gentlemen. The crops will thrive here; I guarantee it."

The bankers, who had been financing Ceres operations for generations, needed to be treated with style and courtesy as he shuttled them between the various available farmlands he was seeking to lease. Sexton assured the lender associates that selected land had been fallow, and minus the banned crops at least three years to legitimize the Zehlen crop leases to the bank's specifications. It was Sexton's job to sell the landscape his crops would be growing on in the Dakotas. On special occasions, Sexton especially loved to play Pisador's *"Pavana"* in E minor softly on the surround sound system of his sedan, relishing the unaccompanied guitar passages from that particular Segovia sonata that happened to be playing in the background as Walsh picked up the phone in his Brookings, Marketing Services International office.

"Hello Robert Walsh speaking, what can I do for you?" He did not recognize the voice immediately in the medley of sounds and the inflected words,

"Navidades siega tiempo de la cosecha amigo…ha ha ha, Robbie how are you doing my man? It is I, your friend Hector from Kingston, wishing you and yours a happy new year 1992, in advance."

"For Christ's sake could you turn that damn music down," Walsh coughed into the receiver. "I don't need a deaf aid yet, but I will if uh, uhh," turning away from the receiver for a few seconds he proceeded. "Excuse me for being so grouchy today. I've been dealing with congestion with over the counter products. I may need something stronger if it won't clear up. You know we have different tastes in music. In fact, I was half expecting a call from you, after I received your Christmas card from Toronto. It was very funny indeed, because no one around here can read English let alone Spanish! The way I look at it is, if this is all you've got for me, I have a lot of work ahead of me convincing the Zehlens to buy into your proposition. For what is it, twelve maybe 15,000 acres of safflowers and sunflowers?" Walsh was prepared to argue.

"I already informed you my land reports for that area were not very encouraging. It won't be an easy sell by any means. I read the information on the seminar. It could be valuable in my negotiations with Zehlen, or it might not be, depending on the way you look at it. You only think you know what appeals to him; there's more to it than that. If I were him, I might need to arrange another loan because you are so far in arrears on the last contract Zehlen won't have enough to plant cabbage in the garden."

"But you have some advantages going for you. Think about it. Zehlen loves the whole idea of being a global Good Samaritan; this medicinal safflower whoop dee-do could be the clincher your argument hinges on. I have my reservations, mostly about your character. I am referring to what happened in the DeKalb and Farmland litigation. I recall there were some bribes behind the scenes you and your partners used to dodge a mortar on that one. According to my own research this is not a good idea Hector."

"Yes but this is *your* skill Robbie; the best I do is give them my standard deal. It's up to you to convince him to take it. You're the one who told me about David. It sounds like if you apply some heat, saying now that you've got it–let's use it–take the money and run. After you have convinced him of the indispensable value of your farmland survey information, that there is little risk of precipitation and cool temperatures in the Sully county area in August, we will have cleared the major hurdle. It's ensured, you can buffalo the bankers–all they want is their money–and with the collateral of Pleasant Valley on the dotted line, there will be no problem. When David objects to signing over the PVF collateral, you just say you made your payments on the '91 leases–what is there to prevent you from making them in 1992?"

"If he is as desperate as you claim he is, Zehlen will sign. Play on their faith in God; you have reported that David and his family are devout Christians. I am sure we can count on your leading the little flock to believe it is God's will, and all the nonsense that goes with it. Keep reminding him of a global crisis in diabetes among children in Africa and Asia, helpless infants in need of new sources of insulin as a first cause beyond faith. We work together on this; your pitch is 'diabetes is growing at an alarming rate of one new diagnosis every ten seconds'. By the year 2025, the incidence of diabetes is expected to increase to over 380 million cases worldwide. According to the International Diabetes Federation, approximately 50% of diabetics requiring insulin therapy have limited, or no access to treatment. Next, we drive a lethal sword into the bull's hump from a global perspective: lack of access to insulin is the leading cause of death in children with diabetes. Worldwide media reports 600 people a day die from the disease. That should do it."

"I read the information, you don't need to quote it to me again Hector," Walsh reacted in his typical, dismissive fashion, "Just let me remind you I am on to your game. You can't fool me as I am aware of the Dekalb lawsuit, the phony deal you made there with Farmland. We don't need the FBI investigating the contract with you and Zehlen. You will need to work out a better plan to deflect a justice department inquiry into the diverted ASCS funds issue you are going to be facing soon enough Hector. You will want the usual finder's fee which I presume will be adjusted to your reduction, let's say, of instead of you paying 25% of the net you reduce it to 10%, but by then Zehlen has no choice to accept as you have already been holding out to the tune of let's say half a million. In the process, Zehlen is short two months' production costs during planting season. Zehlen doesn't know he is up against a major corporate scheme. He is playing with the big boys not just trifling with the farmers around Rockland County. He has never had a slippery partner like you before Hector. And I do not say that facetiously, because I have had a partner like that once; you never knew Rick Ritter, he would steal you blind in the blink of an eye," Walsh felt a lone tear of relief

ANTHONY FALLS JR.

flowing over the conjunctivitis-causing mycelium that never ceased scratching against his right cornea.

"That was before our business, at a time there was a creep willing to shake your hand, lie to your face and gamble he could walk off with the money. So now that you have the legal staff of Ceres Lubrizol behind you, that is, if the plaintiffs ever even make it to trial, then you face the risk some judge actually sees through the plot of promissory fraud on the grower's contract you are liable for–and he calls for *trips*. What do you do then?"

"I trust you to work out the legal details Robbie. Like you told me you did with Janklow. You have experience in the field of avoiding detection. You know how organized crime drags innocent, peripheral people into its schemes–squeezing victim like a Burmese python into compliance with its demands. Zehlen is already in way too deep to be borrowing with that MWFSB boondoggle hanging over his head anyway. My theory is, those people should not be expanding. Let's just say we have developed a safety net for the system, and leave it at that."

"You must know by now Hector, I have read of your methods between the lines of your litigation, and of your dealings in the demise of other partners. You suck the blood out of them, one drop at a time by not paying your debts, claiming you will catch up, but you never do. Then they go under for your debt on the grower's agreement. But guess what? Your crop is tested for the company, at the customer's risk, on soil generally found to be marginal at best, on the land you selected. David is held liable for the loss. It's as simple as that."

"Robbie I'm not sure I follow your theory about my business. But I trust you. That's what counts with me, a man's trust."

"Zehlen claims he is a Methodist. You expect me to take advantage of his probity–he is only generous when it benefits him–I'm sure you're aware of that trait. You need to play upon his empathy for the suffering, saying you need more time to pay off your grower's agreement debts; you don't get big chunks of money from the government like David, even though under the contract you are the owner. Your task Hector is navigating your pirate ship below the radar which you do so well. You market what grain you imagine you can get away with, as futures for cash through your company's apparatus, and send Zehlen a paltry percent of what you owe on the contract–never enough to pay your debt, which you have no intention whatsoever to pay until kingdom come," Walsh convulsed in a brief coughing spell before continuing.

"Basically, you know you can disclaim the contract if it goes to trial; because there was no real profit, only loss you can pin on Zehlen with some crafty attorneys. And there need be no mention in court of what you appropriated as grower fees from the government funds–the $160,000 you tricked Zehlen out of for mysterious reasons. Like I said, my deal is with the bank. I will make sure you are never investigated by them, which is where this litigation starts."

"In future court proceedings, that could take up to five years, there will be no mention of shady deals in the South Dakota lawsuit I am preparing pro se, in which I will be doing my own discovery to cut costs for Pleasant Valley," Walsh stated emphatically, ending the conversation and any mystery about who was in control; effectively, cutting the cord with David and the bank for all times–there was no need to inform his partner of more than he needed to know.

It was enough that, without relaxing at all, he could exalt over another victory on the chessboard of life–when yet another rook had fallen to his black knight. He felt no need at that moment to expose the complete nature of the threat he was making to Hector. He would be just as confused as Zehlen if he tried to explain the timing; it would be better to inform Sexton once the actual paper work for the new loan structure, introduced by the bank, was perfected. The documents should be created by Christmas Walsh thought, and then there was a counter-suit to ponder. Hector didn't need to know about that either.

"I'll go this far. I can help you stay out of jail, but it will be on my terms or else. Let me remind you if I tip off any of the Zehlen family I am pledged to work for, about the Farmland fraud thing and what you are up to, the deal is off. I will have power of attorney over Pleasant Valley soon enough. I am working on that at this moment. But let's make one thing perfectly clear Hector–I will personally blow the whistle on your scheme unless you follow my rules. Do you understand me now?"

"Now hold on just a minute Robbie," Hector retorted feebly. "Those days of fraud allegations are behind me. I will make it worth your while to keep that information private–buried in the past–in particular, about that Dekalb Farmland situation between you and me; because it happened just a few years ago. It was just a civil matter, nothing criminal happened."

"Sure Hector that's what they all say. I still can't figure out how you did it: a crooked court, bribery, threats, whatnot, or some kind of deal with the plaintiff? I'm warning you, if some federal judge was informed of what really happened, you would be paying triple damages for conspiracy with your partners Donovan and Ortega." Walsh continued, "I'm sure you wish those days were behind you, but let me remind you I have a photographic memory for details like that. You need my references with the Zehlens. I'm willing to work with you, not for you. But we don't want this matter ever reaching a court, with you opening that can of worms in a court of appeals, when the plaintiff has consistently characterized your payments as 'secret bribery' intended to sway a partner's loyalty away from your dealings with its clients. Legal evidence of fraud in a civil trial stays on the record, if they reopen the case in another jurisdiction–even if there is no criminal conviction: items like your bankruptcy, your divorce, gambling, private settlements and affairs will be public information, unless I convince Zehlen not to do a standard criminal background check," Walsh could wax eloquent when he mixed his memory for details with threats, innuendos and intervals of silent intimidation.

"I include you in my plans because we are in a racket we never expected to be in. Only insiders know the principles legal theft is based on–one of them is documentation. Hector, you and I know it. There are people who have reduced the science of theft to perfection on computers; in other words, experts know how to steal legally. Your guy Pierce, on the other hand, testified that the $26,000 in checks made payable to him, which he stashed, were not 'finder's fees' but payment for consulting services rendered to your client Hector. Pierce admitted that he never met with, or consulted with, representatives of FRS; later he testified that his trading for Farmland was uninfluenced by any payment. You lied in Federal court—we don't want that happening with Pleasant Valley, now do we?"

"You think you have it all figured out Robbie don't you? Your expungement only applies in South Dakota. A judge can open those sealed files. I can overlook your conviction in my negotiations with Zehlen I suppose, too. The bribery issue was a red herring; the whole case was just a business deal gone haywire. I fixed it, just like you did. I was just giving you some sales tips since we are working on the same enterprise. You informed me David is a cautious lad. My suggestions and your omissions of some of these ominous details you are hounding me with, can all be forgotten under the right conditions," he could have used a respirator like his father with emphysema needed, gasping for air, Sexton pleaded,

"I guarantee you we will make a lot of money if you handle my proposal correctly. Work with me, not against me for a change. Again, I urge you to stress the medical benefits for safflower oil as a selling point. You could use that kind of argument to convince the ladies in the Pleasant Valley office since they are running the business anyway. They have kids don't they? Remind them of that, not of my legal issues or some past mistakes if you would, please. You said Zehlen has four children; take advantage of those numbers, and finesse any mistakes you think I have made. I will make up for any losses you take."

"I beg your pardon Hector. I don't intend to take *any losses*. As power of attorney for Pleasant Valley I will be running the show. We do it my way or the deal is off. You quite possibly could go to prison for promissory fraud the way I see it. Or I could just tell Zehlen your deal is not worth the risk based on my research of your character issues. We will find another grower. It looks like Northrup King has developed the Sutton section, west of 75 on the edge of town, as a test plot for genetically modified corn suited for customers in the county. The smart money is not betting on a risky flower production I can tell you that. I told Zehlen about you and the safflower project after I received the information from Toronto," Walsh continued his harsh rebuttal.

"I just want to remind you of one thing, just to make sure you understand what I'm offering you Hector. You need to understand you have been exposed in your dealings with David. I am giving you the opportunity to invest your debt with Pleasant Valley in a completely new venture that I will be the administrator of. I urge you to cooperate in a new entity, giving you a chance to start over with a clean slate as an investor. You indicated you were receptive to a new strategy, but you appear to have changed your mind."

"I'm not completely sure I know what you're talking about Robbie."

"Of course not," Walsh continued to press his advantage. "I wanted to prove that I was wrong and your payment to David Zehlen was complete last year. It is now apparent you don't intend to keep your word on that issue either. I believe you have reported to the bank and IRS that you paid David Zehlen some $1.5 million, approximately, as your contractual share for this year's production. According to my accountant, if you look at your checks carefully, you will notice you paid that sum for your custom farming operation only; but you paid Pleasant Valley a mere $200K, and that was less than the partner LDP input into last year's crop, which amounts to paying 75% of 25%–or about 20 cents on the dollar of what you owe my client."

"I can't believe your figures are accurate Robbie. I would have to speak with my accountants immediately," Hector pleaded with a hint of desperation in his voice.

"Zehlen said he would talk to his MinGo partners over the holidays and get back to me after the first of the year. I'm waiting to hear from him."

"Now wait a minute. You're not a lawyer Robbie, and you can't prove a thing. Don't try to threaten me. I have other customers I can make a living off of. Maybe you should contact Zehlen, my time is wasting. Spring planting is less than three months away. I need commitment and assurances for my bosses about what's happening to their investment in my South Dakota sales region. Can I turn up the music now? You should love this, Moreno-Torroba– 'Fandanguillo' (playing softly in the background), Robbie can you hear me?" Hector was trying to lighten the mood sensing they had made a deal.

"I prefer the 'Tannhauser Suite.' That's all I have for today; turn Segovia up. I'll let you know what Zehlen decides. Happy New Year Hector," with that Walsh hung up the phone.

Hector turned up the volume of the cassette player and resumed listening to "El Mestre" followed by "La Filla del Marxant." He adjusted his drugstore bifocals and retrieved the specifications for SigCo Phase I clinical trial of safflower-produced insulin out of the top drawer of his desk and turned to the chapter "Optimum growth conditions for production of 40% safflower oil: Field test module" as a guitar solo in G minor tinkled through the silence.

Sexton knew what he was up against working with as shrewd and wily an agribusiness man as existed in the Midwest, dealing with Walsh who reminded him of Lee Marvin, or was it Gene Hackman in *Prime Cut* the movie? He had worked with him in marketing before; but never on a safflowers field test of major proportions. They had set up a deal with Chile on 5000 acres of sunflowers and corn along Highway 12 in Grant County; and one contract for 2000 acres of corn east of Paynesville, Minnesota. But neither of them had setup a deal involving 16,000 acres of any crop, let alone the temperamental and unpredictable safflowers. It would take the both of them working in tandem to arrange the extended grower's agreement for the second year, Walsh's takeover plans depended upon.

Hector's deal with Walsh would remain the same, a 2% actual share of the harvest which Walsh was free to market himself or 3% deferred based on what Sexton marketed the crop for in the next six months after harvest. The two cagey partners had worked that arrangement on the customer contract several times through the 1980's. Where Sexton made his deal on the second year of the contract, the same was true for Walsh, his first year of the contract was the lure, a variation of the ageless bait and switch scheme they worked before to perfection, that depended on insider information Walsh was privy to–the priceless or worthless results of the research package he sold Zehlen for $10,000 in January 1992–when he signed on as manager of the South Dakota production operations.

Walsh's job at the front end was accomplished in research. Sexton would never know he was bluffing–the threatened lawsuit was just another pretentious step in the takeover plan. The turnover of deeds would come sometime later. For the time being, the mention of some mystery that Walsh was privy to that benefited what was going on behind the scenes with the bank attorneys Wilbur and Meyer, working for the Walsh design that included Freeman and the bank, was sufficient information to filter Sexton.

Walsh controlled the flow of litigation news, what little there was trickled down according to a general plan to make Walsh and his cronies a profit at Zehlen expense, as he was accustomed to with his other customers. To Sexton, that incentive was enough of a hook to agree to anything Walsh wanted. Each situation was unique. Job one was to determine approximately how many acres of leasing land were available for the joint farming operation. Under his employment contract with Zehlen, Walsh was supposed to determine if the selected land had no history of potatoes or edible beans, or sunflowers grown on the fields the last three years.

Sexton was interested in total acres of land farmed relative to his particular acreage contract. In the case of Pleasant Valley Farms, he needed to know the ratio of acreage he was to contract for to determine what his share of the Zehlen personage payment would be. And it would be a substantial share for owner production costs on 16,000 acres of flowers out of the total of roughly 42,000 acres David Zehlen was planning on farming in 1992, according the initial reports of Robert Walsh–in the neighborhood of $160,000. Both Sexton and Walsh knew from experience that no farmer was going to give them an actual figure for what their cash reserves, or stored grain, and available credit was heading into a growing cycle. A farmer didn't really know an exact figure, as it depended on market fluctuations that impacted both the stored grain and futures valuations. Walsh had access to at least one set of the books from the office files of Phyllis Zehlen who ran the payroll and accounts payable and receivable.

He had no access to David's office system designed for the MAS 90, scaled to a floppy disc to run on his Apple desktop with 10 MB of storage and a Fujitsu printer. Dave was an effective operator capable of using his system for farm income tax reporting purposes, and computing property and equipment values for previous years, each year assuming that those figures heading into a particular year's growth season were always an estimate that was exaggerated, or truncated depending on weather and marketing forecasts.

One figure could be arrived at with relative certainty in the Pleasant Valley operation–Sexton as well as the bank needed to know what Pleasant Valley was expecting to receive in government subsidy payments relative to their contract involving 16,000 acres of sunflowers and safflowers. That figure was possible to calculate and the key knowledge each of the three parties involved in the Pleasant Valley Sexton-Ceres arrangement needed to know, in particular that the 1991 payment was $50,000 per person amounting to $582,000 personage calculated for 11.64 partners, including all corporate officers.

Partners to the allocation were David, Jack, Phyllis & Nancy Zehlen, Rodney & John Oberg, and Tom Adelman, along with a few others. These government funds, as in a few white collar crime cases, were the diverted and disguised means and ends conspirators manipulated through extortion and corruption. Sexton's share of the proceeds was an agreed upon $160,000 which would later be reimbursed to Dave as payment through a system of production billing chargebacks. David was supposed to believe the personal transaction between him and Hector was perfectly legal–under the interpretation he considered Zehlen debits to Sexton would be reflected as accounting chargebacks to Pleasant Valley Farms as they related to the ASCS funds already advanced.

Hector Sexton, relying on his success with other customers, planned to gain a stranglehold on the operating capital of Pleasant Valley, money stashed for future marketing would not be devoted to operations expenses. Instead, the investment would contribute to the deficit, as Zehlen's intended sources of income, various reserves, private lending, credit and sales of privately stored grain dried up, as they inevitably did every season, toward the end of spring planting; there was no telling how many different reasons he had used to convince his partner to shunt him nearly a third of his operating capital, through allocating the ASCS partner payments to himself, knowing his actions would impact the distribution of the remaining personage among the partners. It seemed like only Walsh understood the Sexton method of extraction, amounted to embezzling critical funds that in previous years had been the life blood of the Zehlen farming operation, sustaining it through the long hot summers until the cash from the harvest flowed again.

CHAPTER 10

David Zehlen and his father contemplated expanding their operations beyond the 18,000 acres they owned outright or held lease/options with equity in 1990, to a projected 45,000 acres. It meant acquiring new leases on land upon which they would be planting contracted oil seed crops in South Dakota, and making bank loan arrangements to finance any shortage in production costs. About the time David and his father made the transition from a two-man standard farming operation to Pleasant Valley corporate structure, the rules for eligibility changed. Under revised federal policies, farm owners could establish new entities, involved in the production and management of the farm operations, and each partner could be entitled to personage payments under the new program.

In order to be eligible for a share of the personage allocation, the partners were required to be "capitalized" or invested in the operations to the point of having contributed $50K to the business–in terms of equity: cash, property, and labor, as investment. It was David's plan to pool the Zehlen's and partner's personage payments, and invest them into the crop production apparatus, as he was entitled to; then get paid back for production and receive a percent of the net after all expenses including his labor markup. Hector Sexton managed to manipulate David into allocating the personage payments to him for reasons never fully explained, or understood–a never verbalized threat that he would further reduce, and withhold additionally on his contract obligations already in arrears–further enervating the Zehlen effort in marketing.

From signing day forward, David assumed Hector was willing to pay him as the contract indicated. In his customized interpretation of the contract, Sexton rationalized that since he was the owner of the crop, he was entitled to the ASCS payments. His initial fee was, in theory, at least three times that which David received as an individual. David had, in turn, invested his share into the crop, and his partner's personage in the same convoluted production scheme.

Once he received the ASCS funds, Sexton found various reasons for reneging on his promise to legitimately capitalize the MinGo partners for their contributions, in violation of the Rylance agreement. For that reason, among others the concept of a federation of Dave and his MinGo partners never materialized. Though David filed a tax return on the would-be affiliate, it failed to reach the level of conforming to government regulations in the eyes of auditors from the ASCS committee. The affiliation of MinGo with Pleasant Valley, as a rental agreement for equipment and services, did not pass muster with the county committee that ruled David did not meet the government personage payment requirements. He would be ruled ineligible and would have a penalty to pay. Sexton knew the impact of such a massive loss on operations, with no marketing of the 1991 grain in storage supposedly in Williston.

If the allocation was ever to be granted, the Granite County local ASCS committee was responsible for making a number of decisions that determined a producer's eligibility to participate in a program and to receive benefits; or if the applicant is in violation, whether he must refund benefits paid in non-compliance. In his role as operations manager for Pleasant Valley, Robert Walsh had knowledge of the strict eligibility requirements for the government subsidies program, where the American tax payer was handing out billions to farmers. Walsh was more than satisfied with his unofficial role of watchdog for external banking institution fraud since the banks he had worked for based their loans on expected government funding.

The role of county committees is in determining eligibility; whether or not, if upon a physical audit of the farm records, there is compliance with the program for the initial application for a half million-dollar subsidy to be valid. An audit determines evidence, or intent to misrepresent eligibility for the application amount, suspicions of fraud, or error that has been caused unintentionally. If that ever turns out to be the case, as it frequently does, the committee ultimately decides the culpability levels.

Because much of the Pleasant Valley operation was situated in remote locations in the tri-state area, outside the immediate purview of the local committee, in the Zehlen situation, it was Walsh himself who filled in the blanks where the Zehlen's did not meet ASCS specifications. As it would be, and had been since he sold his land survey to Zehlen, it was Walsh's insider knowledge of the South Dakota operation that became a critical factor in farm program-related issues, disaster insurance, and the tainted information that compromised the upgraded three quarter million-dollar allocation from the government–funds David Zehlen was counting on to sustain his operations–anticipated in June 1992.

The ASCS payments meant life or death to an operation the size of Pleasant Valley that was running expenses upwards of $200,000 a week during the spring planting months of April and May; it was costly coordinating logistics of a 10 to 20-man team accompanying a massive fleet of tractors and combines, mobile communication, management services that included payroll, subsistence, benefits and limited cash for medical emergencies, travel, insurance, office and legal expenses. At such a critical time, capital reserves were badly eroded; there was less expense at harvest which did not last as long, but it was just as drastic on the budget of a huge operation stretched to the limit. By June 1992, the deficit margin was at the point of exhaustion.

Sexton was in breach of contract status by the end of May for not reimbursing the manager Zehlen for all reasonable and necessary production expenses the contract provided for. The importance of receiving the near million dollars from the government Zehlen was counting on to sustain his operations could not be underestimated, without his guaranteed contract provisions, his MinGo machine was bound to grind to a predictable halt.

Where there had been a reduction of the contract obligations by a third, there would be no disbursement from the marketing program controlled by Sexton, coming in either. Like a euthanasia-tech monitoring the fading signal of a patient approaching flat line, it was only a matter of time that Walsh had calculated to the dollar and the day, if and when Zehlen's cash reserves were exhausted. Before a complete meltdown Walsh had a few more tricks up his sleeve.

* * * * *

Sexton and Robert Walsh were the first professionals racketeers the Zehlens had ever met. Among the diverse knowledge that went into their business decisions were the legal technicalities of the government-producer relationship and the manner in which compliance and the right to payment were determined for the Zehlen farming operations. With more knowledge of the regulations, and past success under their belts in the courtroom, Sexton and Walsh were completely assured Zehlen was in over his head. They would be shutting him down one valve at a time, like the method Jack used to shut down the boiler of his pride and joy: the 90-year old steam engine in the barn the Zehlens rolled out once a year for the Corn Festival.

As co-conspirators, Walsh and Sexton were zeroing in on the financial details of the deficit crisis David Zehlen was facing the end of spring planting. With all his credit and cash options exhausted, the future and survival of Pleasant Valley, along with any hope of continued expansion of its farming operations depended on the success of Zehlen's government and bank loan application as of June 1992. Walsh and Sexton were particularly interested in monitoring the program features on a yield and acreage basis for the Zehlen farming operations that might emerge relative to allegations of fraud, or willful misrepresentation of a business contract.

In their minds at least, the objectives were clear. Both individuals were aware of the rules,

> "the government seeks to encourage certain behavior for which it will pay, while the producer wants to ensure that he is treated fairly and shall not be denied the government benefits he has earned."

Previous to their arrival, David had faithfully observed this code of behavior. He never imagined that if anything went wrong with the government deal, every element of the bargain would be affected; or that individuals denied partner benefits–David, Jack, Phyllis & Nancy Zehlen, James & Dale Sharon, the Obergs, Jeff and Tonya Provo and Tom Adelman–projected to be receiving $75,000 per person in 1992 were at any risk. Sexton had already received $160,000 of the 1991 disbursement upfront as a marketing fee a year earlier. With the government money in hand, David estimated his partner was a million plus in arrears toward the two-year production costs. When the damage was subtotaled, the county committee ruled that MinGo partners and Zehlen Farms were required to repay 1991 personage amounting to $582,000.

On top of those hail stones of misfortune, there was the *total loss* of the 1992 program benefits of $873,000.00; that amounted to close to $1,455,000 in forfeited ASCS personage funds. Two years allocations were lost in chaos: the first for 1991, requiring immediate repayment, and the '92 ASCS allocation forfeited–along with uncompensated production losses through the bold promissory fraud withholding scheme invented by Hector Sexton–perfected by Robert Walsh.

Only an organization the size of Continental and Ceres could withstand such a catastrophic hit. The importance of the producer-government relationship goes beyond merely dictating the success or failure of a price support program at the national level. This relationship determines the rights and obligations of the individual producer *vis-à-vis* those of the government under the program, *i.e.* what the producer must do to be entitled to the government benefit or payment being offered, whether it is in the form of money, a loan, surplus grain, or eligibility to participate in another program. The government role in the normal relationship is in determining whether the producer has complied with necessary program requirements and is thus entitled to participate or to be eligible to be paid. Payment is generally conditioned on the performance of a certain required activity by the producer, such as withholding a certain amount of

ANTHONY FALLS JR.

land from production, or agreeing to store grain for a certain length of time.

In reality, the methods in which the two conspirators enforced the regulations, from their point of view, could only be discovered in the crucible of adversarial debate between them–over who had the most *devious* intentions. Both conspirators planned for what their partner would be unable to afford. If he was bankrupt as their plans predicated he would be; foremost among those things–was competent legal counsel. There was little of that available on a tight budget that supplemented the county attorney and prosecutor's administration, while furnishing healthy government salaries and benefits.

Walsh expressed his intentions in his five-page typed letter to Sexton in December 1992, in which he devoted several pages of his discussion to his intention that David Zehlen would become *"penniless"* as a derelict in the gutter, if he had any say in the matter as power of attorney; and that Sexton would have the resources of a five hundred thousand dollar dream team of attorneys arguing for him, confident that if their methods were ever reviewed in a court of law–even the authorities would be confused by the mixed motives of the separate parties.

The one thing Walsh lacked as an independent "lone wolf" criminal was the protective shield of a corporate umbrella that Sexton could rely on to support him in the Ceres stem, when litigation emerged relative to shady business dealings; in his insecurity he depended on the cunning of an animal to survive. As his infamous letter of December 1992 indicated, he had adapted to a fear of being caught and the threat accompanying apprehension and punishment–and the psychological trauma that would follow–feeling no empathy for David, only disgust, and growing contempt for his methods of doing business absent any guilt that might have accompanied his criminal activities. If Walsh experienced any emotions of pity, they were for Nancy and her daughter only–they were the victims of David's reckless expansionism.

In his dealings post Janklow, Walsh for many years had come to depend on his personal attributes, craft, and guile, and what support he could garner from officials he selected to manipulate, and include in his plans. He had subconsciously drifted into an exaggerated delirium of achievement–reliving that instant of pleasure that was never completely extinguished–the joy he felt eradicating cocklebur and bitter nightshade; no man could imagine the non-human reinforcement he received from nature itself.

Like the mafia Dons of *Good Fellas'* fiction, whose confessional methods he had been exposed to in movies–methods of rationalization he had practiced since his youth–Walsh hedged for himself, using the religious dogma for its social advantages. He was aware a "god" principle existed, that there were principalities, power, and rulers in high places. He saw them on the news every night. In his fashion of thought, he associated his power with those same factions and individuals that existed in both the Lutheran and Catholic religious organizations, where people gathered to pay homage to these mysterious sources of power that they identified with somewhere, beyond good and evil, hidden within the mixed messages of media materialism, the constant droning conservative forecast for the lower caste, counterpoised with unimaginable extravagance and cruelty.

Mr. Walsh made use of that knowledge and confidence in judgment, occasionally praying to his individual and ambivalent lord; as, certainly he could not believe that a Son of God would succumb to such an ignominious fate, described in the holy Gospels. Importuning that deity that he was not unaware of, Robbie Walsh prayed at church that its force would reinforce his quest for perfection–because there were times he was not completely sure who he was working for, or with–and what the worth of it was, as his letter to Sexton Christmas 1992 indicates.

Despite persistent doubt about salvation, he found himself praying for pardon that his ambiguous lord would allow him to carry on his crusades on earth to the end, as Jesus had done. He prayed this power would pardon his venial shortcomings, make him feel better so he could receive the sacraments, including extreme unction if it came to that. Taking communion meant being a part of the congregation of believers. He didn't question what they believed in; it was the assembly, and ritual that counted. Because of his intimate relationship with this power he knew he had, because of its will upon his partners–the minute transfer of telekinetic energy–though few spoke of it, the feeling of power, to move people and objects. Walsh believed he could summon that force to work for him among all these people, "while the battle raged in Galilee it was snowing on Mt. Hermon," he recalled the pastor's words. Why else would they be there?

Ecumenism was fast becoming the practicing method of religion emerging in the last quarter of the 20th Century in Rockland. It little suited Robert's personality, as it required him to be congenial with people who might actually perceive that his beliefs were antithetical to Christianity. There was a general consensus *things* were done in its name; on the negative side, it was the true believer's perception of crisis, the impact of so many knights in shining armor, boots on the ground, in a military action accomplishing little more than reinforcing the Moslems–extending the tension, creating Sunnis like Saddam, the Kuwait invasion–reciting the narrative that led to the Gulf War and like subjects. In the general media process, imminent war was rapidly emerging as the only topic of conversation of any value and interest in the community–igniting fear their local boys in the National Guard could be called up for action in Desert Storm.

Amidst the turmoil, his opinions were as valid as the superstitions that ruled the tight-knit community; for good reason there were times Robbie Walsh felt superior in his dealings with less clever and cunning individuals who submitted to the supporting doctrines of a religious community the Zehlens depended on for fellowship–of these rituals none was as visible as holy communion. Walsh participated in the sacrament at one church or another every Sunday.

CHAPTER 11

The 1991 Pleasant Valley farms harvest of sunflowers, soybeans, corn and wheat was in road gear by the end of September. All David's crops had met expectations except that bushels per acre on two sections of corn in Swift county had been lower than expected; at the same time, the market was up 5 percent. David and Jack planned to sell rather than store beans despite lower than average prices in the market; believing that volume on record yields would make up for any lost revenue of spring markets factoring in storage costs over the winter, while continuing to believe in the contract agreement with their partners. By the end of September, David was receiving cash and checks for soybeans, and corn revenue that offset his short payment from Hector Sexton; it was acceptable in early October; but Zehlen fully expected his partner would eventually make up for it on deliveries of semi loads of grain to the Odessa Coop Elevator and PD Products in Graceville, MN.

During harvest 1991, David wasn't worried. But he was becoming aware of the impact short payments on the huge contract his 13,000 acres in Duehl County could mean to the rest of his operations that were meeting forecasts. He believed that it might be necessary to hire an independent manager with a marketing background, one of the original reasons he consulted with Walsh about using his experience to evaluate the land, and Sexton's "reckless abandonment" of the conditions of the contract, leveling the playing field by bringing another specialist on board.

What concerned Dave was that after receiving three quarters million dollars from Hector Sexton on the contract in December, he was still three quarters million behind. By that time the other Sexton partners in Traverse County, Al Taffe and Kelly Miller had discontinued the second year extension, bailing out after Sexton reduced the contract share 40 percent. Zehlen went along with Sexton believing his partner's promise that he intended to pay off in the anticipated 1992 spring marketing boom he expected sometime in May. Sexton added,

"You will be receiving this infusion of capital right about the time the government subsidies will be arriving for you David. Robbie informed me you have enough reserves to make it until then. Let me know if there are any problems with that arrangement? Miller and Taffe just lost faith at the wrong time when you will profit from their losses. I will be offering you the opportunity to pick up the leases they are dropping."

With nothing to lose except the estimated two million he had invested, including his share of ASCS personage, Zehlen continued dealing with Sexton. David claimed later at a sentencing hearing that the $160K Hector required up front, was money to be filtered back to the accounts of MinGo from Hector's marketing program. He had saved and assembled accounts payable receipts that indicated Hector had for a change paid vendor billings that amounted to $1.3M from Pleasant Valley/MinGo for leases and some of the production input; David massaged his records so that both his and Hector's accounting departments would be satisfied that at least a few minor discrepancies could be finessed–in case anybody was checking which they wouldn't be–unless somebody was snooping around. Approaching twenty years in the business, Pleasant Valley had never been audited by the USDA. That was the least of his worries. With the record of compliance, he and his father had compiled, there would be no reason not to take his word for it. Believing he had committed no crime, Zehlen freely acknowledged he had invoiced Sexton for $300,000, under instructions representing Ceres and SigCo, as Sexton had required him to do–to be paid the refund as production cycle charge-backs.

* * * * *

On the road to an inspection tour of sunflowers and discussion of South Dakota operations with his manager Rodney Oberg,

David stopped at Milbank Implement, the same dealership his dad had purchased farm equipment from since the 1950's. After hearing about the way harvest was proceeding across three states, the owner Ken Behrens was always impressed, ready to extend more credit to the Zehlens.

"Okay David I will make you an offer you can't refuse. As you can see I have ten IHC 4WDs on the lot right now, this year's model; at the first of the year I lose a quarter of a million dollars on those tractors; I have to finance ten more next year, models that I guarantee you couldn't tell them apart standing six feet away, and at seven percent interest you see what I'm saying", said Behrens who could have made a living selling snow cones to Eskimos.

"You and your dad have been among my best customers, with me since I took over the business from my father–he still comes around for coffee at least once in a while, mind you, at 87. If you and Jack offered me that same quarter million, and matched the financing, last year it was 6%, I could let you and your men–I just talked to Rodney last week–drive those tractors off the lot with a tank full of fuel from Milbank Farmers Union. All you have to do is park them on top of your flatbeds. Just add a band and that makes a parade," he chuckled.

"You could be using them by the end of the week for harvest. I am trying to make it easy for you and Jack. Mind you, you will not find a better deal from here to Rapid City. You could actually use a new combine or two, but we will talk about that maybe next year." Behrens was not an award winning implement dealer–his office wall plastered with plaques proclaiming him "Salesman of the Year" since the fifties, and signed by CEOs of International Harvester, John Deere and Case–for no reason.

"You drive a hard bargain Ken. We usually buy new equipment on a five year cycle. That will be coming up next spring."

"I can arrange that David. You're first payment won't be until the end of June when personage arrives next year," Behrens extended the deal amiably. As a matter of fact, you are so convincing Ken, David thought, if my dad was here, he would write the check and lay it in the palm of your hand. He has been bugging me all summer about how he spends all his time in the machine shed repairing our old tractors when he could be up at the cabin. That's his joy of life though. Jack loves tuning those engines, puttering around the shop all day, fixing and installing new engine parts. Always frugal Jack claimed he was saving twenty bucks an hour these mechanics are charging now days, when I can do it myself for nothing, if I had their new-fangled tools and equipment.

"You know my dad as well as anybody in these parts Ken. He never wants to admit some of the equipment is too old, worn out for the job. You've seen the old Martin Zummach steam engine at the Corn Festival. That machine is a relic of the Stone Age, over a hundred years old. We have an Allis still running around the farm that your dad sold him while I was in grade school. I'll talk your offer over with my bankers. You can count on that. I will get back to you after I inspect the Brookings flowers."

Dave and Ken shook hands in the office. Before he was out of the pole barn that housed the dealership and repair shop, Ken rummaged around in a steel cabinet near the entrance to the building. Pulling out a crushed burgundy cap, he handed it to David as he reshaped it. There was a white Milbank Implement Inc. logo embroidered on the front.

"We could use some free advertising with what KMSD charges me to promote my business. It looks like your hunting hat has seen better days," Ken quipped. "We order a box of them every summer as a sponsor for the rinky dink baseball program, adjustable for adults though."

David appreciated the humor. Both men were aware farm credit is a scarce commodity in small towns like Milbank and Rockland. They were both very serious business men at heart. The tractors would eventually cost over three million dollars at 6%. Humor was part of Ken Behrens, the salesman's method of communication. A sense of humor was one quality most people in the farming business have in common. It occurred to David, for an instant, that particular quality is what attracted him about Hector Sexton in the beginning.

He headed south on County 15. At noon he snapped on the KWAT farm market reports and forgot about the sunflowers for the next five miles imagining the beauty of ten identical tractors in an angle view of the row parked in front of multiple Pleasant Valley silos, his growing family pictured in the foreground, *I just hope those flowers in Pope County look as good as Rodney keeps informing me they are,* he thought to himself. *I'm afraid Ken just made me a deal I can't refuse, but Jack will argue against. He is so damn conservative now compared to the radical he was when he made the switch to flowers 40 years ago. We could buy seven of them; that would put our costs at a little less than 2 million on the deal. We save taxes on Sec 179 investment and accelerated depreciation,* he thought, imagining the discussion with his father. David glanced in the rear view mirror as he adjusted the burgundy "Milbank Imp" cap on his head.

David detoured by one section of the Duehl County flowers to spot inspect his South Dakota operations without notice. They looked better than expected considering the dryness of the summer. He estimated ten percent had been harvested. One of the red IH combines stood idle with no driver in sight, as if the huge machine itself had lumbered to a halt halfway down the thirtieth row or so, maybe stopped for rain. Its huge spiral blades were poised like a lion ready to leap into the fray of the battle at a moment's notice.

* * * * *

The South Dakota operations revolved around evolving circumstances; Robert Walsh appeared disheveled and tired, as he was bent over looking over reports on the front desk.

"You can help yourself to some coffee David. We have some good and some not so good news. It looks like on a sample of the harvest we are coming in lower than expectations, at about 900 pounds per acre. That's not too bad. The oil content is close to what we need at 37%. I spoke with Hector last week after we test harvested about a hundred acres at Clear Lake. One of his men was supposed to pick up and deliver about a thousand bushel to Williston. He was a bit disappointed, blaming it on that week of rain and 45 degree temperatures that hit us by surprise in August. I told him it looked like the storm dumped rain on the south 4000 acres that we tested."

"I'm not impressed. What's the good news from my southern farms marketing staff anyway?" Zehlen inquired.

"You don't have to worry about that David. I'm sure the production on the dryer fields will make up for any deficits this test indicates. It's the Board of Trade method. Just a small sample. Tells the farmer what he's got before he gets to market." Walsh assured him. "It's your other people I would be concerned with."

You mean like Adelman don't you, Zehlen thought, but never said. Walsh always managed to introduce the vague sense of uncertainty about the Adelman marketing strategy. To himself, David was thinking, *I am getting nothing but conflicting stories from both these guys all the time. Any way I choose they've got me over a barrel. How do I know when Hector is going to honestly fulfill his share on the contract, frankly, when Walsh seems to know? And just because we're harvesting the other crops and there is a trickle of income, that doesn't mean Hector has to stop payments I need, especially with expenses in arrears.*

"You remember when I stopped by Milbank Implement on the way down here and Behrens had me sold on some new equipment. By then, I had already made arrangements, forking over a couple hundred bills on some new IHCs," as he finished the sentence David could see the reaction he had sensed, but never seen so blatantly.

"You've got to be joking David, how many?" Walsh was livid in an instant.

"Well of course I was planning ahead, Behrens said he had to move them with the bank before new models came out. I leased them for harvest," David answered, aware of the spontaneous change in Walsh's personality as he became aggravated.

"You went way out on limb I would say. You can't depend on Hector sending you another cent before the new harvest is settled. Even then he'll fight you for every dime on the contract." Walsh was not surprised David consulted with no one on such a major purchase at a critical time, as he saw it.

"It's none of your business Robbie," Dave retorted, "what I do with my money. I'm paying you to be my marketing consultant. I needed your advice on the productivity of land. I had talked with Ray Rylance about it. Don't worry. It won't affect your money. Ken made me a deal I couldn't refuse as I see it, whatever I can afford to pay Milbank Implement since Hector was holding out–it's also a huge deduction on my income taxes. I will need it if I have any hope of coming out on my MinGo expenses."

The thought crossed his mind vaguely that Walsh, had not trusted Hector from the beginning, yet they were in it together. The tingling sensation in his arm started, and remained an instant as if a dull needle poked his skin but didn't draw blood. Who could he trust? He had a weird feeling about the deal ever since day one. It was as if the man had some kind of unearthly power to control every event.

"I'm not worried about mine David. I trust you," Walsh was at the point of yelling. "Your problem is you can't depend on Hector because of the attorneys, and accountants who run his business. He will pay his obligation to me one way or another. I will make sure of that with my attorneys; but frankly it's a pittance compared to what I'm worth to him in marketing for that matter David. You and I are just ciphers in ledgers to him and his big shot pals at Ceres and SigCo. Hector has been carrying their dirty laundry to the dry cleaners for years. Oh I know all about him–whatever works for the stakeholders. Now this giant Lubrizol conglomeration from Toronto buys them all out. They call the shots and pay him to make them money, not you, David, or me. I'm probably the only one who could make Hector fulfill on this contract if such a thing is possible, which is what you hired me for ultimately, and I intend to do my job."

ANTHONY FALLS JR.

As usual, David was not listening to Walsh's sermon from the desk. Noticing the typical attention deficit response, Robbie popped up nervously from his chair, and began pacing the two rooms of his business suite, looking out the window on to main street of Brookings, storming back and forth across the ancient pink and gray speckled linoleum.

"And I ask you David? What little credit do I get for my contributions? I've helped other farmers in the past as many of them went under. I'm not saying you will David. I know I'll get my money from you; it's all the money Hector owes you that concerns me." Walsh turned an about face and marched to the picture window–*what is lost before I take over concerns me*–was on his mind at that moment. Robbie tested the edge of Dave's borderline defenses.

"You have no idea what will happen. I don't want it to happen. You, your family, Jack, his lovely wife Phyllis are all alike, naïve. Hector is out for number one only, to make money for corporate owners without a conscience, shadowy individuals with no soul whatsoever. These configurations are much more powerful than Pleasant Valley Farms. You will remember what I was warning you about when you see the 'For Sale' sign on your farm. I've heard and read about the way Hector treats his customers on paper at least. You should read the DeKalb Farmland lawsuit. You're no exception. If you don't see it by now you will soon enough. I can tell you right now those ten IHCs are in jeopardy immediately if you finance them from Milbank Implement," Walsh barked imperiously, concluding another of his grim oracles about the future of the Zehlen enterprise.

"Believe you me David, don't get me wrong, Hector is a charming individual. He has the potential to penetrate the upper echelon of management with Ceres and SVO. They need people like him experienced with customer investment and loans; we know he came from Eastern money. You see his tailored clothes don't you? That tells me he has the cash to put down on a limo your guy Jeff the insurance man chauffeurs him around in? Does Hector look like a farmer to you dressed in his creased wool slacks, Madison boots and lambskin jacket?"

"We both know Phyllis notices him; she calls him 'sexy ass' who reminds her of Danny Glover. He's not that good looking in my opinion. Have you ever heard of the Bohemian Grove rituals David? These people are a different breed from us; they came from generations of wealth with Washington behind him, compared to you or me. The Swiss were far better off in the old country; they are risking their fortunes in this economy."

Walsh maintained a stereotypical profile of his non-white partner; until strategic moments or emotional instants he kept his visions to himself. Jewish, Jamaican and African blood lines blended into one image of Teutonic intolerance for foreigners dating back to the colonies. In a few captured moments with David, he attempted to indoctrinate him to the racial ideas at the base of his as yet unpublished version of *The Prince of Fields*, touching briefly on a Zehlen tradition of conservation of mineral reserves passed down several generations–originally a Rothschild-sponsored program–and became involved with importation of indentured slaves to plantation owners in the new world. In Walsh's theory of race, over many generations, individuals with desired physical qualities were selected, intermarried and integrated into the dominant culture that was opposed to distribution of water and mineral rights of the planet, believing such a policy leads to widening the gap between rich and poor.

"I can see it all happening again, just like in the Farmland case. There is always the possibility of fraud in your deals with Hector David. He even has the Pleasant Valley staff charmed with his presence. One time I heard Phyllis comment that Sexton reminds her of Washington in *Philadelphia* with Hanks, who is related to Lincoln, whatever that means. I don't see *any* resemblance."

"That's why I counted on hiring you for 1992 as South Dakota operations manager, and mission: records examination, unobtrusive observation, interviewing key individuals behind the scenes working to straighten this mess out. We expect your influence to offset Hector's policy since you know more about it than we do at Pleasant Valley. So far Hector has been straight with me. He just owes me a lot of money he promised to pay. We have a guaranteed contract. That will hold up in any court in the land. You may be exaggerating the negatives about his personality. Hector has a solid reputation. The safflowers look fine to me. You've done your job well it appears. I will drive by the north acreage, the remaining eight sections, on the way home to inspect the effects of weather you mentioned. There was more rain up that direction."

As David got up to leave, he felt the urge to extend his arm for the usual handshake, but thought the better of it. Their relationship had cooled to the point of David feeling uncomfortable around Walsh for longer than a cup of lukewarm instant. He knew they should be talking about important matters even though he was concerned and the feeling never left; he did not want to discuss those issues with his manager.

Perhaps that was because Walsh was always upset, and in an irascible mood lately. Obviously he did not want to discuss much. And it was like he put a gag on David's voice and ideas in verbal transactions. In those situations, Dave was stunned by the coldness into semi-speechlessness. It was best to move along–it was apparent something besides the tractors was bothering Walsh. Shaking hands–he never forgot the shock of the first handshake–would only aggravate the situation. It had given him a weird feeling before. He chose to punctuate his visit to Marketing International, adding,

"If I were you, I would rent a nice pastoral film with no violence to watch with Shirley and Louise. I recommend *Paradise*. Say hello to Deuce; what grade is he in now? Wish them all my best. I know your bride will love the movie. I know Nancy did; she said it reminded her of Pleasant Valley in the early days. It just came out on video cassette and should be available here in town. Have a nice weekend Robbie. I'll call you next week."

CHAPTER 12

Using his method of hedging upon the deficit his failures of fulfillment created, Sexton had developed a system of extortion that leveraged government program funds from some of his customers into his coffers. The tried and true technique that emerged from his research was not something that arose spontaneously. It was a calculated secret formula that evolved over time that could be applied if the stakes were high enough.

Hector would run a flexible accounting method that emerged over his many years in the business. Using his method, Sexton was able to orchestrate a classic allocation scheme as unique as the Spanish sonatas he loved. There was really nothing to it. He just had Zehlen convinced that unless he accepted the cut-back on the contract as beneficial in the long run, as Miller and Taffe had failed to see–showing a little more faith, David would get his lost margin back on the spring marketing deal that he assured Zehlen was wide open with grain and insulin shortages worldwide. He could be completely confident a long-term fix for world hunger was available through Ceres genetic R&D.

These and other vague ideas to deflect inquiry into the conspiracy apparatus were bandied about in the hundreds of business-related conversations by early 1992. As always, there were no checks in the mail, only unpaid billing notices. Those days of the marketing windfall were yet to come. David believed he had no other choice than wait it out. At no time, including then until ten years later, did Dave gain an understanding of the legal theft that had befallen the farm. He recalled the slogan of infamy well,

"Make sure you make that $750,000 last; at least we got the flowers in the bin this year. We will have to wait until marketing for our shares. I am with you partner," –the dark Jamaican reassured his victim as he slipped another fib into David's troubled thoughts—it was business as usual stalling with the customer on products and service once the deposit is in the bank; meanwhile, "with each passing day the contract black-hole deficit *widens* on our $1.75M deficit, you have *all* my revenue tied up and have eliminated the margin I needed, dedicated to holding a loose canvas over my farming operations?"

David's once clear thoughts on becoming the world's largest farmer from the Midwest region—were being replaced by an emotional morass of anger and resentment. Replacing the confusion with increased knowledge of the crime against him led to post-traumatic stress, of a battle too painful to remember, that weathered his once sturdy frame of life. In reality the hardship the conspiracy caused became increasingly hard to forget even many years later, by the time his completely altered personality had developed denial into a science.

* * * * *

Although he never disclosed the exact details of the strategy or discussed them with his accountants and attorneys, Robbie Walsh had developed a scheme to perfection. Just as he had in the land survey, Walsh had done what research he could, scanning the records of the most prosperous land owners in the area in the courthouse. With the Marxists, Walsh understood that who controls production has authority over society. Along with it came the elevated social status of the once struggling small farmer, recalling his ancestors who toiled for generations with oxen and a plow to pay the landlord rent, or taxes if he owned the land, with little to spare for luxuries. If the Zehlen family at one time mirrored the traditional image, what he saw was a portrait warped into a legacy of greed and expansionism that had nothing to do with rural America.

"Let me remind you again Hector, what I value is that tremendous gross off 40,000 acres. I manage that as power of attorney once David is permanently on the shelf. I will talk with you more later on this issue when you show more interest in it Hector," His voice trailed off, as he thought, "not used to taking orders are you Mr. Sexy Ass nigger from Jamaica. I suppose you have a big...?" The line went dead. We can work together Walsh reassured himself.

His strategy would depend on pressuring the majority owner's, David and Jack, wives to oust David as President of Pleasant Valley production division and hand power over to Walsh who had been working for them less than six months when he masterminded the takeover. Under new management of power of attorney, Robert Walsh, the confidence man from Nundas, had a deep enough understanding of the promissory fraud and the production swindle to manipulate Sexton, much more than David did. The other spy was a tough hombre who laughed at rumors of his family connections with longshoreman's union management, and organized crime on the East coast.

Walsh had always received his share of the booty. Usually it was a generous bonus from the third beneficiary–the bank, or one of its affiliates that kicked back some of the take–as it assumed directorship of the farms Walsh sabotaged before the bank attorneys took over, and in his role as an incognito agent for the firm in capitalizing and foreclosing on its customer's miscalculated risks. Walsh believed if a farmer was so gullible to fall for the scheme, he didn't deserve to be farming. Walsh himself approaching 60, felt like 70. He had quit smoking. But he hid a pint of lemon vodka under the seat to try to deflect his mind away from the obsession that haunted him. This was going to be his last full-scale takeover operation. It would be enough to accumulate some of the assets, in cash and real estate–enough to retire, and put Shirley in a nice nursing home if need be.

He was too old for the hassle of buying up farms and land. That was the bank's job. He enjoyed the details and the personal transactions as neighbors of the generations came to pay their respects at the closing auctions, realizing the man they ignored was now running the farm–up until the auctions were over–making deals for this and that item, after an owner was evicted suddenly and unexpectedly. The triumph oddly reminded him of his days as weed inspector. He would never forget the smell of the hazardous chemicals room where the DDT was stored, or inspecting the wilted weeds the next day. His job never failed to deliver a feeling of accomplishing a job that had to be done. He had been chosen to do it.

There were compliments from prosecutors for the pro se complaints–where he almost sounded like an attorney–but for some minor detail in his writing. Usually it was the unprofessional tone, wanting to lay it on the victim, which exposed Robbie as a charlatan. Nonetheless, it was his background and field work participation that generated material for the prosecutor to warp into a warrant. On his petitions, Walsh would write up complaints, allegations, and evidence along with drafts of a motion he would then pay his attorneys to file with the court. As in a case out in southern Grant County, information from the complaint is passed along to the county sheriff.

"I remember one occasion when the authorities needed my help finding this old man's farm at night because the power was shut off. They had to do an intervention in a repossession of a quarter-section near LaBolt, SD. The sheriff's task force from Duehl County was involved in it–I had to witness the unfortunate farmer as he was being dragged off a four generation homestead against his will in handcuffs–his wife yelling out the door as they led him away, in the headlights."

"Why are you doing this to my husband!! He didn't do anything–he is no criminal!" She screamed unmentionable obscenities at the deputy. Understandably the wife was very upset and crying as the sheriff handcuffed her seventy-five-year-old husband, and hauled him to the county jail. It happened more than once. I recall that poor woman and others screaming their disapproval of state's rights to the police. I tried to help. I risked my life to stand up for him in my testimony as defendant. I spoke to the man he needed to move off the land; it belonged to the bank now. He said 'Oh no it don't.' Then he ran back in to the house to get a shotgun. I got the hell out of there. That's why I had to issue a complaint in my power as financial officer that led to the man losing his farm. It should never have happened if he had listened and filed bankruptcy like I advised him," Walsh had repeated a similar version of the takeover strategy in court a half dozen times by 1992.

"I'll tell you what David, if that ever happens don't resist the authorities; that old farmer, related to the Helgeson family of Milan, didn't know what hit him. They had to use mace to subdue him. In court he was facing an arrest warrant for assaulting an agent of the government and the sheriff. It was a mixed method fraud created by a crooked partner, and a financial institution willing to pay attorneys like Meyers and Wilber who can beat you in court every time with some argument Brent comes up with that sounds legitimate, but is nothing but legally annotated confusion. Like the one he uses and will use again in Sully eventually. One thing leads to another. Soon you have a basis of a lawsuit over crop ownership and liability for bank loans that led to foreclosure without notice. Finally, the bank that held the mortgage on the crop begins collecting on the collateral; the farm itself worth sometimes as much as ten times the value of the loan is lost just as the litigation was by corruption and mental bribery."

No evidence was left behind that Sexton (and Walsh) had been divining the plan a year and a half before the unfortunate farmer wound up in court with a confused public defender indoctrinated by Walsh, supported by the supposedly baffled counselor, donated by the state–that stood squarely against him.

In the Zehlen Pleasant Valley case, as he had done in others, Sexton presented the customer a supposedly legitimate "Grower's Agreement" in which the owner, Sexton, compensated MinGo as a grower/manager, paying $28 dollars an acre labor expense plus all associated costs incurred: rent, seed, fertilizer, spray, gas and associated financing expenses in the operation. After that, Pleasant Valley was to receive 25 percent of the net income from the sale of the crop, which was standard contract language across the industry between grower and manager. The hidden treble hooks of the Zehlen Sexton deal were embedded in the 3rd paragraph on the second page of the contract, where it was stated that the grower would comply with all government program eligibility requirements.

ANTHONY FALLS JR.

Sexton accomplished his scheme through manipulation of the interpretation of the contract; and in knowing he could suppress an audit that would prove he was in promissory fraud. In the first year of the contract, he paid lump sums to ensure planting and harvest; maintenance was a crap shoot, Sexton refused complete payment of production costs–as a twist he extracted what he owed Zehlen by claiming personage funds were to be used in production–when Zehlen on his end of the deal had pumped as much of his capital as he could into Sexton's safflowers and sunflowers.

At the end of the 1991 crop year, and on various grain sales as harvest proceeded, instead of paying costs incurred for producing the crop and a share of anticipated income from sales, Hector reduced the producer margin $10 dollars an acre–if it came down to litigation over the differences between what Zehlen actually received and what he was owed–Sexton gambled on suppressing the contract in a mire of litigation by pressing false charges that Zehlen was stealing from him.

He had done it before in third party deals. The idea was to slowly take the target farmer out on a credit limb right up until the client has signed over the collateral. Walsh had agreed before times to participate in the plot to snare Zehlen on charges he could fabricate when the time was ripe. In the pretrial stage, he knew how to steer the prosecutor, public defender and judge through the confusion that arrived in terms of reconciling the difference between what Sexton actually paid, and what Zehlen had been receiving at a 40 percent reduction to what they had agreed upon. Frivolous litigation at Zehlen expense ensured that subject would never come up.

Imagining a simulated barb of the treble-hook hellcat he and his nephew Jeff fished with for walleye in Devil's Lake over the Fourth; in a similar fashion Sexton intended to embed the lure in the throat of a Christian fish he located with his apparatus, in allocating the partner deficiency payments into the production that he intended to capitalize on. Hector had done the math; he knew if the guaranty contract he signed with Zehlen was strictly adhered to, the estimated value of the agreement was around $2 million. Although a payment of several hundred thousand here and there seemed appealing to the man in crisis, Sexton knew Zehlen was stretched thin across his huge operations–at a time when cash was crucial. He was desperate and could be depended on to deliver on his end of the bargain if it were to collapse in total confusion, and plea bargain; maybe commit suicide, or sell the farm short, manipulating the female partners. He was comforted in the thought that this time, as it had been in the demise of other clients, there was no way out of the trap he and the other parties were preparing to snag David with once the ASCS wicket was cleared.

Sexton, in selecting his victim, calculated his next close personal partner would be thoroughly indoctrinated to the medicinal value element, and naïve enough, to follow through on his manager's obligations, which were basically to plant both flower crops growing in the field, making sure cultivation, fertilization and herbicide applications were completed on schedule–as was the grower Zehlen's more flexible responsibility. Sexton gambled on Zehlen's farming ethic and budget that he would not want to lose his current investment of production costs: labor, drying, storing, delivering grain, financing and maintaining machinery and property leases, along with the additional ten tractors he financed in Milbank for the new growing season.

By then, Zehlen would have invested as much as 70% of his capital in total management expenditures for the contract while Sexton had contributed 50% of the contract obligations with no intention to contribute any more than that by spring planting 1992. The $750K check from Ceres, with a forwarding note from Sexton, sent at the end of December '91, was the last cash David Zehlen actually ever saw from Sexton. He would have to wait for spring marketing, as Sexton so often repeated to end their conversations.

Sexton had determined over the years that dedicated farmers could be depended upon to match and risk their price deficiency support or personage allocation, to compensate for a potential loss on a contract, out of loyalty to their profession. But as an independent business man who did not profit from the government, who paid taxes that reduced his profits to that government–Hector Sexton did not honor those same principles–instead he took advantage of them. The hi-jacked government money was a gold mine for him to harvest up front. He believed he could count on Zehlen to be no different than scores of other farmers whom he hooked into the same type of scheme.

In Zehlen's predicament, there was yet another factor that entered into the feed grinder-like apparatus he felt he was tumbling into with Walsh and Sexton. Walsh knew the way out of any contract, as corporate attorneys are trained to understand, was the "*conduct clause*" written into the fabric of the supposedly immaculate guaranty contract of Sexton and Zehlen. This particular gray area was Robert Walsh's bailiwick; it would be he who originally determined whether or not the manager, Zehlen, had complied with all governmental laws and regulations stipulated (*under bullet 3c.*) of the grower's agreement. If the case went to trial, it would be Walsh's self-described function as a private investigator, who appeared by chance to blow the whistle on Zehlen, at just exactly the right moment, creating a bucket of allegations and false charges against his employer, under the auspices of his power of attorney, as a necessary step to complete his takeover of the Pleasant Valley operations.

In making a series of pro se complaints against unsuspecting farmers in the past, Walsh had entrapped unwary farmers on charges of voluntarily or involuntarily–it didn't matter–violating USDA laws and regulations; and thereby violating contract stipulation "3c." In so doing, Walsh and Sexton had created portals through which the alleged conduct violations of David Zehlen and other farmers before him could be identified in their crimes that were amplified through bogus legal petitions. It was a series of pro se documents and lawsuits in South Dakota that allowed Sexton to void any number of contracts in the 1980's because, as Walsh boasted in the FBI affidavit of March 1993, "he had investigated a number of frauds in bankruptcies and the demise of farmers in the Midwest."

And he had profited by them. Tidying up his arrangements for his eventual complete takeover of the Pleasant Valley farming operations, Walsh followed the course diagram on the scorecard meticulously to the next hole. He set up a meeting between David Zehlen, Hector Sexton and his attorney Mr. Wehde, at his Brookings office tentatively scheduled for the first week of February 1992.

CHAPTER 13

It was shortly after St. Valentine's Day that David returned a Robert Walsh message on his answering machine. He was still recovering from a respiratory infection and the tongue lashing he had taken in the kitchen of the Zehlen farmhouse, where Walsh's presence lingered like a ghost. In David's chair, he positioned himself so many mornings on her day off, drinking cup after cup of Nancy's egg coffee, chatting with her about how he would be running the farm, filling her with baloney about how her husband wasn't taking good enough care of her during those contrived conversations.

David was up early that morning shoveling eight inches of wet snow that blocked the garage. At a quarter past seven, the kids were supposed to be waiting for the school bus at the end of driveway; on below zero days, where the boys and their dad would be squeezed into his pick-up, keeping his kids warm in the club cab of his Ford F150. When the kids were off to school, as soon as he finished taking off his boots in the entry of what had been his great Uncle Zummach's homestead; Nancy started in on him,

"Today is just another example of my ungrateful spouse. This is what I'm talking about," Nancy yelled with her snow boots on, dashing into the dining room, and then back into the kitchen with a vase of long stem red carnations. "You never even noticed, or asked where they came from, did you? No, you completely forgot about me again. Robbie sends me a dozen roses from "Bouquets by Bob" to Dr. Hansen's office, and Bob, who is handicapped by the way, manages to deliver another dozen to Phyllis at Anothene compliments of a stranger? Even the family dentist was embarrassed for you, and you don't even bother to buy me a card when strangers and the boys did? And you, you creep, expect sex from me before breakfast. Maybe it's like Robbie says, I should be looking for something better. You should read the card he left at the office."

"Now wait a minute honey, it slipped my mind is all. If you recall, I was out of town attending a business convention and national grower's conference in Fargo. I talked to Hector there. I was attending the conference to improve our farm, like everything I do–it's for the sake of our marriage, the kids, Pleasant Valley. I just didn't think of it at the time. I got back into town late, the drugstores were closed. I had so much on my mind. I didn't notice the flowers by Rob as I never turned on the dining room light."

Only then did David fully understand the bitter Valentine's root of what happened in the bedroom, at once locating the true source of disconnect that preceded flying stiletto heels and pillows, as he attempted to climb into bed about 1 a.m. the previous evening–and had attempted to forget completely. For an instant David was stunned with guilt over a trifling subject, one he never thought about–a ridiculous myth that had some major bearing on his marriage was unthinkable. Yet he was shamed that he had neglected the sacred rites of Cupid again. He tried to give his bride a hug but she shoved him away, *he thought he heard his wife say, "Don't you touch me!"*

"I'll make it up to you, how about if I take you out for dinner at the Matador this evening?"

"It's like Robbie says! You're always a day late and a dollar short," she yelled.

"Think about it! Where am I going to find a babysitter when it's 10 below zero, to drive out to the farm in a snow storm like this?"

"You could phone your mom or your sister," he feigned, then recovered. His wife should be obedient and not thinking like this. This is rebellion. She couldn't possibly be taking the incident so seriously. It wasn't his fault.

"How could you be so forgetful? My parents are in Arizona; they flew out of Sioux Falls last week. I told you Kris has play practice. What makes you think I want to go out to dinner with you anyway? I'd rather stay home and wash clothes–now leave me alone I have to get ready for work." she stormed out of the kitchen.

"I could drive you to the office honey, it's below zero," David apologized.

"Just leave me *alone*," she hesitated an instant from screaming, "'*you fool!*'...just make sure I can get out of the driveway. There was two feet of snow in front of the garage the last time I checked," she continued, yelling a few more expletives from the bedroom.

David was out of the house in a flash grabbing a shovel from the porch. He was hoping he didn't need to attach the snowplow to the tractor. As he flailed away on the hard packed snow, he felt a pinch near his arm pit like indigestion followed by a sharp pain on the left side of his chest. At that instant, the thought of another phone conversation with Walsh almost made him vomit in the driveway. Too much coffee, he thought, acid reflux. He would take a nap after Nancy had gone to work. It would be mid-morning before David could muster up enough energy to phone Robert Walsh.

"Hello this is Robert Walsh who am I speaking to please?"

"It's me Dave Zehlen returning your call."

"Oh yes, David. I have a client in the office right now and an appointment at 11 a.m. Could you call me back this afternoon? By then I should have something for you," Walsh dismissed him peremptorily as if he had planned to.

"Sure thing Robbie, I'll call you back this afternoon." The conversation of the morning returned to his thoughts. It was like he was in a trance since the clash with his bride before breakfast. He stared fixedly through the shaft of light through space where the sun shined, between the faded red barn and the galvanized tin machine shed. Gusts of snow flashed across the view propelled by a stiff wind. His vision had been subtended by the existential kitchen window view of the barren snowy fields that stretched endlessly at that particular angle toward the southeast, where tufts of boxelder groves brushed against the gray belt of landscape at that infinite point where the land meets the sky in the imagination.

In those moments, he reflected on his sister Kris's painting collection, at one time destined for an exclusive New York gallery exhibition. He preferred the rustic rural portraits of Sloan. Sipping his coffee, he wished there was something stronger in the cupboard. He could use a stiff drink of Jack Daniels like he had sworn off since the Anothene days. Nancy wouldn't allow it in the house. Walsh's line was busy when David called at 1 p.m. Walsh returned his call at 2 o'clock.

"What can I do for you today David–wait just a minute will you, let me look at my files here a moment. I have something to discuss with you. Hang on. Oh yes, here it is. I was a bit concerned when you didn't call back immediately. Hector has been calling me asking when, and if you are going to sign up for the 1992 grower's agreement. What am I supposed to tell him? I ask you that as a manager concerned for the way you are running your business David. Sometimes I don't think you understand how much other people are depending on you to do the job you signed up for when you hired me, and Hector for that matter, to arrange financing for your farming operations. By the way, did your wife like the carnations I sent her? I thought she'd like them better at home than roses.

"She never mentioned any flowers to me," David replied laconically. "What are you talking about Robbie? You are the one that lined me up with Hector's bank partners. It looks like I may be out a million five if you add up the ASCS deal he lured me into on the adjacent deal your people arranged with him."

"This is no time for incriminations. You agreed to the contract not me. My signature is not on that agreement. I told you, you couldn't trust Hector didn't I?" Walsh pressed his argument. "Now what are you going to do this year? I have been looking over these notes from Resolution Trust out of Nebraska, when I mentioned that I handled agricultural financing deals. It looks to me like you still owe them a lot of money. I hope you don't expect to borrow more from them do you David? I'm only telling you this for your own good. This would be the time to be thinking of turning over your property to a trustee, or power of attorney, either way that suits you."

"When I gave the bank that file on Resolution Trust I told you we had offered to settle our account for $300K when the original loan was for $330 or somewhere in that neighborhood. They haven't responded to the offer. If you do a search you will see that debt is not on the credit report. The loan in resolution with a failed S & L in receivership was outside our control, and the fact we were negotiating on it was enough to satisfy the bank that the grower loan to Hector was a good idea," David used one of the patented explanations he would come to depend on in extended litigation.

"This spring Pleasant Valley will need an operating loan. It is my responsibility; the defaulted loan can be finessed because of my business relationship with financiers. It will be my responsibility to cover or cover-up whatever the case may be, dealing with the RTC matter, depending on how you look at the deficit your deal with Sexton and Ceres has cost Pleasant Valley. You say you have the connections with the bank to ensure that loan will be granted, but we will be required to put Pleasant Valley up as collateral. There is no need to be concerned about the Pleasant Valley credit rating. You can check with Milbank Implement, they would not have allowed me to finance those tractors if we had a problem with credit," David argued.

"Alright David I wasn't looking for an argument on the matter. All you have to do is make your payments and the collateral is secure; you never had a problem with the leases did you?" Walsh reacted in his usual cool fashion, "You know what you have to do to salvage the farm. I'm doing my research as part of doing the job you hired me to do when you hired me as a consultant representing Marketing International. That would be doing the job Adelman *isn't* performing at evidently, because we have not shown any gains on the international markets when Russia and India are negotiating major grain deals with Cargill and Continental. Whose fault is that I ask you? Not mine. We showed promise on the Brooking flowers on the Williston tests didn't we? You will receive your dividends soon enough."

"You are being too harsh Robbie. Tom is a friend, working on a deal as we speak for a hundred thousand bushels of soybeans with ADM. So don't be so quick to judge. He has done his job in the past. I am counting on you to do yours."

"I'm not criticizing Adelman but I think he is an *amateur* is all I'm saying." Walsh wanted to say, "*Can your guy increase your credit limit?*"

"I've been trying to make loan arrangements your deals have forced me into, to fulfill my contract to protect your and my interests David, along with those of your wife and children and Jack and Phyllis as well. I warned you about Sexton. I also advised you not to trust a Jew at the head of your marketing operations. I have found it necessary to contact the financiers I told you about in our first conversations, Salomon Bros. Because of the confidential nature of the business, I am not at liberty at this moment to reveal completely who those connections are. I have mentioned a few; but you can be assured they are legitimate, and if I must say '*well-heeled*'–once I get them on board, you and Pleasant Valley will have nothing left to worry about."

"Am I to assume then you have already been aware of the Pleasant Valley A+ credit rating? I have nothing to hide Robbie, my father and I have disclosed all the required financial information on the application material you presented to the bank, including information on what was at one time considered a default on the loan from Midwest Federal Savings and Loan Bank which was frozen in arbitration. As I have explained to you already, currently that loan is in negotiation with Resolution Trust, the banking organization that took over the failed S&L. So there should be no problem whatsoever," David affirmed, confident the forbearance of the RTC program, or default brought on by weather-related losses, left them eligible for government disaster payments, or future financing.

"All that business is taken care of David, in the deal I am arranging. The bank will be compensating for any liabilities in your credit through collateral administration according to FDIC policy. The bank has guarantees on their money, you can bet on that, as I do. As I said, the package I submitted is confidential information between me and First Omaha. At this time, I am not at liberty to divulge the details of the deal I am arranging for the

ANTHONY FALLS JR.

benefit of Pleasant Valley." Walsh reinforced him in his uncertain fashion.

"You can rest assured these clients of whom I speak are trusted associates of mine, with only your best interests in mind. I refer again in passing to my financial connections, namely, Queen Latifa heir to the Spanish Monacan throne. And you must know the impact of her vast fortune share of oil royalties off the West African coast upon the Board of Directors of the Tri-County State Bank of Rockland I have acquainted with her resume."

"The Queen is one of my personal creditors who I have worked with exclusively in the past. Other individuals to whom I refer, who you will meet soon are skilled in financial crisis management similar to the one you find you and your family in. I am here only to help you out of the jam you got yourself into. You have my word on it," Walsh paused, peering at the clock on the wall, an angle of the living room of the Nundas farm appeared before his mind's eyes.

"I am sorry I have to end this conversation by 11 a.m. today David. I have another client waiting in the lobby. We can continue this discussion. Good bye for now."

"Talk to you later Robbie," David was relieved temporarily. He asked himself, *how was it* that Walsh always seemed to convince him serious matters which they never discussed were under control? He knew it wasn't true–but he imagined it could be like Walsh had supernatural powers; it had to be occult the way Walsh made it seem that through his influence anything is possible. He had the women convinced *he* had a strategy in place to pull Pleasant Valley out of a power dive into the north forty– the farm accident in progress.

Dave had never discussed the funds he was out of luck on with Sexton, with Robert Walsh, or with anyone having any knowledge, or authority over the amount of government money involved with such seriousness before. He was shocked how well informed Walsh was on the whole matter. He should have known well enough that Walsh knew all about the miserable deal Sexton tricked him into. The image of the rusty treble-tine pitchfork, its association with the posed family portrait of the macabre

Rockwell image, flashed across his depressed existence, while simulacrums of art thrashed like an overlay film of Sloan's classic sickle and bucket appeared to his super-conscious: the rustic image of a four tine pitchfork standing at *parade* rest in the 9 o'clock shadow of the morning sun filtering through the south barn door, using that tool for pitching manure–or into a rat once in a while–back in the day they raised livestock. The general mental pain associated with his disability occurred most often at moments of stress, when such vague relationships of events, personalities in surrealistic hues, played tricks with his consciousness, and attitude, particularly at times he was stressed out over the situation he was in with Walsh becoming his wife's Rasputin–and as a consequence or cause, not accurately managing his growing addiction to low dose morphine–behavior that pharmacist Bill Hoven carefully monitored as he filled David's prescriptions at the dispensary.

As the crisis deepened, David was even more uncertain now that Robbie was talking loan arrangements with unknown bankers. He wondered how Walsh found out about the RTC resolution issue that had not been publicized, or settled by December 1991, when he suddenly appeared on the scene as if by chance. In the doomsday scenario Walsh was arranging, the family jewels would be required as security on the loan. Somehow the patriarch would have to be pushed out of the way? Above all, David knew Jack would never agree to sign over the farm for another man's crops.

By May 1992, Walsh was running the farm for all practical purposes; he was in the office more than the president himself. Walsh's magic wand working behind the scenes was functioning perfectly; for that reason, the MWFSB loan did not appear on credit reports. And for some weird reason, David began thinking of the over-sized red and white treble-hooked daredevil in his dad's tackle box, the muskie lure Jack always used for big pike up in the cabin on Lake Minnewaska; he needed one, but workaholic that he had become–David had not taken a real vacation, like a week trout fishing in Red Lodge, in over a decade.

Christ Almighty he thought, how did I get into this mess where I don't even know what's going on? Dad is so damn mad at me about Walsh I can't talk to him anymore. Now I have nobody to trust. And I don't want to discuss it anyway. Was there no way out of the maze he had fallen into, as the labyrinth of the Minotaur in his backyard, of his Greek predecessors that he discovered too late? Would he be able to find his way out of the maze like his Greek ancestor, King Theseus, David believed he was related to through his mother's ancestry? He was comforted thinking of the legacy of his great grandfather Nicholas Nepolitos, who emigrated from Macedonia in the 19th century. His only choice was to ride out the storm amidst the blizzards of the winter of 1992. Once the green fields of spring arrived, things would improve as they always had for twenty some seasons before that.

That afternoon he stopped by the Farmers Co-op Service store to check on disbursement of dividends for Pleasant Valley Farms, with bookkeeper Delores Ninneman, wife of one of the farmers David leased from. She checked her files and informed Dave the records indicate he should be receiving a check for $12,500; the disbursements would be made in the first week of March. This news cheered him considerably, enough so he stopped by the Anothene building to review the accounts payable and receivable.

Phyllis Zehlen and David had never been close since his father's divorce, in the months before she married Jack, when she was just the attractive middle-aged secretary with a son in college, working in the office. She had left her husband's Allstate Insurance business in Marshall, MN to work for Pleasant Valley. David knew it was inevitable that she and Jack would hook up, after all it was his mother who had always said, "Sex was for having babies," and there was nothing more to it than that. He knew his dad was more than just friendly with Phyllis, the Zehlens were a hot-blooded lot. He couldn't fault his father for wanting to be more than just friends with Phyllis.

As he parked in front of the Pleasant Valley office, one block off main street Rockland, he could tell the snowplows had been out. He gazed at the spectacle of new fallen snow. The red, white and blue American flag above the Ag Services building that used to house the Granite Lanes bowling alley snapped in the frigid north wind that blew south in gusts off Big Stone Lake. Right off, David noticed the wilted carnation in a vase on the secretary's desk. Phyllis was warm and friendly to David as he entered the office still shaking the snow off his boots.

"Looks like your flowers could use some water Phyllis."

"I never touched them," she apologized. "I don't like taking flowers from intruders like Robbie is turning into. He thinks he runs the farm. I don't trust him."

"Don't worry he's 'hold harmless' as they say," David managed an uncertain laugh for a second.

"You're the only person that's visited me in the office today David. Jack called. Are you staying warm? It must be 20-below with the wind-chill in the air. I'm glad you stopped by, I have something for you. There is a fax for you still on the machine that just came in from Brookings. And I have a letter for you from Fargo that arrived yesterday. I told Jack about it. Can I make you some coffee?"

David was cheered by the Cenex news, and Phyllis could be charming when she was in a good mood.

"Thanks but no thanks on the coffee. I've had two pots already, and I'm going to pick up the kids. They're letting out school early today because of blowing snow and blizzard conditions. The radio station makes it sound like a major winter storm. That's how the *weather terrorist* Bruce Hagevik describes it on WCCO anyway. I think we only had a couple inches of snow on the farm. I guess it's the wind that scares people. I'll take the fax and the Fargo letter and be on my way. I have the truck running outside so I have to keep a move on."

"Say hello to Nancy for me David," she added as he left the office. He was expecting a check from Hector anytime soon. As bad as the day had started, with a storm and a quarrel over Cupid's arrows, he was willing to bet he had hit blackjack twice on a day that had been one of the bleakest of the winter starting out. He looked ahead to the good times he shared with his boys–

something unexpected and strangely good happened on the days he waited for the bus in his warm pickup with his boys Noah, and the twins, Aaron and Jordan.

CHAPTER 14

As David Zehlen prepared for another growing season, he reminisced over his career which had exceeded even *his* expectations as he approached forty years. After his marriage in 1975 he considered some other professions. He had done over the road driving during the off season for his father's hired trucker, driving an eighteen-wheeler for Neil Specter who drove long distance and managed his father's shipping and receiving business in the 1960's. The Specter Dray Line was among the first shippers willing to transport the early sunflowers to developing markets in Chicago and New Orleans, before the Clinton and Odessa elevators processed the product. Like his driving superintendent, David could back a semi into a 13-foot loading dock better than his most experienced drivers.

There was nothing to it for David, after all he had been practicing on his father's shaky four-wheel trailers and wheeling the manure spreader around the north forty since he was twelve years old, having learned the skill after cleaning out the barn back in the day the Zehlens milked 30 head of Holstein and Jerseys. Driving had been his first chore around the farm since the day he learned how to operate the 1948 John Deere his Grandfather purchased, the year Jack graduated from Rockland high school.

His high school vocational interest tests indicated David should explore the teaching profession in his field of expertise, agriculture. He was tutoring his oldest son in Algebra. For a short time, he entertained the idea of becoming an industrial arts instructor through extension courses offered at the University of Minnesota, Morris branch. At one time, the sophomore school counselor, George Elliot informed David he could always teach agriculture if he wasn't teaching shop. For that, his grades would have to improve his junior and senior year if he expected to extend his education beyond high school. Mr. Elliot emphasized David's previous grades, particularly in English and social studies.

"Because David, they won't be evaluating your straight A's in agriculture and shop–you are very good at those things. The algebra average necessary would be attainable, but you will also need trigonometry and calculus to make it into Morris. Accomplishments aside, the fact remains you will need much higher grades in required subjects to be accepted by a college. Your tests and grades since 7th grade have thus far indicated you would have difficulty scoring high enough on the ACT test to meet entrance standards. I have informed your mother of this situation. She would like you to live on the farm in Rockland, and keep working with your dad." His mother hoped David could commute to Morris and attend what used to be the old agriculture tech school, before it became the University of MN, Morris Campus branch, if his grades and test scores improved.

"Marie has called and written me that she would like to see you going to college like your sister Kristin has done, but not in the twin cities."

When his father informed him the farm was growing too large for a one-man operation, if he was thinking about marriage and a family, David could make a lot more money in farming than in teaching. Jack had started out small. In those days, farmers could scrape out a living on 160 acres and renting. Dave's father had begun working with his father John Zehlen farming 160 acres by 1949. But Jack had been working near full time on the farm since he was 14. With little interest in sports, or hanging out in town, he became his father's right hand man before he graduated from high school. Aware that teachers in Rockland were some of the lowest paid in the state, David decided to join his dad in a full partnership in 1979. Between them the two Zehlen's had amassed 3600 acres, expanding to 15,000 acres purchasing optioned leases on cropland over the next ten years.

The Zehlens had a long history of traditional crop rotations with their spring wheat, sunflowers, soybeans and corn, using the latest practices of conservation tillage. Their farm was among the first in the county to employ low-input sustainable agriculture, a technology that amounts to "drilling" seeds directly into the ground that has been chiseled, replacing the generations old method where the soil has been plowed, disked, and raked into a fine bed of sandy loam, the traditional method used since the steam engine was introduced to agriculture, long thought to be the ideal platform for maximum production. By the 1950's soil conservation concerns and warnings of silent springs made an impact on traditional methods of tillage that resulted in major loss of topsoil through wind water erosion. Under ideal conditions, the Zehlen's customized LISA planting methods supposedly reduced soil erosion by ninety percent. The technique depended on performance of specially designed customized heads and planters, only corporations and the most successful and technologically adept farmers could afford to invest in.

As the Zehlen farm management strategy appeared in an industry magazine article in 1992, when teamed up with management consultant Tom Adelman, they were able to develop markets for large quantities of their grain at the capacity they were capable of producing. According to a *Farm Futures* article, progressive modification for greater production of the farming industry became David's specialty.

In the meantime, his right hand man was proclaiming the farm couldn't get along without him after three months on the job. When in fact, in an amazingly short time, Robbie Walsh had cleverly wedged himself into the business arguing that it was his job to be the controller–the situation was *chaotic* with David in charge. Although he was used to managing farms through tough times like David was in, this was an exceptional case; he normally worked closer to his local Marketing International office in Brookings, South Dakota. Instead of heaping accolades on David's accomplishments, Walsh slyly began pecking away at the frivolousness of the projects Dave doted on, believing only a rich farmer's pampered son could possibly idle away so much of his time growing test plots of raspberries, saskatoons and nitrogen fixing shrubs like sea buckthorn at crunch time. Such trifling was David's fault, as much a part of his demise as his involvement with another man's crop, no less pragmatic than planting thousands of acres of oriental safflowers on tainted soil; the whole project as Walsh knew, destined to be written off as failed protocols of Ceres R&D.

* * * * *

As he stated in his letter to his partner Sexton at Christmas '92, the most important consideration in their dealings with Zehlen was that,

> *"There can be no proven scheme on your behalf against the U.S. government or First Omaha through an agent or private contractor."*

For the same occult reasons he lured other farmers to their demise, Walsh needed just enough time to allow Zehlen to build a scaffold, and then string up a noose for himself. He would use this basic strategy, depending on the *naiveté* of the American farmer, leading the victim into the trap it was his fault for getting himself into–then posing as one of his patented "hold harmless" defendants in litigation.

Fortuitously, Robbie appeared to expose Zehlen's problem as he had the others; those he had accidentally on purpose stumbled upon in his private gum-shoe work as an informer for the bank. And it was only in the process of his power of attorney work discovering the trouble David had: a list of various stretches of the rules, compliance, and government regulations–the worst of which was the violation of item "3c."–in the contract related to the ASCS program entitlement issue they discussed regularly.

It was as if the specialized interests, knowledge and skills of the central characters of the farm resembled the society of *The Sound and the Fury* one of the books his brother Ansel recommended on the college reading list, if he wanted to advance beyond the boundaries of Nundas. But his oddly satisfying experience with the weeds had led to another way of knowing the first comforts of addiction beyond cigarettes; he could only identify vaguely with the protagonist Jason's personality and furious temper. He could make no sense out of it for a book report, with no plot or recognizable events. He could immediately relate to the feeble mother theme in the story. As his English teacher pointed out, the class needed to recognize the mother-figure as a symbol of the declining southern matriarchy, loosely related to the graphic image in the novel, *A Rose for Emily*, the topic of oppressed women, unmentionable incest, affairs with vulgar men–the heroine finally yielding to a banker no less.

Ansel had several other books on his shelf by London and Faulkner that never interested him such as *The Hamlet*, and *Sanctuary* nestled on his bookshelf beside *How to Win Friends and Influence People*. Robbie preferred adventure, and struggled to read *serious* books, the likes of *Keys to the Kingdom* that didn't make much sense to him in his formative years, coupled with his attitude toward accumulating wealth on earth.

In addition to marriage counseling in the kitchen, Robert's job resume extended to barter and bargaining with the financial organizations for various chips and nuggets of Zehlen real estate in the boardroom. And yet all this *drama*–less provocative than *Cat on a Hot Tin Roof*, and more uncertain than Faulkner wrote about in *Yoknapatawpha County*, barren of landscape details–occurred tranquilly, behind the scenes in Pleasant Valley, where the ageless spirit of earth, moving its creatures about, capturing the fate of each in its web of mystery and beauty, amidst the pageant of nature as the seasons changed and re-emerged, made no aesthetic impression on Walsh whatsoever as he proceeded on his daunting mission, content in dialogue at transcendent moments with the same spirit that compelled Ned Lud to complete his ghastly mission.

At times of triumph, Walsh became transformed to his highest level of being, enclosed in a custom-created vacuum of a life, fulfilled in his greatest intentions described in the vision of Milton, literally shaking his fist at the social order of paradise valley, when as quietly as cumulus clouds passing east in a brilliant blue sky–unnoticed over Rockland, the fortune of four generations slipped away–as if a Kansas cyclone has cleared the land, smashing cottonwood and box elder groves to splinters, passing over the remnant of great expectations; in the wake of the storm, the yellow brick road was replaced by I-29.

* * * * *

The way Hector Sexton looked at it, he was in business as usual mode. He was a licensed agent engaged in a normal field test for a new product. From the lab to the field he was as professional as it gets, when a mixer (the most valuable player in the small and large elevator business at the physical level) needs no education if he can follow a few simple instructions and ask no questions. Hector had an academic research background and had considered law school. Ever since his research grant, Hector was engaged in quality control and plant genetic research; as an exempt employee for Ceres, he was administrative steps above the grain sampling and mixing physics that led to the most profitability for the producers. His personality was well suited for the work he had been doing since his graduate-assistantship at Georgia A&M, recalling the days he had listened to classic Borlaug theory-based lectures in graduate agronomy class. It didn't matter then that yet another graduate assistant was lecturing him and his colleagues about lessons they knew by heart: the need for an introduction of a new method of pollination that would allow the various disease-resistant genes from several donor parents to be transferred into a single recurrent parent. It was through this process, making sure each line has different resistant genes, each donor-parent is used in a separate back-crossing program. By 1991, Sexton had learned how to digest and process such hypotheses as methods of knowing and controlling lesser personalities; he was ready to move on to actual massive field trials where he made his money on volume and commission.

Putting the risk of experimental failure on the shoulders of Zehlen was not Sexton's original intention. Those anomalies of testing had to be ironed out before production. On the one hand, Walsh was diametrically opposed to the Zehlen's progressive farming campaign, but he knew how to use him as a mule for his ambitions. And at one time or another, recalling Governor Freeman's statement, "all things work together for the greater glory of God," –Walsh would come out on top of this venture. One way or another he slowly convinced the two wives who controlled Pleasant Valley corporate stock that the farm would collapse if they did not oust David from the Presidency, and make him power of attorney.

As Robert Walsh drove his blue Coronet with a clean shirt, and suit hanging on a clothes rack stretched across the back seat around Pleasant Valley, he projected an image of discontent, displaying a different perspective from the various relationship of the marketers he was doing business with, and their connection with private farmers, like David Zehlen, who had an inordinate interest in organic crops: saskatoon fruit, raspberries and the nitrogen fixing herb sea buckthorn; while Walsh referred to the lot as *exotic crops*, nothing more than a display of vanity, a waste of time and money, and even *less* practical than Hector Sexton's fetish with safflowers with one selling feature– *"multiple human applications for the health of the planet"*. Even though he didn't agree with his partner's methods, Walsh could always use a slogan like that as fluff to reinforce the loan application with First Omaha. His task was to finesse the fact that the crop was not exactly a legitimate food crop that would qualify for ASCS subsidies, the all-important *hook* the bank needed for its purposes.

After he received the Toronto safflower seminar information from Hector, the chain of causation that took advantage of the separate interests of the three parties was at critical mass–the experimental reaction was ready to bubble out of the flask as soon as he turned up the Bunsen burner. Coordination of his plot became a spontaneous mental process for Walsh, even as a foot of new fallen white crystal blanketed the frozen fields of Pleasant Valley in January 1992, carpeting the land with a cold veneer but little actual moisture.

Walsh was becoming increasing agitated on the verge of completing his final mission. He found himself shaking at times, that he steadied after a few shots of vodka and Mountain Dew. Hanging out alone in the old Zehlen house Jack had vacated in favor of his home on Big Stone Lake, for once in his life, Robert felt he was nearing complete control of a farm aggregate the magnitude of which he had never experienced or imagined in his depressed youth. The nucleus would expand, catapulting him into control of *his own* communal farming operation, complete with government subsidies–and a federal reserve bank paying him salary and pension to administrate another liquidation operation.

When he was by himself inspecting the grove north of Jack's house, where if anyone was listening, Walsh could swear he had seen ghostly figures in the cottonwood and elm scrub as the sun disappeared in the west, just as daylight savings time ended, and nights his depressing seasonal affective disorder and the flashbacks of winter in Nundas returned. He was sure he had observed human shadows close to the burn pit, where scattered branches, piles of leaves, broken china, pewter ware, and the trash of four generations was buried under fallen poplar and Siberian elm. Traces of history of three generations, that had survived the burnings, could be found scattered in a small circular area at the west edge of the Zehlen windbreak.

There a horned owl nested–at times Robbie could hear the night hunter hooting to his soul mate under a full moon–hidden somewhere in the maze of black limbs, secure on his perch. A predator with no natural enemies he was. That wise image suited his vision of himself amid the naturalistic Darwinian view, his animus hidden somewhere in the mountainous cottonwood at the north edge of the trees waiting for his prey, a luckless field mouse, to emerge from his burrow. On a cold clear day, Walsh could see a mile north of the farmhouse. Beyond the frozen slough, a weak December sunlight filtered through spindly dogwood, box elder and poplar scrub that composed the circle of plants and grasslands at the lowest level of the windbreak stretching far beyond the rows of grain bins.

At certain moments, as he drove alone listening to KWAT, he was obsessed. He would be driving a BMW soon he thought, as he drove back and forth every week between Brookings and Rockland through the dead of winter, and the wind whistled through the slightly cracked passenger window for ventilation as he smoked Pall Mall after Pall Mall. Then too, Walsh began to wonder what it would be like coming down with Alzheimer's–perhaps he would go insane first in his contempt for Jack Zehlen and his accomplishments. He could not excuse the blind ambition coupled with vain pursuits he despised in David. He found more comfort dreaming of his days as county weed annihilator, as if he was still working with his favorite subjects; trudging around in the fallen branches, sticks and dead trees of the old grove fascinated him in the strange way the only job he was ever satisfied with did. He would be over the emotional stage soon enough. Once he had taken over Pleasant Valley, he would become much more practical. He would have pity on the Zehlens and their children,

"You sound like Creon administrator of Thebes to me, after the fall of Oedipus," a comparison Robbie was not familiar with from Ansel, the scholar, who was somewhat of a Greek mythology aficionado, using one of his obscure analogies; but they always made some kind of sense. Zehlen loved to talk about his ancestors in Greece; that's what Robbie was paying Ansel for the professional touches he applied to the Walsh memorandum series–under that title he might be able to convince the despondent wife, their disabled father won't be able to do much for the lost children. In the same fantasy he imagined himself, once and for all, on top by virtue of the remarkable coincidences that had placed him in his rightful position dictating the fortunes of men, more powerful, and financially able than he, dealing with men who were successful, but perhaps no less ambitious. If that's what Ansel was talking about, he was cool with Creon.

One of Robbie's bitches was Jack's lifelong friends never respected him. That was apparent in the church and restaurant society, where the men despised Walsh and the women distrusted his secret motives and manner after a short, palpable feeling of suspicion he didn't belong in the atmosphere of a close knit rural society, where everybody knows everybody else–and what they want. Walsh knew he had only a short window of opportunity to pull it off. He would need to spend that time attending the churches, dealing with the elevators and hardware store, and the local fanfare. Hobnobbing with the sheriff and attorneys about his business running Zehlen's operations was his most effective talent.

It was difficult to remain incognito in a one-grocery-store town. With food and gas prices rising, Rockland represented the perfect marshal law situation, where it was easier for a complete stranger to step up and take control of law and order amidst chaos. The parochial hamlet instinctively recognized Walsh as different, trouble perhaps, a mysterious outsider and person of interest; nonetheless, above all the people required peace and security that comes with law and order–if the police weren't concerned about the newcomer, they weren't that concerned either.

No one noticed Walsh's primary focus was on David and Jack's wives, half owners of Zehlen farms and majority owners of Pleasant Valley's South Dakota acreage. Their simple minds needed to be thoroughly "scrubbed" and indoctrinated by the Walsh dogma system. Within easy reach of his principles, the Zehlen farming operation was of the scope and magnitude he needed. He was looking ahead to his next strategic move. He had in mind a young couple renting one of the foreclosed properties he was administrating south of Revillo, the Baumgartners–they could move in to either vacant house, prepared to farm the Zehlen land until it was auctioned after foreclosure.

Along with his spiritual revival, Walsh accomplished a complete reversal of fortune after the humiliation of being a convicted felon with no hope. He was confident the *force* he could depend on was with him. He had survived at a time when, with two cents in the bank and a decent attorney, he could have been out of that damn jam. He had vowed he would never be in such a predicament again. Over the course of his work, he would make other men suffer for the indignities he had suffered.

He knew he could pull off his plan as soon as he had access to Pleasant Valley's bookkeeping system maintained by Phyllis Zehlen. David had his low-tech farming program passworded; that application posted his production and storage costs, and his share of the stream of revenue for the grain harvest and futures, including a record of all farm expense, and payroll tax accounting–and nobody but David knew the password. That computer supposedly held the hotly contested double-entry books Walsh needed to make a fraud complaint.

From the onset, Walsh was deeply interested in measuring and recording progress of the steadily expanding black-hole deficit the breach of contract with Sexton had become. Together with Sexton, they had a plan that would never allow David to realize the revenue of the 1991 harvest, or benefits of the government support programs he was factoring into his farm operations budget. By the time the only other source of income available arrived, the First Omaha bank loan, he would be power of attorney disbursing the funds.

Long before the crime was detected, somebody would have to solve a Rubik's cube-like configuration his scheme created to recognize and discover his plan to takeover Pleasant Valley. By then he would have a condo in the Caymans. After all the years of servitude to greater fortunes than his, he could finally make something of himself again, feeling as good as the day he signed the receipt for legal service from Bill Janklow. David would be doing time in Stillwater. Hector would be paying Walsh to stay out of jail. In his farm future, Walsh planned to expand Marketing International to rival Ceres and Lubrizol.

The takeover of a multimillion dollar organization was no coincidence, as the courts would see it: instead it was the culmination of years of study and preparation. And ironically, it was possible because of Walsh's tireless mind, burning the midnight oil, increasing his writing skill exhibited on the farmland study which gave him the edge he needed to complement his knowledge of farming. His work ethic would allow him to triumph over the Rockland phenomenon, and the Jamaican matador, boasting about Borlaug and his B.S. in agronomy from Georgia Southern. If the plan worked this time, he was well beyond being mocked by a sheepskin on the wall.

Every day Walsh was even less impressed with the rural Tom Sawyer, boy wonder from Rockland who appeared on the cover of *Farm Futures* magazine that fateful summer in 1992. David

ANTHONY FALLS JR.

didn't need a degree to get where he was. It didn't matter to Walsh that David had created a farm marketing plan for Control Data and that he was using it to manage his massive farming operations. What good did it do him? The program had not been able to protect him from a breach of contract with Hector Sexton. The lad born with all the privileges, who at one time projected that he would become the most successful farmer in America, was reaping what he sowed in his judgment; with all his knowledge and skill, David never suspected until it was too late what his onetime hired hand Walsh had planned for him.

At an earlier point in his life coming off the cattle theft incident, Walsh was in despair. He was drinking heavily, pursuing other women, and not attending church. The children were small. He sometimes imagined they would be better off on county assistance, or in foster homes. There were moments when he contemplated suicide. His wife would not have survived the grief if he had left her and the children; there was no indemnity on life insurance for suicides. He confessed to the priest he dreaded eternal damnation worse than a hopeless future. To overcome his fear of the loss of heaven and the pains of hell, Robbie relied on religion, praying with the congregation while attending services, confessing his venial sins, admitting to a representative of the power that he had made an error or two in his life. Of course, Walsh presented no details to the pastor, fearing the information could leak to the parish and tarnish his reputation. His life began to turn around, as if a spiritual force of some kind had intervened in his affairs, after he settled the Janklow matter with the court.

Walsh recalled well what it felt like to have no hope–where Zehlen was bound to be soon–thinking it might be better to take his own life before bankruptcy. I wouldn't be a bit surprised, he imagined, after David realizes the damage he has caused–like he too had once felt the urge to take his own life–perhaps another– relying on the gas pipe method inhaling carbon monoxide with the garage door closed.

In his experience, Walsh took full advantage of his most prominent personality traits, in terms of conscientiousness and its converse, and recognition of some occult principle that existed outside himself. As a consequence of crisis, a major shift to a more covert nature in his personality occurred in the short interval Robbie spent mentally reconstituting his life after the livestock trial and judgment, and the time he was introduced to Bill Janklow through Orville Freeman. Adhering to the memory and principles he shared with influential people, Walsh made a decision to follow the leadership of the great men in his life who inspired him to battle his way through the cold war on the plains.

CHAPTER 15

As tensions mounted, David recalled the last important day that he was actually feeling joy in his life, on a deep and dark December, winter's day when he could take comfort in the farming occupation he loved–usually his feeling about being lucky was right on the beam–inside the envelope was a personal check from Hector Sexton made out to Pleasant Valley Farms in the amount of $750,000. The check was folded inside a note that read,

> *"Thank you for your patience David. I am an independent business man like you. I had to wait until my superiors, my financiers, the folks at SigCo and SVO evaluated the weight and oil on the Williston flower deliveries. It took a while. Our original sample was a bit below expectations, but overall the crop met the specifications my partners demanded of me and you. After all, we knew that this was a field test barely once removed from the SigCo experimental plots. I had to remind them of that more than once, that you should not be liable for testing their protocols. I will be sending you the balance as soon as we agree on a contract for 1992. Hector."*

Immediately his outlook changed. Any hard feelings or doubts up until that moment evaporated in an instant as he gazed at the check he never expected to see. Walsh had been the devil's advocate since day one claiming his partner would default. Hector had proved them both wrong in their doubts. He was still considerably short of expectations if the $160K Sexton allocation from the government payment was factored into the equation; but for the time being it appeared that Hector was keeping up with his end of the deal for a change. Along with the check, David assumed there was a good chance his partner was planning to pay the balance when the spring markets made their traditional rise. Although there was no word on it, along with some local grain sales and harvest revenue, David was confident he had all the capital he needed for spring planting.

The uncertainty of the situation was affecting David's personality and his domestic life; his wife was in no mood for celebrations. The surprise check in the mail would change the atmosphere around the old homestead. David picked up a fifth of Smirnoff vodka and a quart of orange juice at the Rockland Municipal. Later they would send the kids to bed early. Pick up a movie at the video store. He would broil up a couple rib-eye steaks fresh from the Pioneer Meat Market; his propane grill was safer to use out on the porch in January than in the sizzling heat of summer. Top off the feast with baked potatoes and sour cream on the side just like in the good days around holidays and weddings. Steak sizzling in the flames might bring his wife back from the dudgeon of seasonal affective disorder associated with her career.

As soon as Robert Walsh received a share of the Sexton profits, he was ready to proceed with his plans for Pleasant Valley Farms. Planting was right around the corner, about six weeks away when he called David Zehlen at home.

"Good morning David. I haven't heard from you lately so I presume you are ready to get down to business," said Walsh. "I am not concerned about our contract. It was about this time last year that you made your first agreement with Hector. So I trust you are ready to proceed with what we have to deal with and the problems faced at year end. I realize that Hector has not been completely forthright in fulfilling on the safflower contract."

"He has been dealing with me, and has promised that he will even up with me before we start planting," David responded. "I wouldn't be so concerned about Hector. What interests me at this point is your crop rotation planning. Are you absolutely sure there have been no potatoes, soybeans or sunflowers on that land the last three years? Hector has been thinking of adding an additional two thousand acres."

"I have another lease in mind near Revillo. The land has no history of soybeans, or sunflowers the last three years; it goes about 7,000 acres, so Hector will be satisfied. I have already discussed the Duehl County fields with him; they've been in pasture since 1988. He is on board with the expansion." Robbie reassured David. "I have been looking at some financial options we are going to have to consider if Hector does not pay up."

"Listen Robbie, that's not your concern right now. He has informed me, and MN Go partners that he will cover the balance owed by the time we're ready to plant." David argued without total conviction, realizing at $200K per week operating expenses, minus the marketing money he would be on the short end of the stick by May–powerless in a position as pawn in a scheme he could not understand. Instead of the usual joyous anticipation of spring he experienced in his relative youth, at middle age he never expected to be stuck in a predicament he was becoming more aware of every day–what the consequences might be if his partner in Fargo did not completely fulfill contract expectations by the end of planting season–with the ever growing deficit in the back of his mind, his fate depending on the fluctuating spring grain market.

"And what are your partners like Rodney and John saying about their share of the promised capitalization from Hector when he hasn't even paid you your share? I ask you that David," Walsh drove the inevitable point to the hilt. "I just hope he sends you enough to pay off each one of them. You need money for wages to put those men back to work on your leases, when you have barely enough of your own capital left over to put equipment back in the fields, and that's about all. Frankly, I don't think you have planned far enough ahead to avoid the consequences you face,"–*investing money that doesn't belong to you in another man's crops,* Walsh thought to himself–that argument could wait its turn.

After the conversation David was distressed. Walsh, *curmudgeon* that he was, had once again managed to take as much helium out of the party balloon Sexton had floated him as possible. Continuing to be cursory rather than congenial, Walsh had personally subtracted as much joy as possible out of the only glimmer of hope for a successful 1992 season David retained. As if a voice in the background was warning him, "Take good care of my money David, because this is the last you will ever see of it."

"What do you have in mind Robbie? I'm listening."

He was hearing muddled growling sounds, faint echoes like they were connected by the old-fashioned party line, garbling Walsh's statements. His back was contracting in spasms. He recalled the night back in a prosperous 1980's right after Christmas, with his boys, having so much fun unwrapping their toys; during the celebration one of the twins left his miniature John Deere parked on the living room stairs. As Dave descended in the darkness, to the better heated bathroom downstairs, his right foot flew out from under him as it landed on the mini tractor. At the shock, his legs bolted out straight forward, and he bounced down the bottom two steps on his butt to the polished hardwood of the dining room floor. It felt like he had broken his back; in fact, he had fractured two bones in his coccyx. He screamed out,

"Call the ambulance!" David yelled.

Nancy dialed 911 and filled in the operator on what happened as he writhed in pain. After that accident, he was laid up a week in traction in the Rockland hospital. The injury he sustained that frigid winter's eve would continue to plague him, even as the bedroom and the boiler in the basement cooled down on twenty-below winter nights. The pain spontaneously erupted related to the very thought of it. He imagined the *Procrustean* bed his adversaries, Walsh and Sexton, had stretched him out on, like a patient strapped to a gurney. Extreme stress brought on the pain medication's black and white hallucinogenic effects. The old injury was flaring up as Walsh tormented him over the land line.

"Go on, yes I'm listening. I told you these pain pills I'm taking for my back do that to me sometimes. Makes me ADHD the doctor says. I drift off. I'm sorry Robbie could you repeat that financing scenario again for me," Dave continued. After a few months of meeting his mortal adversary face to face, he was paralyzed by doubt and confusion. He felt as though his South Dakota operations manager had him under some kind of spell. "I lost the connection there for a moment."

As he recuperated in late January, David imagined he might be experiencing the vague consequences of rural life immortalized by author William Faulkner, that English teacher Leo Nelson urged David to read about in *The Sound and the Fury*, and on the college reading list that was about the subject of agriculture. He didn't notice anything about farming in the story. "So what, maybe I didn't get it," it was just another boring story in American Lit II to him. David wasn't interested in the stuff Leo mentioned in his lectures, irrelevant to Granite County. Maybe this situation was what Leo was warning the class about–stalking around the perimeter, looking for? *Whack!* "*Class, let us be at the required attention level!*"–before finally slapping his ruler on the desk;

"Class your attention please. I am sorry to interrupt you, Mr. Zehlen and Miss Mulligan, there will be no talking, or passing notes in class! These are relevant lessons in American Literature about the world we live in out here on the prairie. We should be thankful the Yellowstone Trail runs down main street or we could be the next town to evaporate off the map, like Nassau or Barry. You could show a little more interest in the rural topics famous authors like Steinbeck, Lewis and Faulkner write about, and turn in your essays on time. You lose one grade for every week your paper is late. That doesn't leave much time for some of you to get a passing grade." Senior high English instructor Leo Nelson never let up on the topic of rural sociology as it affected literature during class and homeroom.

The fact that the new era of narrow specialization and industrialization had dawned on tradition in Pleasant Valley was of little interest to the class and generation the 1973-75 grads David and his wife represented. He was prepared for it technically speaking–Zehlen's owned the business–but his short course in addiction counseling had not prepared him for dealing with an American *sociopath* like Walsh.

"What don't you understand about the situation is what I'm asking you in plain English about David. I have looked over the books. The farm is in dire straits. You will not even have enough cash, credit, or stored grain the way the market is moving" – thinking to himself *thanks to your Jewish consultant who you were paying more than me before I drove him off*–"to complete spring planting. I see your expenses running over $200,000 a week. Where do you expect to come up with that kind of cash? You are going to need financial backing from the outside, from people in my organization network to make it through planting in South Dakota this year, let alone 30,000 acres in Minnesota and North Dakota. You can't put up with Adelman much longer." He was thinking–*if I arrange financing he has to go, that's part of my deal.*

David began wondering, dreading the worst possible, "Why does this man never mention a word about the expected ASCS funds coming in sometime in June that will take Pleasant Valley over the hump? "

"Lay off on Adelman will you Robbie? He's a good man and done a good job for me–it's not his fault the markets haven't opened for specialty crops. It's not up to you; Tom has done everything I've asked him over the years. Let me run my business elsewhere Robbie, I hired you to run the South Dakota operations," David insisted much more mildly than he should have.

"I'm giving you fair warning David unless you follow my instructions, there *won't be* another year for Pleasant Valley. You need every bit of financial advice I have to offer. You notice I haven't even discussed my contract for 1992. I might not need to the way things are going. By next year I might be in retirement on the French Riviera. I have made enough off my business connections in Europe. I have never revealed my connections with the Borbon dynasty; and I won't until we get things settled. I don't need this. I could be set up the rest of my life as administrator of her Spanish inheritance," Walsh became irritated as David showed no attention to the sirens. "I am offering to help you through a crisis you, your family and Jack are facing that you are not even aware of. Hector works for a conglomerate that makes Pleasant Valley and all its leases look like so many dots on the map. Take my word for it I know what you are up against. If you don't act soon it may be too late." Walsh rambled on about his accomplishments, his study of land productivity, contacts and skills, always reinforcing the stimulus and response that Pleasant Valley Farms could not survive without *him.*

David did not recall the climax of the conversation. The valium he had taken along with his low dose morphine was working on his nervous system. *My God,* he thought, *is necessity really the dictator's plea? Have I become like a character in the greatest heroic poem of English history?"* He thought of his love hate relationship with English class–those lessons can't possibly be relevant in the Twentieth century; the postmodern art era his sister is always talking about–and never defining. But she must know something as a graduate of the Minneapolis College of Art, which so much influences her always stalled painting career. He was only an expert on one thing; it was obvious in his writing skill, that math was his strong suit.

"Listen Robbie, this is too much for me right now. I'm having some issues with pain this morning. I've been having one continuous back spasm, a full body cramp is what it feels like today, I might have caught a chill in the night upstairs from my partner. I can hardly stand up straight this morning. Send me the financial information we are discussing. Pleasant Valley can always use some more credit, now that the RTC issue in settlement is frozen, some of our money is locked on that debit account. I'm expecting to hear from them in the next few weeks." With those remarks he ended the call and leaned back on the couch–for the first time in his life *dreading* the thought of what lies ahead in spring planting, working with his two conniving partners.

CHAPTER 16

Although Robert Walsh and Hector Sexton had never worked together on the same project before 1991, they were familiar with each other's reputations–the wariest farmers referred to them in gossip as "shysters." At the time of the first alteration of the contract, his partner excused himself, notifying David that because of lower than expected yields in the harvest, he would be adjusting his share of the costs from roughly $28 to $18 dollars per acre. Going farther with his reasoning, Sexton explained he expected to split the difference, and pay off any balance when the crops were marketed in the spring, claiming the market prices would rebound by then.

Based on undelivered contract expectations, David was in a seriously compromised position expecting to sign another contract for 1992. He didn't believe he could absorb the 1991 loss as easily as Taffe and Miller had–he was forced to stay in the game, or lose his investment. As Walsh wrote later, there never was an explanation why Sexton received a marketing fee, while the MN Go partners ASCS funds were allocated into PVC production costs rather than their bank accounts, with David responsible for the application and distribution of government money. In the meantime, Hector assured his partner he would be sending along a generous payment to compensate for 1991 arrears; it was scarcely mentioned that the deflected ASCS disbursals would be compensated for, and leveraged by a system of charge-backs, considered as payments on arrears on both the ASCS partner funds used in production, and the unilateral contract reduction–regardless of Zehlen's approval.

Ironically, the one taboo subject around the office was the contract loggerheads–a subject becoming increasingly less popular as the Pleasant Valley force was slowly losing territory to *underground* power. The $750 grand had vanished in the field production as if an *avatar* from the dust bowl days had swept across their business account balance. With that account dried up, and Hector as the only viable source for whatever crumbs he parceled out to Zehlen, the situation looked grim, as Cinco de Mayo, a national holiday Sexton celebrated, approached. David had stashed a month advance on his salary in a personal account in the Beardsley State Bank for emergencies, only he knew about.

Walsh was prepared to use his contact on the inside, and an explanation the board of director whose representative he spoke with on the phone would not understand, before transferring his call to a Mr. Martin Boersma in senior account administration for Omaha bank—to extend a loan to Zehlen on Hector's crop—or *the investment the three parties had in it at harvest in year two would be lost.* The finesse on fine details of the contract would be done once again because all parties were aware of what was going down, not the normal collateral guarantee, since the crop itself was owned and insured by Hector Sexton and his partners with Ceres. The distinction that makes a difference this time is: Zehlens are required to sign over their farm as collateral on the operating loan they will invest in Sexton's crop. David is convinced this is the right thing to do as he will be able to pay off the note when Hector fulfills on the contract terms for the Brookings sunflower harvest and receives his share of the net profits. Sexton never failed to bring up the subject of the ASCS personage payments as if he knew more about them than Dave did.

"I am not worried about my money—oh what a relief it will be once the government money arrives in July," he encouraged Nancy as he chatted with her and she summoned David on the intercom in the machine shop; in those brief moments, Sexton assured her they could settle accounts up to the penny. Last year's $160K marketing payment would barely cover his costs for settling the mixing and processing expenses at Williston. Hector apologized. "And that was why it took so long to pay David. Once again I apologize for the delay, and will make up for it in marketing this spring."

As the deadline approached, their conversations became more focused–in every discussion if doubt entered, Hector reminded David he would be receiving a healthy chunk of funds on those second year personage payments to the partners, and that considering both his and his wife's share would be approaching $150K, he and the family could take a trip with the kids to Disneyland; add on Jack and Phyllis shares the sum would be nearly $300K for the Zehlen family and their associated business interests that were eligible. Hector indicated he was having his secretary write up the papers as they spoke, he just needed a few more details and a little more time. Once paper work was submitted to the government, it was a sure thing.

Unfortunately, that would be the contract paper work he *neglected* along with the "large payment" he supposedly was forwarding Pleasant Valley for the partner's "personage" shares used in production, and lawyers to set up MN Go as a legitimate entity in Minnesota where it would be easier than setting it up in North or South Dakota for business and legal reasons. If Zehlen had any evidence to prove it, for all practical purposes he imagined he was ready to send his partner to prison for swindling him on two fronts by December 1991; foremost on the list, an extortion of the ASCS appropriation and promissory fraud on the contract violations. But he held his piece and buckled up for another rocky ride with Sexton.

No one was more aware of the vulnerable position David was in with Sexton, before he set up a meeting to discuss the quicksand the Zehlens were up to their necks in, than Robbie Walsh. At the end of the year he received a list of loan account delinquencies Resolution Trust had posted a *"red flag"* on. The list included a six-month past due account that applied after the RTC took over the Zehlen loan; at the end was an unpublished credit status report of customers Walsh's contact believed were vulnerable to immediate foreclosure because of a number of financial issues related to the MWFSB default in his enforcement region.

As they sat in the Marketing International office on a frosty morning in late January 1992 in downtown Brookings, discussing strategy for an hour before the scheduled meeting, Hector Sexton and Robert Walsh were confident in the offer they were about to close with David Zehlen. Sexton had never met Jack Zehlen. He knew of the old man Jack's reputation as a successful progressive farming entrepreneur, and from the talk about town of the productivity and the sunflowers that had replaced corn on the land Jack rented near Sisseton, South Dakota, planting his crops close to the Sioux Indian reservation on fields that had never known any crop but corn, wheat, oats, barley or soybeans.

Jack was a slim, good-looking man who appeared ten years younger than his 50 years; his sister was a high school homecoming queen who became pregnant, married young and afterward served many years as a stewardess for Northwest Airlines. He was a sharp-dressed man, only Jack's conversation indicated he was a farmer. He had become rich daring to raise an untried crop in conservative farm country. Jack Zehlen was envied, despised and begrudgingly admired by the local farmers of Granite County and the various farmhands who gathered with him Friday after work at the tavern, as was his custom buying rounds for the house when harvest ran through his grain handling complex and filled the storage bins. Jack would make an occasional appearance at the local ON|OFF Municipal liquor store in Sisseton, chatting with various farmers he rented from or living nearby in the area. That is where Hector Sexton was first introduced to David Zehlen, at the White Buffalo tavern on the north end of town, just west of what would later become Interstate 29 in the 1980's. Hector was probably the first black man Jack had ever seen in the farming industry.

At the winter solstice meeting at his office in Fargo between Walsh and Sexton, that was all about the Zehlen safflower contract, Walsh immediately cut to the chase. To extend another year, he would need to exaggerate the positive, not estimating risk factors in discussions involved managing 16,000 acres of crops his client had invested millions in; or lose Zehlen like he had Taffe and Miller and their government money along with them. With that in mind, he might weigh the risk-free contract vs. profits version, instead pushing the global benefits angle. It would be easy to convince Nancy as the mother of three healthy children, and one disabled using anti-seizure drugs, the importance of the medicinal benefits and humanitarian advantages the SigCo safflower brand had to offer.

Hector forwarded Walsh a summary of the Toronto protocols, indicating that after the seminar he would emphasize the importance of his product to mankind in general, versus the rising global menace of diabetes and its deadly toll on the already starving, vaccine-poor children of Africa and Asia. It would be an initiative worth billions, and Zehlen could be a pioneer in the development of a hybrid safflower specially developed to withstand harsh weather of the Great Plains, all the way from the eastern slopes of the Rockies to the foothills of Summit, SD.

Walsh inferred that Sexton gradually bring up the not too far-fetched potential Zehlen's children would soon have something in common with the displaced families of Africa and the middle East–if he didn't do something about it–it was his true Samaritan responsibility to intervene for the greater good. The fact that David had experience with the flowers, already raising unusual varieties of organic specialty crops–Turkish safflowers fit under the same parasol of expectations. In addition, Zehlen was practiced in LISA conservation techniques that would bring additional benefits, silencing the critics of his operation by utilizing proven-effective production methods, controversial as the Borlaug protocols were once treated in the Mexican Sierras.

The research question was resolved; it was found through trial and error that genetic varieties could be altered and adapted to meet requirements for UNICEF funding programs similar to the ASCS subsidies producers benefited from in the States. Walsh firmly believed that if Sexton convinced Zehlen–along with the United Nations he would be doing a far greater service to humankind–that solemn *duty* would become more important than the money for him and *Providence*, the God of the Methodist Church. I know his mother thinks she and her son serve as religious models, consequently a higher goal is much more important than mere food production where there was already a huge world surplus and corn is being marketed in futures for ethanol production. But if he made a successful pitch for high oleic medicinal safflowers, arguing that Pleasant Valley could be considered for international funding under the auspices of the tax payer funded non-profit world health organization dedicated to improving the human condition–it was a no brainer–Zehlen would bite hook, line and sinker on a second contract.

On that morning in late February, Walsh and Sexton were in the midst of discussing a preliminary takeover strategy as David Zehlen unexpectedly showed up early, snow crunching under his boots in sub-zero temperatures that jammed the iced door of Walsh's office, and walked into the reception area of the small undecorated two room office about the size of a two room mobile home. In the outer office was an unoccupied secretary's desk littered with magazines, folders, a rotary phone, and an "in basket" overflowing with papers, facing a large map of South Dakota on the interior wall. The only artifact in the suite was a faded daguerreotype that reminded David of Sloan's "Sickle and Bucket" that hung slightly to the left and behind Walsh's desk.

Shaking newly-fallen snow off his roughed leather coat with fake sheepskin lining, stomping his boots lightly, Zehlen raised his voice a notch as he entered the pressed maple wood-paneled reception area that had not been remodeled since the sixties.

"Hello-o, is anybody out there?"

"Sorry I've been too busy to shovel the sidewalk this morning David," Walsh yelled from the inner office. "Come on down partner, we're in here chilling near the zone heater. We've been waiting for you David. It's warm in here. Let me hang up your coat," said Walsh, walking into the lobby and greeting Zehlen, taking his coat with his hand extended, being polite and cordial as he had ever been in front of either man.

"The Folgers is brewing. Hector made it in from Fargo. He knows all about the Pleasant Valley farming operations, and is dying to meet you. Come on down and have a seat in my office."

Hector Sexton was engaged in extracting what he thought was the contract out of his brief case as Zehlen entered Walsh's inner sanctum. When Sexton had finished searching through his papers and laid the grower's agreement on the table, he realized he had made an error in his haste to be on the road early, and to be on time as Walsh suggested he be for once, since Zehlen usually arrived early. Not thinking clearly and in a rush stopping by his office in the dark at 6 a.m., as chance would have it, Sexton learned too late that he had pulled the wrong file. Instead of the Zehlen safflower contract, he had grabbed the file of next man up and closest to it, that of Elroy Zellner of Webster, South Dakota.

Reaching for Zehlen's hand as he realized his mistake, Sexton apologized superfluously. Walsh was furious–he wanted to scream, "You damn idiot!" but that time his better judgment intervened, where his temper would have once flared, the way he ruled the roost with women in the household of faith in Robbie; in his fifties, Walsh had learned self-control is more important than raging out at an inferior when there is enough uncertainty in a business decision to capitalize on the intermission of *tension* involved.

Rather than being disappointed, Zehlen was relieved. Though he didn't show it Walsh was angry. He could imagine David making that kind of mistake, but not Hector; maybe he was losing his concentration too, like everyone else around him. Believing he was the only sane person in the partnership. In his psychic constellation Walsh believed the *event* was not an accident, more of a coincidence with meaningful consequences; his plan was curtailed, but not foiled completely, a mere setback when he knew the other parties would have been foolhardy to jump in immediately out of desperation–the vulnerable state Walsh took for granted in most cases when he intervened on the bank's dime as the diversified confidence man. With such thoughts he consoled his momentary office *rage*.

The Zehlens were leerier than some, more careless than others like Taffe and Kelly Miller had been, who refused Hector's bargain, and threatened to take it to court in Traverse County if Hector didn't split the difference on the $18 vs. $28-dollar share discount Sexton was offering, ending the partnership after the first year–realizing there was a chance to double their losses continuing with Sexton's deal.

Unlike the Graceville farmers willing to take a loss and bale out, already in dire straits David Zehlen was in no position to resist with his money, or with his intellect, being impaired by confusion, stress and pain. His condition rendered him unable to resist Walsh's emerging deal, when he believed he needed it to succeed as a financial venture to profit in farming. The Omaha bankers who would be quick to collect on their first lien investment *and* Pleasant Valley real estate, would have to wait. The signing of the initial contract changeover would be delayed briefly, until a time there was even *more* at stake.

David was more cautious as his uncertainty grew. He was ingesting a cocktail of drugs for pain every eight hours, living with a nauseous feeling, clouding his perception like he had dodged another mortar round, acting slightly concussed in social settings with others involved in the situation. He was affected by ringing in his ears, like the aftershock of an M-80 exploding too close to an eardrum, at the annual fireworks display–after the meeting Zehlen was even more unsure about committing to yet another agreement that placed Pleasant Valley in deeper jeopardy. In the meantime, he was dealing with the anxiety that bankruptcy might be the only legal option left if something went awry with bank financing arrangements.

That chilled morning, he was feeling a different form of gravity, external pressure to sign another supposedly immaculate contract with no risk to his business. He felt pressure to make an agreement with a man he barely knew that involved the exchange of upwards of two million dollars during the course of eighteen months from planting to harvest; after that, the marketing would be in the hands of Sexton, Adelman and now Walsh. And, if the contract was extended to two years he was looking at least a 30-month commitment before an accurate accounting of profit and loss could occur. The only man he was confident he could trust was Adelman. He would make at least a million dollars if the risk paid off, if it didn't–the farm could be lost.

Farming had become the same gamble every year since he came on board with his father. He was reminded of the legend of Laocoon and his sons, swallowed by serpents on the beach, a legend the student's discussed in Mrs. Brewster's mythology class. He had almost forgotten the image of the prophet crying out a warning, offering the Trojans one last chance to back out of the deal with the Greek nation–before it occurred to him he was facing the same grim situation.

"I am so sorry David; I don't know how this happened. I was in a hurry to sign the contract. Without my bifocals on that early, I opened the cabinet, pulled the file ahead of yours by mistake, and shoved it in my briefcase. I must apologize. I am very glad to meet you. Robbie will tell you we run a smooth operation; this doesn't normally happen in our dealings–in the dark this morning something went wrong. We can reschedule a meeting on a warmer day hopefully?" Hector gestured his frustration, throwing up his hands in disgust, rummaging through his weathered satchel one more time just to prove his intentions were good.

"That was so careless of me. My lawyer approved it. I had it all prepared for you to look over. I didn't expect you to sign immediately. I wanted you to discuss my company's proposal with the bank Robbie has already reviewed. What this means for you is, I will be able to make you an even *sweeter* deal next time we meet." He glanced at Walsh who had his back turned to the conversation, mixing creamer into his coffee, masking his disgust with both men.

"We have only this little matter of the ASCS funding I wanted you to take care of before I send you, shall we say, my 'down payment' on the safflowers and I wanted to talk to you sometime about that anyway. These are matters that Robbie and I have already covered in our discussions that I don't need to repeat with him, but I will go over that material in our next conversation."

But that was a slip of the tongue. In fact, Hector had deliberately avoided discussing the subject of the government funds, and how they related to the contract with the Zehlens. It was all up to him–the conspiracy would never have happened without his ideas. In those moments of betrayal, Walsh became unglued, *outraged* rather–that a single critical feature he nurtured along like a precious cultured pearl–the critical detail upon which he knew the deal hinged, was going to be a matter between Sexton and Zehlen alone. Walsh, of all the parties involved, held the *active* currency because the bank was his handmaiden, with the power to act swiftly and decisively if Zehlen and Sexton ever even thought about leaving him out of *any* detail of their personal transactions.

On the other hand, David was aware of the potential success and wealth a pharmaceutical industry patent, with a quality brand name like Pfizer represented. If this deal worked out, Zehlen could be looking at exclusive contracts to grow medicinal safflowers in the states for generations to come. To that end he would be grateful to his partners for shielding him from something he was up to his neck in the pool with, submerged in an occult situation, explained through art like religion; he didn't really understand what the Lennon song referred to, rotating ideas from phrases that revolved in his mind he could align with his *own*, streaming out of the white cassette he played over and over again. David could see himself as a performer; on his many journeys he never left behind the aging music of his generation that represented the mystery like no other media, capturing the mood of the delayed Zehlen road show, as it slowly ground to a halt, like the hurdy-gurdy man predicted it would.

"David my friend, thank you for being so kind and patient with me; we will call you first thing next week. I have it all set up for you, it just needs a signature. I can mail the contract or fax it to you, we only lost a few days; spring planting is still almost three months away, plenty of time."

As he left Walsh's office he noticed that Robbie's his face was strangely distorted in a grimace he had never seen before– as if some unseen force was twisting his visage grotesquely.

"I will call you David," Walsh added in a scarcely audible growling sound.

Realizing there was nothing left to accomplish Zehlen got up to leave, shaking Hector's hand again courteously, managing a smile of relief scarcely visible under his full mustache. The results were not tallied. David felt incredibly relieved at not signing another contract under duress, not angry as Sexton himself would have been, or he could observe Walsh was–if either of them was under intense pressure in the race to make payments on his vast operations. As he left the office, David was looking ahead to the one pleasure he could count on, driving alone with his thoughts along the road he traveled on the return trip of 125 miles in his warm sled, not worrying about the way things might have been.

As soon as he was out in the brilliant sunshine, the reflecting light of the bright snow made his eyes water. The sound of tires crunching, the white exhaust plumes of the cars idling in the street, awakened his senses. The glowering image of Walsh vanished. The feathers would surely fly between those two as soon as I leave he assumed. The spectacle he imagined was hilarious: grown men raising their fists, and screaming threats at each other. In contrast he and Nancy never fought, David reflected.

In the outdoors his spirit was refreshed, very glad he *was* to escape the clutches of a force that seemed to control the partnership. He was thinking in those terms as he left Brookings in the rear view mirror that morning with no hassle, in no mood for making a decision he might later regret, as if Sexton revealed his consumer attitude which seemed more genuine in contrast to the Hyde personality that Walsh projects when he loses his composure. Was a Sexton Walsh conspiracy involving the loan possible? The idea floated across his consciousness for an instant, and just as rapidly the discomfiting possibility disappeared.

Thank you Lord" he thought, *I wasn't ready to sign that blessed agreement.* This non-event was no coincidence and proves it. He would not sign another contract with Hector unless he was absolutely desperate–he would find a way around the deal somehow, someway. But he couldn't think about it and keep his mind on the icy highway back to the farm. As for now, he thought he had the whole day to himself with no major decisions to make. He drove north admiring the arching red sundog that formed a shroud of water vapor and dust around the sun in the eastern sky: a matchless image of chilling beauty filtering through the stained glass effect of frost on the windshield. David recalled his dad explaining to him what a "sun dog" was; he would have to look the word up in the dictionary for a more accurate explanation of the phenomenon some time. His father was the only other man on earth who could possibly understand the dilemma he faced, but David and Jack weren't speaking to each other much, since Walsh came on board.

The KFGO weatherman, Dan Jurgens, reported that the temperature at 11 a.m. was five below zero with no wind chill. He lit up a Marlboro menthol. David was anticipating the farm market reports on the mighty 790. At least he had more time before deciding on details of the contract, and the dilemma he faced if they had to sign off the farm as collateral. He didn't want to think about it. During the drive home to Pleasant Valley, David had a few hours to himself to contemplate what accepting the contract and signing would mean to his operations. It was better to contemplate and appreciate the peace and beauty of a frigid day than think about what might happen in the future.

Back at the office in Brookings, Robbie Walsh stewed believing he had a right to be angry. He had informed Sexton of David Zehlen and his executive position in Pleasant Valley farms as South Dakota operations manager. But he had fudged a bit in revealing what he knew of David's partners and the personage payments from the government that the Zehlen organization counted on receiving, which was critical information that all three individuals needed to understand. If David was supported by the government, Walsh's plans were *foiled* again. He knew Sexton was shrewd; pulling the Zellner file was an accident, another *occult* reason the early signing didn't happen. They needed more signatures on the loan anyway–the important thing was that Hector was ready to make the deal immediately that risked both their careers in another shady venture. It was *better* this way; he apologized to his partner for his poor hospitality,

"I was off my usual game okay? What can I say? It won't happen again I can assure you of that," Sexton apologized disingenuously.

"Then I assume your attorney informed you that I am appearing in the case pro se in Sully County. Because of that I will do my own discovery, with access to a court reporter and professional staff with insight into the memoranda I am writing at this juncture. David is aware of the lawsuit, but unaware of any implications for Pleasant Valley Farms at this time. We need to exclude him as much as possible in our private enterprise discussions."

"I hear you Robbie," Sexton answered calmly.

"It appears your guy Rylance, who advised the MN Go partnership custom farming operation that you controlled, was involved in fraud. The real trick was slipping the application past the Rockland ASCS committee last year, making sure they approved it when the deal might be illegal. We needed that decision to elevate the penalty to a felony. With that, Jack's pal Harlan was over a barrel; either he admits the ASCS didn't substantiate the information as legitimate on the application that the custom farming operation in South Dakota was not eligible, or the committee is at fault. It was you who convinced David and your Latino friends the government money had nothing to do with custom farming relative to that same ASCS allocation, indicating you were entitled to a share–and now their green card status is in jeopardy. They may need that money for fuel to make it back to Chihuahua. And do I need to recite the reasons you are not entitled to personage as one of the MN Go partners–while you filtered nearly a third of the government allocation into your personal account in Fargo?" Walsh paused to let Sexton comment.

"My question is, why are you telling me this information if you believe I am guilty of these allegations you are making; and not reporting them to the authorities, when they are untrue in the first place?"

"Before I respond to your question, I will make a few more critical points. This is my final request for you to join in a solution that will benefit you and the Zehlens in the long run. The first question to be avoided at all costs is, 'Where did the money go and why? Who stole it from the Zehlens?' because it is apparent that not only is David broke and negative by millions of dollars, but so are his father and stepmother. Making the situation worse, his mother is an invalid in a nursing home; and land that was in trust for her care is now being litigated relative to the MWFSB loan default, and the RTC settlement. Need I say more?"

"No, you can go on with your analogies forever Robbie. I enjoy hearing your far-sided evaluations of my business practices. You've got nothing on me."

"Then let me explain what all this background on your methods dating back to the Woods Elevator case has to do with the Sully lawsuit I am preparing for; and exactly how these people and events fit into the lawsuit over some sunflowers in South Dakota? Well I ask you Hector to read the letter that was written to me on Ceres stationary postmarked in February of this year–that was sent to me, Robert Walsh, ordering me to walk into the ASCS office in Rockland and sign up for the government subsidies program on the South Dakota flowers for the year of 1992."

"I do not recall that being exactly as you describe it. I saw it differently, believing David would sign the papers himself under advisement. We talked about it."

"Not enough, apparently, to avoid suspicion of fraud. David and Jack entrusted you to pay for production and market the balance of their share of the crop; and that hasn't happened. That is your problem in my estimation." Walsh jabbed at Sexton's weak defense knowing he had his opponent against the ropes.

"May I remind you that I was a member of the surveillance committee of the Chicago Mercantile Exchange in the past? Under that authority I ask you Hector, as representative of my client: Who? ...is responsible to the customer in the event a broker's buy and sell cards are not punched at the time the market reached certain prices that were *quoted on the liquidation of a customer account?*"

"Robbie I can never be sure if you are being serious in your accusations of me, or my associates."

"If you say so Hector; but if you choose not to cooperate, I have no other alternative than to have my people in the SEC review all the trades in and out of certain brokerage houses to make sure that absolutely no trades in the name of Pleasant Valley were ever made. You will learn how hopeless your position is if you go back and review the ASCS decision that ignored your participation in the swindle to spare Jack the trouble his son caused–and whose fault is that? And who do you imagine deflected the committee investigation completely away from an audit David was entitled to that would have exposed the issue of how promissory fraud affected all the custom farming employees and partners, in comparison to the guy or investors who ended up with all the ASCS money? What their intent was? Who do you think controlled the flow of information at the hearing Hector, when nobody knew what was going on in all the confusion? Keep in mind the letter mentioned above is a clear and direct order from you to me or David, it doesn't matter in the scheme of things, when it was you demanding that I take advantage of the ASCS payment program for the exclusive benefit of *you* and your investors. Clearly based on the ASCS hearing testimony, none of the custom farmers received a penny. They, along with David, were all being used by you, Hector, as a front to deceive the government."

"I regret I do not have my lawyers here today Robbie; it sounds like you are threatening and slandering me for some grudge you have against David Zehlen, and I'm supposed to be a scapegoat or something? You are really exaggerating. I will go that far in denying every word you say."

"I'm just forewarning you it is not in the best interest of the parent company of Sigco, Jacques, SVO and numerous others to have all this information exposed to a prolonged court battle, because certainly a multinational company will not receive good press; that is, if it is found that they are doing business through contracting agents who take advantage of peasants of the land."

"You *are* starting to sound like Stalin criticizing the commune system this time around Robbie," sensing some light at the end of the tunnel Hector tried to inject some cold-war humor into the dialogue.

"To put this matter to rest for the time being, I have just one more item on the agenda for you today Hector. As you know, I am aware that if it is ever exposed that it is your intent to own and control high-oleic technology through custom farming contracts, it would be devastating press for Ceres, and SVO particularly, if it is found that the company is wholly owned by a *foreign* corporation."

"As far as I can tell Robbie you keep describing all these illegal actions of me and my associates; but so far I have heard nothing I cannot easily disprove in a court of law. There is no end to your confusing ideas about my operations while you are planning to takeover David's farm, am I correct or not?" Sexton's analysis did not faze Walsh.

"Let's look at it this way, just to cast a different light on the matter. If Ceres is the owner of the flowers in South Dakota, is David not an agent of yours? If so, are you not responsible for his activity, and if so what risk are you at with regard to what you think you know about this matter? In the past you have claimed, via your attorney, at our last meeting Friday that Ceres is the owner of the contested flowers. You want the opportunity to sell them. If you forward-contracted to MN Go for the production of specific crops and they defaulted on the agreement, then there is nothing more than a bad business decision on your behalf; but then the previous issue of the letter directing me to the ASCS office exists when Pleasant Valley had all the leases."

"And you believe you can threaten me with false accusations when my two attorneys have advised me on a legal course of action in the South Dakota lawsuit?" Sexton argued feebly.

"You rejected my settlement offer directly from the bank's legal officers," Walsh snarled. "To fulfill my pledge to the Zehlen family and others affected, I have been directed to withdraw the offer of ownership in the name of a company owned by American citizens who are members of the Christian faith, who are of the nature that we shall *forgive* and forget; and that if something is wrong, then go forward and *fix* it. If someone is injured, then it should be that we take him along to a better life. This was the reason I made the offer to come along and be the marketing agent, but it is apparent that this was not acceptable to you based on the information I have received from discussions with the MN Go partners."

"I should have my tape recorder with me Robbie, to record these ridiculous accusations you keep saturating me with," said Sexton grimly.

"You won't need it Hector," Walsh sneered. "In another month you'll come groveling back knowing my alternative is the only one you've got. I remind you of the call to Pleasant Valley's registered agent in South Dakota to verify that a contract for 30,000 metric tons of corn was accepted. I believe you should look in the mirror to see who made that offer, then decide if he is an agent of yours? If so, you should arrange a meeting with the Zehlens because they surely know nothing of the deal."

"You're way off base Robbie, accusing me of business transactions I never heard of in my life!" Walsh had taken it to the limit–against his better judgment he reacted. "Before this discussion goes much further regarding the problem you have caused with my business partner, I should inform you of my attorney Russell Freeman's advice in my office a week ago, when I promised him not to say a word of his theory–unless I needed to–*arguing* with you. In our last discussion, my attorney clearly defined the position of power of attorney you are in, similar to that on page 361 of Black's Law, as felony embezzlement. Look it up. I couldn't believe what my attorney was telling me about your character Robbie. At first I doubted what he was telling me was true, up until the moment you came out with this indirect confession of your intention to harm my business. Without Russell's counsel, I had no idea that the money you have plans to embezzle out of Pleasant Valley, will affect my grower

ANTHONY FALLS JR.

relationship with David," Sexton sensed his message was going in one ear and out the other, as Walsh scurried about the office.

"Listen Robbie I'm telling you for your own good; evidently only real lawyers understand the legal issue. I do not have the skills to conduct a discovery; but for one reason or another that conversion of property and money you have in mind, in Freeman's opinion hinges on blackmail of Ceres. According to Freeman by virtue of your power of attorney, you are defrauding my partner. Furthermore Robbie, that action, not true partnership–was your original intention; the supposedly no risk proposition Zehlen thought he was getting into and I did not think about–also discovered by Freeman, who claims he can prove it in a court of law if it comes to that, which it *does not have to*. Under the circumstances, I am much more willing to negotiate, not ready to accept Freeman's argument against you, for reasons neither side has presented me so far. Look at it this way, you can consider yourself fortunate; my stakeholders are not willing to press the issue, realizing I am a neutral partner in a scheme, you are much more vulnerable, and liable for than me." His voice trailed off becoming inaudible. "I don't see you raising the fee for a half-million-dollar team of super lawyers, like Omaha has on its legal staff Robbie."

"Don't you worry about that issue...," Walsh was a split second from muttering *sexy ass*! Taking a stab at humor, he raised his voice a notch, "*They're pre-paid.* Keep this information in mind though, because it is my last warning against more reckless behavior, just so there is no mistake about it, no one by the name of Zehlen knew of the Kenya deal being offered in the market; but I have it in hard printed evidence to prove where the offer came from–and who it was from," Walsh sounded like he was reading a script.

"Why are you repeating these vague threats? I have no idea where this argument is going Robbie."

"First of all, Pleasant Valley had no corn to sell, let alone export; why would somebody named H–– be offering what they did not have to sell, through an order for phony train loads of corn again–from Woods Elevator? Or were they going to do it from someplace in South Dakota Hector, and then run to bankruptcy like they did five years ago?"

"You're way out on a limb Robbie; now you know why I did not accept your offer," Sexton conceded.

"Don't worry about a thing Hector. We can make sure the mess is all cleaned up by Christmas Eve. We start to celebrate in the Walsh household at around five with Tom and Jerrys. Preparing for Midnight Mass has been a family tradition for generations. I certainly wish you all the best this New Year and I hope this confidential information will be of some consolation and comfort for you in the trials ahead, as a relief from the turmoil; we wish you a joyous holiday season whenever you begin to celebrate. Our home is always open to you if you want to continue our discussion in person. As you know, hospitality is one of the Walsh virtues. If you would like to talk privately, the office downtown is close to our house. You can bring your friends Tonya and Jeff, and we will break bread together for a fine evening and try to make a better year in 1993."

CHAPTER 17

As he patrolled the country roads between his fields, to reinforce his faith in the farming operations that he had been a successful part of for seventeen years, David often reviewed the deal of the previous year–now he was uncertain and apprehensive about the original agreement with his partner by late summer of 1991. Other than the reduction in the terms Sexton was proposing, he felt confident as harvest approached across the Pleasant Valley farms; what had mainly concerned him were agreements relative to the ASCS application, when the local field office had approved the initial PVC application underwritten by his attorney Ray Rylance of Rapid City. Under the first year of the contract, David and his partners received personage payments totaling $582,000 around about Father's Day from the US Department of Agriculture. David recalled the celebration by taking his family out for the prime rib special at the Matador supper club in Rockland.

At dinner that evening, David unexpectedly bumped into one of his detractors, an acquaintance from Appleton, Minnesota Rep. Charley Brown, who had campaigned on the DFL ticket against "special-interest" farming, argued vociferously in his campaign ad on KDIO that subsidies should be eliminated altogether because they did nothing to lower food prices, as the program was intended to do. Brown was irate that small farmers were entitled to millions of federal dollars for crops with marginal food value. He could accept the idea of subsidies for sunflowers; but with those allowances, there would be no government supports for medicinal safflower oil if he had anything to say about it. As a candidate for a second term in the state house of representatives, that idea was out of the question. Nonetheless, at one point during the evening out at the dinner club with his family, David walked over to Brown's table and shook hands with the auctioneer turned politician, and wished him luck in the November election.

Conservatives like Walsh and Brown did not share the belief with affluent society member John K. Galbraith that modern farming, although it is technically outside the industrial regulation system, is a necessary and collateral system which cannot auto-correct to adjust itself to the vagaries of the ever-shifting, fast-paced economies of all western countries with advanced agriculture. The United States has intervened in its own and the world's markets, to the extent of establishing price supports to ensure a continuous supply of food to the nation; this policy has been the direct result of advancing technology and increasingly heavy investment in capital infrastructure.

David had more faith than the politician in the obvious benefits of the programs the politician proscribed, believing Charley Brown cast a blind eye on the expanding market for medicine producing flowers in Granite and Swift County, potentially popping up alongside the ethanol plants that provided *scarce* jobs in small towns like Appleton, Louisburg and Correll. If he had been more open minded, Brown might have noticed improvements in the quality of county roads and bridges that provided better transportation, tax base expansion, more revenues from new agricultural products–instead of being an ultra-conservative demagogue, oblivious to the changing economy of rural America, as he moved up in rank at the State legislature.

The fast talking auctioneer made his living at those final auctions. Had he been a bit more sympathetic to those who had to depend on such skills and ingenuity to make a buck in *their* profession, Brown might have been less opposed to government subsidies for struggling farmers he represented, adapting for survival amidst market downturns, as production costs were soaring. Just before the State Fair, David was shocked to hear on KDIO, that scarcely two weeks after the auction sale on the foreclosure of the Clarence Adolphson farm near Beardsley, Minnesota, House Representative Brown had collapsed while performing as a clown in the Appleton Memorial Day parade, and died in the ambulance on the way to the Montevideo hospital.

* * * * *

With the government money in hand, David did not have recreation on his mind as he went about the practical matter of his tri-state business, depositing the Zehlen shares of the ASCS funds in a Pleasant Valley account, then sent Sexton a PVC check for $160,000. David retained the balance for partner production, not compensating to reflect the growing deficit and *disconnect* in their contract; at that time, realizing if he had kept the money he may have to cut ties with his partners, as Miller and Taffe had, losing over a million five in the current conditions.

David informed Hector in a note clipped to the check, that he would be immediately investing his personage, needing a 3% deduction for cost of living expenses, and subsistence in remote places. In their conversations to follow, he assured Sexton that his own and his partners $50,000 went into producing the safflowers; some of the money was deducted for outstanding bills for fuel, fertilizer, unpaid wages to the men dating back to spring planting, and some equipment leases; he itemized each billing and sent receipts. As David later recalled about the confusing discussion of the futures in spring 1992–farming is a nonlinear event, things get mashed together in the production process. Hector kept most of his promise, using a method extracted from his experience with other customers, sending a portion of the balance, in small payments occasionally from sales of stored grain.

With the ASCS money in their respective accounts at midsummer 1991, both men were satisfied with the deal–already thinking ahead about extending the contract another year. Spring rains had been good followed by an accurate *Farmer's Almanac* prediction of hot and dry weather for most of the summer. Up until combining, Sexton had been true to his word fulfilling on the contract guarantee. In the meantime, David Zehlen had received checks totaling close to $600K from the government, believing it was his privilege to keep his dad, his wife and Phyllis unaware, or guessing about where exactly their share of the remaining $400K was being deposited amidst tens of thousands of acres of crops, and piles of unpaid bills. David made all the decisions–his family trusted him as a shrewd executive, never spending a cent on anything but what he determined was necessary for the welfare of the farm, and maybe a six-pack of Grain Belt.

CHAPTER 18

In his skeptical forecasts, Robert Walsh proved to be an oracle of doom, divining privately and publicly that David Zehlen would sooner or later discover that he could not trust his partner Hector Sexton. It was such a shockingly cold idea that David was in conscious denial of it; after all they talked nearly every day on the phone.

He felt increasingly powerless as his long established verbal repertoires reinforcing himself and his coterie were proving useless. How could Hector be cheating him any worse? He suppressed the thought. Though he could not shake it, he routinely dismissed the obvious landscape of what seemed like general betrayal of all the faith his rapidly disappearing supporters had shown before times when trouble appeared. Was he at fault for the expansion? The family applauded his idea to build the farm up to 45000 acres in the beginning. The whole community had profited by his decisions, and his father's before him.

Ever since fall 1991, David had a sense he was in too deep, with not enough capital to compete in the skin game he was in since he gambled on the Werner elevator deal. On top of his contract worries David was pre-occupied with setting up operations on his other 20,000 acres of sunflowers, soybeans, wheat and corn, relative to his Ulen, MN based operations where some new tractors, and minimum tillage machinery was committed. The third week of May, David managed to shoehorn a week of his time into his northern acres inspecting the leased land managed by the Obergs.

That weekend, Rodney informed David that Hector had not set up the ASCS required capital accounts for him and his father John as he had promised to do. In fact, Hector had not sent him a penny for over five months; he mentioned there was no way he would be able to answer ASCS inquiries and fill out the current information he was supposed to submit relative to the capital accounts David had said Hector supposedly set up. In a phone conversation, David assured Rodney there must be some kind of misunderstanding and he would be coming up to Ulen to discuss the matter personally. There would be no problem David assured the Obergs; he had a guaranteed contract with Hector.

According to David's interpretation, fulfillment of the contract amounted to capitalizing the individual partners. That agreement was the basis of the "custom farming" deal as he saw it. If Hector wasn't fulfilling he was breaching the contract; and he wouldn't dare to do that, David told himself over and over again. That contract was immaculate; he could use it in a court of law if he had to.

On a lighter note, he discussed purchasing the new tractors with his father who was busy in the machine shed greasing the heads on the combine they used on the homestead and local acreage. Jack complained the blades were wearing out; they might make it through one more season. In David's estimation what they needed most was one new combine for the Dakota acres. Though his father wasn't buying his rationale, at that time and for many years after David believed the ten tractors were a reasonable equipment investment under terms of the contract with Sexton.

David noticed that Jack appeared to be distracted thinking about something else; there was an older IH waiting to be repaired outside the garage; once he got going on a project he didn't like interruptions. The old man was in no hurry to listen to a speech. He turned away as Dave explained to him that the savings would show up once they wrote off depreciation on new equipment expenses on their taxes; his dad was noticeably unimpressed even as David explained meticulously, how at the same time the farm saved money by buying $3 million dollars of new equipment at *used prices*. He felt oddly like a child, as if he was compelled to recite his reasoning over and over, carrying heavier tools and wrenches around the shop for his dad, helping like he did in the old days, before the tribulations arrived. It didn't

ANTHONY FALLS JR.

seem like Jack wanted to discuss much, or that he cared one way or another about the issues his son was raising.

"You do what you want David," his father sounded tired and defeated, beyond being irritated and angry with the way things had turned out. "Nobody listens to me around here anymore anyway." Jack continued thinking, *you're going to have to learn some hard lessons about these shysters on your own David, there's nothing I can do about it this time; we just have to ride the storm out and hope for the best.*

"That's not true. I consider everything you say in view of the circumstances. I should never have hired Walsh or trusted Hector–we're in it too deep to back out now. We need that bank loan Robbie claims can get us through this mess Hector created–now the women want him in as power of attorney." Dave apologized not wanting to create another scene or argue as he did constantly with Walsh and Sexton.

"It's your deal, you take care of it," Jack retorted turning back to the harvester head he was wrenching on, as if he had more important things to do than get involved in the mess his son had created.

* * * * *

By the late spring of 1992, Robert Walsh had arranged a deal with one of his contacts in the private sector. The week before Memorial Day 1992, David Zehlen met with bank officials and took them on a tour of his farming operations in the Brookings and Duehl county area. As he later reported to the FBI, Walsh contacted First Bank of Omaha which was conducting a search on the Zehlen South Dakota operations. On a guided tour, a group of their bank representatives learned that the Sully land was leased by Zehlen, and the crops were owned by Hector Sexton.

The day after the South Dakota tour, First Omaha loan officers met with Hector Sexton in his Fargo office. According to Sexton, the purpose of the meeting was explaining the work he did for Zehlen, and the work Zehlen did for him. Apparently there was little discussion about contract details. Sexton understood that the bank was considering a loan to Pleasant Valley Corporation. Sexton informed the bank that he worked as a marketing consultant for Zehlen; and that David farmed approximately 16,000 acres of safflowers and some specialty beans for him on land near Brookings, SD and in Sully County.

According to his 1993 FBI deposition, Walsh claimed that on or about June 15, 1992 Zehlen had requested that he could use his Marketing International office in Brookings, SD, to meet with representatives of First Omaha Bank and Trust to complete the loan signing. The three bank representatives that included Vice President Tom Jessen, loan officer Alfred Eastland, and bank attorney Will Anderson representing the Meyer law firm, met privately with David Zehlen, Jack Zehlen, Phyllis and Nancy Zehlen. At that time, they agreed to a revolving line of credit on the South Dakota operation only, that eventually grew to $1.5 million.

In the *pro se* Sully lawsuit that followed the case, Hector Sexton claimed he could not recall whether or not he ever mentioned the MinGo partners "personage" deal he was pressuring Zehlen into signing up for to the bank inspectors; or the fact that he had contracted specifically with the Zehlen custom farming operation rather than Pleasant Valley farms or Zehlen individually, in his discussions with bank officials during the Fargo meeting. In confusing court proceedings that began in November 1992, bank officials claimed that Zehlen indicated he owned the crop's production contract; and that the grower's agreement was sub-leased to his MinGo partners.

Zehlen stated that in the proposed charge-back billing arrangement Sexton claimed that he had no actual deficits to make up for; if he did, he intended to make up for them in marketing and services. Westlaw reported that consequently, Sexton had never informed the bankers of his interest in specific collateral offered to the bank, or his contractual relationship with MinGo partners, rather than Zehlen who was President of Pleasant Valley at that time.

Walsh would later claim that David Zehlen told him that he had been notified that he was a finalist for a position "managing 30,000 acres on the behalf of First Bank and Trust in Sioux Falls, SD." On that basis, the court ruled that Zehlen had ownership rights to the contested safflowers which allowed the bank's security interests to attach to the collateral in what was interpreted as a defaulted *lending* arrangement.

In the same FBI affidavit of March 3, 1993, Walsh informed the FBI that in the summer of 1992, David Zehlen had instructed him to "go to all of the ASCS offices" (there was only one in Granite County) "and change the loan deficiency payments from Pleasant Valley Farms to MinGo," an organization Walsh believed was little more than a frivolous title given to a group of David's seasonal farm employees, that didn't qualify for subsidies, exploiting a loophole. Walsh claimed he refused the order because the action was illegal, since MinGo was nothing more than a list of seven partners and *their* equipment which amounted to less than $50K per personage. In the Walsh oversight inventory, even if the paperwork ever was completed, he viewed the partner's shares as invalid in the application, based on depreciated equipment valuations of machinery that was certainly not being used on the Zehlen project.

CHAPTER 19

David held out hope that if the weather cooperated, prices could be higher than ever for beans and flowers. By the time he pulled out of the driveway, turning north on Highway 75, he had forgotten all about the conflict; nobody was home, the wife was at the dentist's office, kids in school–instinctively he glanced to the east noticing the red flag was up on the mailbox. Inside was one letter from Hector Sexton. He decided not to read it immediately sensing it might not help his mood any after the usual gloomy conversation with his dad in the shop; he put the letter in his inside coat pocket and snapped on the mighty 790 hoping that the soybean market had held steady.

At Wheaton, MN David pulled into the Cenex truck stop to refuel; in that hour, he had placed any worries about his dad's objections behind him. He didn't want to upset his only partner any more than he already was by bringing up the subject of new technology he was not going to understand. Jack was not about to learn the new tricks and computerized electronics these new machines were coming out with. All his father would be able to do with the new equipment is kick the tires, change the oil and keep the diesel tank full.

David kept abreast of the new technology; after all it was he who had created the Control Data accounting program the Zehlens and many other farmers depended upon to manage production, marketing, and expenditures. He realized that his father, like most other farmers in that generation, was light years behind his hi-tech approach, with no interest or intention to learn advanced electronic farming techniques, rendered totally incapable of fixing and fiddling like on the Farmalls, as he had been accustomed to for a generation before. Out of courtesy and respect for propriety and appearance's sake, it was necessary that Father Jack's signature be on any major loan transactions.

ANTHONY FALLS JR.

At the gas station he refilled his thermos. The time on the road had calmed him down enough that he was ready to absorb another shock if he had to. He scanned the Sexton letter,

Dear David,

I have been discussing the '91 safflower crop with Robert Walsh over the past month or so while you were busy with your other leases in Minnesota. I was disappointed to learn that both the weight and the oil content were too far below projected expectations. Robert informed me that the previous lease-holder may have grown potatoes and soybeans on the land without informing Robert that those leases had a history for some years he didn't know about. The lease owners had changed during the years in question, and so on before the present lease was arranged, saying that his three-year study indicated only those crops grown from 1988 through 1990 when the ground had been fallow; he believed that cool moist weather in late August last year may have reduced yield by as much as 40 percent on specialty oils like oleic and safflower. I appreciate that Robert was honest with me, but because of his report I will have to explain to my bosses at SigCo and Ceres why the weight and oil does not meet expectations. It will not meet minimal experimental specifications for a genetic base. For these reasons explained above David I believe it is necessary to adjust the agreement as the crop will not meet expectations I once projected and may be substantially a loss on gross product sunflowers and safflowers combined.

Therefore, David I will be forced to maintain a reduced percentage as of last year, though it remains constant, falling from $28 to $18/acre costs until further notice. In addition to this reduction David I have found it necessary to delay funding on the capital accounts of the ASCS partners, because I could be audited by the USDA. Because I have had to divert the payment you sent to other sources including wages lost to MinGo when the men claim you promised I would compensate them which is not altogether true.

I have contacted my insurance agent Jeffrey Provo about this matter; he indicated that he believed the policy would not cover marginal losses on expectations related to unanticipated soil conditions; but that the loss of expected yield will be compensated for by diverting at least some of *the USDA funds away from marketing. These contract adjustments were necessary because my employers SigCo and Ceres have notified me that due to lowered oil content, the Pleasant Valley contract has an effect on their arrangements that depend on us as 'manufacturing and commercialization' partners; our failures to produce a marketable product affects the contract future which benefits diabetic children worldwide.*

I make this adjustment knowing you must have other money and credit sources available, because Robert informed me you had added 10 new tractors; and, that led me to believe you have remaining cash, capital and storage reserves; so I presume you are successful and prospering in Pleasant Valley on your other leases. These things happen in the industry. I am not saying it is not your fault or it is. Please believe me David it is not my decision alone to make compensation and capitalization adjustments, but I am forced to do what I must do. I will do everything I can to negotiate with my superiors so that we will be able to maintain the "Grower's Agreement" in a more successful year as we approach a critical production cycle. I will be much closer to balancing accounts with you for your work after the safflowers are harvested, delivered, and fully evaluated in Williston.

Very sincerely yours, Hector Sexton

Well at least he had the courtesy to ramble on with his excuse. I give him that much credit" David thought after reading the letter. He had to suppress an urge to vomit; it might have been motion sickness replacing the elation he had felt upon heading out on the highway that morning. He reached for the tin of Dramamine in the glove box; the letter was just another feeble request for more time, to be patient as he was being extorted; the thought hurt as much as the sharp pains he felt in his chest at unpredictable times related to stress. This ploy for patience was as low as a snake's belly, exploiting his sympathy for sick children.

The pain medication for his back did not sit well in his stomach when mixed with bad news and a quart of coffee. Should he turn around, return to the farm and talk it over with his father, or proceed to Ulen, MN beyond the halfway mark at

Crookston? Should he move on to the north acres and explain the dire circumstances to his associate John Oberg, why his son Rodney, somewhere in South Dakota working for two millionaires, was asking to borrow from him, instead of those who promised to finance his business? And what about their "no risk" mutual partnership agreement with Sexton that never happened, when John and his son assumed money they received in small sums was wages from Hector or Zehlen–not the USDA. There was no way out unless he terminated the contract with Sexton; there would be no solution to his problems versus the lopsided promissory logic on the contract, or on the ASCS position his partner hedged. He would have to tell John, who he loved at one time like a father, there would be no deal any time soon for Dave and the partners he had promised a share of the business to.

Predictably, John was as upset as an alienated farmer could be. There were no explanations for *his* partners, as to why the capital accounts were not funded. Hector had been equivocating for nine months in his convoluted explanations, each one a little different, about why he needed the ASCS funds–or he insinuated he would not fulfill on the contract; now he was doing neither. It was harvest 1991 and David was already looking at promissory fraud from his partner; by 1992 his partner was urging him to embezzle money to make up for his 1991 loss–and there seemed to be no way out of the snare.

In mid-October, as Halloween overlapped the harvest season in the Zehlen household, when the corn was husked, the children tried out their masks before they went trick-or-treating at Grandma's. That event, placed temporarily before Thanksgiving in importance, in terms of macabre drama for a few weeks–when life imitates the art of dying–occupied David's beleaguered mind as he chauffeured the farm kids in their costumes door to door at the senior's residential development on the north side of Rockland as the sun went down on the 31st.

During the daytime hours shortened after daylight savings ended, David swore he could see spirits, the little dust devils in the ditches and land hollows bordering scrub groves, where animal and human-like shadows moved with the passing clouds in a steady wind out of the northwest.

His wife was coloring her hair a dark auburn. Hannah watched spellbound as her mom carved the teeth of a happy face from a bright orange pumpkin in the kitchen. David was asking himself why his dad, who he had depended upon so often in the past, had been rendered so ineffectual in the deals of the present–when he was the only wise man of the bunch.

Altogether it was a *sickening* thought if he dwelled on it, stress caused by two outsiders who had become menacing specters where all the troubles and headaches began–David could feel tension building behind his eyes, like an infernal being was applying pressure–an invisible hydra composed of his partners' intentions had actually evolved into a persistent and gnawing evil tumor in his brain with multiple symptoms. He could not completely dismiss the image as just another myth his sister brought home from her sculpture class, believing nothing like *that* could possibly be happening in the postmodern world of successful farming. He had become his own therapist for lack of any other. Though his eyesight was 20-20, David was worried at times he was experiencing early symptoms of glaucoma which were being constantly discussed in the media as health concerns among people his age.

Even with Angus's guitar squealing in his ears David feared he could doze off; losing consciousness, any second he could be in the ditch or the other lane. He recalled the warning label, knowing he shouldn't be driving on his pain medications. The truck wobbled a few times as it hit the shoulder; the shaking was ten times worse at 65, but it kept him awake. As he passed over the concrete sections of the highway north of Breckenridge, the road surface changed, reminding him of the ten mile stretch, a one-piece asphalt slab they cruised on as kids in his friend Del's green Chrysler sedan, exactly like the one in *Prime Cut*.

The Pleasant Valley road seemed like a stretch of the *Autobahn* in comparison to US 75. *That's what successful farming can do to community* he thought, almost falling asleep as he remembered the soundless drive, stretching twenty miles from the diagonal three miles northwest of Rockland to a dot on the map named Clontarf, at the intersection of US 9 north of Benson, Minnesota. Racing along that stretch of road with his pals Del Silberstine and Mark Schultz, both now lying in the Rockland cemetery, on moonlit nights as clear as a cloudy day in Del Sr.'s big sedan—had to be one of the greatest thrills of his youth. Those days were gone, where once the only danger was an occasional hay wagon or combine traveling at 5 mph in between fields—but in the reality feature he faced two seasoned con men taking over his business; and he had no idea how to stop them. That thought kept him vigilant as his tires cackled on the pavement.

Listening to KFGX didn't help the way his head felt as he drove north on US 75. It was at moments like this—when he no longer felt in control—like it had been in some classes, that his education began to interest him when it began to apply to his life, in a situation like the *Merchant of Venice;* where an individual something like Romeo, was on the verge of losing a pound of flesh for defaulting on a business contract. The lesson seemed like an absurd premise at the time, as Leo struggled to apply the foreign principle to the lives of his students and their parents.

Now it made him think, on the road alone when he had some time to meditate, when there was nothing *else* that made sense. Did the current events have some relation to the present dilemma, and perhaps even his son's struggle to pass English in eighth grade? And why did these forgotten phrases he thought were meaningless at the time, seem important now? It couldn't happen here, huh? Thanks, I get the message too late.

David could not recall whether it was Sinclair Lewis or Upton Sinclair that wrote about what he was going through. For a few captured hours on the road, at least David felt secure in his golden GM pickup, steel belted radials clacking to the beat of *Sin City.* The mechanical rhythm mixed and amplified, reminded Dave of nothing more than the clatter of the shingle gun roofers used when he was remodeling the barn; in his fevered imagination, the cyclic sounds blended in perfect dissonance with the inexorable process eroding his farm.

David and his father were peaceful people; he had never picked a fight in his life except when he was joking with his identical twin sisters. Now he was thinking of the irony that the oldest of his sisters was disabled like he was, as a result of a broken vertebrae she sustained from being bucked off one of their two horses.

When he rolled down the window for a smoke, the clickity-clacking wheels echoed along with AC-DC live, a tape he loved. On the highway to hell he met the silver-tongued devil. Hector's explanation about medicinal safflowers was nothing but a smokescreen of why the bills for labor, fuel, fertilizer, and fungicide were not being paid.

David was certain that he did not want to discuss details of government liability he was not sure of with John or Rodney; it was time to talk contract with his father's attorney Ralph Rosenberg. Even so, he was not exactly sure what those matters were; or if a lawyer could do anything about them. Late in May, he thought about discussing the problem with Cub Wiley recently retired from the ASCS office; first he needed to consult with Ray Rylance about what was holding up the disbursal of the funds; and if there was any reason for a stoppage of the personage payments.

David maintained that he had made it very clear to counsel Rylance at the time he was discussing the ASCS program with Sexton, that if they were to participate they would have to develop a company partnership to access the program benefits by adhering to ASCS conditions and any particular business arrangements, taking all necessary precautions to maintain a high level of accountability in terms of accurate documentation of the money trail. There would ultimately have to be an accounting of their mutual arrangements to see that they were maintaining proper ASCS "personage determinations." David believed that despite his failings on the ASCS applications, whatever they might be, the audit would ultimately prove Hector owed him over a million dollars; and that he had a valid contract to prove it.

What good would it do to tell Rodney the hard lessons of history? He didn't want to admit that the year before, David had reluctantly agreed to a reduction in payments–or he faced getting nothing at all from his partner. It was an embarrassing situation. As his wife later testified in the Sully lawsuit, David and Hector spoke often and transparently about the progress of the maturing crops, discussing the planting schedules and blooming dates as the contract stipulated on a daily basis. During those discussions, Sexton continually spoke of and requested documents from Zehlen that identified any changes in the companies involved in the contract and crop ownership, and business operation practices of the various contracted partners and parties including Ceres, Sigco, and the ASCS along with the various financial institutions involved. That unspoken voice of betrayal was continually being denied in what David was yet to understand, let alone explain, as if the cover up and the crime were the same. It would take a criminal psychologist to explain Walsh's role in the conspiracy to a wise old farmer who had him pegged as a shyster from day one, and his son who had treated Robert like the strong older brother he never had.

The two men agreed that the shortages David was experiencing would be reflected in several accounting charge backs to Sexton from Pleasant Valley Farms. These chargebacks were to be related to funds already advanced by PVF. These funds would then be advanced to the partners such as Rodney and John Oberg as loans to the partners that were to be used to maintain ASCS required "personage" determination rules and separateness of entities for the company that would ultimately be formed–MinGo Partners–as their contract consultant Ray Rylance had advised.

There was no formal contract for the second year of the partnership, or adjustment of percentages in his favor as David hoped there would be. The Sexton camp argued that expenses were high and that a lower rate was necessary relative to increased fuel and labor costs; but no actual agreement was reached beyond the original contract. There was no disagreement among the partners that the 1991 season was successful, when stored grain and potential marketing could increase revenue a third in the coming year.

Based on that forecast, Sexton and Zehlen decided to proceed with a 1992 production agreement that depended on settlement of the 1991 contract deal they agreed would be concluded when the final delivery of the safflower crops in May or June of 1992 was sold. Minor contract adjustments would be made at that time. As his wife would later testify, these were the matters of genuine material interest she overheard David and Hector discussing on a seemingly friendly, daily basis as midsummer meltdown approached–as if they both wanted her in on it or as she implied in the Sully hearing–they would have been less transparent.

Hector Sexton advanced funds sparingly; rumors spread by Walsh suggested Sexton actually paid MN Go employees as much as $500 cash to complete particular assignments involving shipments of sunflowers and soybeans, in personal transactions, and perks that didn't appear on invoices. Thinking it was his obligation, David kept his partner well informed of costs and alignment of costs to expenses in production, refusing not to believe against all odds, the parties were in it for mutual benefit. Both men were able to monitor the progress of production by a visible inspection of individual sections. Despite continuous requests for critical documentation needed to validate the partnership, his obligations for paperwork relative to the Rylance ASCS stipulations were consistently neglected by Sexton.

Under the assumption of the payment being delivered in a timely fashion, it would have been applied as the correct documentation for 1991 applications showing the individuals designated as "personage eligible" in determinations related to the existence of the MinGo partnership structure, only legitimized through capitalization participation by Sexton–and the supposedly legitimate features of the accounting chargebacks system David agreed to–that came back to bite him in the butt.

The projected allocations never happened because Hector Sexton failed to provide the formal documents, according to

David. Adjustments amounting to $330K of the $582K were accounted for; the rest vanished into the partnership apparatus, as Sexton interpreted it. A superficial ASCS audit determined the 1991 allocation was filtered into a non-existent partnership arrangement.

Behind the holocaust was Walsh, the confidential informant who tipped off the USDA Zehlen was running a custom farming operation in South Dakota that was not eligible for funding. By that time, Hector had already received 160K and the rest had gone into unpaid production costs. Both Zehlen's 1991 and '92 applications were ruled ineligible by the ASCS review board in Minneapolis. As a result, David was required to pay back over half a million dollars to the ASCS while he lost the next allocation, the 1992 payment. In his vague interpretation of the rapidly deteriorating situation, Zehlen believed that his partner's mistakes alone were responsible for the ASCS disaster that was unfolding upon Pleasant Valley Farms.

In his chosen field, Walsh made it easy for people to misunderstand his multiple personalities. He succeeded in projecting an innocuous image with a dash of mystery about what he was doing that attached him to the people he chose; he could be aggressive at times to gather attention, if in some instances the locals ignored him altogether. Those that did not, he toyed with, disarming them with the harmless, fatherly sounding authority like comedian Bill Cosby, commenting on the one family show Shirley never missed, distracting his audience with references to the weather, society and the media.

Walsh had perfected a sarcastic tone similar to that of Mephistopheles scolding Faust; using a slightly threatening inflection of sound in his voice had become his preferred tool in manipulating the partner wives in the deal. Nancy was easily intimidated. Phyllis, the more mature Zehlen wife wasn't buying Walsh's line, but she had few options as creditors kept calling the office with complaints of unpaid bills. In one of his frequent visits, Walsh arrived as the girls were discussing why there was no check in the mail yet from Hector so she could close the books on his deal. As Walsh entered Phyllis cupped her hand over the phone,

"Can I help you with something Robbie?" Phyllis inquired in a shrill voice.

"Nope just checking in, I wanted a discussion with David about the ASCS payment; but I see he isn't in."

"He is out of the office this week at a Farmer's Union convention in Minot, North Dakota."

In his key role as South Dakota manager, Walsh had immediate access to some of the books; along with that information he presumed an accounting existed of the USDA payouts. He was aware David never used the standard filing cabinet. Like a prospector looking for gold in the outback, he knew those reports from David's computer would be about as useful as the *Farmer's Almanac* predicting the next year's revenue forecast; what he was looking for were the original 1991 bank loan papers. Eventually he would discover where David had stashed the *golden fleece* among the clutter of bric-a-brac on his desk, the numerous portraits of the Zehlen family and farm–perhaps in a wall safe behind one of them. He would tear up the floor and walls to find those documents. As close as he was to the fountain of wealth, Walsh could only imagine where those reports existed.

In 1991 David had no trouble convincing Nancy and Phyllis they were legally entitled to a seventh of the total personage, just like the rest of the partners. He convinced them not to worry about a thing, the money would be flowing through him to MN Go; he would distribute their shares. As David was coming into his own at explaining why nothing was happening, he had learned to repeat Hector's slogans of assurance just as ineffectively on the domestic front,

"I'll take care of the government honey. Why don't you just try and be a loving wife to me, and fulfill your vows to love, honor and obey your husband for a change. Lately all you do is listen to my hired hand; then you lock me out of the bedroom. I've given everything to you and my family. Haven't I?"

"Robbie claims it was sin; you groomed me like a little lamb for the slaughter!" Nancy countered in a flash of brutal retrospect.

"I don't care what that man says it's all a pack of lies, what he says to my friends, to the whole town. It's a bunch of crap. Only a lecher like him would bring up something like that to the mother of my three sons and Hannah behind my back in my own kitchen. I always honored you as the mother of my children haven't I?" David reacted cautiously knowing Walsh had touched a tender nerve on that verboten subject.

"He says you raped me, when I was a virgin and made me your sex slave when I wasn't legally of age," she was sobbing now. "He threatened he might tell everybody in the Methodist Bible Study group we attended, you committed a crime against me and my family. Robbie claimed there's a curse on our marriage and that our family will fail because of it?"

"How did he come to *that* conclusion?" David raised his voice as he seldom did. "Did you tell him that we had sex before marriage? There were no children out of wedlock were there? How did he know anyway? It's not like ours was one of these shotgun weddings around town was it? My dad and yours spent ten grand at least on that wedding. There were 150 guests. Including a famous Hollywood movie producer–did you forget that?"

"I don't know how he figured it out," she cried. "He asked me a bunch of questions, and took it from there."

"That damn pervert made you confess to something we agreed *never* to talk about for the sake of the children didn't he?"

"Stop please David." Waving her arms like a referee, Nancy was calling for a time out, tears streaming down her cheeks; she was not apologizing for the way Walsh had brain washed her, or what that meant to their marriage of over a decade–there was always some truth to what he said. It was always the shocking doubts Robbie raised of the spouse she had entrusted her life to that caused the present trouble.

"I don't want to talk about Robbie ever again. He makes me sick. It's not your fault David. I know you love me; but I am so confused right now. I need to be alone. Because I get more confused by what he says the more he talks; that's when I have all these doubts about you." Like, *how can I trust you out on the road?* she thought silently, as Nancy hugged her husband of 17 years, then quickly ascended the stairs to their bedroom, and shut the door noticeably.

His wife was in no hurry to leave him yet; like a queen under siege in a game of chess, she was uncertain where to move next. To David it felt like his wife was already packing a suitcase. Weathering another crisis, Nancy was thankful the children were staying with their grandparents and sister at the Hoven lake home. In his deal with Walsh, David had not bargained on Robbie becoming the unofficial marriage counselor of the Zehlen family. At the time of his hiring, Robbie projected the image of a relatively successful agricultural businessman seeking to expand his business. Two years into the meltdown, David tried to explain to his partners the Zehlens had fallen into cahoots with Walsh by default on the South Dakota management deal. Sexton was hooked because Walsh had the inside dope on the ASCS swindle. Now he had to fulfill Walsh's plans before they both went down.

David's father, a quiet and wise man who had been around the block a few times, having spent some time at Fort Ripley with the guard–knew men better than Dave. Jack recognized what a ruthless brute his son's hire had turned out to be; the *snake* in the grass he had recognized in the beginning, had become an anaconda strangling the breath out of PHC. By harvest time 1992, Jack had absorbed and accepted the consequences of David's expansionism; his son had virtually taken over the farm when Jack believed 3500 acres was enough. Now it was too late to do anything about it. He had been just as foolish writing a check for two hundred fifty thousand dollars for safe keeping to Walsh, who coaxed him out of his quarter million-dollar pension stash, claiming Jack would lose an IRA to the inevitable bankruptcy he would be facing if things didn't shape up. Like his son, Jack had never met a truly evil person with multiple personalities capable of manipulating him.

From their first meeting, Jack Zehlen could see through the facade Walsh projected, but felt strangely powerless to do anything about it. Walsh had to be cautious with the patriarch; he patronized Jack around other members of the family-owned business, referring to him as his "older brother"–but privately he steered clear of Jack as much as possible. Robbie was much more comfortable in the church of true believers, where he could rub elbows with the hierarchs and powers of the various parishes he visited.

Rockland was the largest community Walsh had ever worked a scam in. It was the ideal size to have all the social advantages of a large city on a miniature scale. A man could make a name for himself overnight by creating a bio and sending it in as a "Letter to the Editor" introducing himself to the community through the Rockland *Independent* newspaper that reported local news, high school sports, and published court and police reports, highlighting a two-page entertainment section.

If a person was not looking for much excitement, Rockland had all the advantages and infrastructure of state, church, and general main street business, plus a municipal pool and golf course. The pragmatic loner, Walsh realized he could never be successful in a city the size of Watertown, St. Cloud, or Mankato. Under the right conditions, Robert Walsh had learned to infiltrate and take advantage of a modest closed society, through golf membership, attending events like Crazy Days, Corn Festival, and the annual Fireman's Ball, and making appearances in the culture celebrations in a city the size of Milbank, Redfield or Rockland for a relatively short time. In Walsh's experience, small towns were easy places to pull off an *Ocean's 11* style scam, with plenty of isolated money, and virtually no security system.

Once Walsh had outfoxed his only opponent Jack Zehlen, the patriarch of Pleasant Valley had become increasingly invisible in the farming operations, preferring to tinker on the machinery in the tool shed, or spend his weekends with Phyllis–where she constantly complained about Walsh's presence in the office–at the cabin on Lake Minnewaska. After Walsh was in control, Jack was brushed aside except for symbolic purposes–as the Walsh regime began to consolidate its power. David's father had become obsolete overnight in the Granite County empire he had built from scratch.

Until several years later, Jack did not know the extent of the mayhem the outsider from Nundas had created. Walsh dealt exclusively with Nancy and Jack's wife who ran the office; and with David as seldom as possible while maintaining the delusion everything was under control, as if the family trustee was coming to their financial and emotional rescue. Walsh imagined himself in his new office on the third floor with a magnificent view of Rockland's central park; his executive office remodeled in the historic Anothene building on 3rd and Washington, a block off main street Rockland, in sight of the Carnegie Library built in 1918 by the famous Minneapolis architect Herman Ellerbe. The 80-year old library was of pre-Sullivan structure without an internal steel frame. Despite its age, the dark red clay brick structure remained well preserved in its original early 20th Century design, and was recognized and annotated on the emerging world wide web for its collection of Lakota tribal art. Walsh imagined he would someday put a million-dollar price tag on the old hospital.

As long as a man didn't steal openly in Rockland, he was generally accepted. Money was always tight. The real estate was tied down; there was little a man could make off with without being immediately apprehended by law enforcement; theft of automobiles or farm machinery was rare. Law and order prevailed in the province; there was no reason to distrust Robert Walsh who deposited ten thousand dollars in a business account at Tri-County State Bank.

There were few businessmen remaining in Rockland by 1990 except the franchises, Pamida, Holiday and Penny's run by imported managers for a couple years before they moved along. It was to Robbie's advantage to be temporary, not required to mingle with any of the town fathers, who had accumulated wealth in construction, and agriculture; he unobtrusively observed the local establishment people who gathered every weekday morning at Cashtown or Hilltop. Walsh saw the closed community and parochial life style as advantageous to his scheme; there was little interest in outsiders in general and less in a fifty-year-plus man looking like an overweight Nick Nolte in need of a shave; a rumor circulated up and down main a grim looking man was preparing to set up an income tax service in the old Hanson's Hardware building.

At the Rockland Senior Center at 2nd and Madison, on the site where once a cafe owned and operated by Jack's mother Grace stood, an alert senior citizen reported that a mysterious stranger playing gin rummy with Rose Conrad had started and encouraged a rumor that the Zehlen's farming operation would soon be under new management. The same man pinned up a business card for Marketing International of Brookings, SD on the bulletin board in the lobby. One of Dave's closest friends Steve Stern, owner of Radio Shack, reported that Walsh claimed his friend, and one of his best customers, Dave Zehlen was a fraud and an anarchist like John Lennon who also happened to have long hair–and that he was going to bring Zehlen down a notch or two before long.

Behind the scenes, Walsh informed elders of the Catholic faith that David Zehlen and another parishioner Thomas Jorgenson, then living in Minneapolis, a former altar boy and lector were involved in drug smuggling and trafficking, flying in bales of marijuana from Mexico in broad daylight to SD fields. According to Walsh it was very possible Colombian drug lord Pablo Escobar himself was involved in the operation, shipping cocaine and marijuana to a leased property with an airstrip not more than a hundred miles southwest of Rockland. Of course there was never any proof the allegations were true or false. And they were never investigated. But the hearsay spread and came to the attention of the local law enforcement officer Joe Bernard who informed County Attorney Bill Watkins about the allegations Walsh was making.

As a child, most of Robbie's early reading material was Ansel's comic book collection; as he matured, his fascination turned to his father's monthly editions of *True Detective* magazine. His taste was more toward violence as he spent the idle hours of his Sunday afternoons paging through the cardboard boxes of pulp fiction stacked in the basement. Once he moved beyond comic books and crime magazines, his fetish turned to movies–fascinated with subjects like the *Black Dahlia*, and films about robberies, murders, and gangsters. Unlike his brother, Walsh did not enjoy reading. The only book he ever recalled reading was *Call of the Wild* he received as a Christmas present from Ansel. He would not soon forget the image of a magnificent wolf on the cover; on a clear winter night, he could still imagine the howl of that wolf under a full moon.

Evil bullies like Edward G. Robinson and Jimmy Cagney fascinated him. Strangely, those were the characters Walsh admired, even if they generally died like John Dillinger in a shootout at the end of the movie. As he matured, his taste for violent action became more refined; he claimed Humphrey Bogart deserved an academy award for *Desperate Hours*, although the movie itself was very boring. In his opinion, the greatest film ever made was *Ocean's 11*, the 1960 classic with Frank Sinatra, Dean Martin, Peter Lawford and Sammy Davis Jr., co-starring North Dakota native, Angie Dickinson, who appeared regularly on the *Johnny Carson Show*–by 1960, the sinister warriors owned half of Atlantic City.

Another movie that Walsh found intriguing, was *Prime Cut* with Lee Marvin, the tough star of *M Squad*. He commented on the movie often to David. As his hair skipped gray and faded to white, Shirley and Louise agreed that Robert, when he got that serious look on his face, reminded them of machine-gun-wielding FBI special agent Marvin–mowing down criminals in the cornfield war–against Gene Hackman and his henchmen who were prostituting pubescent girls.

The excitement of knocking over small town banks amidst a hail of bullets and glass appealed to Clyde Barrow and Gene Hackman–but there was too much risk in it for Walsh. Robbie had been imagining different ways to commit the illusive perfect crime since his youth; he had faith that if the right opportunity came along, he could put his plan in motion, abscond with the funds, and disappear in cloud of dust. Before his victims, and their ineffective attorneys and judges understood the scheme, he would be laying on the beach in Nice with a new identity, and a playboy reputation.

The ultra-conservative side of Robbie's personality took offense at the Zehlens' supposed empathy with the rural folks losing their farms, as that perspective appeared in the media. Walsh believed the pampered rich kid could not possibly identify with the displaced farmers affected by expanding operations like Pleasant Valley farm corporation. Walsh agreed with the notion that large farming enterprises–like major corporations in general–exploited their employees. His particular beef was that the Zehlen's success depended on large government subsidies that took unfair advantage of the personage payment programs that arrived for the 1980's generations–too late to save Father Walsh's farm that failed in the aftermath of the Depression, when such government support was unavailable.

In his chosen line of work, Walsh flashed back in unpredictable moments to those cornhusker days he patrolled the ditches for his targets, performing his daily rounds of weed control inspection. The big screen spectacle captured the perils of the cornfield like no other in the film archives of Robbie's memory, as years later the scene flashed back in vivid detail; in his frequent nightmares, revolving blades of a monstrous combine loomed above him, closing in on him–gobbling up an automobile he had escaped from–spitting out the metal pieces chunk by chunk.

What surprised Walsh the most about the Zehlen clan, and he may have resented it all the more–Walsh's victims lived somewhat frugally–with only a few of the *visible* signs of the massive wealth he expected to see. Nevertheless, his goal was the same; complete his assignment for the bank, and skim the remains for himself. This time nearing retirement, Robbie was in it for *all* the marbles, transferring money he conveniently allocated and then appropriated for his "fiduciary" services; funds that would someday be deposited in a Cayman Islands bank account where his company Marketing International would be opening an extension of his South Dakota practice in the near future.

* * * * *

Robert Walsh had no intention of being snared in his scheme; even so he felt vague guilt only in that he had not been more effective in this trade, which meant making decisions about life and death, his *own* and *other* people's. He attended confession regularly at St. John's, where he effectively infiltrated the local parish while at the same time maintaining membership in another congregation in Madison. Devout man that he was, he confided with Father Wolfe he needed the fellowship of other Christians while spending time away from his family and church. His remorse for sin was accepted by the priest who recognized his voice in public, that at first had been unfamiliar in the confidentiality of the booth.

After several months of regular attendance, the priest knew the new kid on the block as the reformed pilgrim from South Dakota. A Walsh interview on Saturday offered a refreshing change to the monotony; like the other male parishioners, he had no sins of *mortal* nature or consequence to confess. What he heard was Robert Walsh earnestly confessing to the venial flaws of his behavior. He admitted he had forgotten his wife's birthday, he felt inadequate in meeting the spiritual standards of the new ecumenical council–his mind at times wandered from the message of the sermon–he didn't call his ailing wife long distance often enough, and so on. Walsh was adding a new wrinkle to the usual confession; the penitent sinner he knew himself to be going to the well one more time, wishing and hoping that the Good Lord forgive those sins he had forgotten or *neglected* to confess,

"Amen."

"Your sins are forgiven my son. Go in peace. In the name of the Father, Son, and Holy Ghost, Amen."

Walsh made the sign of the cross and exited the booth feeling a tremendous sense of relief. Of all the rituals that were accepted within Walsh's belief system, there was no room for the Catholic ignominy theater, the priest taking off his socks and washing the feet of the celebrant on Good Friday; or the culminating ceremony of the passion of Jesus Christ–the ultimate shame of the "Stations of the Cross." That ritual above all others did not appeal to his personality; the experience, that sacrifice of dignity, was much too palpable to be a model of Catholic behavior. Pious Walsh preferred the escape of dogma where parsing passages of the catechism for application and conformity was more reassuring in group bible study sessions; those discussions eventually led to reports of numerous blessings, amid reflections upon the "gospel of prosperity" as Bullock and Copeland taught it, that related ever so vaguely to the ecumenical movement of the 1970's.

The cleansing feeling of fellowship in small groups with other Christians, where he actually had an audience for his ideas, and the right to disclose them if he chose to, was the one aspect that appealed to Robert. Through constant attendance, Robert discovered that voicing his opinion at the Rockland stage of his odyssey was why he attended church regularly, and for no other reason after the lure of skirts had diminished considerably from the urgency of his youth.

The religious side of the man was curious to learn of the realities of other believers–it was as if the bible sessions allowed him to test the validity and assumptions of his fellow Christians. Group debate over religious topics allowed him to explore and adjust religion to his psychic need for–if not forgiveness– *reinforcement* at least, from the principalities, the powers, the rulers of wickedness in high places that he knew *existed* were not going to come down on him too heavy, at least for the moment. He knew that sense of power and determination–because weird things happened when he put on his priest costume, a little bit of white dickey showing above a black shirt collar, wearing a low-brimmed hat as he circled Rockland in his faded blue Coronado on the day of funerals and religious feasts. Robbie's hopes were set on purgatory, not the Kingdom of God immediately, praying often to the various powers he was aware of, that he not be judged too harshly for his deeds in this world in the afterlife. Most times when he was alone or in transit between Rockland

and Brookings, Robert was speeding. It is a little known fact that he accumulated 8 speeding tickets in the 34 months he worked the Zehlen swindle with his partners. During those cruises, Walsh was constantly rationalizing his actions religious zealots might call "sins" as *corrections* of a greater menace; he couldn't actually judge David or Jack as "evil" per se. Ill-defined as a man's flaws actually were in desperate and uncertain modern times, making critical judgments that affected men's fate didn't torment him.

In his peculiar brand of religion Walsh was a believer, and he believed if and when judgment came, he would be able to stand up to whomever it was judging him–God, Christ, Peter at the gate–he could explain his side giving explanations for the necessary acts this life had imposed on him; in short, explain why he had done the things that needed to be done for the sake of humanity, acting as he chose for that improvement of the human condition, always aligning himself against those interests opposed to improving the common lot of humanity such as he observed in the Pleasant Valley management system. In a similar fashion, he stood opposed to the gratuitous investments in the planet by powerful green giant organizations like Ceres, SigCo, and Lubrizol–entities that projected their medicinal safflower program was for the benefit of the earth.

On his confessional Saturdays, Robert appreciated the serenity St. John's offered. As shafts of sunlight filtered through silver maple leaves, waving in a slight breeze, creating tiny sparkles of gold that shimmered in the stained glass windows of St. Johns, Walsh valued the peace of religion dearly. It was at those moments he felt he had succeeded in convincing one holy man he was worthy of the sanction of his mission on earth. Allowing the holy sacrament to intervene on his behalf made the release of information on his behavior a much more dignifying process, unburdening himself through the general act of contrition of all the acts he must atone for–as a fallen man–that he was not willing to reveal publicly. Judgment time will come soon enough he thought, confession was a celebration of forgiveness; he was justified, in that he did what needed to be done. Under those conditions he was willing to forgive what others, his partners, and rivals in the farming business had done to him.

* * * * *

That fatal spring of 1992 at the urging of Robert Walsh, David Zehlen approached the bank about obtaining a loan for his farming operations. The concern he had that Sexton had not been forthcoming on the contract contributed to his decision to take out another loan, this time with farm collateral on the line. It was David's interpretation that the loan was justified under the conditions of the contract as another manager's expense, and therefore covered under the guaranty. Having secured the First Omaha note through the influence of Walsh, David felt relieved considerably that it would be possible to salvage the operations for another year. Once the personage payments were disbursed he could satisfy his creditors. It would be possible to live and sleep with Nancy again. He recalled the earlier years when his father had joked with him that *a farmer faces bankruptcy every spring.*

CHAPTER 20

For one out of thirteen pristine weekends of spring, everything seemed to be falling in place for David Zehlen. Pleasant Valley itself is a beautiful stretch of native grass, rolling farmland, soil bank, and shallow inland lakes; a natural wildlife refuge, it is home to abundant species of muskrat and ducks, dotted with wetland game reserves, populated with song birds, pheasant, hawks, owls, crows, an occasional eagle, whitetail deer, rabbits and fox–along a well maintained tar road that extends twenty miles northeast of Rockland on a diagonal to Clontarf, MN, a tiny town with one elevator, and about 160 people nestled at the junction of Granite County 22 and US Hwy 9.

On Mother's Day 1992, things were back to a semblance of normality. There were a number of unspoken issues that had been partially resolved by some good news for a change, but Nancy's lack of enthusiasm was apparent; she was being a mother to her children, having heard the check was in the mail too often to trust the messenger completely again. In honor of the occasion, Nancy made potato salad and coleslaw. David fired up the grill. Jack and Phyllis planned on dropping by around noon. Nothing could interfere with Dave's celebration after learning the Omaha loan had cleared the first wicket. There was a slight chance they might be able to consolidate the RTC default if the farm deed and custom farming equipment was assigned as collateral on the note in the new deal. Later in the day David was surprised by a phone call and some unexpected news from his marketing consultant Tom Adelman in the Twin Cities.

"David I have some good news for you for a change," Adelman was unusually cheerful.

"You cut a deal with Cargill for 20,000 bushels of hard red spring wheat?" Dave could only imagine.

"Not quite but close. This idea could be a major marketing opportunity for Pleasant Valley Farms. I wrote to the publisher of

Farm Futures Magazine we subscribe to in the office–he offered to write an article about your operations," Adelman was gushing compared to his usual brusque style.

"I thought that was just your imagination running away with you. I never even heard of that magazine until you brought it up. Now they want an interview? All the good news is refreshing for a change," David was joking knowing the bubble could burst at any second.

"*Farm Futures* is a marketing magazine with circulation in the sun belt," Adelman continued. "It appeals to the progressive farmer interested in new products, innovations, and technology, for sale or investment, at a time when many Midwestern farmers are very conservative, unwilling to invest and reluctant to take any chances in this economy, while your record of risk speaks another language. So I called the publisher Ron Nelson Jr. and spent some time on phone with him discussing your operations. He surprised me with his interest, saying there are not many young farmers with such a large, private operation in the Midwest these days."

"I mentioned you partner with your dad Jack, and his early successes growing sunflowers when it was considered an experimental crop. He asked if you are practicing intensive low input sustainable agriculture. I said I thought you were. Nelson said they are running feature articles on new trends in agriculture–LISA happens to be one of the new technologies Iowa State is researching, where the emphasis has been on genetic modification for the last decade; he said it was always interesting to hear of a new technology that might increase production and soil conservation at the same time. He offered to send one of his reporters up to Pleasant Valley to interview you for a potential article, with your approval of course. I gave him your number. Ron was saying they would like to see how your sunflower fields are looking about Memorial Day," Adelman concluded his remarks with a positive tone in his voice. "The magazine would contact you and make all the arrangements. This is how they do all their features based on an interview with their best reporters he said."

A few days before Memorial Day 1992, Ms. Colleen Nelson daughter of Ron Nelson Jr. the publisher of *Farm Futures Magazine,* turned right off US Highway 75 and pulled into the driveway of the Dave Zehlen farm. David walked up to the car extending his hand as the publisher's daughter stepped out of a late model Toyota, wearing a khaki shirt, blue jeans, adjusting a "Cyclones Baseball" hat over a blonde ponytail.

"How do you do Mr. Zehlen? I am Colleen Nelson from *Farm Futures* magazine."

"Pleased to meet you! And thank you for driving up to Minnesota country. Why don't you step inside and meet the family? My son Noah is so excited to meet you he forgot to do his chores this morning; he will show up any minute and wants to ride along with us, if you don't mind?"

"Sounds good to me," she responded in a professional manner, with a practiced tone of command in her voice that belied her age that appeared to be about 17.

As it turned out, the young woman destined to be editor of *Farm Futures* was doing field research on a doctoral in agricultural journalism out of Northern Iowa University. Colleen was a graduate of Northern Iowa where she lettered in fast pitch softball. She had the slim attractive face of a sports model that was beyond being merely pretty, there was immediate, and noticeable depth and intelligence in her demeanor. David could tell right away Ron Nelson's daughter had the experience and training a woman needed to be successful in a public career that might turn political. Reaching back into the front seat for her oversized purse, that served as a carrying case for her mini cam outfit Colleen extended her hand and said,

"Thank you so much for inviting us Mr. Zehlen. I'm Ron's oldest daughter; he sent me all the way up from Iowa City to write an article about your farm. How nice is that? It's been a gorgeous drive. When I started out the sun was just coming up at 5:30. I stopped for a break one time in Luverne. Just like your directions, Mr. Zehlen; go one mile north of the city limits of Rockland. Look for a large white farm house on the right. I didn't need a map once I hit Highway 75 at Pipestone."

During a brief visit and a cup of coffee with Nancy and David in the kitchen, Colleen explained another reason why she was there–because the work matched her credentials; as an agricultural journalism major, she was doing her graduate studies in the field laboratory out of Iowa State, partially funded by a research internship focusing on intensive farming techniques in northern Iowa. Most of the graduate work was behind her: today her assignment was to begin a feature series of articles about low-input sustainable agriculture for the *Farm Futures* summer quarterly publication.

After a quarter hour in the kitchen, Dave announced he was ready to go whenever she was. But he asked permission on behalf of his son who had just appeared in the kitchen, because Noah was very shy around pretty girls–could he please ride along on the tour of Pleasant Valley. Another quarter hour passed as the folks chatted in the driveway before the threesome was on the trail. By 10:45 they were winding northwest along Pleasant Valley road. Colleen opened up her tote bag and pulled out a portable tape recorder.

"This is some beautiful country David. Thanks for showing me around."

"And we have an exceptionally nice day for you Colleen. It's been raining a lot this past week, with a light mist over the prairie in the morning. Then it is clear by evening. You picked the right time for an interview."

"I can't use my camera with this on," Colleen commented as she unbuckled her seatbelt. She turned acknowledging Noah in the club cab.

"Are you enjoying our company Noah? I like your name."

"Right out of *Genesis* Colleen," David laughed. "We wanted to start him off on solid ground didn't we? Right son?"

"Right dad," Noah was tired of that joke about his name when he had no choice in the matter. Dave chuckled.

"You guys don't mind if I record some of our conversation, do you? I'll use this tape for the transcript of the articles I write about Pleasant Valley. I'll just ask you a few questions and you can respond to them as we drive along. I am particularly interested in your low input sustainable agriculture technology program. The Agricultural College of Iowa State has asked *Farm Futures* to work with them on a study of large scale LISA farming operations in the Minnesota River basin and Iowa. Pleasant Valley Farms would be a great place to start a series of articles on the subject. And I agree with the idea, at 40,000 plus acres, yours is among the largest family owned operations in the tri-state area."

"The privilege is all mine Colleen. I will give you a brief description of an exciting day in the life of a farmer. Noah is our oldest boy. Nancy and I are approaching our fifteenth anniversary. This is a typical Saturday in Pleasant Valley: at six this morning I was up at Dad's south quarter in Steven's County. As I fixed a couple fertilizer hoses in the input drills I could not help but notice the sublime beauty of the morning you are noticing today. I could hear a meadowlark perched on the power line as he pitched his song. From a half mile away, I heard his mate's call from the grove echo across the slough. Or maybe I imagined I did. Have you ever heard the song of the red-winged blackbird Colleen?"

"There is nothing like that inversion in modern music. My hands smelled of fertilizer, so I walked down to the edge of the pond to rinse the chemical off my hands. At that instant a muskrat mama with four little ones trailing her suddenly splashed out of the reeds not more than ten feet ahead of me. I watched them swimming into the rising sun as I dipped my hands into the cold water. This was a typical scene we don't see on the farm every day, but a lot more often than you do in the city; experiences like that are why I am thankful farming is my occupation. But I digress. Both my consultant and the publisher agreed your magazine would be an excellent source to advertise our unique market programs at Pleasant Valley." Dave began projecting as if he was Bruce Hagevik the most famous representative of the Rockland baby boomer generation, who started out sounding like *Claudius* on KDIO. After a long unpaid apprenticeship his pronunciation improved and Bruce moved up the ladder to WCCO. Better yet ladies and gentlemen, today we have Dave Zehlen–farming superstar–speaking for Pleasant Valley farms. As he spoke Colleen turned the microphone his direction,

"My dad started farming with his dad on the original 160 acres in 1950. By the time I joined the operations in 1979 the farm had grown to 3500 acres. My father was one of the first farmers in the community to plant a large percentage of sunflowers, and that had a lot to do with his success, and mine frankly."

"Besides helping Pleasant Valley Farms find financiers and investors, Tom Adelman our consultant has lined us up with customers for organic crops including foreign buyers in Japan and Europe," this was no time to squander an opportunity with the media,

"One of the problems smaller farmers face is finding buyers. A lot of farms have given up on alternative crops that we sell a lot of because they can't afford to set up markets for their production. Our investment in large quantities for sale has helped Pleasant Valley clear that formidable hurdle. The farm forward-contracts 100% of its organic production," Dave elaborated.

"The size of our operation depends on a number of factors in including expanding markets. This year I am looking at 45,000 acres with the North and South Dakota leases. Such a volume of profit allows me to offset expenses connected with our investment in low input specialization that requires conversion to air and oil compression technology, specially adapted nozzles, and expensive equipment which has only become available the last few years. At Pleasant Valley Farms we carefully micro-manage fertilizer, and pesticide expenditures. We employ a full time soil scientist during the growing season. This year it will be a graduate assistant out of the University of Minnesota, St. Paul agriculture campus. Using the computer software I designed and sold to Mr. Gunther at Control Data, we correlate our data with the county extension programs. So far we have been able to convert University soil and erosion input data maps to our computer applications."

As the ride progressed, Dave ushered his passengers around several sections of sunflowers and soybeans in Akron township, and made a physical observation of several inches of just emerging organic white wheat. In that same section 80 acres of corn stood about knee high on Memorial Day. By then David and Colleen had chatted for two hours. Colleen looked up from her work, informing Dave she was running low on tape as she pressed the stop button.

"Off the record, now that we have the farm business documented, I just wanted to mention a few things that might be included in the video about our Pleasant Valley vision. We have a global technology mission that we share with environmentalists to keep the planet clean; for that reason, I plan to invest in a broader theme of decontaminating polluted water in the Minnesota River Valley. We can get into that in our next interview. I have a substantial investment with one of my research partners in the Mojave Desert Utah branch of UEON–that's a name I created for the project which stands for United Energy of Nevada; we have a facility located at the edge of the Great Salt Lake in Utah that is developing 'Vortex-ology'–I'll fill you in on the details of my program for globalization before we schedule a video interview. Thank you for visiting Pleasant Valley Colleen. Do you have anything to say to our visitor Noah?"

"Yeah dad! Thank you very much Colleen."

Back at her desk in Iowa, the young writer reflected on the interview; while writing the article she recalled being a bit surprised at the tone perhaps, and the seamless transition to a different subject at the very end. Why was she thinking of the specialty crops like purple saskatoon berries that seemed so fascinating to David? And why had she noticed the boy seemingly so bored by the tour routine–or perhaps that was understandable because similar to other males she came in contact with in her work, Noah was absorbed by Colleen's sports fragrance and personality and not unlike the boys she was used to being around among her nephews and friend's kids.

David's final remarks and those anecdotes about UEON could have been developed into another chapter in her article; at the time though they seemed to change the focus of the interview. Her host's concluding remarks didn't fit the image of Pleasant Valley as she conceived the organization. Those comments seemed a bit incongruous with the way the storyline was heading, before those words emerged from David's mouth that seemed like misfits, with the interview and tour de force of the farm. Notwithstanding, Ms. Nelson's one-page report with a picture of Dave as the cover page appeared as the July 1992 *Farm Futures* feature article, "LISA: Sustainability is About Change."

CHAPTER 21

In the week that followed notification of the ASCS violation, Robert Walsh was very active. One of the first connections he made, after David Zehlen informed him of the decision, was to contact Harlan Anderson, the committee chairman of the ASCS county board. Walsh had tipped him off that–even if he was power of attorney for the family, if he discovered violations by the Zehlens, it was his duty as fiduciary to inform the government that illegal activities were being conducted.

Privately Walsh and Anderson agreed not to be too harsh on Jack, and take it easy on David, because it was his first offense; there would be no mention of the Sexton fraud–too early for that issue to enter the dialogue. Various methods and motions were established to deflect the government review; by obstructing any such inquiry, secrecy was ensured. Any information that was bound to reveal evidence detrimental to the cause of conspiracy, such as a TILA audit, or such investigation into financial issues behind the demise–was the bane of the conspiracy–matters of genuine material interest would be forever concealed under the elaborate cover-up that continued to operate in the background. It was equally important, that if an investigation was conducted–as to why the ineligibility issue was raised above a penalty–the sinister takeover plan must never be revealed. So the many hen houses of *Orwell* remained tacked together invisibly, like a chain-link fence surrounding a perimeter. It was necessary to maintain draconian measures against the victims, to suppress questions about the mechanics of judgment; that evidence of a conspiracy would be proscribed in a similar fashion, using depositions submitted before a selected courtroom and prejudiced judge–leading up to a prison stint for David.

A legal factor in Jack's favor in any decision, was his untarnished record of compliance in his dealings with the Granite

County ASCS programs, since the 1960's, without a single violation that could influence the county board. The elder Zehlen had done jury duty on the highly publicized Barton Flowers murder case, the result of a duck hunting dispute in Artichoke Township. Jack was a member of the local Rod and Gun Club, and Ducks Unlimited, and a retired member of the Rockland National Guard artillery battalion. David's father was a highly respected, but reticent leader of the farming community; in addition, he was a heavy contributor to the new church built in north Rockland during the 1960's, and served ten years on the Board of Directors of the Methodist Church.

Behind the scenes, Walsh and Harlan, along with Cub Wiley of the Granite County Commissioners, discussed the ASCS determination; although the violation was serious–$582K was a lot of money–nothing illegal happened, the government's money was invested in crops, wages and equipment. The commissioners decided that the Zehlens had enough capital assets, cash and credit to be able to pay off the ASCS refund if they were forced to. Walsh insinuated David had cautiously stashed at least $10K of the funds in a private account in unnamed bank, knowing he was bound to over-draft his Pleasant Valley account. The auxiliary committee didn't take Walsh seriously in his initial allegations, agreeing privately the mismanaged "personage" was in violation of the rules requirement, but a mere gaffe by the wayward son–that could have been overlooked in the complexity of a 41,000-acre operation–and was therefore forgivable.

In the decision of the committee, the combined Zehlen actions did not rise to the level of a criminal violation in view of their history and other factors. The sanctions would be severe enough; the Zehlens would be required to pay back a half million plus dollars. To make matters worse, they would not be eligible to receive any payments for the 1992 growing season. Without the need of a full blown audit, influenced by Walsh's opinions, Harlan believed his friend Jack Zehlen had more than enough cash and credit to roll back operations and ride the storm out on the original 3500 acres.

Walsh was resigned to being the incognito "whistle blower" with no visible presence in the process. He and Anderson agreed it was best for him to keep a low profile–at that time there was no reason to disclose who broke the news of the ineligibility issue to the Granite County committee. In August, Walsh and Anderson agreed to keep Walsh's *informant* role and the link to his power of attorney discovery confidential to preserve the dignity of the Zehlen family; until it was fully evaluated, the wives didn't need to know how their husbands affected judgment, or how their actions related to the future of Pleasant Valley farms.

According to Walsh's interpretation, the ASCS problem was solely David Zehlen's fault because of the way he had bullied his father and his wife into the Sexton contract. For a generation later, Anderson would agonize over penalizing one of his best friends in what increasingly began to look and feel like Walsh had something to do with the situation Harlan couldn't put his finger on.

In the August heat, it was obvious David was wilting under pressure of mistaken risks in marketing grain through a third party; under extreme duress, with no criminal intent David had faltered, that's all it was–a big misunderstanding–or was it something else? On top of that was a psychological issue of clinical depression in the boy he had once known, that now needed to be treated. Rumor was rampant. Some drugs–Valium, and Percodan–were unaccounted for in an audit of the dispensary by the bureau of drugs and alcohol.

One of the Anothene night staff, practical nurse Delores R–– of Corona, SD accepted a plea bargain to theft of class "A" narcotics; a charge arranged through the County Attorney with no jail time, in consideration of her three school-age children and divorcee status. Before the hearing, Walsh voiced his concerns for the Pleasant Valley connection to Bill Watkins, not actually implying David was involved; it may have been a coincidence that the drugs disappeared during David's late night babysitting hours at the detox center.

In discussions that would last another year, about the various ASCS issues at stake, it became clear that Walsh was not satisfied with the ASCS decision in Granite County; it became apparent he was not done creating havoc, but his objectives became less obvious.

* * * * *

Before the Watkins interview and for the next 8 months, Zehlens remained in the dark, unaware of the facts that it was Hector Sexton in cahoots with Robert Walsh who had created the means and ends of the crisis. In his manner of always feigning that what he did was in the best interests of the Zehlen family, as manager of their leases in South Dakota–and projecting a palpable anima of caring and concern–had given Harlan the impression he was acting as trustee for the *benefit* of Pleasant Valley.

"I hate to inform you of this Harlan, knowing you and Jack are close; but because of the trouble David has caused, the Zehlens will be penniless. That goes without saying," Walsh finished the bad news with no empathy. *Maybe it's because I know how badly the son has mismanaged the old man's property*, he thought. *I pity Jack most because he loses most.* Although he was not specific about the details, Walsh told Anderson that he was working on a deal with his private contacts on Wall Street related to agricultural finance and marketing in the Middle East, through whom he might be able to sell the farm to an investor from Saudi Arabia who wanted to emigrate to the States–before the aftermath of the invasion of Kuwait and the Desert Storm War spills over into his country, Dubai–fearing he might lose his property to enemy insurgents.

During the discussions about what he predicted was the eminent collapse of Pleasant Valley, Walsh relegated Tom Adelman, a member of the Minneapolis Grain Exchange whom Anderson had met, to the scapegoat role, claiming that if he had done his job as a consultant in grain marketing in Asia and Europe as he said he would–the Zehlens would not be in such a jam. Anderson was very upset at being in the middle of a crooked deal where it looked like his own son, was taking his old buddy Jack, the most successful farmer the county had ever known–down–in the wake of bad business decisions with his partner.

The leaders of the community were as baffled as every farmer in the county by an outsider who spoke of agricultural policy enforcement like a corporation lawyer. Confusion reigned supreme as Walsh administrated the farm into ruin. At the same time, Wiley and Anderson saw no need to bring on another controversy for the government to be involved in, when the community was seeking funding for a multimillion dollar health services center.

Hearing more contradicting details of the calamity didn't help, as Clinton-area commissioner Sandberg voiced his distrust of the information Walsh gave the committee from the beginning. Under the circumstances where David was as confused as the board, the majority was forced to go with the flow of information that tended to label the Pleasant Valley Farms operation as illegitimate. Board members sensed power-of-attorney Walsh's concerns for the Zehlen's welfare were disingenuous; but the local damage was done, and Walsh was carrying the ball as far as he could take it–beyond Granite County.

Within hours of concluding his preliminary business with the chairman of the ASCS committee, Walsh contacted Thomas Jessen, a key bank official who participated in both contract-signing events involving the four Zehlens. In researching the financial situation the Zehlens faced, Jessen became aware of the stalled credit of the Zehlen-related RTC loan problem, which had developed when their previous Pleasant Valley lender Midwest Federal was frozen in receivership during the savings and loan crisis of the late 1980's. He was first introduced to the plans for expansion of the Zehlen operation while the default was supposedly in resolution status. Nonetheless in January 1991, the defaulted MWFSL loan did not appear to be an obstacle in providing another loan, when the Sexton custom farming contract was considered in the deal–and the crops were designated collateral.

In the conspiracy spin, when the bank examined the state filing system and determined there were no financing statements, or other lien documents evidencing superior security interests in the safflowers, sunflowers and soybeans, a loan for $1,350,000 was issued. In future litigation, David Zehlen insisted that he had disclosed all debts on the1992 financial information Robert Walsh submitted to the bank on his behalf in loan negotiations. During the January 1991 discussions, David claimed his loan defaults were stated at fair market value; the bank was fully aware the RTC debts were in arbitration as part of an intervention by the USDA to remediate damages to the farming industry caused by weather-related losses in 1988 and '89, and well before the bank accepted the original loan application in 1991.

At the same time, the Bank was bidding on distressed loans at reduced market value–while thousands of customers were forced to pay back the loans at principal plus interest. Walsh himself was cognizant of every detail of the information the bank required on the equity evaluation, including an income worksheet that validated the 1992 line of credit, with all the numbers ensuring First Omaha would have first lien on the crop.

Jessen had previous dealings with Hector Sexton in 1989, on an experimental GMO contract failure near Revillo, SD leading to a foreclosure Ceres was involved in, and had working knowledge of his recent history of SigCo safflower leasing arrangements. Updating his resume, Sexton informed Mr. Jessen that he had become a marketing consultant for Pleasant Valley Farms, acknowledging David Zehlen farmed approximately 15,000 acres of safflowers, sunflowers and some soybeans under contract in Grant Duehl and Sully Counties in South Dakota–Sexton's sponsorship was the main reason why the bank was considering a loan for David Zehlen's custom farming operation–while the bank would have 1st lien on the crop. Although it was required by the contract, Zehlen had no crop insurance on the 1992 loan. By signing off on a *contract waiver*, First Omaha's VP Thomas Jessen allowed Sexton to change the insurance provision of the contract, lapsing coverage through Jeff Provo.

* * * * *

The tenor of conversations between Walsh and Sexton increased in pitch as each man addressed the situation as they perceived it. When Robert Walsh and Hector Sexton spoke with each other thereafter, once the agreement was reached on the subject of the South Dakota safflowers, neither of them was overly concerned with the ASCS default; yet neither man was willing to back down a centimeter in terms of what they were trying to accomplish in the numerous conversations that followed.

"Hey Robbie my man, how is it going on the safflowers? Don't they look healthy in all that Dakota sunshine? My brother Jeffrey Provo has been bugging me lately about the ridiculously high cost of the risk premium he is paying on those safflowers. Is there any way we could steer clear of that last payment? Security Mutual of Illinois is asking for $65K by the end of the month," Sexton was gambling that Walsh would be more affected by the loss of government funding issues Zehlen was facing.

"Look Hector I have before me a letter from you on Ceres stationery telling me to walk in to the ASCS office in Rockland; and sign up for the program. So don't try to suggest that you have nothing to do with David's predicament," Walsh reacted.

"Believe me Robbie. I was sorry to hear about David's problem. I want to remind you Ceres and SigCo are my employers, not Pleasant Valley or David Zehlen. I have just been trying to manage my end of the owner's manual and contract with him and Jack. It's not my fault that he over-extended himself on his other fields in Minnesota and North Dakota. I have been paying my share," Hector corrected Walsh with his patented responses, perfected through years of practice.

"Let's just put it this way Hector," Walsh knew the game Sexton was playing as well as he did. "You have been dealing with David at a fraction of your obligation to him, trickling out just enough cash and credit, most of it going directly to his vendors to keep the skids greased, so that a crisis like this is inevitable, and *invisible* I might add to Zehlen who is an honest man, naively believing you will fulfill on the contract. I know how you operate–like some kind of mysterious wizard behind an iron curtain of Lubrizol and Ceres. Now you expect me, not David who is in total confusion, to manage the crisis you have created through your aggravated promissory fraud."

"Wait just a minute Robbie! That is a misconception. I'm not asking you for any favors. I said *Jeff* was wondering if there was any way we can all avoid that last insurance payment before harvest? You told me the crop is in excellent shape. There is nothing that could go wrong at this point. If the insurance is canceled after the loan disbursement is made and the crop is perfectly good I don't see a problem," Sexton had an anxious edge to his voice.

"The only problem is that your methods are in breach of a legal contract," Walsh responded. "David is in no position to deal with the government or the bank at this point. He is no longer in control of Pleasant Valley after this month. You have that to your advantage; you and Provo can try to convince Jessen that the safflowers don't need the insurance. I won't put my neck on the block for you again. You have Vice President Jessen's number don't you? There are still a few weeks until harvest to gamble on your brother-in-law's insurance policy; but it's your risk not mine if anything happens to those safflowers. David still owns all the leases and he has sunk all his money into the black hole you created. In my role as power of attorney, I will have to deal with the crisis you caused by your deficit-creating program, and I fully intend to do what I can for the Zehlen family."

On selected evenings, sipping his lemon vodka with Mountain Dew at the front window of his apartment above main street, with a truncated view facing the south end of the lake–a mild ecstasy descended upon Robbie as if he was experiencing what Pleasant Valley would be like in the future–when it was under new management. In the vision, he would be appraising the galvanized silos and corrugated steel pole barns that housed ten spanking new red IHC tractors from Milbank Implement; he imagined the mechanical herd, poised and ready for an oil change and lube job outside Jack's machine shop. By sundown the thirsty rigs would be in the barn, filled with diesel fuel, ready to tackle the bounteous harvest that lies before them in the morning, as the once green fields slowly turned a hazy shade of gold in the August heat.

On the shaky side, he would snap out of his stupor, stumbling to bed, discomfited by flashbacks of his inspection work for the county; in his nightmares it was like he was still on the job, constantly rinsing his hands with oily liquid hand cleaner. After a day's work, he could never wash away whichever stench was worse, the petroleum smell, or that of the stale pool hall where he spent Saturday afternoons drinking with the customers at the Madison on-sale. His mind drifted back to those youthful nights time and again; among friends he was buying rounds for the house, celebrating, announcing he was marrying his sweetheart Shirley–then the lovers waltzed to her favorite tune, "You picked a fine time to leave me Lucille..."

* * * * *

Although he was unsettled in his unconscious, Walsh was confident the Zehlens, law enforcement, and the courts would *never* figure out his scheme in a million years. Walsh was not about to allow the opportunity he had waited a lifetime for elude him again–if he could help it. With that objective in mind, on the eve of the Corn Festival, Walsh pulled out his wallet and thumbed through his business cards until he found the one from his Janklow connection, Ray Clark, who had given him an aerial tour of his farm west of Milbank. During the plane ride, Clark had mentioned a peripheral business, and in a later conversation had given him the name of his son-in law who ran an aerial crop spraying system, on the back of the Clarkdale Nursery business card: "Shannon Custom Application Services, Stockholm, S.D. – Miles Shannon, Owner"

Ray Clark was not particularly proud, nor embarrassed when he mentioned to Walsh that his former son-in-law had spent military time strafing rice paddies and dousing the jungle foliage of Southeast Asia with Agent Orange. They both had heard the horror stories about the defoliation of Viet Nam, and the damage the chemical causes to exposed skin and lungs. Had he hung around with Ray any longer, Robbie would have had to admit he was "scared-to-death" of flying. Walsh kept the business card Clark passed along recommending his former son-in-law Miles Shannon, who ran a crop dusting operation out of Stockholm, SD.

CHAPTER 22

The June 1992 notification–a violation of USDA rules–and its accompanying sanctions, changed the business structure of Pleasant Valley Farms. As Robert Walsh reported the situation to the FBI a year later, a meeting was held in Rockland at the end of July, 1992. Preliminary to the meeting with state officials in St. Paul, Nancy and Phyllis Zehlen told *their* side of the story to officers of the county committee at the ASCS office in Rockland. According to Walsh, the major issue of the meeting was evidence he presented that David Zehlen had manipulated the ASCS funds.

Using the defense strategy that Walsh had prepared for them–if they hoped to avoid prosecution for participation in the "scheme" –Nancy and Phyllis Zehlen were instructed to plead they were "not properly informed by their husbands of the consequences of their names being submitted as applicants eligible for a share of the half-million-dollar government support payments." If either of them was required to testify, Robbie coached the girls to report "*they were very upset and concerned by what David had done with the ASCS funding.*" Neither woman was aware of the circumstances under which David had been forced to divert a third of the government funds to Hector Sexton. No actual accounting was ever made of where the housewives' shares of the personage were invested. In the contingency, the Trojan women divided the Pleasant Valley books among themselves, Phyllis taking over billing and accounts payable and receivable while Nancy handled MinGo timekeeping and payroll.

Meanwhile, Walsh made it as difficult as possible for the county committee to understand how and why he had completely reorganized the ideology, commerce and various domestic pressures and prejudices that affected Pleasant Valley management once the takeover was in motion. David was physically unavailable, increasingly responsible for equipment operation and maintenance as his remote crews diminished. There was never a record of Jack agreeing to the Walsh takeover as power of attorney. With his vote abstaining and David not in attendance, as majority board members, Nancy and Phyllis voted to remove David as president of Pleasant Valley Farms, and replace him for all practical purpose with the new boss, Robert Walsh, in July 1992.

At the informal board hearing, Walsh reinforced the general idea that David was incompetent, at the same time introducing the idea it was necessary that David relinquish the directorship of the Pleasant Valley farming operations for the sake of its survival. There was plenty of work to be done maintaining and harvesting the remote leases. Walsh assured Jack's old cronies at the county ASCS hearing David would be retained and assigned to prepare those areas for growing crops under his directorship when the 1993 growing season arrived.

From that time on, Walsh would be using the president's office for the phone and the fax while David was out of town on business. Behind the closed door, Walsh was compiling an evidence folder based on digging around in David's papers and the accounts accessible through Phyllis, head bookkeeper, who became much more cooperative once the government was involved. Walsh scoured through her files for delinquent bills to reinforce the idea that David's conduct should have been under investigation by the FBI in connection with FDIC fraud on the Omaha loans months before Walsh arrived on the scene the end of 1991.

As he reported to the FBI in the coming months, Phyllis and Nancy Zehlen had completely lost confidence in David after the ASCS issue surfaced; the oppressed women asked Robert Walsh to intervene for them in further meetings with the ASCS scheduled for November 1992. Walsh assured the office staff that before that series of hearings relative to the lawsuit he was preparing, he would produce hold-harmless agreements for Nancy and Phyllis to sign; in the legal dealings, Walsh claimed he would be their advocate and state's witness about David's reckless behavior that had caused such a huge loss. Walsh would argue for their cause–keeping them out of prison–because it was David who had created the crisis. Walsh calmed the hyper-feminine fears he had created, claiming he would be the informal trustee of the family business, fully capable of proving the owners of Pleasant Valley were neither liable nor culpable for their husbands' actions, or the $50K personage payments from the government that went into David's crops.

"If it ever gets to that point in the interrogations," Walsh cautioned, "b*oth* of you must indicate you believed those funds went into Hector's, not David's crops; that's why you agreed to the arrangement, under pressure from your husband. Let's just say he bullied you into it; if the interrogation goes beyond that, you can claim it was *all* his idea–you objected to it. As victimized spouses, *we*, Nancy and Phyllis–got *nothing* from the ASCS. We had nothing to do with David's scheme–it was *clearly* a fraud."

As a reward for his services above and beyond those of the ASCS penalty hearing and his indispensable counsel to the organization, Robert Walsh was elected to be the successor to President David–by Nancy and Phyllis. As power of attorney for Pleasant Valley Farms, Walsh received authority to dispose of real and personal property of the corporation–for his own benefit, or the benefit of others, enabling him to dispose of interest which is vested in another–in an *extra*-legal fashion he took full advantage of it. Once Walsh had gained control of the corporation, he used the sense of danger that Nancy believed she was in, because of her husband's actions, to control her. On a routine basis, he made sure Nancy remained aware she faced potential prison time for what could be viewed as *her* participation, alongside her husband in a scheme that involved embezzling half a million dollars from the United States government–as long as Nancy cooperated, Walsh would make sure *at least* the Rockland committee would continue to ignore that her signature was attached to the application for ASCS payments in 1991.

"David and Hector talked about their farming business over the phone every day during the spring of 1992," Nancy stated in the Sully hearing. To Nancy Zehlen, it was a mystery why she was constantly being made aware of the contract that existed–between her husband and Hector Zehlen as a result of those conversations–as if the domestic security of the family had some bearing on the legal status of the contract.

Walsh never bothered to explain to his victim that in a particularly devious fashion, the issue of the guaranty was *reversed* under a false assumption; instead of having contract indemnity–David Zehlen would be ruled liable for "loss on a loan" the grower contract has been converted to. In the interpretation posted by the Westlaw quarterly, the contract guarantee agreement in place after February 1991, was ruled a "lending arrangement" and enabled Hector Sexton to enforce *his* guarantee–allowing Ceres to collect on a reinterpreted contract liability into a Zehlen *loan*–in the *kangaroo* court restitution appeal of 1994.

* * * * *

"I have set up a schedule for you to discuss matters with the County Attorney David. You will need to control your demeanor better than you have around the farm lately. You should not be drinking while you are on your medications," Walsh counseled assuming that the contract conversion would not become an issue in the complaint if the more serious charges of "loan fraud" suddenly entered the discourse.

"You will have to prepare a statement because you can't explain what is happening between you and Hector for the past year. If you act like you do around me, the county attorney will assume you are trying to hide something with your usual vague responses."

Walsh was familiar with the hardline county prosecutor's ambition, seeking to enhance his resume and reputation, thinking of creative ways to increase his points toward a judgeship. He would listen to David Zehlen's spin, for a while. As soon as the prosecutor noticed David's usual evasiveness and equivocation on the critical issues, followed by quack opinions about subjects he knew nothing about, legal matters–there was good chance Watkins could become more suspicious, involved, more interested in the case than he appeared to be. In most cases what little actual criminal activity there was on the part of the victim, needed to be exaggerated; if he found that domestic intervention was necessary to enforce the rule of law, Bill Watkins would be a first responder, always there, enforcing the law that *violence* against women was #1 on the intolerable list on his watch.

* * * * *

On a muggy day in late June as he sat in the office alone, Walsh scanned through an article in *Modern Farming* magazine that reported promising results, as scientists tried a variety of new pesticides to increase productivity under drought conditions. He moved on to the feature article that discussed BASF protocols in aerial fungicides that are typically applied in the form of liquids rather than dry chemicals, while little information is available on their toxicity;

> Advocates for crop dusting say that as the planes have become more expensive and sophisticated, pilots are less likely to be reckless about spraying. Global positioning systems, for instance, by 1995 will be enabled to increase efficiency, according to an extension agricultural engineer with Iowa State University."

He reached for his billfold. Like a man possessed, Robbie began fumbling nervously through his business cards as he perused the article,

> ...all part of the risk package of being in a high profit production business based on rates of spreading toxic chemicals in the environment. Modern pilots might be spending more money on equipment and have access to emerging GPS technology, but the chemicals are still being applied in the same principle way: once released into the atmosphere the chemicals in a light oil-like suspension drawn through the air to the ground by the force of gravity, when dusted over the crops ideally. But when the wind is strong, chemical drift is inevitable, and

there is always room for human error. There are plenty of cost effective alternative methods for combating fungal disease. Progressive farmers seeking to increase production through methods such as ground applications are worried about efficiency and maintaining production levels without the need for spraying toxic pesticides and chemicals. Purdue University Cooperative Extension Service recommends managing high-oleic leaf spot and similar fungal infestation using a combination of hybrid features to increase absorption of the chemicals by the plants and the soil.

* * * * *

"Hello. Who am I speaking to?" Miles Shannon inquired in a military tone.

"Hello Mr. Shannon I assume, how are you? My name is Robert Walsh on behalf of Pleasant Valley farms that I represent in Granite County Minnesota. You probably heard of us; we know your reputation from some of your customers in the Clinton, Graceville area. What I am calling about is a certain government contractor you know, Ray Clark of Milbank, recommended your services to me citing your twenty years of experience in the trade. I am inquiring as acting president, Miles, would you be interested in an aerial application of a DDT derivative on our acres in Sully County? You are probably aware the mobile dicamba molecules commonly used in chemical compounds are known to be subject to volatilization this late in the season."

"I heard that," Shannon responded. "If possible we would be looking at an early morning application, about 4:00 a.m. or so; my spotters will be out there with headlights on before the fireworks starts." Miles coughed for a few seconds as his mind flashed back to the cockpit of his C-123, escorted by fighter jets as it streaked across the Cambodian border into a combat zone.

"Normally we apply herbicides later in August to test our experimental borer-resistant genetically modified plants. We have changed our strategy to increase yields next season."

"I agree with your strategy Mr. Walsh. We have been dealing with an unusual amount of moisture this August. On top of that it looks to me like another wave of root worm is invading the territory. You know the pesky little buggers thrive on those wet, cool conditions. You can give old Ray all the credit for my occupation–he must be pushing 80 by now. He taught me to fly that old Piper Cub on his farm when I was courting his daughter after I graduated from the university. I enlisted in the Air Force in lieu of being drafted. Ray's training put me in harm's way, and pulled me out of it. I mean nothing could touch us above the jungle, never saw a MIG in 20 flights. A friend of Ray's is a friend of mine. You are in luck this late in the season Mr. Walsh. We have had quite a few cancellations. We can arrange that mixed herbicide-pesticide application for you," Shannon reinforced his *commander* as if he was debriefing him over a carpet-bombing mission of a Viet Cong rice paddy.

"Frankly I am a bit surprised Ray Clark still recommends me. No doubt we had it out a few times over his idea of my perceived mistreatment of his daughter Susan, and our son Gregory, his first grandson–since our divorce. I realize he had to take her side. Father-in-law, you know the drill; he had some influence over his daughter. We separated after 7 years, and then split entirely. I was pretty messed up after Nam I guess. Now I channel a lot of that negative energy into my profession. Just send me the coordinates, we deliver the goods." Shannon opened up as if the brandy in his coffee had warmed his feelings toward a valued comrade in the industry.

"I'll send you that information as soon as I have it. I'm not a high-tech guy. If I circled the area on a map would that work for you?" Walsh negotiated in his typical homespun fashion with Shannon. He could afford to be generous with Pleasant Valley money.

"We can probably use those logistics Mr. Walsh. I can check the courthouse for the coordinates once you send me the information. Early morning application gives a better chance for the chemicals to soak deep into the plant tissue before the 95-degree heat bakes the ground another twelve hours; when the dew point is at 77. Could you hold on for a minute?" thinking of the conditions on the ground on the Mekong, if he were shot down, the air force pilot cupped his hand over the receiver and coughed a spell.

"Thanks for holding sir. As I was saying, we could do ten sections in two hours between four and 6 a.m. For day jobs my fees can run anywhere from $375-$550 dollars an hour per rig. There is a ten percent differential for night flying. That's a big parcel of land out in Sully that will require at least a tanker of fuel. There were some telephone poles, and a few power lines the last time I sprayed in that area. No trees though. My new plane is very quiet. I don't believe a soul lives within ten miles any direction from those sections Mr. Walsh. Night adds risks and costs with my spotters. I'm guessing it could run you around $8500 for close to the four hours it would take plus chemical. My costs vary, depending on weight of the chemical you want applied. You get the pilot for no charge–as experienced as there is in these parts," Shannon was in a much lighter mood after sealing the deal.

"Whatever it takes is fine with me. The job needs to be finished by Labor Day. We're talking maximum application. Those oleic root-borers are killing my flowers. High Oleic leaf spot is taking its toll on the crop as well. We dusted over that. The standard aerial double-dose should finish off the job of the eradication, increasing the efficiency of our operations" and Shannon's treatment would be accelerated by the atrazine and 2-4D applied the first of the month on the ground, Robbie thought to himself.

"Clark was correct in his instincts, yours is exactly the kind of service I am looking for. Send me your billing as soon as possible. We want to make that deadline," Walsh concluded. In fact, the Sully land was already stressed before Walsh salted it; nothing would grow on that land but cocklebur and crowfoot grass for the next two years. Walsh had also fudged a bit on the Brookings summary: 7000 acres of sunflowers had been grown on the land two years earlier rendering the land unsuitable for the growth of safflowers, which was a violation of the original Sexton contract stipulations.

"Then we will be expecting you sometime around the third week until the end of August to make the spraying deadline," Walsh ended on a confident note. "I'll contact you with the coordinates."

"I look forward to doing business with you in the future Mr. Walsh. I checked my records. You are correct, Shannon Aerial has done some custom spraying around Beardsley, MN. I see on the map that is close to Clinton," Shannon confirmed the reconnaissance report.

"Thanks for informing me of that detail. I'll call you to confirm when the check is in the mail Miles."

CHAPTER 23

It did not dawn on David until several years later that as Pastor Jerry White of the Methodist church often reminded his congregation,

"We do not wrestle with flesh and blood, but against principalities, and powers, against the rulers of darkness–against the rulers of darkness of this age–and my dear people those days of lawlessness are upon us and about to overtake us if we do not believe in Jesus."

Beyond that point of teaching, which was largely a generalization about a mystery, there was very little detail added by the preacher about what those various levels of evil he spoke of were to be expected or experienced in the life of the average Methodist. David was as confused by religion as he was by Robbie Walsh's personality and purposes. Were these elements somehow connected? The occult elements of the situation did not escape his thoughts as he dismissed them quickly. But it did seem weird that in the same summer he was the featured progressive farmer in a farm industry magazine–his life was spinning out of control–the success story Colleen Nelson was writing about to be published, at the very moment his organization was *crumbling* at the foundations.

The *Farm Futures* article expressed the challenges and finessed the dilemma Pleasant Valley Farm faced eloquently. The magazine presented a one-page synopsis of the roots of the Zehlen operation in Granite County with a picture of David smiling on the cover. The report was well written but limited in scope, basically scanning the topic of low-input sustainable agriculture. In many respects the article proposed more questions than answers about the survivability of a large privately owned farm–"*the David Zehlen farming operation could be the ultimate nightmare of the sustainable agriculture movement.*"

                                    * * * * *

As part of the penalty for the defaulted 1991 allocation, Pleasant
Valley would not be receiving ASCS payments for the 1992
season. In the final decision of July 1992, Pleasant Valley Farms
were declared ineligible for the government programs they had
depended on for a generation. David Zehlen was charged with
violations, through mismanagement of federal subsidies; he was
being held responsible for the violation, however he was not
found to be guilty by the county committee of a *criminal* act such
as the "fraud" Walsh claimed against him.

David was convinced the problem was a matter of
incompetent record keeping caused by Sexton's refusal to
provide the necessary paperwork–documentation he had been
requesting since March 1991 when Zehlen decided to form a
business of his own that included his partners in MN Go. At that
time Sexton encouraged him to do so. The information Hector
Sexton finally did submit to the ASCS was inaccurate. In
committee June 1992, the ASCS determined the incorrect
documentation indicated "co-mingling of funds" in the joint
operations; as such the organizational units did not meet
government requirements to be counted as "separate" entities.
As a result of records management errors, David and the various
partners who were never clearly advised of what they were
getting into, were required to repay $582,000 to the
government.

When he learned of the ASCS decision, Sexton feigned
innocence and ignorance, claiming he had made payments to the
MinGo partners. He argued that David caused the problem in his
failures to organize the paperwork properly–by the time David
sent him the papers it was basically too late to do anything. The
silent partners who had not received personage payments were
charged with repaying the ASCS. David unflinchingly believed the
defaulted arrangement with Sexton could be presented as
evidence he had complied with all government regulations. He

was confident his patented software system accurately reflected his records of crop production if the case ever went to trial.

His conspiring partners Walsh, and Sexton advised David to appeal the decision to the ASCS as a formality. In private conversations with David, Sexton defended his actions, blaming his secretary for losing some of the government forms, but not to worry. He had made arrangements to repay individual MN Go partners based on stored grain sales and futures; by the time he was ready to fund it, the organization had been mismanaged and disintegrated. To appease David and not cause an uproar, Hector agreed he would compensate David for the 1991 ASCS loss through a system of arranged charge-backs that would be billed as 1991 costs for crop expense and fertilizer in the same fashion he had dealt with some of his other customers in the past.

Up until mid-summer 1992, David Zehlen, as president and administrator of Pleasant Valley, had complied with all the conditions of the bank loan and a succession of redeeming notes relative to leases that dated to March 1991. The loan agreement Robert Walsh had arranged for in the spring 1992 was not completed until June. The bank retained first-lien position on the crop. Sexton held the second lien on the crop he owned. The main purpose of the operations loan was borrowing additional money to account for previous year's loss of Hector Sexton's obligations under the 1991 grower's agreement. On top of the ASCS doppelganger losses, the bank loan became the *issue* the survival of the farm depended on.

David believed there was no way on earth he could be held liable for Hector's share of grower's expenses; besides that, the guarantee built into the contract was valid and would be upheld in litigation regarding what Sexton had, or had not invested in the contract. The slim hope he retained, reinforced by a guaranteed contract agreement, kept his spirits alive after the ASCS default–as the conspiracy upped the ante. In the Walsh-manufactured contingency, a note for $613K was issued to Pleasant Valley Farms under the new administration of Robert Walsh, power-of-attorney on a sublease of 9500 acres of safflowers in South Dakota.

After the note was signed, David's infernal rival would have the ex-*officio* authority he needed to dispose of real and personal property, for his own benefit, or others he manipulated. A sense of dread like no time in life descended upon David. Opening up the Bible at page one, he would meditate on Pastor White's ominous words in the general sermon he recalled bits and pieces of, "He cast on them the fierceness of his indignation, sending Angels of Destruction among them."

In the Zehlen household of his formative years, it was natural to wonder about such realities given his mother's tendency to discuss the preacher's performance, sometimes for an *hour* or so after church. On particularly dull Sunday afternoons, David speculated that perhaps this devastation brought upon him by outsiders with evil objectives could be an expression of the wrath of God for his behavior, in the form of a *curse* for having sex before marriage. "So what I loved the woman didn't I? – proving it a thousand different ways–*some rich sheikhs in Arabia marry their second and third wives at the age of twelve don't they?*" With such thoughts he controlled his conscience.

David was not unwilling if he knew who or what to pray to; like everyone else in junior bible study, he was supposed to be finding some kind of reality, or empowering relationship with the church; something *tangible* from fellowship he, or his mother in a wheelchair could see, or had experienced or witnessed; not the ecumenism some fraud like Vern Bullock preached–who charmed his audiences with Christian rock music. David sensed more than recognized the uncertain belief; at other times the charlatanism caused him to automatically be dismissive, and resistant to all religious authority. In future conflict, Dave would insist upon managing his own therapy, attempting to understand the curse that passed over his land.

As he patrolled the rolling green acres of Pleasant Valley *post-presidency* in his pickup, as depressed as he was, the view of the sunset over Big Stone Lake on a Saturday evening was gorgeous. As he passed the Sioux Historic billboard, he noticed the Labor Day dance ad for the known locally-only band he followed at one time. The band once called "The Derelict

Brothers" was playing at The Cove the last time he saw and chatted with some of the members. Whatever happened to those boys he wondered? As the dilemma he faced became more ominous sounding every day, Dave thought of the past as he inserted his "Violent Iron" rhythmic rock album into his CD player; soon, immersed in the stereo sound of his newly installed JBLs, David found himself listening more carefully than ever to the fateful lyrics he had heard a hundred times, unplugged, live and recorded–the tenor vocals of his friend Tim Cassandria would be ringing in his ears for hours,

> "Winding down the spiral staircase
> Where no one's allowed to escape their fate"

CHAPTER 24

Sexton notified Walsh that his brother-in-law Jeff Provo had personally inspected the safflowers in Sully County. Both he and the insurance man were satisfied with the growing and blooming progress at mid-summer. The weight and the oleic oil content of the seed had met specifications. The point of their discussions was that both Sexton and Provo were contemplating cancelling the last insurance premium payment of $55K with Security Risk of Illinois due August 31st.

"Maybe we don't have to worry about that last payment, Robbie? Unless you have that kind of money just lying around gathering dust; you might as well save yourself some cash. It seems like kind of a waste of money if we don't need it."

In the bartering process, Sexton implied that Walsh and Provo were committed up to their necks already as partners, and Walsh owed him a favor. As power of attorney, he could finesse the cancellation issue best with Jessen and Eastman of First Omaha, convincing them to look the other way and trust Sexton's years of field experience, when the loan was invested– and cash was *tight* before harvest–naively believing Walsh was actually accommodating his wishes without the usual resistance whenever cash was mentioned; he was more than happy to accommodate Hector's decision to drop the insurance.

Walsh had inspected the crop on a bi-weekly basis since the sprouts broke ground in May, the weather was beyond expectations, hot and dry since early July. He had other leases to ensure and administrative functions on his mind as he mouthed another oracle,

"You will do it your way regardless of what I say Hector. Just like David. He hired me as a consultant; but he never listened to my advice from day one. It's your crop and your risk." Walsh was not about to blow the whistle on Sexton at that point; he had another trick up his sleeve, another idea that involved using both

Zehlen and Sexton again to his advantage. The conversation resumed,

"I would rather have you pay off some of these unpaid fertilizer invoices and sift in a few pesticide accounts payable David has been requesting from you, and complaining to me about since last spring. I have some ideas about what we can do with those invoices to discuss with you, but not at this moment."

By June 1992, Robert Walsh was generally managing the Pleasant Valley office, overseeing the PVC billing with Phyllis Zehlen as his assistant, while Dave was assigned to road work, meandering around dozens of leases stretched across three states, imagining Walsh was actually effectively handling the farming operations for lack of understanding the personal, and financial extent of the takeover–and amidst the dense confusion the conspiracy depended on. It was like his mind was spinning a surreal version of reality he had not prepared for, or experienced in his previous life, brought on by stress, pain, and side-effects of low dose morphine.

"If you have final authority as power of attorney Robbie, you need to recognize that I have paid what I believe is my share on those bills. You need to put on your bifocals, and examine the fine print of the contract I signed with David in 199l Robbie where it says, 'the grower will reimburse the manager' that would be Pleasant Valley and their employees including David Zehlen–for all *reasonable* and necessary expenses incurred by the manager in carrying out his duties for me. I need to see a combined statement of those expenses on clear and understandable documents, not assorted notes and scraps with a few comments here and there that show the nature and scope of David's expenses on the South Dakota leases. I haven't bothered yet to expose a rumor that somebody's men have engaged in what might be considered 'illegal' activity. I'm not saying who these men were, or if this report is evidence of a violation of the grower's agreement by those unidentified employees hauling my soybeans and sunflowers to the Alberta Cargill elevator for cash without my knowledge," Sexton attempted to apply his negotiating skills as far as possible,

"Now then if you Robbie, sitting in the administrator's chair could finally establish some kind of order in that organization, it might be a different story. I might be able to reconfigure some of those bills into my system. I have been waiting for the *opportunity* you might say, to make some decisions on how to rectify the situation. That is if you as power of attorney were to review the supposedly overdue invoices and supporting documents; and along with their reproductions, you could instruct David in a method I have used in my previous dealings, implementing the technology we need in your office to produce documents that reflect legitimate and necessary expenses for production of my safflowers. We have encountered similar situations in our work, previously have we not? I am confident you can coach David how to do it." Sexton knew from experience minor adjustments would be necessary; there was no consistent design–no two white-collar crimes were exactly the same.

"I'll see what I can do Hector. Call me if there are any more problems," Walsh was satisfied with input to the daily grind, with one ear tuned to the broadcast of the *Sioux Jackrabbits* game crackling in the background.

"You bet Robbie. I will talk to you later."

* * * * *

If David Zehlen had studied his cultural anthropology lessons he might have learned what he sensed, that in the final decade of the 20th Century, the model of ultra-successful farming the Zehlen story reflects, contradicts the traditional models of life in America that history and literature reveal. The remote Minnesota country culture, as his social studies teacher Ron Kleven tried to explain to the disinterested class of sophomores, in reality, was *not* the paradise it seemed. David recalled the spectrum of humanities offered at Rockland High.

"The last test results are on the books; let me repeat class– if you students are ever to understand morbid religious frenzies, lynch law and other devastating phenomena of contemporary Americana–we must look more closely into the psychological tissue of our rural life. For that reason class, this year we are moving forward with the cross-studies curriculum, linking history with Mrs. Brewster's English II, full semester course on the subject of agriculture in American Literature; when we move ahead we will be reading *Under the Lion's Paw*, by Hamlin Garland, as an example of oppression in rural society. When we study *The Scarlet Letter* we learn that a secret illegitimate pregnancy is at the heart of the plot; for the drama portion of the semester Mr. Furan will be directing and selecting the cast for *Cat on a Hot Tin Roof* in preparation for the Junior class play, and so on." Don't be overly excited class, the baseball coach thought to himself as he delivered the message the first week of classes. David could read his teachers' minds in his halcyon days.

"At the end of the semester we will read and study a few novels from Faulkner's exhibits that need to be supplemented by the sober case-history and by the economic-*psychiatric* appraisal of the conditions of life in our rural sections."

David had no idea what Mr. Kleven, his B-squad football coach, was talking about at the time. English was his worst class; history was a close second. Could those lessons possibly be relevant to current events of the 1990's?

* * * * *

There were a number of "psychiatric and cultural pitfalls" that littered the steps of Mr. Zehlen's abrupt fall from *grace* and the "gradual cultural impoverishment" of his personality that contributed to his deteriorating mental condition. After receiving his license in 1969, Robert Walsh's brother Ansel became a practicing psychologist operating out of a clinic that specializing in research on post war trauma in relation to married life in the civilian environment. Ansel agreed to perform an analysis of David's "mental" health as it affected his domestic life and management of Pleasant Valley. In February 1993, Dr. Ansel Walsh conducted a psychological evaluation complete with a Myers-Briggs battery of tests, administered in person over the course of two days in the Anothene presidential suite.

By the end of the psychological testing sessions, David's counselors had him convinced the research would be used in developing a mental incompetence defense in case Hector hauled him into court over the contract. Instead the psychiatric report concluded that David was an unconscientiously, emotional sociopath, with below-average intelligence, capable of any sort of "mischief" short of homicide. Phyllis Zehlen added a few choice anecdotes to the final report about David's forgetfulness around the office, confirming that David had been asking questions about what Robbie was doing snooping around his Anothene closets and drawers when he wasn't around.

There was absolutely no doubt according to the psychological profile submitted to the court later, that David was capable of theft and violence, particularly against members of the opposite sex. He had as much as admitted it under the probing of psychoanalytic technique. Sealed files of Nancy Zehlen's contributions to the psychological profile of her husband still exist; but have been kept in locked storage in the files of Granite County Attorney William Watkins, supposedly to protect David's wife from further damage public revelation of the information could lead to for her, and her four children.

From the psychological perspective of his adversaries, it is reasonable to assume that David Zehlen, born successful, had never learned how to deal with failure. As the condition drove him over the edge of the forty-year reality that no longer existed–he continued to fantasize that things would work out. Accustomed to control, it was unfathomable he must depend on Walsh as power of attorney. There was small comfort knowing that after July it was his former employee–Walsh's obligation to collect on the guarantee. Was there that much difference between a trustee and power of attorney he asked himself over and over? His doubts gathered momentum as symptoms of angst interfered with his thoughts–in psychiatric terms David's interior monologues validating multiple realities about unexplainable mysteries–where culture, language, and the power of adversaries, mix and matched within treacherous circumstances shaped his personality, now hobbled in the "walking psychosis" stage. In the process, the emerging vocal persona asserted a new ideology, constantly reciting a script that sounded a bit like quackery, as it incorporated legal terms indiscriminately. At the bottom line, the altered David persona insisted that he had a contract indemnity that protected him against all odds. As far as he knew that agreement and guaranty had never been canceled; and that reality became the core issue as Walsh consolidated his control over Pleasant Valley.

* * * * *

"Alright Hector the time has come," *we have a few secrets between us,* Walsh was thinking. "You have suggested I never do you any favors. Now I have one for you. As you know I have been in discussions about the loan David Zehlen took out on your crops. We don't need to go into too much detail. There is another issue you may not be aware of now that the note was cleared. You need to know the issue of the RTC default was not accurately described in the application. We had to finesse that obstacle or David could not borrow a dime. Although Zehlen and I have discussed the matter I did not advise him not to disclose that debt. That's not the point."

"It's hard to believe that detail escaped detection by the loan officer," Hector responded.

"That's where my influence with the bank enters the picture. I am not authorized to inform every person involved of the details of the foolproof design. You are an exception Hector, welcome to the infrastructure," Walsh demonstrated the tone of command he reserved for dealing with subordinates.

"I spoke with loan officer Jessen about the application fraud and the insurance issue, and sent him some snapshots of the high-oleic safflowers; he agrees that the insurance is not an issue. You can cancel the premium with Jeff Provo if you choose to do so; he will sign a contract waiver. It's a risk. We know that, but Zehlen's conduct over the last few months has deteriorated his credibility. If it comes to a lawsuit you're better off taking the loss on a bad loan to Zehlen rather than facing promissory fraud charges. I have a long time relationship with Tom Jessen soon to be a bank President who observed the crop early in June. So he's in on this decision. If the paper work indicates purpose, Zehlen is already facing criminal fraud charges on the loan application for not disclosing the Midwest Federal S&L default, after the bank attorneys finish their assignment."

"Just what do you intend to do Robbie?"

"I can't inform you of every detail at this time because the situation is too complicated. I don't want to discuss it over the phone either. But put it this way–you don't want to be facing some judge in district court who suspects a fraud and calls for three times the money now do you?"

"Of course not, but I already have $350 grand invested in that crop. I don't want to lose it. SigCo has been one of my best sponsors over the years. What am I supposed to tell them when the bank claims my crop?" Sexton's confidence wobbled, knowing he had been used as *bait* in a larger scheme, now he was hooked.

"You will think of an excuse Hector. Your partners can write the experimental seed off as a loss. I have the power of attorney to draw up the papers as soon as I can work out the details of his separation with David and his wife. I need you to be aware Phyllis Zehlen will be our new director of operations for the 'Interwest' division of Marketing International. In the new organization we ensure David's complete removal as president and director of farming operations. Think about it–what is a third of a million loss to your billionaire partners that have insurance– what you and I both know is nothing more than a drop in the bucket compared to what David estimates you owe him Hector?"

"And that would be?"

"David says over $1.75 million. I say closer to $2.5M if you factor in non-collection on the 1992 harvest, along with the loss of *all* ASCS funds you are causing by your crimes Hector. You're not a very good bookkeeper are you? Or are you running two sets of books, in your system? Like David. In your accounts, you are ahead at least $1.2 M–but you have failed to fulfill by breaching the contract. You are liable for the bank loan Hector. Only with my help will you escape that pitfall by the skin of your teeth."

"I see where you are going with this Robbie," Hector thought of saying *take me to your leader.*

"One day at a time, you remember the old motto of Anothene don't you Hector? I have the plaque in my bottom drawer."

"No I never attended their sessions."

"We go by the golden rule at Interwest, he who holds the gold *rules.* So remember that. I'm letting you know the Pleasant Valley loan disbursement will be indirectly routed to me through Tom Jessen. I am in charge of the PVC account; he knows the details. We had to structure the bank investment this way because Zehlen is already in default on the loan I am disbursing. With thousands of acres and millions of dollars worth of crops in the field, most of them in South Dakota mortgaged under this loan. I am administrating the account and running the farm through harvest. By then the bank knows I have taken over completely for David, and running the farm on bank money. That's really all you need to know for the present. As I said Jessen, Provo and I say the crop looks good enough to drop the insurance. But it's up to you. Do you understand?"

"I hear you Robbie. I'm depending on your *counseling* at this point. I need to review the details of the deal I put together in '91 with Zehlen again with Jessen. We can't afford any screw ups at this stage."

"We discussed that problem. Jessen said he would like to discuss the situation with you at the end of the safflower harvest–if there is one. If you wait patiently you can cut your losses, and make a restitution claim against David on the South Dakota loan."

"What loan are you talking about?"

"You will learn about that soon enough. I have to move along to another customer.

Good day Hector."

"Okay Robbie whatever you say," he had no idea what Walsh had up his sleeve.

CHAPTER 25

After Walsh was assigned power of attorney for Pleasant Valley Farms, and he was deposed as president, David spent as little time as possible around the homestead; he was sleeping over at his dad's cottage awaiting repercussions from the ASCS penalty, completely avoiding the office in Rockland where Walsh had taken his chair. David was on the hourly payroll. Phyllis, who was having difficulty communicating the new policy, notified Dave through the mail he was expected to turn in a time sheet to account for his working hours. He knew absolutely nothing about where the *rest* of the bank loan was being allocated.

On one of his trips into the City of Rockland, buying parts for his dad at the local hardware store, David bumped into an old friend Jim Ferguson who had been teaching out of the state a number of years. For the summer, Ferguson was hanging around town working for his father-in-law, waiting to learn if his application to teach middle school in Eau Claire, WI was accepted.

In a brief conversation in the nuts and bolts aisle, David filled in Ferguson as best he could about what happened to him. They would need to spend more time dissecting the situation. He didn't have much to discuss because frankly he was unsure what was going to happen. The case was bound to end up in civil court.

"Last time I heard Pleasant Valley was on the verge of *incredible* success David. My father-in-law Vince showed me the magazine article. How's it going man?" he patted him on the back lightly.

"Well Jim we missed a few curves in the road and wound up in the ditch, out of the farming business since 1992. The bankers were successful in claiming the collateral as being theirs, and belonging to them; however, on the collection of the collateral, as it is given on the note, the case only provided for the collection of the soybeans and the sunflowers under the contract–there's no accounting for the loss of the safflowers. The income from the safflowers was a complete loss; however, that did not prevent the bank from collecting on the debt owed by the owners of the crop at that time."

"I'm not an expert Dave. Just briefly can you explain how this lack of collection on the safflowers affected the bank foreclosure on the farm in the coming years?"

"It was because of the lack of collection on the contract at that time that caused the error. It appears that they collected on the collateral; the contract had a guarantee that provided for the collection of the collateral that would have applied to the Sexton contract and all their costs at the time; the bank failed to do their job to collect their own collateral from those who owed it. Under this interpretation the collateral appears to be owed by me when in fact it is owed by Ceres," Dave concluded as his face returned to normal after grimacing through what sounded like a practiced script, "The way I see it, amidst a lot of confusion about who profited in this misunderstanding about a contract one of my employees caused, he created suspicion and false charges. We have no documentation per se of the date the formal foreclosure process started. I assume it was in motion by the middle of October 1992. Robert Walsh, the main conspirator, wrote a letter to his partner at Christmas that year; he mentioned the conspiracy was in progress by then, but didn't mention the foreclosure specifically," Dave would often ramble on at least five minutes at a time on his conspiracy theory.

In the wake of the tale, Ferguson encouraged David to keep an accurate journal that documented the ordeal. If nothing else, Dave should store and manage his records; the cold files might keep the case alive in the future. This was the first decent advice he had heard in five years from his 40-year-old mentor with a Master's in English and a minor in philosophy. Emerging out of the religious chaos as a spokesman for moderation, as one of the first of the local youth to enter and just as quickly exit the dialectical materialism debate, Ferguson viewed the conspiracy in the words of *Jaspers* as another "inscrutable configuration of sophistry." What little that definition meant at the time he read, it made more sense when he came in contact with white collar crime on the border.

It would take a very cunning and intelligent being to eliminate major commercial players David and Jack in the blink of an eye–something must have gone haywire. It would be easier to deceive the king's court than the progressive father and son duo he was familiar with, before misfortune had plagued them. David kept mentioning this "Machiavellian" archetype that was running the farm, with vague descriptions of how that situation developed. To Ferguson, these characterizations of an ultimate nemesis reminded him of names tossed about in graduate English seminars, the wicked administrator Creon, Iago the false informer, and Chillingsworth, mysterious nemesis of the *Scarlet Letter*.

"Now then David, here we may have a fleeting glance at Jung's *daemon* described in *Late Thoughts*–Carl's take on the hitherto undefined creature of the subconscious apparently with enough power to influence life changing events."

Ferguson could go on for it seemed like hours with this analytic psychology jargon that made no sense whatsoever to Dave in his PTSD condition; but it was concerned counsel of a friend that mattered most at a crisis time that seemed to linger on and on. If there was ever such a thing as an intellectual leader of the Rockland post-Christian movement–it was Ferguson the teacher philosopher who evolved into one of the few friends David Zehlen had after the farm was *lost*.

More of an agnostic himself, Ferguson recognized what he called the "phony fervor" leaders like Bullock demonstrated, indicating they had *no relationship with God* whatsoever in their hypocrisy; at the same time, they were not true believers in Jesus, because none of them had any spiritual depth either. Lay leaders dominated discussion with other subjects, trivia and trifles in church, where there was more open discussion and free speech than in school. Conversation about such ideas–as God, the Holy Spirit, and instruction in the catechism–the topic of senior-high religious instructions were not considered necessary components of secular discussion of wealth, ethics, and morals in the community and media.

Out of such methods and meditating upon them, Ferguson managed to escape personal controversy over belief, secure in the idea that learning throughout adulthood was the *only* valid form of therapy. Realizing Jung had over fifty therapy sessions with some of his clients, there was never any question in Ferguson's mind, of the value of continued therapy. Over time, Ferguson believed he could ultimately determine a man's character and mental development through assessment of degrees of religious experience and a person's relationship with the "higher power"–he shared these fundamental beliefs with Dave Zehlen who continued to believe in the twelve steps to sobriety.

* * * * *

After videotaping several interviews and reviewing the charges against David Zehlen, Ferguson determined his intervention was necessary because psychological factors were involved in the swindle engineered by the conspiracy–because Robert Walsh, Prosecutor William Watkins, and public defense attorney Holbrooke used various psychological methods, duress, intimidation, insinuations and threats to confuse Zehlen into a series of bad legal decisions–in the process David became unstable, and a dysfunctional manager of his own business. The rapid deterioration of his universe contributed substantially to his declining mental condition.

Ferguson was unaware of the details, but could have guessed the contents of an affidavit Ansel Walsh submitted to the Granite County Sheriff's department;

Dear Attorney Watkins,

Mr. Robert Walsh of the firm of Marketing International LLC has recently inquired about my counseling and psychological testing services; he informed me of his concerns for his client David Zehlen, once executive officer of Pleasant Valley Farms. During the normal course of his work my brother discovered and observed evidence that Mr. Zehlen was engaged in criminal activities. For that reason and the injustice being done to his wife and four children he asked me to intervene and requested my services. My assessment of his personality supports the probability that Mr. Zehlen stole money and property from his partner.

Attorney Watkins I strongly recommend the court review Robert Walsh's reports of David Zehlen's criminal activities. I agree with my brother that David Zehlen has an over inflated ego, and an exaggerated opinion of himself. In my opinion he resembles a predatory con man that misled the government, using his business and wife to cover up a personal enrichment scheme. In my professional opinion, it is the dominant Zehlen personality traits clearly associated with dishonesty and conscientiousness that are responsible, indicating David feels no remorse for the crimes he has committed, or the widespread financial damage he has caused. With the Prosecutor I agree that mandatory sentencing guidelines call for stiffer penalties where no remorse is shown. And then there is the issue of the magnitude of loss suffered by his partner to deal with in restitution court. Though David has shown no tendencies to seek revenge against those who have accused him of crimes, he does not yet admit guilt.

David has a history of addiction to pain killers for his heart and back conditions that restrict his movement and impair his consciousness. In his condition he cannot perform normal farm labor that require strength, lifting heavy bales, shoveling grain, changing oil and tires on the farm equipment, any longer according to Robert. For those reasons he is undependable. David is nervous and evasive, fearing inevitable pressure when the bureau begins interrogating him. Uncertainty renders him incapable of making decisions. Long term use of prescription drugs such as low dose morphine David has used regularly since back surgery can damage the brain. That may be the source of David Zehlen's personality defect. With no meaningful work to look forward to, considering repressed anger and frustration involved, it is possible Zehlen could pose a terroristic threat to the community if he becomes more alienated.

Sincerely, Ansel Walsh, M.D. Clinical Psychology

There was little doubt according to the independent psychological profile provided by the Walsh tandem, that appeared on the Rockland County Attorney's desk in late February 1993, seamlessly submitted with the "sealed" depositions of spousal sources Phyllis and Nancy Zehlen, to whom David had demonstrated irresponsible, criminal behavior in the demise of Pleasant Valley Corporation. In their depositions, Nancy and Phyllis provided critical information to the Granite County court that David alone was culpable. Combined with Ansel Walsh's assessment, David's *fate* was confirmed.

CHAPTER 26

As he appeared at the office of Robert Walsh in Brookings, South Dakota on the morning of August 8, 1992–David Zehlen was a weary and desperate man after another sleepless night, when the temperature never dipped below 87 degrees, followed by an eighty-mile drive.

"David! My god man, are you ill? You are sweating *torrents* and need to cool down after a drive through this sweltering heat. Radio in Watertown claims the dew point could reach a record today at 72," Walsh reported like the KDLO weatherman. "Have a seat in my office, sit next to the air conditioner; make yourself feel comfortable. I'll make you some Taster's choice. You need some caffeine to unwind after *that* drive from Rockland."

"The air is out on the truck, haven't been able to fix it."

Walsh wasn't serving iced tea that day. Nothing made Dave feel any better after the *Farm Futures* dream-scenario evaporated on a muggy morning in July, the day the red flag on the mail box appeared, when Shorty Belgum dropped off the last of his rural mail. He would not forget the moment he opened the envelope containing the latest news of the imploding disaster with his son's Swiss army knife, using it because he had mislaid his Barlow somewhere in the tool shed. David recalled the symbolism as he delivered his oldest son a legacy lesson now and then.

He would not soon forget the moment he opened the envelope containing the bad news, and how it contrasted with the Swiss heritage of wealth and savings that enabled the early founders of the family to emigrate to America with some cash in their pockets, ready to stake their fortune in Granite County as Noah's great grandfather had, on and on, down the ancestral line that he felt he could preach about if it came to that. In David's version of events, the Zehlen lineage stretched back to the Black

Forest region of Germany bordering Switzerland in about the years 14-1500;

"It was near Bavaria where the legend of the Zehlen name became storied for its generosity. Even today the community holds a celebration for *'goodwill to all men'* similar to May Day in this country. At the continental divide, the family roots crossed the Luchsinger family line of farmers, related to your great Uncle Martin Zummach we bought the house from, who was originally from the same district in the old country–by chance or design, they all settled in Traverse and Granite counties in the late 19th century." His eyes watered a few bitter tears as he stared into the bleak news, outlined by the orange ball in the east. "The red handle embossed with a tiny cross symbolizes the peaceful yet potent power of the Swiss; this small gift is my sign to you that *agriculture* has been the Zehlen family tradition since the middle ages. Always keep that in mind son."

In retrospect, it was ironic that such tiny details mattered. Was it a coincidence he was using the gift he had given Noah for Christmas–as a letter opener on a day of doom? How could he forget that event, scarcely two weeks from the day his interview was published in an industry magazine that had to be one of the greatest events of his life–when less than a month later he was seriously contemplating taking drastic measures against his own–perhaps *another* man's life?

For a few days in late summer, news of the *Farm Futures* article, and benefits of the publicity, though the magazine was not widely circulated, coming on the heels of the crushing days of spring seemed to rejuvenate family spirits; over the course of the '92 Memorial Day celebrations in Rockland, there was a family outing followed by fireworks at Lakeside Park. Mom, David and the kids spent Monday afternoon visiting with grandma Grace who lived in the Lakeside Manor Apartments on the edge of the park. Later that night when the kids were all tucked in bed, the stressed out husband and wife shared a rare moment of connubial bliss. Since those blessed days of relative peace and harmony, David's Pleasant Valley existence had turned into a complete nightmare like nothing he had ever experienced, or was prepared to experience in a lifetime.

* * * * *

While there were rare moments of marital bliss and harmony at home, there was an important series of tasks awaiting David in the business office. Robbie Walsh was taking full advantage of the confused state of his *victim* as he puttered around David's mahogany desk. As if fixated on organization, Walsh was constantly sorting and shuffling through papers on the desk, and in the drawers. He spent five minutes preparing a mug of coffee for David Zehlen who sat silent, staring vacantly out the window of Walsh's office with a mournful look on his face as if to say, "What am I going to do now Robbie? Oh, thank you *for a spoonful of water.*"

"Here you go David. No need to look so somber, everything's under control. You have nothing to worry about any more. The bank loan has been approved, what more can you expect under the circumstances?" Walsh's voice boomed, amplified by the high ceiling office. The new boss was in complete command of the situation. Before training, he just needed to make a few adjustments for darkness on the copy machine.

"I wanted you to be here today David because you need to know exactly how much Hector Sexton owes Pleasant Valley Farms. Mind you I'm not exactly sure how much he owes; but I do know he hasn't sent Pleasant Valley a dollar on the contract since spring planting," Walsh carried on a one-sided conversation as he scurried about the office organizing the items he expected David to assemble.

"To collect the debt Sexton owes you there are a few simple tasks I have arranged for you according to classification and category. All you have to do is follow my instructions. It is necessary to do these things before the three parties involved can come to any kind of resolution. I believe we have come up with an amicable solution that will benefit all the parties involved."

"According to Hector the billing situation is the result of a problem you created. He claims he has paid you enough. You never did have an accurate system of accounting on the personage," Walsh expressed little sympathy. "No business can survive with such a flimsy accounting structure. That's why you are no longer director of Pleasant Valley Farms."

"Nobody said there'd be days like this Robbie," David reflected on Lennon's idea, "like I am having with Hector *collecting* on the contract. I handled the invoicing with Hector. I know it is accurate. This crisis didn't happen overnight you know. Sexton owes me close to a million five; but he has only paid about half of that. I invested the ASCS funds in the partnership. And then you factor in the June loan for a million two that went into his crop. He owes me that too."

"Hector says the accounts only show figures based on your projections of revenue, never showing the actual invoicing and producer management; along with that, he claims are your extravagant expenditures of his money. Hector claims he paid $750K straight up and thousands of hourly cash wages to MinGo custom operations employees that don't show up on your accounting spread sheets. He has a different version of the contract." Walsh paused, coughing to clear his throat. "Sexton claims your men were skimming grain, running it late night through back roads to elevators across the border for cash in Odessa and Bellingham. A lot of wages and fuel expense went with those trucks. I'm not saying I believe the rumor. You can't prove it's not true either. From now on you have nothing to worry about. Working with Hector we came up with a plan so you can salvage some of that cash you claim you have lost."

"I hope you don't believe that nonsense about those phony deals Robbie," David reacted, stunned into submission by the remarks of the man he had known less than a year, who was now *mocking* him as a final insult. "I have never committed a crime like that in my life, and neither have my partners in MinGo. If Hector had been fulfilling on his contract obligations I wouldn't be this desperate. It's his fault this all happened. An audit would prove it."

"Yes David I hear you. Just who do you imagine is going to pay for a TILA when you have no money? I wouldn't be so quick to place the blame on Hector. According to the stakeholders–that would be Nancy and Phyllis–they claim you made all the decisions about where the money went. That's why they elected *me* power of attorney," Walsh stated with a military tone of authority in his voice like David had never noticed before.

"As I will demonstrate, we have come up with a method of correction that will *even* the deficit. Now that you're relaxed a little and cooled off from that brutal drive in this August heat and humidity–the dew point reached 78–highest they've seen this summer; you can just step over next to the machine. Let me show you how we run this operation. The coffee is on me. It will only take a couple hours, and the whole infernal business is finished," Robbie conducted his lesson to the novice.

"This is a method we have developed based on our past experience in similar situations as an efficient system to recover some of the money you believe you lost to Hector in the last year. I assume you know how to operate the photocopy machine. Would you like a refill David, before we get started? Or do you prefer instant?"

"No thank you, I drank a thermos full of ice tea on the way down here. But I would be interested to know what you have in mind. I'm ready to get to work, but first I must use your restroom to wash my hands," *I must have a fever*, he thought to himself. In the john he gathered his thoughts. As he looked in the mirror that was so old and dirty, it was almost as if he could make out tiny moving figures at the corroded edges where the metal frame met glass. After he washed his hands, avoiding his face with the chemical smelling gel, he took a leak and flushed the filthy toilet. Back in the office Walsh was rummaging through a filing cabinet behind his desk. He turned around with a folder in his hands, placed it on his desk and sat down.

"I have this much information for you. I must say Phyllis performs her job effectively for Pleasant Valley Farms. When it comes to business that concerns the safflowers contract, I make sure of that to protect our company interests," Walsh attempted to reinforce his new trainee.

"Your step-mother sends me copies of all the accounts payable and receivable for the corporation. You handled the billings until things went haywire. I was never that concerned with your farming operations in Minnesota or North Dakota for that matter; but she sends me the stuff anyway. I like her work. Phyllis someday may have a stakeholder's interest when I expand my marketing business, but that is beside the point today," he walked over to the copier, holding up a paper in his right hand.

"I so seldom use this machine these days. Just last week the service repair man put in a new toner cartridge; that's all it needed. What I have in my hand is an invoice of an advance from Hector's company Ceres in the amount of $177,000 for fertilizer to be applied on farmland that was to be used to produce the safflower oil seed crop. The method we are using today is a common business practice that takes advantage of modern technology."

"First we create a template by making 30 copies of the front side. After that we flip one of those papers over and put it on top of the new pile of white paper, found in this drawer-like compartment, below the scanner bed I am showing you. You are now ready to proceed. Next we place the first of your 30 new invoices to Hector for $10,000 each on the copy plate, face up and push down the cover, and hit the green button like this. Presto! Let's see how your new billing looks?" Walsh pulled a fresh copy from the output slot. It appeared the training exercise was successful as David and Robbie examined the document that had become a two-sided invoice, on one side was the paid bill for fertilizer; on the other side was the new invoice for 10K.

"This looks very good David. Professional job if you ask me. Now all you do is repeat this same process thirty more times. Remember to keep flipping the template document. Let's see how the next ones look? Then you stagger the dates over May through June and sign them. That's all there is to it. To save time you can use the Pleasant Valley Farms stamp that Phyllis furnished me. Make sure you change the dates so there are no duplicates." Walsh continued to tinker on the machine, adjusting the darkness as he spoke.

"Now then, if you see a signature from Hector on the back side, just trim it off. Just like that your new billing statement is created setting forth an itemization of fertilizer used on the fields upon which the safflowers are being grown for Hector and his company," David was in such a hurry to complete the task his mind was not functioning critically as Walsh led him through the clerical steps.

"I'll be watching over your shoulder. Once we have created the new billings, let me look them over before you sign. This process is going to take some time. Along with this document I have several invoices for work on some other leases that I just received from Phyllis. Just a few of those I wouldn't worry about. Let me know when you get to them, but we use the same process. Once each new billing is created, stamp it with Pleasant Valley logo. If you get lost I'm here to help you," Dave was feeling nauseated as Walsh finished hands-on training.

Under the stress, feeling side effects of his medications, David felt like a *zombie* after going through the motions on the weirdest day he had ever spent in an office, where clerical was never his line of work. It did occur to him more than once, he was being a fraud, but he was not exactly sure how, or why he could be guilty of any kind of a crime since all three parties were involved in the little charade? No money was lost if the deal went through. For the next two hours David stood at attention as his back ached continuously, following commander Walsh's instructions. What could possibly be wrong with following the PHC power of attorney's orders? Or, was he being *manipulated,* like the Brooklyn shopkeeper selling fake lottery tickets–and laundering money–trapped by the mob into doing whatever dirty deed they forced him to do for the loan that apparently could never be paid back; he–they–he wasn't sure who anymore? ... forced into the swindle, to ensure the *good fellas* wouldn't burn down his grocery store.

As he worked feverishly, David never suspected the invoices floating through the U.S mail would be dragging him deeper into the fraud Hector had created; and that the additional charges were for acres that he had already been reimbursed for–and those expenses were exaggerated to compensate for other layers of fraud Hector had shuffled him through.

"I've got the postage covered David. Don't worry about that!" Walsh yelled from his inner sanctum.

David argued with himself. Walsh must know what he was doing? He always handled the paperwork on legal issues, even before assuming power of attorney over Pleasant Valley. Under some scenarios the whole idea seemed sane, a series of legitimate personal transactions involving three partners made some sense, as Walsh explained his instructions on a day David fell–unconscious victim to an outside force–not understanding what he was doing could backfire on him, naively assuming the situation would improve once Hector complied with the charge-back plan.

The simple task turned into an agonizing process as David pushed the buttons and arranged papers on the flatbed of the printer. His back pain felt like an ice pick sticking in his spine, while he rationalized in between the repetitive steps that he was doing the right thing for Pleasant Valley–at the same time he was doing the *will* of Walsh who he knew he couldn't trust. He was uncomfortable violating his own principles in his deals with Hector Sexton, not applying sound and legitimate accounting principles in his business. If any fraud was ever charged against Pleasant Valley Farms, it would not be completely his fault. It was the best he could hope for.

Before he finished, David was feeling the drowsy side effects of the synthetic morphine he was taking to alleviate his back pain as Robbie popped in and out of his office to keep the coffee brewing. For two hours David kept plowing through an uncomfortable and unfamiliar chore, using every bit of his strength to remain standing; his ruptured disk was inflamed after standing for what seemed like all day at the copy machine. After 120 minutes of monotony his head was spinning as he yelled back into the inner office,

"I think I'm done Robbie. We've got a few extras. I'm ready to sign them; should be out of here around noon." He felt like he would collapse if he stood another minute. His head was spinning, his body was numb except for the stinging pain in his coccyx he aggravated every time he bent over, or moved suddenly.

Walsh dashed out of the office and quickly cleared a space in the midst of tape and scissors scattered around the small work area. Leaning over the pile of papers for a closer look, adjusting his bifocals, he began quickly sorting the wheat from the chaff, one stack for the good, bad copies consigned to the waste basket. Still sweating, David returned from the restroom to the task, as Walsh directed him to sign a half dozen papers, the ones he judged had the best overall appearance. He was ready to proceed upon Walsh's orders as if he were obeying his industrial arts teacher Mr. Fowler;

"These invoices look good David. Go ahead and sign them. Then you just fold and seal them in envelopes. Hector will be more than happy to get this debt settled." Walsh seemed unusually pleased with David's work for a change.

"I can tell you are tired David. You did a lot of work today. Just sign the billings and you can take off. Be home in time to milk the cows." Walsh chuckled. "I'll drop them off at the post office for you with my outgoing mail."

Within minutes of the time David exited the Marketing International premises, Walsh was on the phone dialing up Hector Sexton in his Fargo, North Dakota office. By the end of August 1992, Pleasant Valley Farms with David Zehlen still listed a director, received a check for $40K for the earliest chargebacks from Hector Sexton and Ceres, Inc. The extra ten grand was to be viewed as the excess reimbursement for charge-backs that David Zehlen claimed for billable hours worked specifically related to the South Dakota sunflowers that both men had their claims relative to. Of course, Robert never sent the invoices through the mail; he hand-delivered ten of the best copies to Hector Sexton at Trevett's Cafe in Milbank a week later.

Driving back to the farm through ninety degree August heat, David was looking ahead until mid-September harvest when 1992 elevator revenue starts pouring in. Along with the rest of his family, he believed the crisis had stabilized; the loan that Robert Walsh had negotiated for them with Omaha Federal would allow them to make it through another harvest. Another good year would *right* the ship. Jack's dollars invested in IRAs, which at one time he planned to use to bail out the farm if all other crisis averting measures failed, were available. David was expecting his dividend of $12,000 from Cenex to look forward to; that along with his Wells Fargo checking account with a few thousand dollars remaining in it would have to last through harvest.

"If we make it through December," David soloed in his pickup as he drove home in the sultry heat; in a rare optimistic mood he found himself singing along with Merle and the Strangers. For the time being, he was satisfied he had done something positive for Pleasant Valley.

* * * * *

As if anything else could possibly go wrong, in the tumultuous summer of 1992, in the middle of August a series of high cumulus clouds descended upon the Great Plains. Violent thunderstorms generated in the high Rockies rumbled across Nebraska, Iowa and the Dakotas; strong winds, thunder, lightning, and large hail stones battered eastern South Dakota over the course of two weeks. At night the temperature dropped to a low of 44 degrees. The unseasonable cloudburst delivered the Sexton safflowers a beating they would never recover from. Though he disguised his sentiments about the disaster, Robert Walsh was *secretly* delighted.

CHAPTER 27

In the meantime, Robert Walsh maintained steady correspondence with his brother Ansel who was editing a college text book entitled "Applications in Gestalt Therapy." Ansel's research reinforced the Walsh theory that David was engaged in criminal activities, providing direct evidence of psychopathic tendencies, and potential violence. The psychologist's report was based on evidence of behavioral issues directly supplied by the power of attorney who was acting as a private investigator for the FBI, and the bank. Once the county attorney became engaged, the information evolved to criminal complaints, illegal court processes and judgments against David Zehlen. Professor Walsh's opinions provided the stamp of *professional* approval the success of the Zehlen swindle depended upon. Ultimately, it was Ansel Walsh's evaluation that reinforced a series of interventions by Granite county welfare authorities, alerted they could be called in at any minute to prevent domestic violence involving David and Nancy Zehlen.

* * * * *

After the unfortunate passing of his two best high school friends, Jim Ferguson remained David's closest friend in Rockland. Functioning as a psychological counselor and tutor that crucial summer of his career, entering his 7th year of teaching Jim was hoping he might finally achieve tenure, as he prepared to sign a contract to teach Senior High English at one of several Wisconsin High Schools he applied at.

"I'm not going to be around forever you know. You will learn in a hurry judges do not accept handicaps in writing ability as excuses for presenting incomprehensible reports. If you expect to litigate the case pro se, you will eventually have to learn to write persuasive sentences and paragraphs yourself if you ever intend to present a legal argument against the partners. Unfortunately, lawyers around here won't touch the case. There are too many conflicts of interest with your dad and wife involved."

* * * * *

Before David showed any promise in communication, an informal assessment by the English teacher indicated competency in one key core learning skill, math. Ferguson believed he needed more than normal "brush-up" meaning refresher courses in English, history, and science. Ferguson's partner on Saturday mornings was head instructor George Antonelli who administered the GED program geared for high school dropouts, serving Granite County in the remodeled basement of the Rockland library.

After reviewing the initial evaluation and interviewing him, George suspected that David had a more serious psychological problem–basic alienation–he was losing his homeland like many immigrants Antonelli had encountered in his teaching experience in urban centers. Applying the philosophy of adult education, Mr. Antonelli believed that David, approaching 50, remained capable of accomplishing greater things, graduating from failures of youthful aspiration and great expectations– through learning development.

In the classroom an heuristic method was used, with appropriate reading material applied to computer-aided training, and empirical analysis to assist David in dealing with the identity the new social order fashioned for him that he no longer had the desire to identify with. He was trying to escape the painful memory in denial of, that George estimated occupied as much as 80% of his conscious awareness, and had to be subordinated to a higher principle–or the student faced the reality of being categorized as illiterate in postmodern society.

After a few conversations at the library, Ferguson, a former high school drama coach, and amateur actor himself, was struck by the classic resemblances of the Zehlen downfall with some dramatic literature he was familiar with. Of course David's lovely wife, close friend of *his* wife, became one of the *victims* of collateral damage of mendacity on a "hot tin roof." In the aftermath of the collapse, the English mentor imagined Sophocles' Creon taking over the kingdom through subterfuge, the tyrannical Walsh using his power of attorney over Pleasant Valley Farms, claiming the incompetent president was unfit to run the business. To achieve his objective, *necessity* was indeed the dictator's plea.

In his literary imagination, Ferguson imagined the exiled sisters Antigone and Ismene in lock-step with Walsh's plan, investing the remaining financial resources, and confidence into their personal Creon, while David was being deposed as President of the Pleasant Valley. At Mother Earth's command, the farm was entrusted to their faithless trustee. In less than three years, Walsh was in complete control of the women's thoughts and administration of an agenda they knew nothing about. The Trojan women could only shake their heads in disbelief as the Zehlen farming empire, spread over an area almost as large as Macedonia where David's maternal ancestors emigrated from in the 19th Century, crumbled. While Dave faded into the wilderness over the course of 30 months, *Mephisto* Walsh became Nancy's constant confidante and advisor, and her husband's constant informer, as his mental health deteriorated in the face of powerlessness, and unconscious awareness of the hostile takeover he could do nothing to prevent.

The writing center gave David hope. If nothing else, he was anxious to improve his writing skills to communicate with his son Noah who was attending the University. He began keeping a journal. An initial assessment of the student Dave showed he lacked basic writing skills in e-mails and personal correspondence; according to the rubric every other element of content, formatting and organization, style, usage, mechanics and grammar, coupled with his lack of reading comprehension on short passages indicated he was below eighth grade level in writing. David soon learned George was very serious. There was little room, and limited time in his conversations for a student to illustrate exceptional farming skills; Antonelli considered applied technical skills, and technology-specific reports did not always equate with a high degree of literary. According to Ferguson, the first attribute of communication could be finessed by a good secretary.

But when the efficient little lady at the desk, who can type, is not handling the correspondence, a general lack of content and organization, along with persistently irritating tones of authority became limitations of effectiveness in legal correspondence and documentation. It became apparent David had the writing ability of a mid-school student, that quality along with a projected attitude of allegation and accusation in general in his writing would later result in admonitions of judges and attorneys that his work was "incomprehensible gibberish;" his letters projected an angry tone–not a trait in writing to be *trifled* with–that David did not begin to understand he was doing, though he claimed he did. Ferguson warned David of the potential for a negative reaction, and "prejudice" ruling, should he not observe the etiquette and format required in legal writing.

Ferguson believed that a reading and writing assessment reflects the level of intelligence of the individual being tested. If there was some discrepancy from predictive data tables, the learning gap could ultimately be corrected through training and practice. In David's case, it became clearer according to theory, learning development would need to be a precedent to professional development. In corrections educational settings, periodic testing could prove the defendant did, or did not have the reading ability to understand legal documents, and therefore demonstrated a lack of knowledge of the scope of the problems. His counselors at the learning center came to believe educational gaps probably contributed to David's decision to *capitulate* to false charges.

He was no legal scholar, but Ferguson believed that as a result of his literacy disability a legal argument existed that David had made an unintelligent and legally "inadmissible" plea to false charges because of his reduced ability, and lack of understanding of the charges he faced–which were not intelligently *defined* in the first place. The conspiracy itself was based on *confusion—that a lot of money had been lost, and somebody had to pay*—when only a shorthand generalization explains why David Zehlen pled guilty to bogus charges in the Granite County plea bargain.

CHAPTER 28

Hector Sexton listened faithfully to the farm market reports at noon, followed by sports, and then the weather reports on the mighty 790. To Hector the reports spelled disaster for the high-oleic safflowers battered and beaten by unexpected storms. At the time he made the decision, Sexton did not consider how much he might regret that he agreed to allow his brother-in-law Jeff Provo to cancel the insurance. What poor judgment he had shown when he had the money. It was pocket change for his lifestyle; it seemed like such a remote possibility they could lose the crop a few weeks before the freak storms.

The first week of September, Sexton made a special trip to Sully to examine the remnants of three sections of safflowers that were nothing but hollow empty stalks not even worth the trouble of cultivation, shredded and reduced to silage, he believed under the storm clouds that ravaged eastern South Dakota in mid and late August. With the canceled insurance issue staring him squarely in the face, Sexton realized he was in serious trouble if anyone but he and Robert Walsh discovered the extent and scope of the activities the two of them had collaborated on.

On the defensive side, Hector was not terribly concerned that his dealings with David Zehlen could reflect negatively upon him, because it was Zehlen who had been found to be in violation of ASCS regulations. The insurance and the ASCS conduct issue were independent variables, depending on whether the contract "item 3c."–compliance with all regulations–was finessed, or amplified by his attorney in litigation that favored the bank and conspirators if the case ever came to trial.

Sexton was confident there was no way a plaintiff could ever prove promissory fraud against him. He had records of direct payments that were in Zehlen's accounts by January 1992. The actual percentage those payments amounted to–relative to the deficit he created–would not be disclosed. The estimated three million dollars in cash and credit Jack and David Zehlen extracted from accounts in Granite, Traverse and Stevens county in Minnesota and the Big Stone State Bank in South Dakota–and invested in production to plant an additional 15,000 acres of sunflowers, safflowers, corn, wheat and oats across three states–would never be accounted for in Walsh's calculus.

Zehlen's capital investment was micro-managed around a slick multi-layered application of technology and manpower that depended on contract fulfillment from his partners. Zehlen's ASCS funds were deposited in the Fargo account around the same time Sexton had written other checks and made production transactions with MinGo partners in 1991. His invoices amounted to $1.5 million to David Zehlen for expenses when he needed to match or exceed Pleasant Valley costs and contributions including personage, knowing ahead of time Zehlen would be short because of market share and contract deficits in the coming year.

* * * * *

Both Walsh and Sexton assumed David ran a separate vaguely-legal set of books in a virtual duplicate entry accounting system that could be accessed on his computer; if the case ever made it to civil court, which it most likely was headed toward, the Ceres attorneys on Hector's team were prepared to prove that cashflow of money from SigCo/Ceres and Sexton indicated the arrangement between Sexton and Zehlen was a lending arrangement, and not a custom production contract-based relationship.

Walsh would leave the details of the sleight-of-hand methods needed to convince a hearing judge the contract was a loan, to Myers and Wilber, the bank attorneys he was working closely with. The attorneys, as they had in the past, relied on Robert's knowledge of agriculture conspiracy methods; Walsh needed the appearance and power of legitimacy lawyers provided. After moving up the ladder to power of attorney for PVC in less than six months, Walsh was confident in the intricate strategy evolved that would grant Sexton immunity and himself invisibility as they pursued their personalized objectives.

"Of course Hector, it is obvious to me David is powerless to oppose our plans. You are vulnerable in two key areas I would like discuss with you before I reveal my future goals in the deal. First, David Zehlen put all his chips, including the ASCS funds, along with the loans from the Omaha bank into your crop; that would be the safflowers which have been completely destroyed by forces of nature. If you don't intend to fulfill on the contract I see big trouble ahead for you." Walsh laid his trump on the table.

"With his current system of accounting, anything can go wrong. David keeps everything in his head. Then he leaves the leftover fragments on paper for his bookkeeper to sort out. To me, David's management style is closer to chaotic than effective. It feels like he is trying to take over my business by manipulating MN Go. He could never prove that I was not fulfilling on the contract." Sexton retorted, not the least bit worried.

"Have you ever heard of an audit Hector?" Walsh explained. "All these farmers operate the way you do. They never want an audit until it's absolutely necessary. By then it's too late usually to save the farm. Look at it this way. The Zehlens are basically penniless after the ASCS default. It took Jack's savings and his IRA to bail David out. The bank's argument for its total entitlement on the foreclosure in court will stand, while the contract guaranty will not. The subject will not even be referred to in court. That's strike one–David will soon be on the hook for your loan default; and by the way, so is the farm for the note he signed on a *loan* for *your* crops mister."

"The way I've seen it in the demise of other farmers in our area who went under before Zehlen came along, they all rob Peter to pay Paul. Then they run a devil-may-care operation expecting dad, the bank or the State Department of Justice to bail them out–when Granite County is *not* the state's jurisdiction. His rich old man won't be able to bail David out of felony charges. He was too big for his britches this time. He should have started on 160 acres; and he might have learned responsibility. A couple thousand bucks, even ten thousand shifted back between owner and manager among the parties involved doesn't matter all that much when money is available. But that's what a decent attorney will cost when it is not. At one time it appeared as if Zehlens had a fortune stashed in marketing futures; but if the grain isn't moving, Zehlen is stonewalled, paying interest on borrowed money." Walsh had taken the podium.

"There is not enough cash to operate if a partner like you, Hector, drains the well and doesn't pay his obligations a quarter of a million at a time. And you know it, shutting down his business, slowly squeezing his operating margin down to nothing. Within a week of it happening, you had the timing down–to the day, to the hour–when the combines roll or the tractors grind to a halt. You as well as I know what that means to an operation of his size; you can imagine what the drain of a hundred grand a week in operating expenses means–don't tell me about fraud, you strangled PVC! We might be the only two people on earth that know that Hector my friend," Walsh replied with unusual intensity. "Now then if we're talking audit, a RESPA securitization audit, with appraisal verification, would be a greater expense than a TILA audit–that might work for David. But I'm not about to let that happen either. Who has the money or time for an extensive audit? The state won't pay for it, certainly not you or me."

"I am confident Wilber and Myers for the bank will have their investigation completed by the time Zehlen and his public defender have learned a word about the South Dakota civil case. We can depend on the county attorney to write a complaint if we provide evidence. It appears David *still* believes the contract justifies his expenses just as we assumed he would, to validate the Spriegl charges. I don't intend to interfere with David, who will be writing illegal checks on the Pleasant Valley account until the law stops him. You see where I'm going with this?" Walsh proceeded with no compassion whatsoever in his voice.

"All the bank will ever have to do is present the unpaid bill for the loan and the collateral under *their* guaranty contract in court in front of Judge Silas, who is more confused than David. We will need to hear your Attorney Freeman making motions in court, gathering with counsel at the bench, informing the judge the FDIC will back up the bank's claim. You don't want any publicity connected with extended litigation either. There is always the possibility some judge could see through your scheme and call for trips. The longer our claim is exposed in public court the more chance it could fail. The last thing we need is a trial. We need you behind the scenes in Granite County innocuous and incognito. You are the defendant, a *victim* of a swindle by David, remember that. At least *try* to be humble. Maybe you should stay in Fargo Hector, and just send Freeman." Walsh paused for a second, expecting a reaction from the partner who had gravitated from being manipulated to being used.

"So what do you want me to do about it Robbie? I know your history. You've been here before. We know the method in place from experience; the bank forecloses for some mysterious reason: that would be the neglected MWFSB default information that somehow escaped detection in your, shall we say, negotiations with the bank? Examining the nexus more deeply, you have made sure no documentation to prove the bank actually foreclosed by October 1992 exists. David was never notified formally of the foreclosure although you were aware of it as his power-of-attorney. These personal transactions could be linked in litigation with the undisclosed default every credit agency in the country knew about, if it was necessary. I doubt seriously that will ever happen. Next, factor in you were the controller for a half year, who for some reason decided not to make the loan payment when there was substantial revenue available after harvest–would that interpretation ever come to the attention of the fraud unit? It might. Who would believe there is no connection with fraud in your actions as power of attorney Robbie? Or are we all fools? Funny, nobody notices the connections, the *little* details of your administration that give you away. Do you believe I'm the only person on the planet who knows you haven't put a penny of that loan in David's pocket, when you knew his income and savings was exhausted by June? The same man who made over a million five with me last year, I heard it from Phyllis–is begging for lunch money from the wife."

Sexton knew the game but he had never lost a huge crop without insurance before either.

"Before you accuse me take a look at yourself Hector. Your interpretation is subjective and gratuitous. The truth is David's wife begged me to help the family so they wouldn't be bankrupt and in court for a generation to come. According to his own father, David was a menace and his own worst enemy; so they had to do something. I accepted the appointment to Pleasant Valley Farms because David has been completely dysfunctional in business for at least six months previous to my arrival, according to his wife." Walsh paused, letting his message sink in. "I intend to use that power to the best of my ability. You, like nobody on earth can accuse me of doing anything illegal Hector and you know it." Walsh added a climactic summary as if he was making a prepared statement for the Rockland Independent.

"The timing couldn't be worse–or better–depending on how you approach the situation; if it is a coincidence as it were, an act of God that the crop is uninsured, let me remind you it is *your* loss under the guaranteed contract you signed with David. Frankly, isn't it amazing the damage occurred exactly two weeks after I warned you against the risk you were taking if you dropped the insurance? You see where I am going with this Hector? Jeff Provo hasn't inspected the flowers yet. You should tell him to hold off an assessment of crop damage until a week or two after Labor Day to determine if any crop is left standing; it may not be a complete loss after all. As long as you keep in mind you didn't listen to me and you are paying the price we can work on a solution. I just did my job, and what do you know? Things worked out for me. That's all you need to remember. If you do that much, maybe I can help you."

"That's what I'm talking about isn't it Robbie? We are in this together aren't we?" Hector was eating out of Walsh's lunch box. "Maybe I can find other ways to help you. I know I gambled and lost on the insurance deal; a miscalculation that's all it was."

"Listen Hector I don't need any excuses. What you did was illegal; the contract specified insurance was required. The reason the bank backed the risk was because you paid the premium. I was there all the time, unobtrusively, observing the process you might say. How do you explain that you received the kickback on personage and gobbled up the rest in production, and left David Zehlen liable for the deficit *you created* and maintained, so unscrupulously? Answer me before you face a federal judge for fraud!" Walsh noticed his partner's confident tone receding, scarcely audible.

"As long as you understand your position Hector, with nowhere to hide from your treacherous acts upon my client, who has basically been eliminated from the profession by your actions–that is unless you listen very carefully to the plan that I have in mind–if you do exactly as I say I might be able to finesse the insurance issue with the bank. The first thing I want you to do is to arrange a telephone conference or a meeting, either way is fine with me, with your attorney. I believe his name is Freeman, the lawyer you refer to often in our discussions. As soon as I hear from him, I will initiate civil action with the Omaha bank," *after all, I arranged the loan–I can certainly manage how that loan is collected*–he thought to himself.

"Okay Robbie anything you say. I never intended any harm against David. The MN Go partnership turned into a bad business deal all the way around if you know what I mean." At that moment, like never before in the deal, Sexton realized and appreciated that Walsh was going to let him survive, while they both hung Zehlen out to dry. He could not be sure why Walsh was doing him such a favor. He wasn't about to inquire deeply either.

"I sincerely believe you didn't mean to cause any damage to the Zehlens Hector. Just give me a call when the meeting with Freeman is set up," Walsh dismissed Sexton with the note of disgust in his voice he reserved for people he had outwitted.

CHAPTER 29

What had once been forecast as a promising fall harvest in year two of the grower's agreement contract, turned out to be an uncertain nightmare for Pleasant Valley farm which had come under the directorship of Robert Walsh as power of attorney by August 1992. The 12,000 acres of safflowers that Walsh had originally been hired by David Zehlen to manage, had been completely demolished by cold and wet conditions supposedly in the last two weeks of August. Early bloom had been excellent; but that was one sample of the flowers taken in July–before the thunderstorms had ravaged eastern South Dakota. The small sample of plants that remained standing after storm damage was declared unsuitable for testing. After an aerial assessment, the blackened crop was declared a total loss by SigCo. To its customers, the parent organization acknowledged the complete crop loss, sending letters to all their regional growers, notifying them of the effects of rain and moist conditions in eastern South Dakota. Under program guidelines, yields affected by similar weather would be eligible for disaster payments under their risk insurance and policy provisions.

* * * * *

There was never any question about who owned the crop. An affidavit related to the Sully FBI report states that bank official Thomas Jessen, "first became aware of a problem when he was contacted by Hector Sexton October 23, 1992. Sexton claimed to have some agreement with David Zehlen which gave Sexton ownership of the crops grown on Zehlen's South Dakota Farm."

Behind the scenes and behind closed doors, Walsh was discussing with bank official Jessen how the bank was going to reinterpret the financial information to indicate that the David Zehlen, dba Pleasant Valley Farms, had failed to disclose the

Midwest Federal S&L default on the loan application for additional operating capital supporting the Sexton Zehlen partnership in 1992. In FBI affidavit FD-307 of Thomas H. Jessen, Vice President, First National Bank of Omaha, on 3/5/97 stated:

"First Omaha required David Zehlen to submit financial statements. In addition, Jessen also obtained a current credit bureau report for the Zehlens. Jessen stated that the financial statements of the Zehlens had failed to disclose their default on loans from Midwest Federal Savings Bank. Jessen stated further that he first was informed of the Zehlen default on the Midwest Federal Savings Bank loan after First Omaha Bank started litigation to recover the Bank's collateral from the Zehlen loans. Jessen claimed that if the bank had been aware of the loan default they would not have approved the farm operating loan. In the same affidavit Jessen repeated that First Omaha relied on financial statements provided by the Zehlens that were inaccurate and unreliable."

According to David Zehlen, the statements Thomas Jessen V.P, First Omaha Bank made to the FBI were false. David later claimed that he provided the information relative to the Midwest Federal Savings Bank loan default in the loan application package that was presented to the bank in May 1992–by Robert Walsh; as a government document states, relative to the loan application package that was presented to the bank in 1992 by David Zehlen (re: FBI Affidavit 87D),

"During May 1992 Pleasant Valley Farms and David Zehlen began asking for manager Walsh's help to obtain loans from banks. Sometime in April 1992, Walsh informed the FBI David Zehlen asked him for a copy of his resume to include with a loan package for First Omaha."

In his developing theory David Zehlen imagined, what if the bank planned all along to use the federal loan default as the issue the foreclosure without notice hinged on, and future litigation depended on–having used the same method before many times– in the demise of other farmers. The initial step in the process was approving a loan package, the first of two on income from leases, the second loan granted on the basis of the collateral assignment. It was a formula for disaster that David believed he had no other choice but to accept; the whole scheme was managed brilliantly by the "dream team" of super lawyers led by Brett Wilber, making it appear the loan was granted legitimately, while the loan officers were being deceived and unaware of the MWFSB default problem.

The alpha male Robert Walsh continued leading the pack, making key moves and bold decisions, daring to tamper with the S&L default issue the promissory fraud hinged on. In the Walsh version reported to the bureau, he became involved on a conflict of interest matter related to the Woods elevator deal revolving around Zehlen defense attorneys Faegre and Benson whose role in the case was conditional; First Omaha was looking for a person to manage 30,000 acres in South Dakota on their behalf. Walsh suggested that David Zehlen contact John French, Senior partner of F&B, and tell French that he would expose the entire scheme surrounding Woods elevator if he did not get the First Bank position. In March 1992, Zehlen informed Walsh he had been notified he was a finalist for the position."

The board determined the loan would be allocated in segments; disbursement of funds would be administered by Walsh instead of David who had failed a vote of confidence. Where there had been scarce recollection of the original loan indemnity within fair business practice law perspectives, there was even less concern, or regard in understanding its relationship to the conspiracy among the Board of Directors of First Omaha that furiously debated the merits of the Zehlen loan extension of another million five.

Once the collateral had been appropriated, it would be placed under the secure administration of Robert Walsh who had taken over the management of the farm as the bank's unofficial agent. The bank had agreed to the plan in the past, working independent deals with their special agent in the field who was efficient in the office as well. On the basis of that trust built over a decade, with money to burn, the Jessen group allocated the loan to Pleasant Valley knowing Robert Walsh would be set up as administrator through power of attorney for Pleasant Valley

Corporation by the time the loan was disbursed the end of July 1992.

In the confusion about whether or not the flowers were going to reach market, and who they belonged to–whether they were to be or not to be harvested–the heavy heads of a million plants wilted and dried, picked clean by blackbirds and sparrows before the first snowfall of autumn, 1992. Walsh claimed full credit for salvaging the operations. It was his early warning and friendship with the county sheriff that may have prevented violence in the sunflower fields; he had done his clandestine work. creating the ultimate confusion over crop ownership.

Later that fatal fall, Sexton produced documents in Sully civil court that reflected that he had paid over a million dollars to Pleasant Valley Farms for leases on the crops. The affidavit indicated that Pleasant Valley Farms had already pledged the crop to the Omaha bank; and that the bank was *"at a loss"* because it did not verify that Hector Sexton *already* owned the crop under contract.

To clear the lease and earn a few buck after New Years, David finished combining the remains of the stalks and stems of the South Dakota flowers in mid-January 1993. Grinding the naked flower stalks under in light snow and ten-degree weather– facing a stiff wind out of the northwest–was the last time David ever drove a tractor under the auspices of the Pleasant Valley Corporation. The new straw boss Robbie Walsh, issued him a personal check for $1500 for his services at the end of the month.

In Orwellian terms, Robert Walsh had all his hen houses tacked together. In reality, three collaborators were involved in an elaborate conspiracy against Pleasant Valley Farms. David never knew what hit him as all three parties closed in for the kill. Walsh, Sexton and the bank were collaborating to foreclose on the Pleasant Valley Farms $1.2-million-dollar loan without notice for a series of frivolous causes. Ultimately, the bank was willing to spend a half-million dollars to perfect the scheme Robert Walsh initiated to claim their prize in the most corrupt lottery the farmers of Granite County had ever witnessed–as the century was grinding to an end. It would take many years of litigation, relative to civil rights violations, to unravel the diverse means, ends, and objectives of the scheme Robert Walsh had assembled. In a feeble gesture of submission to a higher power, in the fall of 1992, Hector Sexton solidified his claim on 16,000 acres of flowers that never made it to market–by agreeing to take a loss his partners upstairs would cover through insurance and tax write-offs.

With the MWFSB issue hanging around his neck like an albatross, conspiracy expert attorney Wilber was preparing the judgment David would be held liable for on Sexton's huge loss– completing another phase of the takeover operation. Behind the scenes, Walsh was keeping busy micromanaging both a criminal and civil case against his client; never a particularly good writer, as it was in the beginning, Walsh's greatest skill remained his ability to organize piles of papers, graduating eventually to legal documents, sorting them into classes and categories of thought that reflected his interpretation of the way things should be. In his simple fashion, he perfected the cover-up by succeeding to convince civil court the flow of cash between Zehlen and Sexton *appeared* to be a loan.

David Zehlen, whose farming operations had been designated as one the most successful in the Midwest by a leading farm industry magazine a few months before it imploded, wasn't the only person fooled. He was sick and tired even thinking about the incomprehensible reversal of his great expectations in the blink of an eye. His unheralded rival, Robert Walsh was calling the shots, sitting in the cat-bird's seat of Pleasant Valley Farms. Despite his doubts, David maintained his belief that the contract he had signed with Sexton in 1991, which was reaffirmed in 1992 by a few jottings and an illegible signature on a napkin–was the one shred of hope that remained to pull the farm out of the disaster it was headed for.

As always, Walsh was a step ahead of any planning or assumptions that David Zehlen once had about contract protection remaining on the 1991 agreement with Hector Sexton. His indemnity had been erased behind the scenes, unknown to him. The next step in the takeover involved security and validation of the key process the conspiracy depended on. The first step was notifying the Myers Legal Group of Sioux Falls, SD that the bank would be pursuing a civil lawsuit in Sully County Court; their job was to establish that the contract, with its attached *guaranty* on the original agreement between Zehlen and Sexton–was nothing more than a loan.

Walsh himself had drawn up a few pages of a pro se memoranda as a first draft and forwarded his ideas to First Omaha Vice President, Tom Jessen for his suggestions. The week following the conversation between Sexton and Jessen, he forwarded page two, paragraph one of his pro se countersuit that stated there never was contract involving the bank and Sexton prior to June 1992, legally erasing any doubt, eliminating any evidence that the crop was owned by Sexton; in the process, indicating Sexton had loaned Zehlen close to a half million dollars–and the money was owed to him.

Jessen stated in a 1997 FBI affidavit that he first became aware of the Zehlen violation upon receiving a stack of phony bills via UPS. The truth was, the bank had provided the loan to Pleasant Valley based on the fact there was a *contract* between Zehlen and Sexton in the first place; and that David would be entitled to substantial USDA subsidies on the basis of that agreement. The contract conversion then became linked in the confusion with the falsified First Omaha loan default when Walsh was in control of accounts paid for at Pleasant Valley. An important but overlooked detail of the foreclosure was the role of administration. Had Walsh willfully chosen not to pay the mortgage? Or was that an under-performed, unperformed personal transaction what might be expected of the power of attorney? Or was that part of the bargain with First Omaha, another default mechanism the conspiracy hinged on?

If David was not undone by the omission, perhaps the Sully lawsuit to come, presided over by counsel of First Omaha attorney Wilber could be considered his undoing. There Robert Walsh and Nancy Zehlen provided depositions that affirmed that the contract between David Zehlen and Hector Sexton was indeed a loan, not a contract, accomplishing the major share of the damage. Such a series of false premises, integrated into court judgment, was a part of the internal mechanics of the system; in the confusion element Wilber's argument depended on to validate the conspiracy strategy, such false argumentation allowed the redefinition of the contract as a loan. Forgotten in the process is that by virtue of a changed definition, and accompanying breach of judgment–David Zehlen became liable for a $375,000 loss Sexton sued him for in Granite County Court a year later.

CHAPTER 30

Once Robert Walsh gained power of attorney over Pleasant Valley Farms, he began to exercise his authority to dispose of real and personal property of members of the corporation. In December 1992, Walsh convinced Jack Zehlen to cash in and turn over his $190,000 dollar IRA pension to him during the crisis, reasoning that once creditors began to make claims on the rapidly diminishing farm accounts, as counsel for the farm and power of attorney–Walsh advised Jack that he would be better off turning the money over for safekeeping. Jack never saw that money again.

In the years that followed, Walsh would gain control over a $600,000 Zehlen children's trust fund and use that money to remodel the Anothene office building in Rockland, extending his form of *aid* to a community improvement project the Zehlens had invested $385,000 of their farm profits in the 1980's restoration period. Walsh never acknowledged that he appropriated the children's fund. In future litigation he would deny that the trust fund ever existed.

Walsh told Jack specifically he would make a deal with the Affiliated Bank Group, one of the major creditors Jack had been dealing with for many years. Walsh claimed that he would use the money to redeem the farm in the event of foreclosure. Instead the money was appropriated under Walsh's power of attorney, and deposited into his Marketing International accounting system; his heirs would retain ownership of the Anothene building at Washington and 3rd, downtown Rockland, after Robert passed away from complications of Alzheimer's disease.

In an exaggerated display of generosity, Walsh presented Nancy with a mink coat for Christmas 1992. The unexpected gift from Santa, bulging out under the tree, was a year-end reward for good behavior, following his appointment as chief executive of Pleasant Valley by Nancy and Phyllis Zehlen. During the next year he would purchase their shares of Pleasant Valley Farms for pennies on the dollar. David's latent explanation was that the women sold the farm, and split twenty thousand cash Walsh paid them for its depreciated value at below ten percent of the market. Walsh probably used some of the money he swindled from Jack Zehlen's IRA account for the combined twenty thousand dollar payments to Nancy and Phyllis, co-owners of Pleasant Valley Farms.

Though David depended on his computer for over ten years as if it were a genie assigned to perform his wishes and will, there were no preferences, menus, or features in the basic program he relied on, that represented percent of attrition due to loss of contract–the black hole Walsh realized was on the verge of imploding.

Although the expectations of the agreement between Sexton and Pleasant Valley Farms outlined in the contract were $1.2 million a year, the computer printouts from David's program provided no measurement, or correlation of payment with expenses due after two months of planting in either spring by PVC. In early protocols, the CD program fell short of providing charts or tables, or content reflecting billings to expenses during the critical plant to harvest span the small farmer kept track of in his head. A serious weakness of the software was that it did not reflect "grower-adjusted" accounting for reciprocal expenses in credit for advances the manager made on ASCS funds used in labor, fertilizer, and pesticide applications. Designed for a small farm, Dave's software was not capable of analysis and input of an expanded operation with thirty times more logistical problems than the average farmer dealt with in the yearly cycle of labor and material.

Before critical mass reached meltdown, David was confident his platform managed the farm *efficiently*; confident enough the IRS would accept its findings on his taxes if he punched in the production numbers correctly. Demonstrated by its shortcomings in its early stages, the software was not sophisticated enough to throw up multiple "red flag" alerts when Hector Sexton was showing a deficit in his share of production costs, as David Zehlen's operations budget *diminished* by the hour; the program he depended on with basic word processor features, and few analytic applications, providing reports at best–was obsolete before it became effective.

Zehlen assumed his expectations for expenses of the grower as accounts receivable would be at least $600K, or a payment of one third on anticipated costs for each spring of the contract; that would in the future be adjusted back to him on the basis of finalizing the accounting in June or July 1992. Looking forward to 1993 sales on the second contract, he resumed his expenses covered under the continued agreement his "management" would be compensated for, receiving 25% of the difference between the costs incurred for growing the crop, and the income received from the sale of the crop by the grower.

When the proprietary software he was using proved to be incapable of reflecting the complexities of the farm management task at hand, David Zehlen as director of the corporation apparently became unable to manage what seemed to be unenforceable contract arrangements with a partner who was engaged in promissory fraud. He had taken algebra and geometry; but the mind-boggling *calculus* of Sexton was transparent to Walsh alone. Relying on flexible lending arrangements from financial institutions like Midwest Federal Savings, farm credit with institutions like Affiliated, the government's own Resolution Trust, the ASCS programs, and the profits generated from previous years–the Zehlens operated a "showcase" farming operation until *Walsh* arrived.

While David Zehlen was operating his farm under the assumptions that his partner Hector Sexton would be fulfilling his obligations as owner of the contract, obtaining fuel, fertilizer, pesticides, and herbicides–at least compensating him for his expenditures on a daily, weekly and monthly basis during planting–which along with labor and production expense was at an all-time high: equipment costs were in the tens of thousands per-week range for operations the size of Zehlens–by July of

1992 Robert Walsh had already factored Sexton's *predictable* behavior into the PVC quadratic.

Walsh was not accepted at SDSU because he had no record of algebra on his high school transcript. Without a formal education, Robbie Walsh believed he had the mental capacity of his brother Ansel who managed to overcome the fragmented learning he had been provided in the Nundas, Madison school district. Unlike Ansel, Robert experienced the thoughts and feelings of alienation over loss of his roots. He became oddly sentimental about the topic when Shirley summarized the TV series *Roots* over a rooster dinner. He could not take the idea seriously because it was about the other *race*.

Nonetheless, Robert Walsh understood the basics of agricultural engineering. He knew that if the first week of planting the South Dakota safflowers required ten men working 60 hours a week at adjusted rates for machine-operator to laborer averaging $15 per hour, and a supervisor working the same hours at $20, those hours and expenses had to be aligned against a fixed ratio of time allocated for the growing season, planting, maintenance. Within that alignment, material costs for the operations (fuel, chemical, overhead) paid for either by the grower or owner as accounts payable or credit had to be factored into costs of production at roughly $50K per month more. Hector Sexton had a much better idea of how to run an immense project than David, in his first year of custom farming, at a scale ten times larger than he was used to. Sexton had been in a complex business for almost twenty years, while his partner was wet behind the ears and proving it.

Although the reports from his managers and employees consistently indicated the 1991 crop and custom farming arrangement between Zehlen and Sexton was successful, Walsh knew that was standard short term speculation, projecting Sexton was fulfilling the contract and the *shaky* marketing agreement. As informant he was aware of the background–the melting iceberg the farm was floating on–in a situation where the Zehlens no longer had the Midwest Federal Saving Bank lender to rely on for operating capital they had during the successes of the 1980's. Walsh just happened to arrive on the scene because the Zehlens were having difficulties finding a lender as a result of the MWFSB bailout into the RTC treasuries. To Walsh and Jessen's advantage, First Omaha Leasing, the equipment lending subsidiary was in no hurry to resolve their collateral issues related to *any* S&L default, despite the Zehlen's offer to settle the *original* farm debt in October 1991, for an additional twenty-five thousand cash.

* * * * *

True to form, Robert Walsh claimed credit for discovery of fraud within the organization–for its own benefit, to the FBI. Walsh became indignant that the bureau lieutenants were intelligent enough to not take him seriously, performing his duties, informing them of David Zehlen's conduct that was contrary to both his partner's and the *bank's* interests. The interviewer was not convinced Walsh was squealing for none other than moral and ethical reasons–the ones he felt *obligated* to blow the whistle on his employer for. Nonetheless, by their neglect, federal agents allowed Walsh to blow the "horn" as persistent as the Great Northern diesel cutting off the Zehlen west pasture, on steel rails that stretched to Fargo, signaling the dying breathe of an era that lasted into the next century. Walsh, engineer of infamy, would ride that train to the depot, and pull that whistle chain on demand, implying the FBI *knew it all along*–Walsh was a quack performing as a private investigator. Notwithstanding, the bureau recorded his dramatic performance in meticulous detail.

For all legal purposes, by March 5, 1993 the bureau had washed its hands of the matter and hung David out to dry; by that time both David and Jack had voiced their objections, contacting and informing the police and sheriff, and the bureau that–they had been *swindled* by Sexton and Walsh. But no investigation was ever initiated, presumably because enforcement and apprehension in general was controlled by the conspiracy–*authority* if there was any–was under the assumption that David Zehlen had committed bank fraud. Pressing their lawsuit with the Walsh's $500,000 "dream team" of attorneys, First Omaha was forcing the criminal theft issue as part of the cover-up. In the process of obfuscating the contract, the *bank's* interests *trumped* concerns for the criminal and civil rights of the Zehlens; if there was any analysis, it reflected nothing more than mind control and manipulation by Walsh leading to the Zehlen demise. Thorough investigation of the matter was declined by the bureau; however, in its diligence (the Omaha bureau) forwarded a copy of the suspicious activity report implicating Walsh in the conspiracy to the Minneapolis investigative branch of the FBI; but substance of the Zehlen complaints about Hector and Walsh was *deflected* in favor of the bank's interests.

Because there was no evidence that a crime had ever been committed, the bureau declined to prosecute Zehlen or his father *either*–when every legal professional on both sides should have known the real issue was the "phantom" South Dakota *civil* lawsuit–there was no need to attract attention to the case, the FBI was claiming,

> The bank suffered no loss in the Zehlen transaction; furthermore, there was no language in the contract that prohibited the Zehlens from entering into a custom farming contract.

The bureau report continued,

> Walsh appeared to have strong influence on the Zehlens because of his power of attorney; on the record Walsh gave every appearance of being a manipulator who realized an opportunity to capitalize on the problems being experienced by Zehlen entities.

The bureau stated that in the same interview Walsh insisted on talking about his contact with a "high official" in the bureau; it was apparent Walsh believed that information would be intimidating to the interviewing agent. Walsh was obviously agitated at the bureau's lack of interest in his ideas. The report noted that Robbie was indignant, and angry, short of being belligerent, exhibiting noticeably reproachable conduct and attitude toward the interviewer–in his assumption a recent law-school graduate with zero knowledge of agricultural crime–had no interest whatsoever in the identity of Walsh's high level contact in the FBI organization; the bureau was maintaining its previous position of "nondisclosure" of its assumptions of the Zehlen culpability relative to the bank fraud charge, and in subsequent statements the bureau summarized. Walsh had successfully manipulated the entire Zehlen family into poverty and dependence. The bureau noted, "*only Walsh profited by the entire matter.*"

When he and David discussed the MWFSB loan default privately, it was Walsh who suggested that all unencumbered assets of the family be placed under his control under power of attorney protections. A few months later, he convinced Nancy and Phyllis Zehlen to divorce their husbands. Jack was forced to file bankruptcy and settle with the bank. Moreover, Walsh convinced Nancy to swap her half-interest in Pleasant Valley Farms over to him for a couple thousand down, pre-paid rent subtracted from the price he paid for her share of the farm and a free residence in a remodeled house owned by Walsh overlooking Rockland city park, within walking distance of Anothene and Dr. Hansen's dentist's office. When she remarried, Robbie retained ownership of the house.

In its summary, the bureau concluded Walsh gained control by buying a share of the farm and liquidating the assets. The bank's clandestine involvement at every level of the conspiracy trumped any diligence for a legitimate investigation; evaluation of the actual text of the information set forth in the investigative report indicates the bureau's real relevance (and relationship) to the conspiracy as its actions denied, conformed to, and at the same time–*reinforced* the progress of the conspiracy.

Despite the cover up, there remains the possibility that at some echelon of the bureau, some layer exists over and above the agent interviewer stage of authority. Walsh may have been referring to an actual person, identity unknown, the bureau insider linked with conspiracy through the bank's involvement, extending the probability of a special agent contact with *knowledge* of the bank's involvement with Walsh–adding suspicion to the mysterious FBI and bank collaboration in previous cases he referred to–in the March 5, 1993 affidavit.

CHAPTER 31

By the end of December of 1992, Robert Walsh had such a stranglehold on the operations that he was taking measures to ensure the internal security of his takeover campaign against Pleasant Valley Farms. While David was basically in a state of shock, he later described this as a period of his life he spent dealing with *demons* of alcoholism and tobacco while suffering through post-traumatic stress syndrome because so many things he had taken for granted and taken advantage of that had been the foundation of his life, had been snatched from him as it were by a *thief in the night*. He recalled Pastor White warning that a man can lose his soul at the crossroads of life when the Lord sends angels of destruction among the naive lambs. It seemed like such an irrational fantasy to imagine–he dismissed the thought almost as quickly as the words passed through one ear and out the other.

Until it happened to *him*, who could have guessed something like this could happen in such a peaceful valley, and the tiny hamlet at the foot of it. Here he was sitting in a pew, as he had most Sunday mornings his whole life, and losing control of a business he himself had taken over from his dad the last ten years. He didn't want to be reminded of his problems in a church sermon about withholding his tithe from the church. My wife gives our ten percent at First English he thought–And for what reason? He had no one to ask, *"Why is this happening to me?"* – as the scriptures reminded him *Job* had done.

During those desolate times, Dave came to realize he had no clearly-defined image to pray to. *I have been loyal to the church* he thought, *just as my father was, now on the verge of losing what he worked for his whole life.* David was there with his dad the day they poured concrete for the foundation of the new Methodist church on north Otto Ave. He barely remembered the old one, a block from the armory, salvaged and demolished long ago. In his current perspective, it looked like another loyal supporter of religion was on the verge of losing what he had worked a lifetime to build; after expanding the farm into a 3,500-acre bonanza over two generations, dad and I are no longer on speaking terms. The blessings he once had were turning into curses. By 1993, David had no faith to lose, and going to church during the crisis reinforced his unbelief.

In the Zehlen household, Walsh's words of authority reigned as powerfully as those of the Christian minister's in regulating the secular lives he controlled. With the ASCS issue hanging over their heads like the *Sword of Damocles,* he advised the desperate women their only option was to sell the farm to their designated power of attorney at as close to cash value as he could offer them. He claimed his offer was adjusted to compensate for the existing corporate debt based on combined loans from the bank and Sexton approaching two million dollars; the farm was reduced in value at least eighty to ninety percent in market value compared to what it once was,

"In my sworn duty as power of attorney, I am arranging an agreement with my partners in Interwest to absorb the Pleasant Valley debt that involves issuing extended lines of credit for the members of the new organization we are forming; once you have agreed to cash out your shares with Marketing International we will open accounts for you with my Wall St. Brokers Morgan and Stanley."

In the wake of the success of the takeover, Walsh began making more public appearances, strutting around the corporate offices like a cockerel rooster, openly flirting with Jack's wife Phyllis who was looking for the shortest route out of the marriage that Walsh had sabotaged.

"Now that the end is in sight," Walsh advised Phyllis she should think about advantages a younger man, one who was rich and had renounced smoking and drinking, had to offer. The new company Robbie was forming on the ruins of Pleasant Valley would be on the *Fortune 500* list of the best companies in America in no time, implying that if she consented to having an affair with him, or at least becoming warmer to his advances that were becoming more and more aggressive, she could play a greater role than she *ever* imagined in his next venture.

His script was always the same, according to the gospel of Walsh it was only because of *his* intervention that both Phyllis and Nancy had been granted a separate hearing on the ASCS fraud he had exposed. Otherwise they could be facing prison time in women's federal penitentiary at Leavenworth, Kansas. This absurd premise became the basis for his control of the women's lives. Life would not be easy, if they followed his instructions neither woman would be culpable because of Walsh's *influence* over the review board; his warning acted as a *stay* of imposition, the girls better stay out of sight and out of trouble the next year. If their behavior was satisfactory, the victimized women would be ruled hold-harmless in the agreement for their involvement in the personage swindle. Nonetheless, the farm would be sacrificed. By then they were completely indoctrinated, both women testified to the FBI that David was *solely responsible* for the violation of government rules Walsh had reported to the ASCS. In the informal 1992 hearing, both wives claimed they had been *misled* by their respective husbands and received nothing out of the deal.

* * * * *

It was December 7, 1992 when Robert Walsh met with the board, Hector Sexton, his brother-in-law Jeff Provo and his wife Tonya who was Hector's half-sister, in the Anothene corporate headquarters of Pleasant Valley farms in Rockland. At that meeting Walsh, acting as power of attorney for Pleasant Valley Farms, chose to summarize his findings presented to the USDA County Committee.

"We know David made terrible mistakes in South Dakota. He is a naïve farmer who misunderstood the rules that is all. This is David's first violation. We will recommend leniency on his behalf with the state prosecutor who I was forced to inform, to let him off with a penalty rather than place him in prison with violent inmates," Walsh had accomplished his goal using effective if not eloquent prose.

In his role *du jour*, Robert Walsh confronted Sexton and his two associates as he referred to them with a list of allegations of fraud relative to the safflower contract he had signed with David Zehlen. According to Walsh, he had asked Hector Sexton's attorney John Freeman if he was aware of the Sexton debt to Pleasant Valley Farms. Freeman was evasive, but he indicated he would be more than willing to create the documentation for the transfer of all property and assets to the new corporation Walsh was planning to establish under his authority,

"Today I am informing you in my position it is perfectly legal to do whatever I decide to do from now on," Walsh paused, his eyes scanning the board room. "I am not a trustee Hector! That is the distinction that makes a difference. My reinterpretation of the contract will make it possible for each of you to refinance with me. You might consider consolidating your obligations; specifically, your unpaid debts to Pleasant Valley into the new business I am creating called Interwest. In return you will be offered a line of credit through the bank at a below-market interest rate. I called you to the office today for one purpose," Robbie cleared his throat.

"This morning I propose a solution to you in the presence of your *in-law* and sister Tonya, out of great respect for your business acumen and your ongoing associations with Ceres, Lubrizol and SigCo, powerful organizations that have been placed in a predicament with First Omaha; first of all, I have great concerns relative to your obligations to the stakeholders as first-lien holders on a decimated crop, and regarding the insurance policy that was cancelled, when I advised there were risks involved."

"The bank is well aware of that weather-related event; we all know the circumstances surrounding it as well. A settlement has been reached with First Omaha. Together we have hammered out this deal in meticulous detail," he wanted to add– "*Do you people think I brought in a business printer for no reason?*

Why do you think I hired Miles Shan...?" –issues better left unmentioned.

"I know your concerns after 13000 acres of safflowers fizzled out in Sully. You didn't lose that much. SigCo lost their seed. The MinGo crew was not involved; no wages were lost. Zehlen paid you a hundred-sixty grand of USDA subsidy money–now *he* has to pay it back to the government. What are you worried about? I'm the only person on earth that knows *you* caused the problems; if those links were leaked to the authorities, it would be devastating to your career, Hector." Robbie glanced up from a notepad, looking for a shadow of doubt in the room.

"Again like I say, we are not discussing that particular issue today; nor, are we mentioning the canceling of the insurance issue again with the knowledge of the bank which links Jeffrey in on the deal–that is also beside the point of the arrangement I am about to propose to you," Walsh's tone became more amicable in a second. He rose from his chair in the board room and left the room for a moment, returning with a manila folder in hand, and his new associate in tow.

"I would like to introduce *you* my partners, to Phyllis, our newest member of the Interwest team," Walsh announced. "I informed her all about my plans and she will be excited to join us as soon as the South Dakota lawsuit is settled. Phyllis has been working as hostess and corporate secretary until now. And she will be serving as acting vice president of our new enterprise."

Phyllis Zehlen appeared radiant for the occasion wearing a pastel green ensemble with matching jade earrings. The previous day she had added a light auburn tint to her trim from the Allure Beauty Shop before accepting her new title publicly in what sounded like a promotion; like any professional, she could take an increase in salary seriously. On the day of the meeting, her duties included serving lunch featuring a jelly roll *fresh* from the Mittlestead Bakery less than a block from the office.

For a variety of reasons Phyllis was excited about her new appointment. No doubt her attitude was affected by new incentives introduced to her compensation package in the weeks preceding her appointment under the Walsh administration, when he bribed her that if she cooperated with him he could convince Jack to pay her upwards to two-hundred grand as a pre-divorce settlement. Walsh assured her he had access to those locked funds.

"Of course this won't be happening overnight. Just spend a moment with us Phyllis. I know you have a load of work to do with the harvest receipts coming in and all." Robbie pulled up a chair for her right next to his, evidently proud of a new trophy added to his cabinet. "I would like you to become acquainted with our corporate partners Jeff and Tonya Provo. You have met Hector."

The information conference proceeded like clockwork. Walsh laid the financial numbers on the planning table in a practiced speech using every cliché he could think of, in a 45-minute presentation that lasted what seemed like *hours*, telling his listeners he didn't believe in passing the buck, or blaming people for past failures, but a professional organization needs checks and balances, inquiry into dysfunctional business practices, and eliminating them was the main focus of his speech. Walsh stressed the point that if David had carried out his agreement with Hector,

"There would be no need of me standing here today as administrator of Pleasant Valley that you are both aware was once upon a time a highly profitable farming operation producing food in the breadbasket of America," Walsh assured the group all errors in management would be corrected under the new administration; adding that his *cabala* of outside supporters could not be penetrated by anyone in the room except himself. Once the agenda was established Walsh brought up some specific details of his plans for reorganization.

"I want to put this issue to bed once and for all Hector; you know my interest in this matter is getting it settled; in order to settle it the easy way, as I have stated in other words, the first step should be to sign over all the Dakota sunflowers and safflowers to the Omaha bank in order shut down the suit; again, if I ensure the bank appropriates the collateral they won't have a problem." Walsh continued confidently. "I am quite sure this arrangement will make life much easier for you and my clients and numerous others you are acquainted with."

"We are gathered here today not to denigrate or criticize the previous administration's performance, rather we are here to discuss the offer of settlement I am preparing at this time, with Attorney Wehde arranging discounted letters of credit for affected parties in the lawsuit, though I am not prepared to release those documents at this moment. The delay is caused by the people who offered me the umbrella deal. Let's just say they are financial sources who told me some years ago, to investigate and get this mess settled. The stakeholders had no desire to let the controversy become an issue that gets tangled up with the U.S. government and the families involved. We are here to ratify an alternate agreement because I made your attorney Freeman an offer I believed he couldn't refuse some time ago," Walsh sighed in relief as if the knowledge had some bearing on the situation.

"Mr. Freeman informed me it was your desire Hector, not to accept my offer; then without my knowledge you held a private meeting with MinGo about taking over ownership of David's custom farming business once he was removed from the presidency of Pleasant Valley Corporation; and that David had no idea our discussions involved him. David by the way is working near Williston closing out some leases for me as we speak."

"As a consequence of the imminent collapse of Pleasant Valley that is upon us we must be prepared for the worst; today I am notifying you that within the next six months," Walsh's voice echoed in the room as if Goebbels was bullying the Junkers in the Reichstag. "I would like to consolidate with your partners in total ownership and operation of the current 40,000 acres. In addition, we should plan to lease 20,000 more acres this year and next, under a futures contract to SVO, Ceres, Lubrizol. As an independent contractor, I would like you to make arrangements with Jacques Seed for a corn and soybean contract for the production of 20,000 acres in the event that Jacques decides to enter the competition with their new nitrogen enriched hybrid soybeans and high-oleic corn that will be in full production within 3 years."

"For that very reason we are fortunate to have Jeff and Tonya on board Hector, as our risk insurance providers. As we have experienced this past season, if the weather turns on us we are out of luck–unless we pay these overpriced premiums through bank insurance sources which means we need to sacrifice more scarce capital. I should say *cash* expended to ensure against loss; the banks won't risk *their* money unless we go out on a limb. Don't believe for a second those loan officers are not aware the potential for profit is much greater as risk increases. These conglomerates like Ceres and Continental know how to leverage the capital. For one thing, they don't lose interest on borrowed money invested in production. Essentially, they can write-off loss against massive profits while Zehlen can't." Thinking of the tractors as he stared across central park, Walsh was beaming with the confidence success instills, as his speech approached a climax.

Hector appeared to be listening to the presentation though at times his thoughts were elsewhere. Realizing Walsh had him backed into a corner with his knowledge of the swindle on the Zehlen contract and ASCS frauds–a partner to it–he had no choice but to march in lockstep with the scheme.

"Of course Hector," Walsh increased the intensity of his voice. "My deal is much more generous than any offer you can expect, versus the chance this case ever makes it to court and some zealous judge calls for an audit. What rock do you hide under then? I'm sorry to bring these issues up in front of Jeff and Tonya, but some leadership needs to be shown here. If you research the issues I have presented to you in our discussion today and previously in my office in Brookings, South Dakota, you must realize change will be required under new management policy." He cleared his throat.

"Because of that I will not be as noticeable around the office, spending most of my time in discovery in the courthouse library, writing my argument in the South Dakota lawsuit that ultimately will affect David's future in farming. In my research, I have been gathering information over many hours sifting through the chaos in Dave's office. I had to change the locks. David is welcome to haul his computer out of basement storage. I don't use one. Not even a calculator. I just use an NCR adding machine and photocopy the tape at the library if necessary," Walsh composed his remarks with precision. At that point in the meeting Phyllis excused herself from the corporate board room, apologizing she had year-ending reports to complete.

"In my pro se depositions and documentation, I am listing any contractors including your bosses Ceres, SVO and Lubrizol Hector who have lost money on the deal with Pleasant Valley in my mission to square the debt David accumulated. My task from now on will be focused on using my power to alter the personal transactions involved in changing the original contract offered to David Zehlen by Ceres, to a loan after Zehlen already invested roughly a million five of his and the bank's money the first year, and was suffering the loss of his corporation the next year– because of litigation–funding and supporting documentation from the bank. Not an easy task I assure you, when a slightly different interpretation of the grower's agreement would certainly create a devastating situation for *you* if a judge figured out what the conversion mystery is all about" Walsh looked directly at Sexton staring out the window. "Just so you understand what I'm saying and doing is for your benefit, don't you Hector?"

"That sounds like tampering to me. But like I said in Brookings Robbie, I am listening to your ideas. I just don't completely understand what you are saying yet. Perhaps what you are explaining is beyond my capabilities. Can you inform the three of us in plain English, what the purpose of me notifying Jessen that I am the owner of the safflowers is, when he already knows that information?" Hector inquired with a puzzled expression on his face.

"Bear with me and thank you for your patience on that critical issue Hector," Walsh continued. "You sent him the phony bills didn't you? There is more evidence to come. That is why we are all gathered here today. Why I have offered you the opportunity to vent your frustration about your disagreements in the deal with Zehlen that went south."

"Okay Robbie. What can I say? I'm listening seriously to your proposal am I not?" Hector played along with the farce as Jeff and Tonya looked at each other and nodded as if they too were amazed at the persuasive ability of their new leader.

"And now Hector if you would be so kind as to put this First Omaha situation behind you by assigning the flower income to them which means you agree to accept the loss of the crop as a formality. It will cost us less to plow the bird damage under–than salvage the silage," Walsh declared.

"In the meantime, I will be making arrangements with David to settle the government situation the Zehlens are in–with hold-harmless agreements. His actions in illegally allocating the government funds will be merely declared violations. Zehlen will be forced to pay back the government a half million dollars in penalties. Unfortunately, we can't help that, we all know by now, the farm will be sacrificed."

"You need not wonder how this is done any longer. I accomplish much of my work anonymously, using insider influence as a professional investigator with private bank contacts and contracts. My background includes inspection for the Mississippi River board of trade, acting as a watchdog over agricultural marketing service practices, working side by side with ATF and customs agents, undercover at different times in unofficial capacities since my relationship with South Dakota Governor Bill Janklow who I was proud to number among my associates at the early stages of my career," Walsh emptied a glass of water, without missing a beat.

"Don't get me wrong; I'm not threatening you or David. You both made illegal personal transactions that under a different interpretation can be vaguely defined as, against the law–that made you both vulnerable to prosecution for–embezzling government money you weren't entitled to. In the solution I propose, you catch a break in the new deal. I'm sorry to report David's marathon for the money is over," Walsh's words reached toward a toastmaster's peak of eloquence. "In your case Hector,

I'm here to help you avoid being indicted for fraud by a grand jury composed of Jack Zehlen's friends in Granite County. Instead I will be offering you shares and a refinancing option to be a part of my newly formed corporation Interwest. Are you with me Hector...Jeff? Tonya? Is it a deal?"

"We hear you Robbie. Maybe we do not understand the meaning of what you are saying? It will take time for it all to sink in," said Hector. Jeff Provo nodded in agreement with Sexton. Tonya stared blankly at Walsh. Hector's in-laws had no idea what direction they were being led in the wilderness.

"What I'm saying is this: if the money David Zehlen and Pleasant Valley Farms borrowed from First Omaha was invested in the South Dakota safflowers by an agent of Ceres, SVO/Lubrizol and you don't intend to deliver on your obligations– then I see real trouble; if you advanced a *loan* to Pleasant Valley, that is a different story. But if it is apparent that it is a bad loan and you are willing to accept the loss which will eventually be made up to you in restitution, and in your associations with me personally in Interwest in our future dealings; again, what I'm saying is if you do it my way at least there can be *no proven scheme* on the promissory fraud, or ASCS issues with David Zehlen. Do you see what I mean Hector? I don't expect Jeff to understand every detail at the moment. You need to believe that I am doing this for your benefit as much as I am doing it for the Zehlen family. Trust me and every promise I make on your half of the deal will come to fruition," Walsh sounded unconvincing as he raced through his prepared statement.

"Could you slow down a little and please explain this plan in plain English Robbie? You are confusing my associates Jeff and Tonya. This is a difficult second language material for them to comprehend."

"They will catch on soon enough." Walsh argued decisively. "I am appearing pro se in the South Dakota lawsuit over ownership of your safflowers Hector. For that reason, I am doing my own discovery. I feel the case deserves the spending of some $500,000 in fees to prove the argument, because if I am right the case could be beneficial to both me and you in the future. The bank will prove David is liable for the loss. I was recently faxed correspondence between the bank and the Brent Wilber firm regarding the new interpretation of your agreement with David Zehlen," Walsh paused a few seconds before forging ahead to the punch line.

"What I suggest you do Hector is, you and your company agree to hand over all the South Dakota sunflowers and safflowers to FNBO in order to settle the suit. At least you won't be facing a Leavenworth term for government fraud. If the bank gets all the collateral, while you Hector, Ceres, Lubrizol are determined to not fulfill on the contract obligation to my client Pleasant Valley–how can they when there is no crop? You can see why there is not much I can do unless you cooperate. As you know Jeff, there is no coverage for the loss because the insurance was canceled; there is some uncertainty if insurance coverage exists for the sunflowers; so it appears to be a total loss on both crops."

"So I'm not sure Jessen can back you up on that one either. That means *you* Hector, and your group is liable for that entire loss. Again I mention that if your organization has no intention to fulfill on the contract and pay the bill to the bank and they claim the collateral–that would be the Pleasant Valley assets, equity, property–they don't have a bitch. I have discussed this potential arrangement with Jessen and the bank attorneys"

"The only thing uncertain about the upcoming foreclosure on Pleasant Valley is the date. It all depends on what you and your partners intend to argue in the bank lawsuit. I know in the long run this solution will keep many errors from being exposed to the public. And I am sure this will make life much easier for you, my clients and numerous other associates you are familiar with in the course of your dealings with Ceres, SVO, and Lubrizol," Walsh scanned his followers, looking for any disagreement with his ideas. When he saw there were none he continued.

"Perhaps those companies approve and reinforce your methods. I for one do not; but I intend to do what I can for victims of your business practices, because I am pledged to do what is right in preserving the dignity of the Zehlen family. Are you with me on this arrangement? It must be kept confidential. Not even Phyllis knows the complete details at this time. I'm not sure she needs to know them frankly," Walsh proceeded with confidence, if not caution.

"As far as other activity that may have caused harm to the Zehlen family and Pleasant Valley Corporation, it is apparent to me that this information must never be discussed in front of a judge with sympathy for Zehlen; because *that* judge will be obligated by their oath to call a state's attorney or prosecutor for immediate examination–and I am referring to the extraction of funds from the government through limited partners in 1991–and your persistence Hector in this conduct becomes the issue again, a year when you were giving orders to MN Go partners working on your South Dakota safflowers and sunflowers," Walsh was driving ahead on cruise control.

"It is reprehensible that at such a critical time, when the ASCS had already challenged the supposed restructuring that was reviewed and only benefited you in 1991–you ignored my warnings. You had it both ways, as the only person who benefited by the scheme of things. I don't condemn you for it; but the state's attorney's office and the courts might if they get wind of it. I assure you they won't from me," Walsh adjusted his bifocals, and began peering at another document from the file.

"However Hector I must inform you of the potentially volatile nature of these issues, which absolutely must be resolved before we authorize a charter for Interwest," Walsh paused a moment, took a sip of water and checked his notes before continuing. Walsh scanned the board room as if to determine if it was bugged. Hector was crestfallen but managed to keep his composure in front of his sister and her husband. Walsh continued speaking somberly,

"I will be involved in recording your depositions required in the South Dakota lawsuit I am pursuing pro se; that work will involve many hours of diligence on my part, and gathering witnesses for depositions is my number one concern. We must build a solid argument that the contract is a loan, simple as that.

I will need to write a series of legal motions, supported by a solid argument, with numerous cites, then forward it to the banks attorneys for finalization," Walsh explained.

"At this juncture I am thinking particularly of David's wife and her children specifically, aware there will be other casualties in the chaos David created. SigCo seeds would be one, Ceres another, his neighbor Glen Bergen among many others. In any event, if there was a 1992 grain contract offered to Pleasant Valley as we know there was, or any agreement of a binding nature–it would most certainly be devastating to the lawsuit if some nosy judge or attorney started snooping around, examined the structure of what we are trying to accomplish here, reversed the judgment; in the process you became liable for 3-times the money. Do you see what I'm driving at Hector? The risk we are taking."

Walsh paused and walked over to the window, noticing a queue of neighborhood kids, bundled in parkas and scarves, dragging their sleds to the edge of the snowy park hills across the street from the Anothene building, before rocketing down the steep hill known as "Three Post." It's a miracle someone's kid hasn't been killed on that damn slope that must be a hundred feet long and at least 60 degrees steep, he thought for a moment before resuming his presentation.

"What I would like for you to do Hector, is to contact your attorney immediately. I refer to your counsel, the law firm of Esq. John Freeman of Fargo I am acquainted with. That may have changed. I believe you mentioned the name of another attorney you work with, a Mr. Hanson from Devil's Lake. We need a good attorney supervising and organizing legal depositions for the hearing. Furthermore, I have informed you and your attorney in the Sully litigation, in a private conversation that the payment of the entire obligation you have withheld from Pleasant Valley Farms and the Zehlen family for whom I am speaking, could be absorbed as debt and restructured in loans from your financiers, letters of credit, whatnot as need be, for the necessary financial stability you need to establish and maintain your initial investment and operating capital in Interwest."

"Of course this deal I am offering is completely legitimate and validated by your lawyers Freeman and Hanson. In previous discussions with your attorneys for Ceres, SVO, and Lubrizol my offer was subject to review of your people and mine who have backgrounds with, or are involved with Salomon Brothers brokerage house out of New York. There is a chance certainly, the investors that you have relied on in the past would know how to handle a discounted letter of credit so the contract could be completed with extensions and layers as is shown in the Wall Street Journal article I will photocopy and send to you. The necessary information is in the handout I am passing out to you now as our two-hour session is coming to a close. I want you to remember these things in the brochure that outline the structure of the new enterprise I am forming upon the foundation of the old one." Walsh was talking at a volume that echoed, just fast enough so there would be some difficulty in translation and transparency of his message to the foreign ear.

"This information will be helpful when you apply for your green card Jeff. I remind you to keep the enclosed business card in your wallet. Keep that folder handy as part of the letter package when you need to provide documentation to prove you are not an illegal alien to this country. Without a high school diploma from Mexico you do not need other problems. You will need to prove you are holding a permanent job in the United States, working for Hector, employed full time, not just as a seasonal temp on the application, to the immigration bureau before your visa expires."

The ancient radiators in the conference room were clacking in staccato as if they needed to be bled soon. Beads of sweat were standing out on Walsh's reddening forehead as he continued his speech. He cleared his throat, taking another sip of ice water. The Provos were whispering in Spanish, apparently shocked that Walsh was so well aware of their *iffy* immigration status.

"In taking over as power of attorney for Pleasant Valley Farms, I have given my word to the Zehlen family that they will be free and clear of all their debts when I am finished with this matter. If need be I could prove, and you know this all too well Hector, that the Zehlens have been taken advantage of. In the process, they have suffered the loss of all Jack's assets." Walsh's words slipped off his tongue as smooth as Johnny Walker Red, the liquor in particular he had sworn off at 40. Ice water on his tongue brought back the experience and taste of whiskey on the rocks, embedded deep in the recesses of his memory. He glanced out at the hedge of conifers lining the bluff of the city park. Invigorated by the landscape view he had inherited, on a gray day in the winter season Walsh resumed his speech, gathering momentum for his climax.

"I know you are as fond as I am Hector, of Nancy and the four Zehlen children. We are concerned that David's mother is ailing with MS. As part of my offer to the family of David and Jack, I have agreed with Nancy and Phyllis to help them get out of this terrible mental stress they are under as owners of Pleasant Valley Corporation. I do what I do so they don't suffer the embarrassment of a Chapter 7 bankruptcy–after being once known in Rockland as wealthy, highly respected citizens, while living large as any on Highland Highway, distinguished members of the church and community." Walsh paused a moment and wiped his brow, as a beads of sweat perched above his eyes, then he drained his glass of ice water before continuing, pondering over his notes, to make sure he covered all the details.

When the radiators hissed, the building temperature had risen to 72. It was *cold* out–at least Walsh knew the boiler was working. He wished Phyllis was pouring him another glass. The adrenaline was pumping. Though his shakiness was under control, invisible, Robbie was rushing forward on the dry drunk he had resisted so many years. His career had reached his peak in the conference room of the Zehlen's Anothene alcohol rehab center that he would soon claim as his own personal property. He scanned the room again for dramatic effect as if to check which way the drafts waft, before resuming his speech.

"As I have informed you previously, we all realize the Zehlens will be penniless; it is fortunate that Nancy will retain her position as a dental assistant with Dr. Hanson. Nancy asked me just the other day, if I could help her avoid the tremendous hassle they are going through. No one has suffered more than her. I had pity for the woman pleading with me, if I couldn't help her just put aside the grief for the good, once and for all; just let the family live so that they don't have to be in and out of court for many years to come. As David's long suffering wife Nancy knows, the Sully lawsuit will require many hours of painful litigation. Is there any disagreement on that issue?" Walsh glancing down at his notes inquired of his listeners. After there was silence for a moment or two he resumed the message,

"We all know Nancy will have to fudge a bit about the truth and her involvement in the personage issues as she and Phyllis were forced to with the ASCS committee in August. I have been mentoring her, discussing her role in it on a daily basis. When I took over power of attorney as a favor to the Zehlen family, I told Nancy and Phyllis I would do what they want done regardless of the effect on my income." With no ventilation it was hot and stuffy in the conference room by two o'clock. Walsh retrieved his handkerchief and wiped his eyes to suggest he had shed a few tears for the Zehlens; it was all a part his greatest performance on *earth*, as it is.

"Are there any questions, remarks, new ideas to add? –final thoughts before we put this matter to rest?" Walsh inquired of his tired guests, scanning Hector, Jeff and Tonya Provo's expressionless faces to determine if there were any restive notions left in this organization. At that moment almost as if Phyllis had read his mind, she reappeared in the board room with a pitcher of ice water. For an instant Walsh rejoiced over his choice for vice president–of the *phoenix* that will rise from the ashes of Pleasant Valley, embracing the thought they were on the same wave length, as Phyllis poured him another glass of ice water. Moments like that reaffirmed what Robbie believed was his ability to move people and objects by powers of *telepathy*.

"I have no further questions Robbie," Hector was submissive. Knowing he was whipped, he stuck to the script, retaining a shred of dignity, he commented. "You evidently have done your homework on this assignment. You are way ahead of us on this one. Let's give our new leader a hand my friends." He and Jeff clapped. It was not clear if Tonya understood the significance of the occasion or the *command* of it. Her reaction was unsure as she may have been reticent to clap for Robbie because the terribly serious expression on his face all the time made her nervous.

"The man never smiles; he scares me," Tonya later told her husband.

Sexton wasn't prepared for a lecture on ethics and morality either, from the ringleader of what he knew was a corrupt deal he couldn't back out of.

"We will all have to see how this whole new deal you are telling us about here today shakes out Robbie. It sounds like a lot of speculation. Today you have presented a great deal more of your strategy than in our last discussion in Brookings before harvest," Hector had his usual doubts. "It will take some time for me and my relatives with me today to digest everything you have said. But I can tell you this much. My associates and I are behind you a hundred percent for the long haul you can be sure of that," said Hector concluding his remarks, anxious for some fresh air after the Anothene II debriefing, where he could be comfortable again in the luxury of his Lincoln, rehashing the meeting with his *chauffeur* during the drive back to Fargo.

As his guests were leaving Walsh pulled Hector aside, saying he didn't choose that day to discuss in detail the issue of Sexton's conduct on the ASCS problem–either of them could explain that situation to the Provos at some other time–if it was necessary. On this special day, he wanted the ladies in the office to understand he was a gentleman at heart, but a serious business man. Patting Hector on the shoulder as he left the board room, Walsh reiterated his confidence in the scheme.

"You are wise and a shrewd businessman Hector, I recognize that. We can use your skills in Interwest," said Walsh. "No disrespect. I knew you would see the light sooner or later. I will have Phyllis fax you a full report on all the issues we covered today. She is working on a draft of the letter of credit I am talking about. You should have your copy in the next week or so. Thank you for coming Jeff and Tonya."

Hospitality conscious, Robbie shook hands with his new associates as they left the conference. After a smoke in the furnace room, he stepped into David's executive suite that had once been a doctor's office in the first Rockland Community Hospital, and closed the door. As he reclined in the director's chair, Robbie felt a tremendous sense of self-satisfaction. A few years past fifty he was one step closer to seeing the dreams of his youth–to create his own agricultural empire big enough to compete with the Continentals, the Peaveys, and Ceres–come to fruition.

It took more insight than Zehlen or Sexton had available at the time to understand–many of the Walsh slogans were simply revisions of the dictator's plea. Sure he had to expand on what he knew of Sexton–that he had committed what could be considered racketeering under a different lens.

There was a chance he would be declared civilly and criminal liable for those acts unless he listened to Walsh's terms for a subtle takeover of the Pleasant Valley farming operations. As he became more control conscious, Walsh felt the constant need to make those people under him beware that he held their fate in his hands; he had learned later in life than most people to make his associates *fear* rather than love or respect him–when there was always the threat, the potential for Walsh to blow the whistle on Sexton as he had done already indirectly to make his points in the meeting. His thoughts pleased him, allowing him to feel omnipotent for a change. Unconsciously, Walsh had succeeded in becoming the politician he aspired to be–disposing of his rivals through abdication of the electoral process.

Walsh did not have the sheepskin his brother had; his cunning nature had more to do with feeling and intuition than Ansel's. At his age, urges and sensations did not arrive at the physical level as they had in his youth. The enervating condition that resulted was an indication Robbie was battling what might have been diagnosed as male menopause, if it was brought to the attention of a physician which it never was. By 1990, Robert's pleasures were more of a cerebral nature.

Basic principles of biological assumption confirmed that he shared the same genes related to intelligence as his brother; he had put as much time, work and research in his discovery on the Pleasant Valley Project as Ansel had in writing his doctoral thesis. He was proud of his work. He felt he was ready to take his place with the great men he associated with in his past. Walsh would soon become the wealthy man of prestige and esteem he was entitled to be. Robert had resigned years before that he would never hold a government job because of trusting a crooked partner. In the restoration process–Robert had recovered from the depths of despair to achieve *unimaginable* success in private business. Walsh was confident he was on the verge of making more money than he *ever* would have realized in any civil service job, short of the Senate.

Sitting back in the captain's chair, he reflected on the solemn events of the takeover as it evolved from the larval stage. Walsh was satisfied and gratified by his presentation that frigid afternoon. After all, he had no professional speech training, or philosophy background, yet had done a hell of a job today in Pleasant Valley's one-time board room, now the headquarters of Interwest. The secret of his effectiveness was his *absolute* mastery of the subject matter. He had learned his lessons from the school of hard knocks in his younger days, putting the counsel of his mentor Bill Janklow to good use. Like him Walsh had survived what could have been a career ending incident; once that episode was covered up, the suspiciously rogue attorney went on to be Governor of the State of South Dakota. It had taken a somewhat corrupt but very clever attorney to expunge Walsh's records. *Wild bill* as they referred to the Governor was the single man on earth Walsh owed his revitalized career to.

The meeting had been an exclamation point in his meteoric rise to the top, an unusual display of absolute authority necessary to create solidarity within the organization. In his finest moment, he laid his portfolio on the table of the conference room, announcing the formation of a new entity leaping like a spring calf from the crumbling ruins of Pleasant Valley Farms. It was Robert Walsh's hour of destiny, the time to make an unusual show of power like a sudden bolt of lightning through the dead of winter. No one on the planet except Robert would be able to appreciate or comprehend the historic triumph Walsh accomplished for the country December 7, 1992, "*51 years to the day since Pearl*" he jotted in his notebook.

CHAPTER 32

Within weeks of the success of his first public announcements about the new management arrangements, Robert Walsh announced the annual corporate meeting to the principal stakeholders of Pleasant Valley Corporation to be held on Fat Tuesday 1993 at 2:30 p.m., in the Anothene board room; he was now chairman of the board of directors on top of administrating his other duties since taking over the corporation in July '92. He had never actually toyed with his customers before like he had with the Zehlens; never before had he been in such a naturalized setting run by two attractive women who would be available soon, amidst the scarcity; they were not your average housewives–they dressed and acted like *city* girls running the business for the owner.

In Walsh's estimation, though they were not the *Sports Illustrated* caliber swimsuit models he preferred, Nancy and Phyllis were without a doubt "trophy" women by local standards. Walsh had observed as much in a provincial society where hunting the prized 36-point buck was an established ritual among the sons of the community who had successfully completed gun-safety training as early as twelve years. The young guns of Rockland were proud of when their pictures appeared on the pages of the Rockland Independent, carcasses in hand; such accuracy was possible after many hours spent, each summer plinking tin cans in the pasture, practicing for the three-day season with their .22 rifles. Such training rituals were the norm passed on from father to son; the young huntsmen graduating from duck and pheasants, prepared to take advantage of the rutting routine of the buck, each hunter hoping to end the reproductive cycle of an overpopulated species with a 12-gauge slug to the ribs. Ah yes, Robbie inhaled–to the male whitetail, nothing is more beautiful than a little brown doe.

"We are gathered here today to commemorate the recovery of Pleasant Valley Farms under new management and new title. Forgetting the errors of the past we move forward." Sounding *eerily* familiar, Walsh proceeded beyond his standard introduction, getting to the *nitty-gritty* quickly.

"Thank you for excusing my lack of an entertaining icebreaker for you today. As both of you know," Walsh stated grimly. "I have been in constant contact with the Omaha bank since these events developed relative to the ominous financial situation; I have researched the jeopardy that your husband David placed your corporation in. Of course I was just performing my duties in the role you assumed I would as power of attorney. I am doing my best in a very difficult situation. And in view of the dire circumstances your husband's acts have placed you in, it was the only choice because as you both know the government was on the verge of criminal prosecution of David and the other officers of the corporation in the ASCS fraud." Walsh took a sip of his coffee. The two Zehlen wives sat silently as if awaiting a jury verdict in a kidnapping case.

"It was only because of the relationships I have developed over the years with various levels of government that I have been able to accomplish what I have. Of course my friendship was compromised with Harlan Anderson of the ASCS county committee. I assumed he was with me. At the very end, I felt threatened he would change his mind. If I may add also, that Phyllis has a right to feel terribly betrayed by Jack, in that he took advantage of their relationship, allowing that marital trust to be destroyed by the covert methods he and David used to *mislead* the government on program applications." Walsh hesitated again lifting his mug to his lips for a full gulp of coffee before continuing,

"Ladies I ask you, for the sake of what remains of the relationships you have with your husbands, marriage or business-wise, be patient. I don't want to bring up the government problems David created again. I know how you both suffered through tremendous angst over those government hearings, in which you both were under pressure to testify against your *own* husbands; if you failed to do that, you could have been facing time in Shakopee. I understand what stress can do to you. I am thankful I had enough influence with the board in the power and authority of the office you handed me to intervene on your behalf. Another reason I chose to conduct this meeting with you here today is to celebrate the *macabre*, Halloween of springtime, the Mardi Gras being celebrated a thousand miles due south of Rockland, in the Big Easy where I inspected the public elevator for mixing fraud. David and Nancy spent their 10th anniversary there. What a coincidence isn't it? I would request you keep the proceeds of our meeting confidential, because there will probably be criminal charges arising out of the mishandling of the South Dakota government financing arrangements between David and Hector Sexton. That is why I called you in to the office today, even though I hated to pull Nancy away from her career at the dentist's office."

"I can only imagine the stress you are under, what your job and career means to you now that you are the only breadwinner in the family–my apologies to the dentist for allowing you some time off. Trust me I will make up any financial loss of your salary in the offer I am about to make you. Are there any questions from you ladies today?"

"None than I can think of right at the moment Robbie." If her attention wavered she risked a scolding from the boss for not paying attention to his sermon; she secretly glanced at her watch, worried about Hannah who arrived home early on Tuesdays from her special education classes. Then she remembered David was at home that afternoon. Nancy was trying to understand why it was so important to Robbie that the contract between Sexton and David be *reinterpreted* as a loan. She was reticent to bring up the subject in front of Phyllis, who did not seem to be under the same scrutiny and pressure she was feeling under Walsh's directorship.

"Alright then if there are no questions I'll continue where we left off with the new business agenda," said Walsh making as much drama out of the meeting as possible. "Just as you both were not held accountable on the ASCS scheme that David and Jack put together against the government, when you very easily could have been unless I mediated the situation at some risk to myself I might add, which I was more than willing to take for the sake of resolving the situation you are in. I have some very good news from the Omaha Bank I will share with you later in our meeting."

The *charlatan* in the man was at peak performance level, as Robbie raised a glass of ice cubes to his mouth, relishing that last cold sip and paused for effect. Over the years he had developed a repertoire of strange expressions and gestures learned in automobile sales and *Toastmasters* of Brookings that were oddly effective when they accompanied his well-developed skill to utter the vague corollary idea at the right time to *think* about– that could interrupt a serious chain of thought–as it was intended to. Using such a method, he was able to succeed in imposing his ideology by making it appear as well designed, practical solutions to impossible situations, inserting shorthand generalizations at every stage of an argument over irrelevant issues–a skill not learned in academe–although some professors are known to use the same technique. Familiar with his patented method of exaggerating issues that should never be discussed among the remaining stakeholders of Pleasant Valley Farms– while obstructing their main concerns–the audience became bored with Walsh's gratuitous dramatics by the time the first cubes in his glass melted.

"What I am about to tell you is strictly confidential, I need you to understand that," Walsh continued. "I could require signatures from both of you on our confidentially form; but we'll let that go for now. As I have mentioned in the past, when in spring 1992 Pleasant Valley began experiencing cash flow problems, it was then that David began asking for my assistance to help obtain loans from banks. It was I who came running to David's assistance. For a short time, I was his right-hand man. That was before I realized that as soon as the bank loan was issued I was expendable. I know for a fact David was planning on handing me my walking papers right up until you women stood up to David and impeached his presidency of Pleasant Valley by declaring me power of attorney. David probably suspected I had tipped off the FBI that he may have had something to do with the Woods Elevator incident; the bureau was thinking of re-opening that case under a RICO investigation," Walsh pretending to be unsurprised by his discovery, took a moment to wipe his brow with a clean handkerchief for appearances sake, and continued matter-of-factly.

"At that time what I did not reveal to you was that David may have been involved in a similar international grain scam that he was running with his partner Pete Werner through Woods Elevator in North Dakota. Believe me I don't want to delve too deeply into this matter with the bureau at this time; but as I told both David and the FBI, his name was linked with *kited* trains in a fictitious scheme that involved stolen box car loads of corn, headed for the Middle East–specifically Turkey. U.S customs examined receipts and other activities related to the marketing of commodities in international trading out of Woods. I didn't mention that incident before because I thought that among all the other troubling issues, it would upset both of you too much at the time." Walsh took a sip of his water, wishing it was something stronger.

"And about that time," Walsh continued, "that's when I learned David's name and his credit was being used in an illegal PIK-certificate trading scheme running out of Woods Elevator. I'm afraid this is the void where some of the money Hector was liable for on the first contract was disappearing to. All I'm asking for is some kind of explanation for why David needed more money, loans and credit from banks when he had all that cash at one time? Where did it go is my question? Before I learned the truth I trusted David like a son. He is frugal but naïve. We know he didn't spend that money on himself. It went into Hector's crop and paying those leases. I was involved in forwarding David's resume to First Omaha because they were looking for a person to manage 16,000 acres on their behalf in South Dakota. This is where the loan involving Hector's crops comes into play. So you can easily see how involved I became almost immediately, with millions of dollars on the line," Walsh concluded on a persuasive note.

"But what does this all mean for us, and our future Robbie? I don't understand what you are trying to say," said Nancy. "I mean what is the point? We made you power of attorney so we didn't have to think of these matters we don't understand. We are not farmers. I never spent time on one before in my life before I met David; he took me horseback riding out at the farm. I hate horses. Phyllis knew more than I did about agriculture because she worked for Farmer's Coop in Marshall for five years before she met Jack. We hired you because at one point you convinced me it was the *only* way to save Pleasant Valley, making you our trusted power of attorney. You offered unsolicited advice on our marriage which was on the verge of failing at that time. So that didn't help either. It is obvious we still don't understand the mess my husband and Jack brought upon us, when they named us as officers of the corporation that did not even have a charter. On top of that we got nothing out of the deal. And could you please explain why it is so important for me to testify that the safflower contract with Hector was a loan?" Nancy continued wondering why Robert wasn't pressuring Phyllis like he was her, why she said so little at such a critical time?

"Don't worry I'm coming to that part Nancy, and I will explain *everything* to you in due time so that you may know the background and the reasons I do what I must do to help you and your children out of the terrible jam David's management of the corporation has created for Pleasant Valley Farms," Walsh changed the subject in typical fashion but clipped his words because Nancy Zehlen was listening closely to learn more about the fate of her husband that seemed to be in Walsh's hands.

"Phyllis do you have any questions? You are about to become secretary to the president of the new corporation." in a senior moment Robbie's mind wandered as his voice trailed off, "… *rising upon the ashes of the old* …"

For that minute interval, no one in the room seemed to notice his consciousness had revisited the Nundas city limits of his mind, dealing with signs and the image that flared up now and then from the recesses of time at unpredictable moments. Regaining control, he ignored the sudden *spell* that may have lasted three to five seconds when he appeared to be completely normal; Robbie resumed his train of thought.

"You need to realize from now on–you must have complete confidence in me–my advanced experience and my decision-making ability; believe me I have been through this before with other farmers in the Midwest. I know exactly what I intend to do in your case."

"You know we trust you Robbie," Phyllis answered mechanically. "We had no other choice. That's why we made you our power of attorney; but I'm not completely confident I understand what you are getting at any better than Nancy. I hope you understand we are just housewives. I never lived on a farm in my life until I married Jack. Neither did Nancy, her father was a pharmacist. Our kids are in school or in college. I come in to the office three days a week to be the secretary weekday afternoons and answer the phones. Accounts receivable went through Dave. I pay a few local bills; that's all I do. Between us we know less than zero about farming. We hired you to run the business since our partners obviously don't know what they are doing."

"Thank you Phyllis, you are correct. What I am about to tell you will probably change your lives; but it is better that way. I guarantee it," Walsh knew how to reinforce doubt. "Let me explain something to you so you both understand how this works." Phyllis raised her hand feebly. Walsh ignored her gesture a moment as he scanned his notebook. In a perky tone he replied,

"What is it Phyllis?" Walsh was beaming, his way of indicating he was pleased the *girls* as he referred to them were responding to his vague presentation, never intended to answer the obvious questions about what happens to David and Jack.

"My husband, Jack I mean, says we will lose the farm now because there is no money left to pay off the loan. Is that true Robbie?" Phyllis inquired carefully. "That doesn't make sense to me. Jack says you..."

"Which loan are we talking about Phyllis, the bank loan or the Sexton loan? Take your pick?" Walsh retorted instantly.

"Please Phyllis can't you just keep your faithless doubts to yourself for a change? Robbie is just trying to help us get through this mess?" Nancy blurted out unexpectedly, defending Walsh.

"Your husband did nothing when he could have stopped David from his schemes. His son can do no wrong in Jack's eyes. He just doesn't like Robbie running the farm; isn't that true Robbie? All we are asking Robbie now is if these problems just cannot be put aside for good and let us live in peace. My family, my children, my parents in their retirement; let us live so that we don't have to be in and out of court for many years to come–you warned me unless we do something about these horrible decisions made by our husbands–we faced *prison* time. The discovery that Robbie is doing voluntarily, will cause others so much discomfort we won't be able to bear it. Isn't that what you told me Robbie?" Tears were welling up in her eyes; her contacts were irritated by the salty tears as she concluded her pathetic plea.

"Dysfunctional domestic affairs are not my bailiwick Nancy. I was just commenting on my observations nothing more. You both have an understanding of the problems you face. I think Jack drinks too much. He spends too much time in the machine shop fixing things that don't matter anymore, more like a hobby for him now. The equipment he keeps repairing is worn out. That's why David financed new tractors on Hector's guaranteed contract. I believe he actually thought of MN Go as an organization capable of competing with growers like Hector; that was a *fatal* mistake," Walsh was livid for an instant, pupils literally dancing in his eyes.

"David has always been spoiled rotten and never listens to anybody including his father, me, or any of you. He created the problem. Jack is correct, Pleasant Valley over-extended itself on the First Omaha loan," –(Walsh had embezzled his IRA) –"there is nothing left to pay off the bank with *except* the collateral security they assigned on the loan."

"We heard all that Robbie," Nancy was close to tears. "We expected you to fix that as power of attorney because you told us you could prevent the disaster we were facing in the ASCS. I never thought we could lose the farm because of the Omaha loan. It was always our understanding the crops were the collateral. We thought Hector seemed like an honest man. David never mentioned the possibility things could go wrong. What can we do if it's too late according to Jack?"

"Don't tell me either one of you read the fine print on the agreements you signed, before you went out and bought some new clothes and celebrated at Foster Lodge. I heard all about the venison and wild rice banquet, free to the public. At the time I was not invited. On top of that omission, your husbands never explained that by *then* the conditions had changed drastically, and the farm was 'on the line' with First Omaha. There is more to it, but now you know why I stepped in to help you out of this jam. Both David and Jack were fools to take out a loan on Hector's crop," Walsh acted disgusted as he secretly rejoiced.

"I told them what the risks were but they never listened. Then David asked me to arrange financing with my long-time financing associates. He was on the verge of destroying my credibility with my backers. That's history by now; water over the dam. But the reason I called you in today was to discuss exactly what we are facing now. I am negotiating the predicament you all face with Mr. Jessen. The bank has offered us some generous terms."

Walsh paused and poured himself a glass of water, carrying it in his hand as he walked over to the window that faced the spruce trees lining the high ridge of the snow-covered park to the southeast of the headquarters building. Phyllis and Nancy who had never been close until the crisis, could make up at will, as the performance required, figuratively curled up in the fetal position like David's identical siblings appeared, when they were faced with a crisis. Walsh resumed his place at the conference table squarely facing the two women he was manipulating.

"I have some good news and some bad," said Walsh laying his cards on the table. "I am afraid that Hector has no choice but to go to court over the money lost in the Woods Elevator shortfall which can be linked to the current Pleasant Valley circumstances. But he will go after Pete Werner, not David, because he has no money left. Although it is off the record for now, Hector believes that David and his men in South Dakota have been covertly swindling him at least two years, skimming grain, delivering it at night on back-county roads into Minnesota and then selling a couple thousand bushels at a time in the local elevators in Revillo, Odessa and Bellingham. We've all heard the rumors, now I have proof from Curley Novak manager of the Odessa elevator. Off the record he confirmed reports of a few late night shipments, but offered no details when I chatted with him briefly at the White Pony café during the Odessa centennial. There are rumors about town that David and Jack have been flying under the radar for years to lower their income taxes. In my view the scheme is similar to what happened in South Dakota; the distinction is that at the Woods Elevator we are talking lost *boxcars* at Hector's expense. There is no proof. In addition, Hector has shown me phony billings on fertilizer and chemicals amounting to $330K, he claims is direct evidence of intentional theft of his grain," Walsh stretched the criminal implications as far as possible.

"I can't believe my husband would stoop that low," Nancy reacted meekly, though she was approaching hysteria. Phyllis had her arm around her step-daughter in-law Nancy who looked as if she had aged a few years in the course of an hour.

"He fooled me. Like the others I believed my husband. I thought David was clever and innovative in his farming practices; we all thought he was a successful farmer like he appeared to be on the cover of *Farm Futures*, not because he is a damn crook. Pardon my French. Is David going to prison Robbie? What will my boys think of their father behind bars? They are on the varsity next year." She burst into tears.

"I hesitated to disclose this information for a reason. You are my closest friends in Rockland. We are business partners. I waited as long as I could to reveal this information to you. All Hector wants is his money back that he loaned to David."

"Loan? For God's sake *what* loan are you talking about Robbie? I thought we had a contract with Hector that David was putting his money and the bank's in to. The Zehlens don't need any more debt," Nancy sobbed inconsolably. "I didn't know of any loan David had with Hector. Don't tell me he lied to me about that too Robbie?

"Unfortunately that's the way Hector's attorney staff and the court will look at it Nancy; that is something we will have to work out in the lawsuit Pleasant Valley will be facing from the Omaha Bank. And that's the last thing I just want to mention to you girls today, Nancy, Phyllis. This is important, I had to tell you the worst first," Walsh continued. "I go back to the first question Phyllis raised. And that was what Phyllis?"

"Excuse me Robbie I don't recall what we were talking about then," Phyllis answered methodically. "You have talked about so many things today."

"The foreclosure sweetheart, the foreclosure," Walsh refreshed her anterograde memory. "The foreclosure Jack was worried about. Now you remember don't you? Your husband acted unconcerned as a matter of fact; but he sensed it was coming. I am not sure the exact date the paper work and the Wilber Meyer motions began in October of 1992. I warned him he should be worried with nothing to pay off the huge debt with the Omaha bank. I preserved some of his IRA money for him, maybe for your benefit. But as I said that is what you hired me for."

"As I have mentioned many times," said Walsh with renewed vigor. "I worked with the bank to procure the loan for Pleasant Valley; there were some conditions and adjustments involved that we never discussed, and I won't get into the details at this meeting. But I am pleased to inform you I have been working with the bank and its attorneys to settle this debt. We discussed my plan back in December Phyllis. Do you remember our discussions with Hector, Jeff and Tonya Provo?"

"No I can't recall what you said exactly Robbie. Could you refresh our collective memory?" Phyllis responded mechanically, bored stiff with Walsh's theatrics. "Maybe you could repeat the part about why the contract has to become a loan explaining to us so we both understand your reasoning, since Nancy was not at the same meeting I was. You're alright now aren't you honey?" She smoothed Nancy's recently curled locks.

"Oh sure!" Nancy exclaimed. "I'm always ready for more bad news. I might as well know my husband's *dirty laundry!*" Her temper flared, oddly strengthened in her ire; before the crisis she and David never fought, as the estrogen she was unaccustomed to contributed to a bundle of unfamiliar emotions, in discord with income security, socialization, and esteem considerations that accompanied a floundering marriage.

"I'll see what kind of deal I can work out for David with the prosecutor's office; if he cooperates fully, your husband might just be facing probation. It all depends on how sincere David is about accepting punishment and restitution for damages if a harsh judge wants to go that direction. Granite County judgment depends on how serious Hector is about pressing charges," said Walsh replying to his own question. "That's a ways off yet, so try not to think of it right now."

Walsh paused and left the room for a few minutes, enjoying a Winston outside the building in the patio area on a 17-degree day. The Zehlen women talked intensely during those moments Robbie was out of earshot–venting their anger at David for ruining their jaded lives. While he was outside the boardroom, the girls discussed their dire circumstances. They agreed it would be wonderful to finally put the unsettling situation their irresponsible husbands had placed them in behind with a nice trip to Phoenix, Arizona where Phyllis's sister lived. Walsh returned invigorated by the fresh air and two cigarettes, the second of which he snuffed in the snow after two puffs.

"I would give anything to get out of this terrible mental stress if we don't have to file a humiliating bankruptcy in this community. It would be in *The Independent.* My parents would die of embarrassment. The boys are such promising student athletes; what would their classmates think? My mom is just sick over this latest episode of David's irresponsibility that cost us the farm. I can't take time off from work, not for spending hours in the courthouse. My employer won't tolerate that. I can't afford a lawyer either–can David? He would have to settle for a court-appointed public defender according to you Robbie. I don't want to spend the best years of my life and yours Phyllis wrapped up in court like Robbie says we will if we don't settle this thing right now," Nancy complained bitterly.

"I want this mess over with as soon as possible too pumpkin. We just want to see you happy again," Phyllis consoled her as sincerely as she could.

More than a few tears flowed as Nancy's mascara trickled down her cheeks; checking her compact mirror, she continued daubing her swollen eyes with tissue. The girls settled down as soon as Walsh entered the board room, fully aware of his power, knowing the bewildered housewives depended on him for words of encouragement, and some kind of a *solution* to the dilemma they faced, brought on by their *derelict* husbands.

"Now my final point I want to make with you girls to think about is this," Walsh resumed his important strategic update. "As I have repeated, I have been dealing with First Omaha. They are willing to forgo charges of bank fraud against David if…"

"If what? Don't tell me we are facing bank fraud charges too! We never had an extra cent. My sons were wearing hand me downs. What do you mean Robbie?" Nancy sounded angrier by the moment. "My God Robbie, this can't be happening. We all signed for that loan in your office. David said it was perfectly legal. What else did my husband do to screw that up? Why didn't you tell me this before?" She was weeping profusely, the tissues piled up as Phyllis put her arm around Nancy's shoulders whispering,

"Calm down dear. We can make it through this. Just listen to Robbie. He knows exactly what to do to help us," Walsh had made his "brownie-points" with Phyllis.

"I think we can adjourn this board meeting in a few minutes. Believe me Nancy I know this is a lot of painful news for one session. I have discussed my plans with Phyllis previously," Walsh added a soothing tone to his voice. "If you follow through on my plan, the bank is not interested in pressing fraud charges against David, at least for now. They will be satisfied with the collateral of the contract. Those details will be worked out in the pro se lawsuit and discovery I am preparing for Sully. We don't need to discuss those details at the moment. Mr. Jessen and I have discussed the loan; and specifically, the major problem which is the non-disclosed MWFSB loan default," Walsh cleared his throat.

"According to bank records at that time, First Omaha had reviewed a current credit report for Pleasant Valley Farms. Unfortunately Nancy, as I informed Phyllis some time ago, the financial statements that David and Jack provided during April 1992 failed to disclose their four hundred and fifty thousand dollar default on the Midwest Federal Savings Bank loan–a major detail approving the loan depended on. In granting the 1992 loan, Mr. Jessen, who is a Vice President of First Omaha, claimed he relied on the false financial information provided by David. First Omaha would not have approved the farm operating loan for Pleasant Valley Corporation if they had known about the defaulted loan at the time. Therefore, it is David who is guilty of stealing close to three million dollars over two years from the bank at the point of a *pen*–pardon my pun." Walsh feigned that he was irate over David's faux pas.

"David is culpable since it was he who provided the figures on the loan. So only he is guilty of fraud. But through my influence as power of attorney, I have negotiated an agreement with First Omaha that depends on the officers of the corporation–that would be you girls–agreeing to sign off on the collateral, if the bank in return chooses not to press fraud charges against your husbands, at least for the present. No telling what the bank will do to collect on the actual default on their loan."

"Thank God," said Nancy, "I don't think I could stand being married to a man in prison. I couldn't handle the disgrace of it. Imagine me going to work with Dr. Hanson, cleaning teeth, assisting in dental surgery, thinking about my husband in prison all day long. I can't bear the thought of being married to a corrections inmate. David is not the man I married. It's not my fault. I'm just a naive small town girl whose intentions were good. You both know I have never been unfaithful to David, but he betrayed me and his children in the way he handled his finances. I can't be held accountable for that can I?" Phyllis comforted Nancy who continued sobbing over her losses.

"We know you were a good wife Nancy. None of this mess is your fault. But from now on you need to follow my advice. If you do, your tribulations will be over before you know it," Walsh assured the women. "The bank has informed me they will not be pursuing a normal foreclosure procedure on the loan. The turnover of the records, the keys to the farm so to speak, will be accomplished privately between us three, since you two are the only credible financial officers left in Pleasant Valley. I have been discussing a deal with my associates based on the assignment of the collateral since I am administrating the loan now. I will have cashier's checks for $10,000 dollars made out to both of you in my office whenever you want to complete the paper work Nancy."

"The only charges David will face presently are the theft-by-swindle charges Hector is forced into filing because of his and his company's major loss of the safflowers and sunflowers. David is liable because Hector cannot account for the lost crops to his partners Ceres, SVO and Lubrizol, a loss that Sexton claims David is solely responsible for because of his mismanagement of the South Dakota operations. So we have the good news mixed with bad. You can rest assured there will be no complaints filed against the stakeholders of Pleasant Valley Farms. Once you sign the 'hold harmless' agreements–you will have *nothing* to worry about."

CHAPTER 33

In mid-February 1993, Robert Walsh notified David Zehlen that he had a check waiting for him for the work he had done for Pleasant Valley farms raking the remnants of the Sully safflowers under in late January. Walsh left a message with Nancy that David should stop by the office. He would be there to discuss plans for the upcoming growing season. In the confused state he was in, David remained unaware of the *plot brewing* against him that had been initialized by his partners.

For at least six months, Dave continued his work under the same *false* assumption as Nancy and Phyllis–that Walsh as power of attorney actually intended to pull the rabbit out of the hat and *save* the farming operations from a complete collapse–by *David* making a voluntary statement about the problems he was facing: *promissory fraud* he was dealing with collecting on the partnership with Hector Sexton. They agreed the next best option was a conference with county enforcement, addressing a variety of complaints–a meeting with the county attorney was necessary to keep Pleasant Valley afloat relative to its debt load and mortgage based on the Omaha bank loan. In their discussion, Walsh coached David he must state his position clearly, explaining why he was forced to apply for loans specifically to handle the deficit Sexton had created by not fulfilling on either the 1991 or 1992 grower's agreements he signed with Pleasant Valley corporation. It was obvious after two years, Sexton had an obligation he apparently had no intention to fulfill, and so on.

In the office briefings before the voluntary statement, Walsh urged David to concentrate on describing the consequences of Hector's failures that not only had an effect on David and his family–they severely hindered his attorney power in trying to help the farm out of a crisis that threatened the livelihood and the very survival of the farm–just as Hector's actions had adverse effects on the South Dakota flowers, the ASCS issues, and the dropping of the insurance had interfered with his management of the South Dakota branch of Pleasant Valley Farms. Robbie continuously reassured David his intervention was *only* a temporary phase. Once matters of genuine material interest were settled, Pleasant Valley operations would be back to normal. David would be able resume his former duties under new management, but his responsibilities would remain the same on what would now be a 60,000-acre operation through Jacques Seed Co, instead of SigCo.

During the winter lull, Nancy and Phyllis maintained a code of silence on the proposed formation of Interwest. To ease the critics, David reiterated in minute detail describing why and how the bills were created; and that he had received little or nothing from Sexton since the charge-back billings he had sent out in August '92 from Walsh's office in Brookings. Dave complained that had received only one check for $40K from Ceres *for deposit only* in the MinGo operating account, dedicated to payment of past due accounts and wages. Amidst these events, Walsh convinced David Zehlen that he believed in the family's best interest he should walk in, and talk over the Sexton situation with the Granite County Attorney, Bill Watkins, setting up an appointment as soon as he could so if possible there could be a settlement on the debt before spring planting 1993.

Walsh stressed that as administrator of the organization he would wrench as much cooperation as possible on the Sexton debt; but the deal ultimately would depend on negotiation, he alone had the skills to mediate a deal for a settlement between the bank and Hector to resolve the Zehlen debt load, since all three parties on the inside were involved from 1991 through 1993. From the administrative point of view, it would be much more difficult to manage the farm because by 1993 there would be no ASCS funds to count on, supporting the extensive Zehlen operations.

David was pleased to receive a personal check from Robert Walsh for $1500 bucks for barely a week's work as Walsh referred to it as, "cleaning up the S.D. flowers mess" grinding stubble off the ground. Like his wife and Phyllis, David naively assumed that

Walsh was in fact doing what he could to sustain the farm, through what was obviously going to be a difficult year ahead for the Pleasant Valley organization. David assured Walsh he would visit County Attorney Bill Watkins at the courthouse, because they had done business in the past and he regarded Watkins as a friend.

* * * * *

The day after their visit in corporate headquarters, Robert Walsh phoned County Attorney William Watkins at his office in the courthouse informing him David was coming in for a visit to talk about the farming situation; the important news was that he himself had written up an informal memorandum about some criminal issues that he and the prosecutor might decide to report to the County Sheriff. He informed Bill these issues had arrived unexpectedly in the course of his discovery work on the financial situation as power of attorney for the Zehlen family, as general manager and now president of Pleasant Valley Farms production operations. He said he would like to stop off at the office, have a short discussion and drop off the report he had assembled that Walsh believed might be an indication of criminal activities of one of the members of the corporation he now represented. He needed Watkins' opinion of the matter in any event,

"At this time I am not looking to make a formal complaint or anything of that nature. I am very concerned for the welfare of the individuals, and the distribution of real property of the corporation I have recently become the director of," Walsh reported. "I would very much like you to look over some of the evidence I have accumulated in my work as a private investigator for FBI and secret service matters as well as power of attorney for the Zehlen family. What alarms me Bill is the devastating effects of these criminal matters on innocent members of the Zehlen family *both you and your wife* know very well, from your work with Nancy in the ecumenical council discussions among the First English Lutheran, Methodist and Catholic parishes of the community; not to mention the $20 million dollar gross revenue the Zehlens expect this year and how that benefits Rockland area mercantilism. I look at how the Zehlen decline affects a generation of children, two marriages, and the church fellowship we are all a part of. Basically, I am concerned about how the loss of all that money affects other members of the community," the county attorney listened attentively, occasionally taking notes.

"I have learned that you come from a farm background in Meeker County Bill, so this matter should be transparent for you. But in my opinion, and, and I have done my share of pro se work, the Zehlen situation should be of interest to you as the county prosecutor for several reasons, those discussed now, and in the future, when domestic abuse, civil and criminal violations and physical violence become serious concerns. It is probably beyond my authority to report this evidence to the county sheriff. For that reason, I'm leaving enforcement and apprehension to you."

"Of course I will need more information before I make my decision whether or not to proceed with an investigation; but I appreciate your concern Mr. Walsh. I'll look into this matter as soon as I can. You can stop by my office tomorrow around 9:00 a.m. Robbie," Watkins concluded curiously. "I could tell you were on to something the last time we talked so I was expecting you to contact me again."

"Tomorrow I'm in court at ten o'clock with Judge Silas on an assault case with liquor and minors involved during Crazy Days. You probably have read about it in *The Independent*. There were several victims, multiple injuries, hospitalization of a local teenager on this one, plus the potential of an unregistered fire arms issue. There has been an unusual amount of activity in court lately for a small town; the docket is full of misdemeanors related to driving violations. But this case intrigues me because potentially it affects our entire community."

"That's the way I look at it," Walsh agreed. "Just doing my job."

"I have some personal business and a conference Wednesday. But Thursday of this week looks like I'll be available. I'll have my secretary make up a copy of the memo and lay it on my desk. I'll read it this afternoon when court is adjourned. My guess is we don't have to file charges immediately. I'll look over your information in the morning. How does that sound?" Watkins was slightly curious about the scraps his new watchdog was feeding him.

"Just what I was expecting from you Bill; we will need an expert to unravel this mystery. I admit it took me a while to figure out what was going on. The scope of this scheme to defraud the American government is beyond my comprehension; it will take some time to absorb I can tell you that much already. I think I discovered the answer. I will be in your office Thursday nine a.m. sharp."

The substance of Walsh's memorandum was anything but straightforward, with vague descriptions of a crime in progress, and some individuals and entities he was unfamiliar with. Watkins was curious enough to read it over the evening before their meeting in his office to get a better idea of where Walsh was coming from. Bill reviewed it again in the morning, as he was a notoriously early riser; which was always something that bugged his wife, he confided in Walsh. But to preface his memorandum discussion, Walsh had another issue he wanted to discuss with Bill before they went over the actual probable-cause facts of the complaint; he mentioned that perhaps a retainer from the Omaha campaign vault would be in order sooner than later. He knew he could wait until after the voluntary walk-in mission was accomplished. Zehlen wasn't going far with barely enough in his personal account to keep a quarter tank of fuel in his pickup.

"As I mentioned before in our conversation earlier this week Bill, I have taken over power of attorney for the Zehlen family and their corporation." Walsh became intense in an instant. "You would understand very well because you are an enforcer of justice in our community. My main concern has become not only the legal but the financial ramifications involved in directing a mammoth farming operation like the Zehlen corporation that now farms roughly 45,000 acres in Minnesota, South and North Dakota. As you might imagine the cost of running the farming operation is staggering."

"Yes I understand that," Watkins replied. "Your draft is vague in certain areas of intentionality. You need to inform the court specifically how David's crime relates to the various issues you presented in your memorandum, including those of the government and financial institutions. Although I must admit the argument for personal injury and spousal abuse was shocking. I would have to see the psychiatric report you mention. But overall your memorandum was thought provoking, written by a man with no formal legal training Robert. But Judge Silas court is good at wood shedding if you have ever been there. Gerry will automatically reprimand what he views in his discretion as argumentative and prejudicial to the man's long standing name and credibility in the community. Though it is apparent you have concerns for violence connected with domestic issues, we need to stick to the facts as much as possible." It's obvious you don't like our local prodigy David Zehlen much Mr. Walsh, was Watkins' immediate reaction.

"Thanks for noticing those characteristics of my writing, Bill. Unlike you, I am not a professional writer. Having stood before Judge Silas in probate, Your Honor sees clearly I am a power of attorney, not a lawyer," Walsh rationalized. "That's why I am putting this case in your hands Bill. We both know the limitations of pro se in civil and criminal court. It is largely ignored; that's why I need you to file the complaint based on your research that I am giving you as my discovery evidence. I will try to make my major point momentarily; but I feel this is critical background information that I have discovered in my role as a private investigator that I have not disclosed to anyone but you. I feel you need it, to focus your investigation on this evidence of criminal actions I have discovered on my watch."

"Sustained Mr. Walsh, I have to keep in mind your credentials. I need to know your rights–are they full or limited as power of attorney?" Watkins questioned further. "You can continue with your reasons if you believe it is important. Looking at my watch; I am due in court again at 10 o'clock, so we have to be aware of the short time frame we are operating in."

"Thank you Bill, for inquiring. This discussion will only take a few minutes of your time," Walsh was surprised at Bill's immediate level of interest, ready to take advantage of the opportunity. "I have unlimited powers under the charter. What I'm saying is compelling because this case involves a Federal Reserve Bank; and an ongoing investigation of alleged FDIC loan fraud, mismanagement of millions of dollars of government money, and additional charges that are forthcoming from the memorandum. As director of fiduciary operations and a six hundred-thousand-dollar trust for the children of Pleasant Valley Farms–of course we are dealing with theft of unusually large sums of money in a small community."

"In other words if you investigate the evidence, the $1.7-million-dollar motive of the fraud is detailed in the memorandum you reviewed involving the plaintiff Pleasant Valley in the fraud scheme against David Zehlen's partner, Hector Sexton. The memo presents evidence that David Zehlen is in possession, custody and title of stolen property with intent to defraud the same person, that would be the defendant mentioned in the memorandum that David had a partnership loan arrangement with. In retaliation, the same person was accused by David Zehlen in the loan-deficiency payment scheme he was found to be in violation of in 1992. This is where the FDIC and FBI have jurisdiction," Walsh paused. Noticing no reaction from Bill who was taking notes, he concluded.

"I do realize Bill this is a very complicated situation that involves giving false credit information to a Federal Reserve Bank. That violation is one of a number of charges that in addition to the motive, intent and causation of a swindle, you will be indicting on theft charges if you decide there is a case–you understand I don't have all the information yet from the bank. I have been informed and have knowledge the Federal Reserve Bank I have mentioned, that would be First Omaha of Nebraska, is about to foreclose on the 1992 farm operations loan in default that has me deeply concerned for the Zehlen family. As you know Bill I have become the director of financial operations of the farm now at the request of David's and Jack's wives. So I thought I would bring that up with you here today as a prelude to the criminal issues presented in the memorandum. I'm just trying to assist the investigation any way I can. Only a competent attorney like you with experience in court everyday looking at the microcosm of crime in the community under a microscope can understand the nature of what is probably the *biggest* case to ever hit Granite County court, next to the Barton Flowers homicide trial."

"David tells me Jack sat on that jury. It takes that kind of trial experience to understand where I am going with this case Bill. The seriousness of the crimes and the damage done to an upstanding family in the community is shocking. I have obligations to serve the family, which is why I was apprehensive and cautious about presenting this information to you today in the court house," Walsh glanced at his watch. "I see we are approaching ten o'clock, Bill. I know how busy you are with all the misdemeanors on the docket. I believe this is felony-level material we are dealing with in the memo. So thanks for your time in the office today. This is a lot of information I am disclosing to you–you will need time to digest it."

"I have been listening to every word Robert; you are making some very serious allegations. I will need to read your report again and have a talk with David before I make my decision. But I thank you for coming in and helping me do a better job keeping law and order in this community," Watkins was serious. "That is a tall order in itself. Our job is to serve the county as best we can. Not every man is capable of doing what you do so well with no formal legal training. I commend you for that. I agree it is surprising that someone as recognizable as David Zehlen could be involved in a scheme like you describe in the heart of our community. I am impressed, no one noticed until you came along. My secretary saved an article in the local newspaper about David in the national magazine last summer. The name of the article, I don't subscribe to the publication–the name escapes me at this moment."

"That would be *Farm Futures* magazine. They put his picture on the cover. We saved five copies for his mother," Walsh recited the classic Hook line. "I may be exaggerating; but David boasts about that article all the time. I'm sick of it. I think it is disgusting in view of his despicable behavior in the context of these matters we are discussing now. But that is beside the point. From the legal perspective what do you think I should do about this situation Bill?" Walsh asked.

"First off I think David will need to make an appearance in my office," Watkins responded favorably. "It can be informal; he will have to explain some of these 'allegations' as you refer to them to me in a legal setting. Let's just say David needs to appear in my office to make a voluntary statement to me and the County Sheriff. You've met my deputy Joe Bernard. At that time, we will learn on and off the record what Mr. Zehlen has to say about some of the allegations in the memorandum you showed me. We don't have to reveal to him that I have ever seen it, as it has not been filed yet. It was just a conversation that you and I had over the phone off the record. How does that sound to you Robert? I see no reason for you to be physically involved at this stage is there?"

"Absolutely not; I'm leaving it to your discretion and your judgment alone." Walsh secretly rejoiced knowing that he had done the damage he wished to inflict upon his impaled opponent anonymously–*incognito* behind the scenes–*always* the best place to be in a case like this; he had learned from experience. His memorandum would never be filed as long as the information in it was preserved until Watkins pressed charges against Zehlen.

"I hope you understand Bill I am just trying to stay out of the way. I have done my due diligence to help the victims of what I can see clearly are crimes of a civil and criminal nature; it is my responsibility to see those people I am responsible for receive consolation and compensation for their suffering. I wouldn't necessarily want you or the court to jump to any conclusions Bill; but all the evidence and information is there. Once you hear what David has to say I think you'll agree. I'll advise him to stop by your office to make a statement. You can take it from there." Walsh rose from his chair, and extended his unusually long arm across the County Attorney's desk, confirming the assignation that was in motion.

"Talk to you later. Thank you so much Bill."

"You are very welcome Robert," Watkins responded. "We need our community leaders to be involved in law enforcement. Without your help I might never have learned what happened out there."

"As power of attorney I take my job very seriously. Sometimes I feel it is necessary to correct what I have observed as nuisance activity which arises from unreasonable, unwarranted or unlawful use by a person of his *own* or other people's property." Walsh sounded like he was reading from Black's Law. "I am on the side of law and order; you can count on that."

CHAPTER 34

The sidewalks around the court house were shoveled. There was a foot of snow on the ground the morning of March 4, 1993, at 10 a.m. when David Zehlen walked into the office of Granite County Attorney William Watkins to make the long anticipated voluntary statement everybody in the legal community except Dave was prepared for. On the welcoming committee that morning was Deputy County Sheriff Joe Bernard Jr. of the Granite County Sheriff's office.

David greeted the two men unsuspectingly, shaking hands with Deputy Bernard, who he had not seen for several years, since he had been promoted from the Rockland Police department to the County Sheriff's position. He had known both men for many years. He had no reason to believe the meeting was not a legitimate conversation among good neighbors discussing a common legal problem in Granite County that involved outsiders to the agricultural community they were unfamiliar with. David was there, he believed, to describe these people and the problems he was having with them.

"I'm sorry I have to involve law enforcement in this situation I find myself and my manager Robert Walsh in–Bill, Joe–my power of attorney you both probably know, has been with me almost 15 months now. We have been discussing what to do about this matter, how to collect this money that is owed to me in ongoing debt since harvest 1991. Robbie advised me to come to the office to talk about it with the County Attorney. I see Joe is here so we have *quorum* on this matter." David had the vague thought his sense of humor would not be effective.

"I am here to help you understand the circumstances I find myself in with my partner Hector Sexton of Fargo North Dakota who works for Ceres, SVO and Lubrizol–billion dollar organizations." David explained. "I just want to get this stuff cleared up, straightened around. Even if it takes an intervention of law-enforcement to determine who owes who what? And once and for all, figure out what this debt confusion is all about, when there was *no money lost*." His voice reached a slightly higher pitch for a second, as he felt a dry, choking feeling in his throat, recalling the script Walsh grilled him on.

The deputy read Dave his Miranda rights. He was not under arrest at any time during the discussion; he had a right to remain silent if he chose to without answering, under no obligations and so on–he could leave any time he wanted. Deputy Bernard also informed David that he could be charged with criminal offenses at any time later as a result of anything he might say that day on the transcript.

"We're glad you came in voluntarily David," Attorney Watkins affirmed. "Let's hear your side of the story."

Dave acknowledged that he understood his rights. He then proceeded to state the reasons why he had decided to make a voluntary statement about his relationship with Hector Sexton, explaining why Walsh who had become power of attorney for Pleasant Valley Farms felt it necessary for him to walk in for the conversation they were having relative to the problems the Zehlens were having collecting on a partnership agreement. As the owner of the farm at the time of the partnership arrangement that went haywire with Hector Sexton who worked for Ceres, SVO and Lubrizol, David labored to explain. He needed Walsh's services when the contract violation occurred on a specialty crop deal, Walsh originally was hired to manage acreage for Pleasant Valley and qualify for a government subsidy of three quarter million dollars on; with that subsidy in mind, he made a risk-free production and marketing deal of high-oleic oil seeds. That's all there is to it.

"In the first year of the arrangement which was 1991, we had a good crop; but Hector insisted that I rearrange my production operations to reflect an operating partnership. That's when Ray Rylance, an attorney from Rapid City, came on board to write the partnership contract that made us eligible for government subsidies. My partner violated the agreement Granite County ASCS approved. Do you see where I'm going with this Bill, Joe?"

David sounded desperate to reach the end of his convoluted explanation.

"I had Ray Rylance write it up to include my MinGo employees so that we would all be able to benefit from USDA programs. Hector insisted on the agreement to the point where he was threatening me that if I didn't go along with his proposal that he believed he was allowed under ASCS regulations, the contract could suffer. Sexton argued he was entitled to benefits of government program eligibility on the crops he owned, as much as I did when applying for and receiving on behalf of the partners. He indicated this was the way he worked his deals with other customers," David stuck with the script he had rehearsed with Walsh a half dozen times.

"It was not my fault when Hector reneged on his responsibilities. His failure to adequately fund MN Go destroyed the partnership structure my attorney Ray Rylance set up so the partners were eligible for personage. That would not have happened if Hector had kept his pledges to me about what he would do to capitalize my employees, who would then be partners. If he had done what he promised none of that would have happened," David could tell he was not making the impression he had counted on with enforcement.

"Hector indicated this arrangement was the same as his deals with other customers. I did not know at the time this was the reason Ed Taffe and Kelly Miller were no longer working for him," David remarked to little effect. "By now I have a good idea how he reneged on his responsibilities, and why those two farmers backed out on the arrangement."

"We have received information from an unidentified source that a statement was given by your wife and your step-mother to the ASCS committee on your government violations. Is that right Dave?" said Joe Bernard.

"They both said they felt a certain amount of terror under duress that was forcing them to participate in the scheme. Is that allegation true David?" Watkins inquired seriously.

"At the time I am talking about there was no pressure from me. I wasn't even around my own farm for business reasons. I was all over the place inspecting leases in three states when Walsh had taken over. He was responsible for the stress and anxiety my wife had if any was created–she wouldn't even listen to me after Walsh took over as power of attorney," David defended himself instinctively.

"Did you at any time ask, request or force your wife to do something she might not normally want to do?" Watkins's eyes lit up at his piercing inquiry. "You don't have to answer the question at this time David; we're going to take a short break now; you are free to walk outside or use the facilities. We will return in a few moments."

David's interrogators were distracted by another nugget. Like a squirrel chasing a peanut, in an instant Deputy Joe disappeared into the dispatcher's room where several pages of results of a criminal background check on a juvenile facing an assault with a deadly weapon charge were arriving on the computer. "This won't take long David," Bill apologized. "We just have a few more questions for you; if you have any more information you are welcome to share it with us. If you need anything, I'll be right back."

A party to a failed marriage, Bill Watkins had the requisite skills to use that lever if necessary in his investigation; all he needed was a deposition from each of the victimized women– once he had their statements in front of him to prove they acted the way they did under false, misleading, and bad advice from David–the domestic intimidation factor would become more evidence against the accused.

A few minutes later, as he waited outside the court house enjoying what little he might of the menthol cigarette he knew he should not be inhaling, David recalled his wife's *weird* remark just as she left the house for work that morning, "Remember to inform Bill the contract was *canceled* David." She said it with full assurance, and yet such disinterest as if it were a done-deal already–that's the way the cookie crumbles David–just as she was exiting the kitchen door closest to the garage. He recalled the odd reminder to inform Bill of what? What the hell was his wife of two decades talking about; no one could believe that nonsense could they? He recalled he had warmed up his wife's Toyota on that dark March day, resigned to his fate. Gone was most of the passion; he was becoming content with any sign of peace and harmony from his high school sweetheart. He had learned not to argue with his once so passive wife–in the very short time when things started going down the tubes–fast.

The sun never managed to pierce through the legal gloom, or penetrate the dense fog, mixed with choking gases and dust pouring out of the smokestack of the Otter Tail plant across the river that morning. The precipitator was shut down for repairs at a time the boiler was running full throttle; the pollution index was at a dangerous level until a blizzard settled in over the weekend, canceling the District 11 basketball playoffs in his twin sons' first year on the "B" team–in eighth grade. There had been some talk of calling them up to the varsity after a 3-12 season if the Trojans made it past the first round of the sub-district seeding against the Clarkfield Cardinals in their first game. One more cigarette was not going to kill him he thought, as he puffed a Marlboro menthol outside the courthouse.

The low dose morphine he was prescribed for his back was taking its toll; his meds made him feel drowsy. Mixed with more than enough coffee, his breakfast cocktail made him feel slightly nauseous, unconsciously if for no other reason, trying to suppress the dread of facing another interrogation over the contract. Nancy was just following her queues; his wife's odd remark that morning seemed so incongruous. He recalled the click of the latch, the instant the porch door closed; he was relieved his wife did not slam it as she would if she was angry about something. His wife's remark seemed so out of context that David forgot it completely–right up until that moment of doubt about the *intentions* of the county prosecutor he at one time assumed was a friend. The doubts returned, at about the time he noticed the warm reception had cooled to a chilling seriousness he did not expect, in the office of the County Attorney and deputy sheriff.

At the time, David was unaware Walsh already had two interviews lined up with the bureau later in March. In his doubts,

David could not ignore the possibility his wife was privy to some of the mysterious dialogue, when he had never felt so alone, so much a stranger and prison-pent as he felt that day in the courthouse–where he had never been in his life except to retrieve his certified marriage license. Now he understood some relationship existed between those events, as he recalled his dad recently mentioning how when he was a young man he sat in the jury box during the Barton Flowers murder case back in the sixties.

In the few short minutes of the opening exchange, there had been a noticeable change of tone and attitude of the inquiry he was experiencing with power figures Bill and Joe–enforcers of the law he previously assumed were in his corner–before he walked in the office. David asked himself where these doubts were coming from–he had to trust law enforcement didn't he? Someone must understand what was happening behind his back; that intuition continued to grow beyond just a weird feeling. He sensed the interview was heading *south*, like everything else, for some unknown reason. He knew he would need to be more cautious as the conversation continued.

"Okay Dave we are starting the tape again. There is no pressure. You can feel free to say anything you want," Watkins assured him. "Under Miranda you cannot be technically arrested yet; but anything you say could be held against you if it is evidence of criminal offenses. You understand that don't you David?"

"Yes I do Bill. I have nothing to hide. That's why I came here voluntarily," David added. "I don't want to lose my train of thought either; so I'll move on. I didn't necessarily come here to discuss the ASCS problems, but they are related, I hope you can understand that. When I agreed to Hector's arrangement of the ASCS structure, as Ray Rylance laid it out in Rapid City, he said he would fulfill on his obligations on the contract; but he never did really. He paid some of his share on the fuel, fertilizer and chemical costs, but not all of it. I didn't have enough of a margin to operate without his share of costs. Instead of his contract paying $28, he was paying me $18 an acre, more than 40 percent less than we had agreed to on the contract, which was my management expenses leveraged against contract expectations of $1.7 million. Instead of fulfilling, Hector notified me that he would only be paying a discounted difference after using our MN Go and Pleasant Valley equipment and LDP allocation from the government–those acts were violations of the 1991 grower's agreement. Do you see what I mean?" David scanned the room to see if the officers were paying attention to his itemization, glancing at Deputy Bernard or County Attorney Watkins, jotting notes on a legal pad. With no reaction or response from either man, sensing the indifference in the room to his interpretation, he attempted to penetrate the thick silence.

"I am not going to pretend to be an expert on farm management," Attorney Watkins commented. "We are listening patiently to your story David." Looking up a second, Bill fiddled with a pen as he scribbled notes. "So would you please move along with the inquiry rather than asking us questions."

"Sure Bill. Like I said," he continued more cautiously with every breath he took. "Hector did make some payments for fuel, fertilizer and chemicals, which was basic needs for his crop. But with him only fulfilling on part of his obligations, and my not having the ASCS money to pay my employees by the summer of 1992 it was getting chaotic. You see what I mean? I knew I would be running into cash flow problems. Around the first of the year in 1992, I received an advance of $153 thousand that Hector said he wanted applied in the spring on the 1992 contract yet to be signed; the money was for operating costs to produce the next year's crop to make sure the seed was in the ground. And that was about all it was good for. At that time, I was still being shorted a third relative to the original contract agreement from the year before. I know this explanation gets complicated, but I hope you see where I am going with this conversation. In my opinion, I see Hector's breach of contract as promissory fraud; that is the sole reason I came in to make the voluntary statement."

"What I am asking you David is–Did you? or, did you not? – send Hector Sexton duplicate invoices for fertilizer August or thereabouts 1992?' Watkins zeroed in on his objective, adjusting his bifocals while examining a document on his desk.

"Yes I did; but it was for the previous year's expenses Sexton never paid. On that basis he did send me an advance," David explained futilely. "But that money did not fully compensate for my losses on the deficit that Hector created, along with my deficits of the ASCS funds. Those limited funds helped put the crop in the ground is all. In June I received a billing statement from Ceres, Inc. that set forth an itemization for fertilizer and chemicals used on the fields where the safflowers were being grown."

"And when did this financial transaction take place?" Watkins queried. "Once we have the time established accurately, along with the other information we can proceed on the transcript, please continue Dave."

"It happened around mid-August 1992 in Robbie's office in Brookings, South Dakota," David responded. "I submitted a series of invoices to Hector which we had previously agreed upon that he would regard as so many accounting chargebacks paid to Ceres related to funds already advanced by Pleasant Valley Farms for operational expenses incurred in the two previous years. In the previous year, these were funds supposed to be advanced to my MinGo employees as partners in order to be eligible for ASCS personage certification–under the contract arrangement–and the requirements and determinations for separation of partnership entities as recommended by my attorney Ray Rylance of Rapid City were *legally* complied with. So I hope you can follow me on this explanation?"

"So then you sent these duplicate invoices through the mail, did you Dave? Wait, hold on; just a minute! Julie is signaling me. Can we wait just a moment while our secretary needs to change the audio-cassette? Julie says it's okay now; she just flipped it. David your answer is on the record. Along with those invoices at that time David, did you submit separate invoices for the work done by these same partners as you refer to them?" Watkins was inquiring much more intrusively than David expected. "And you are saying that was an invoice on acreage that Pleasant Valley

Corporation was to be reimbursed for specifically to the ... (looking at his notes) $28 or rather $18 dollars an acre for the number of acres worked?"

"Well Bill I'm not exactly sure where you are going with those questions. Are we are talking about the same billing arrangement I was explaining to you that Hector agreed on?" David answered with a question. Bill recognized that Dave was being evasive, confident he had another bold offender to deal with by the *vague* explanations and impertinent questions.

"Hector just said *send* me the billings–on the backsides of the old fertilizer invoices–that you believe I am accountable for. I'll settle our accounts on our charge-back arrangement. That's what I thought I was doing. Robbie Walsh was there. He knew what I was doing and showed me how to use his new photocopier. He had the previous invoices *already laid out* for me on the front desk."

"You can ask Robbie about that day. He is the one who stamped and mailed the invoices. So if there is mail fraud, I was not involved. I know it sounds stupid. Only one person in the world could have come up with a crazy idea like this for paying off a debt to Hector Sexton. Do you know him?"

"I have heard of him yes." Watkins pressed the issue. "So would you admit David that the billings were for fertilizer that was not actually applied or received for another farming lease or entity that you had been involved with in another county; and that billing was not actually for fertilizer applied to your partner's sunflowers–and in fact that bill had *already* been paid on another $117,000 contract expense in June?"

"Not exactly Bill, I couldn't say that. Because the only contract I had going on was the year before when Walsh was involved with Hector's safflowers and *other* customers; some that he was managing out of his office in Brookings," David argued. "You would have to talk to Robbie about that because the only billings I was concerned with were those he presented me that day. I didn't have time to determine what the original bills were for; he was in a hurry to get the mail to the post office before it closed at noon on Saturday. I didn't think I had any reason to doubt the deal my partners had setup. My partners both said 'do as we say and you will be paid.' But they tricked me into doing the wrong thing. Ceres never paid a dime on those bills. Hector took the 'phony bills' directly to the bank; and showed them to Tom Jessen. Maybe he sent copies. I'm pretty sure he has some of the billings in his office."

"You offered to make a statement, voluntarily. We are not here to answer your questions David, but inquire into the truth of yours. We're not making any judgments today David, just *answer* the questions." Watkins ordered. His tone had changed from congenial to imperious in an instant. "Your guilt or innocence will be determined later. We just need some answers to these questions for the time being."

"Alright Bill, Joe—I don't intend to create any problems. You just need to understand we are discussing *Hector's* debt not mine," David responded curtly.

"Maybe you could use another drink of cold spring water from the fountain to refresh your memory right now?" Joe Bernard responded to the situation, unsuccessfully attempting to change the mood to a lighter shade of pale, in what had turned into a somber conversation.

"Bill and I need to discuss another issue that just arrived on the scene. Relax for a couple minutes or so. Pick yourself up a cup of coffee in the lobby. We know this is stressful for you. Be back in around ten minutes please, so we can finish off our conversation. We just need a little more information from you is all."

Following the deputy sheriff's advice, David bought himself a cup of decaf from the machine in the basement. He stepped outside the courthouse for a moment to cool off from what had turned from a friendly discussion to a nightmare inquisition of David's curiosity cabinet; there were too many introjects in the background for either side to proceed honestly. When he returned, David had decided to answer Watkins' last query very cautiously; he was intuitively aware something was wrong with the way Walsh had coaxed him through the billing of production arrears at his office; but he went along with the program believing in his partners.

"Okay David, you have been telling us about what happened that day in Robert Walsh's office last August–can you continue where you left off," Joe Bernard entered the conversation for the moment.

"Well like I keep repeating, Hector and I had entered into this agreement that he would reimburse me for his debts on a charge-back-basis so his superiors would not discover how much he was behind on both contracts, not to mention the half million he had squandered of the ASCS funds," Dave answered, with a tone of desperation in his voice.

"So that is what the backcharges were all about. As part of the relationship with his company Ceres, my corporation was to be reimbursed for acreage worked at the *revised* discount rate he figured out; he wasn't even paying *that much* to MinGo really either. It was Walsh's idea to compensate for the debt Hector owed me–that I also billed him for–on approximately four thousand extra acres not actually worked. I did it that way to allow him to account for the debt he owed me by a legitimate billing for the thousands of acres he already owed me for that had fallen through the cracks in his accounting system. According to my computer records and personal audit, Hector actually owed me for close to five times that amount over two years. He agreed to it saying this is the way he covers his bills with other customers. We discussed the arrangement every other day. Walsh was aware I was facing a crisis, hundreds of thousands of dollars short already in my dealings with Sexton; and that Pleasant Valley needed that money for operating expenses for spring planting," David explained. "It was Robbie who specifically directed me to send Hector ten invoices for $35,000 dollars each. Walsh changed the billing to thirty invoices for ten thousand each, that day in his office. I was still $150 thousand short on the deal even if he paid up. We could have worked it out, but he only paid me a fraction of the arrears to Pleasant Valley at that time, so it didn't make much difference anyway," David glanced anxiously at Watkins who was furiously writing notes.

Neither he nor Joe Bernard commented on David's report of the events of the Sexton fraud he was explaining. At the climax of the interview, Watkins brought up one more critical issue seemingly out of the blue. The serious tone of his inquiry suggested this was not a query David Zehlen would be able to avoid by repeating from his typical series of vague responses, that he did not realize were so pitifully inadequate.

"David I just want to ask you one more question before you leave the sheriff's office today." Watkins was questioning him like Johnny Cochran cross-examining Mark Fuhrman. "I'm not making any allegations at this time. I'm just asking. Did you ever think about committing *loan* fraud against a lending institution?

By his own admission, it was at that instant David went ballistic for a moment, but thought better of reacting noticeably. An uncontrollable flash of emotion created an atmosphere of tension in the deputy's office that ended the discussion for the purposes of preliminary apprehension–and intervention Bill and Joe needed. In that split second, David flashed back to the media he was familiar with, witnessing the Travolta and Duvall scene outside the courtroom in *Civil Action*. He was a half second from spontaneously blurting *"of course I did, you dumb ass,"*

"Oh yeah, I'm sure I *thought* about it Bill!" slipped off his tongue in a second of rage instead of making a careful answer, thinking to himself–what a stupid idea! *Bill must be drinking the damn kool-aid.*

"Don't take it so personally David. I have no further questions." Watkins knew he hit a nerve. "It was just a routine question." But David would discover too late Watkins was not joking. By the time of the voluntary statement, Watkins was familiar with Walsh's memorandum. As prosecutor, he was aware of the consequences if Dave did not disclose the MWFSB loan default on the bank loan application for Sexton's crops. In his favor if the case ever made appeal court, Watkins would be allowed to argue he was unaware of the relationship of the case to the *Sully* lawsuit, and the consequences to the accused of the *assumptions* of David's guilt he was making on behalf of the conspiracy.

Fear had replaced the confidence David had before his encounter with Granite County Attorney Watkins. The assurance his sanity depended on–that one person in the community with power and authority over the mystery he was experiencing and describing was on his side–was gone. What little security David had remaining, was immediately replaced with fear of apprehension and dread of the months ahead under the thumb of his underexposed rival.

CHAPTER 35

With Robert Walsh in control as power of attorney over the property, the farming operations underwent a dramatic change in 1993. After his cleanup of the safflower stubble in Sully County South Dakota in January, David became expendable, and in fact, a liability to the new management team that Robert Walsh had assembled–consisting of himself and Phyllis and Nancy Zehlen–neither of whom had an interest in gardening, let alone farming.

Walsh took advantage of the fact that the two remaining stakeholders wanted to quickly dispose of the case, move into town, and distance themselves as quickly as possible from the fate that awaited David and Jack for their involvement in criminal activities. Robbie was their last hope to deliver them from a dreadful public disgrace. For that purpose, Walsh let the girls know often he was in the process of assembling a discovery file to implement the exposure of the fraud scheme as it was unfolding in County Attorney Watkins' office–the result of his private investigative work. In a private meeting, Nancy explained her position relative to reading the fine print to the county attorney,

"David didn't expect me to read them I'm sure of that. He knew I couldn't understand the language of the contracts, or pages of loans he was signing. It was a mistake assuming that he could. Whatever David told me to sign, I just wanted to get through with it, rather than this continuous process of listening to my husband's confusing explanations of what they meant; and arguing about it. I just signed the papers." Nancy was intelligent enough to admit that like many people she didn't make it a habit of reading or understanding legal documents. When Watkins asked Dave if he was aware of the questionable nature of the contracts he was handing his wife,

"Just whatever the bank gave me for her to sign," he replied.

"But you were taking out fraudulent loans then weren't you?" Watkins posed another obvious question. "Were the loans related to the illegal ASCS scheme?"

"That's not what happened–they were indirectly–whatever. Everybody knows the bank loan was based on the contract with Hector," David repeated. "I didn't believe there was anything wrong with taking out loans when they were for the owner's crops. Neither did they at the time; and neither did the ASCS office in Rockland until Walsh stepped in."

David wrote years later in his diary that at no time during the preliminary discussions with Robbie Walsh, about making a voluntary statement to the County Attorney, was there any indication or did David suspect there was any evidence of criminal intentions that were about to be discovered of his participation in a personal enrichment scheme based on the material evidence he was presenting in the voluntary statement. The only reason he was in the Sheriff's office that day was to discuss a bitter dispute that was caused by Sexton and his financiers; he still had no idea the crooked strategy depended on termination of two one-year contracts between Pleasant Valley Farms and Hector Sexton and Ceres in Sully, South Dakota Circuit Court. On page 55, he noted that he felt he was in the middle of something he didn't really understand, suspended in another Lennon McCartney verse, yet he feared gaining more knowledge would lead to more agony over the breach of contract he vaguely knew the details of, because of an inaccurate accounting method. As David recounted the conversation in Watkins' office later, it appeared the County Attorney had *no* interest in the material he presented relative to the promissory fraud he had experienced in his business relationship with Hector Sexton. Dave described the meeting in his journal.

> I was in his office about an hour. We took a short break. The deputy asked me if I would like a glass of water a couple times. During the first half hour of the interview I must have brought up the subject of Hector and the fact that he was not fulfilling on the guaranteed contract at least a half dozen times. I stated that Hector owed me over a million five on that contract. It seemed like every time I brought up the

subject Bill deflected to another issue, or changed the subject. I must have brought the contract violation up at least five times in that first half of my voluntary statement.

After twenty minutes or so we took a short break. Bill and Joe stepped out of the attorney's office and I believe went to the sheriff's office which is right down the hall in the court house. I had the idea it was for a criminal background check when I don't have as much as a parking ticket on my record.

When they came back Joe asked me if I felt comfortable continuing. I said I did. It was all repetition for me. But all I remember is that when we resumed creating the transcript, which is on the public record, Bill started asking me if I had ever thought about committing fraud with a lending institution.

Of course I was a bit ornery; it affected my attitude because it felt like Bill was ignoring my ideas. He waited until the conclusion of the interview, then Bill brought up the bank fraud out of the blue. I blew my cool for a second. He was totally ignoring the point I was trying to make in the first place going in for the voluntary statement.

For some reason I was thinking about that scene in Saturday Night at the Movies. Based on my relationship with Rivkin I consider myself a film aficionado, thinking of the dialogue of Duvall and Travolta in Civil Action when I said, "Oh sure I have," when he asked me if I ever thought about committing bank fraud. I didn't take it seriously. Isn't it strange how life imitates art at times? Evidently that was a big mistake. From that moment on it became very uncomfortable in Bill's office. I could not ever get back to the point of the promissory fraud I was experiencing with my partner.

Until the bank fraud case arrived several years later, Bill, I suspect, combined the two cases in his mind according to the Walsh theory–focusing on his idea I was stealing from my partner. It was like he was cross-examining me on the bank fraud subject, which I thought was absurd, and irrelevant. I probably acted defensive. Why wouldn't I be? Here I was in the County Prosecutor's office talking to someone I thought was a friend, expecting some muscle in my dealings with Hector. Next thing I know they were trying to convict me of something I never imagined. Once the idea came up, I had no idea where Bill was coming from. I was confused and angry. I admit it.

Writing about the subject made David feel constructive in the defense he was mustering in the trenches;

> After about fifteen minutes of grilling on the subject I did not want to talk about, with no mention of the promissory fraud, I felt nauseated and wanted to get out of there. Both Bill and Joe sensed that I guess. And since I wasn't giving them anything on the bank fraud because I didn't know what they were talking about, the interview was over in about forty-five minutes I would guess. The whole transcript of some sixty pages is on the record; and it is notable that neither Bill nor Joe asked me a single question about what I was going through with Hector Sexton. I was out of there in less than an hour I would imagine.

* * * * *

Privately Watkins and Walsh had agreed that if an appeal ever arrived relative to the Pleasant Valley case, they would be able to argue that David Zehlen never presented sufficient evidence of a crime being conducted against him for his office to investigate–while there *was* sufficient evidence to investigate *his* suspected crimes. If the issue ever arose in an appeal, as long as Joe Bernard was involved in the voluntary statement it was his responsibility as a representative of the Granite County Sheriff's department, to investigate. Bill would argue in appeal that investigation was not his *job*–detective work was Deputy Joe's responsibility.

The most egregious error in attorney Watkins' *practice,* was that he never told David Zehlen he had the right to an audit. A simple TILA audit based on the allegations David was making against Sexton in the voluntary statement would have resolved the issue. Zehlen claims he requested that the state provide an audit a half dozen times from his public defender. On appeal, Holbrooke defended his actions, stating he deflected the request because he was forced to press for a plea bargain when David was reluctant to provide critical information related to the ASCS penalty.

The audit was a *critical* measurement–Walsh knew he couldn't allow it to happen. When Bill proposed an audit Walsh argued against it, saying it would be too costly for the state. The Zehlens who were penniless couldn't afford the TILA they needed. The state was forced to be conservative because enough resources had already been depleted by David Zehlen in the investigation of his multiple offenses. Walsh succeeded on both fronts with his argument that economic factors–primarily scarcity of funds–out-weighed David's right to the legitimate attorney his financial officer Walsh could have arranged–had he wanted to.

A psychological purpose–beyond the object of justice–was motivating Watkins to prosecute this man he had known over a decade; as if he had become a believer, swept along in a current of judgment that propelled an obvious charlatan like Walsh on his mission–which was not completely transparent. The county attorney gave little thought to how quickly his assumptions about a friendly local guy with a reputation, and no criminal record, suddenly appeared through the Walsh lens to be number one on America's Most Wanted list. It may have been ambition to advance in the legal profession, that propelled him to indict David Zehlen on *hearsay* alone–as much or more than the allegations of an outsider with no roots in the community. There could have been other more *occult* motives connected to such principles, power and presumptions of invulnerability that united the two professionals against the *"once the most successful"* private farming operation in the world.

In the months following the inquisitions of March leading to the November hearing, the public defender David was saddled with by William Watkins and Robert Walsh, *ignored* Zehlen's repeated request that he review the South Dakota civil suit judgment. If he had, attorney Holbrooke might have discovered that the bank agreed to cancellation of the insurance that would have covered the safflower loss. Or better yet, he might have discovered that the bank attorneys were *converting* the contract between Zehlen and Sexton the bank had capitalized, to a "loan."

The failure of his public defender to understand the case well enough to develop a defense against false charges, could become an issue upon appeal. Zehlen was no legal genius; he was smart enough to know he was helpless without competent legal assistance. Instead of being helped by his attorneys, getting matters straightened out in the voluntary statement, David Zehlen found himself more deeply snared in the plot Robert Walsh had disclosed to Hector Sexton and his various associates during the winter of 1992-1993. Instead of a legitimate investigation to prove or disprove the allegations Zehlen was making in the Sexton contract dispute, Watkins placed bank fraud relative to the MWFSL loan default at the top of a list of what he later claimed were over twenty-six additional Spriegl charges–the worst being that David had written unauthorized checks on the Pleasant Valley account.

* * * * *

On August 30, 1993, Deputy Sheriff Joe Bernard of Granite County and Granite County Attorney William Watkins drove in [Joe's] police cruiser to Fargo, North Dakota to interview Mr. Hector Sexton. Sexton was the one-time partner and financial backer for David Zehlen, president of Pleasant Valley Farms; they first met at a Cenex shareholders function in Watertown in 1989. Attorney Watkins and I met with Mr. Sexton and his attorney Mark Hanson in Mr. Hanson's office in Fargo, North Dakota.

In our conversation we talked about Hector Sexton's background and how he became associated with David Zehlen and his Pleasant Valley Farms operation. Under advisement of his attorney, Sexton told Prosecutor Watkins and I he had worked with David Zehlen for two or three years. During that time, he had faith in David and had developed a trust in him from previous years of business; during that time had never experienced any problems in their farming operations.

Hector stated that he started to have some doubts about their loan arrangement in 1991. At that time, he began to think that's when maybe something wasn't right with their business deals beginning in July of 1992. When he talked with officials of the First Omaha Bank in October of 1992 he found out things were not right; at that time, he contacted the bank and claimed he had some agreement with Zehlen which gave him (Sexton) ownership of the crops grown on Zehlen's leased land in South Dakota.

Hector Sexton then told me and County Attorney Watkins that he had received some "phony bills" from David Zehlen on acreage and fertilizer that was never applied on his land. Hector told us that he had always trusted David up until that point. He had thought of it as some kind of misunderstanding and never questioned the bills even though he had advanced David a large sum of money in March 1992 for operations expenses.

Sexton then stated that he would be willing to testify in Granite County court if need be relative to any charges filed against David Zehlen. Mr. Hanson, Hector Sexton's attorney then commented in the conversation that he had seen the copies of the documents relative to the double billing scheme that he had reviewed and analyzed. They were genuine evidence of a double billing scheme.

Mr. Hanson agreed with Hector's opinion the bills were frauds, and that he would send copies of the documentation to the Granite County Attorney and Sheriff's office for apprehension and enforcement if it was necessary. In reporting the incident, Hector Sexton stated that he had sent copies of some thirty of these duplicate invoices to First Omaha Vice President Jessen so that he would become aware that David was not representing the best interests of the bank.

Upon their return to Rockland, Deputy Bernard wrote up a report which was eventually filed in the Granite County Courthouse and signed by Judge Gerald Silas a day or two before the pre-trial hearing the Sexton complaints had led to, that was scheduled for November 1993.

Over the land line, Walsh advised Sexton keynote counsel was arriving.

"Be generous with the obvious facts, of course everyone on the planet knows you own the crop; but spin it a little, mix in the uncertainty with the evident–confusion is your best ally. Watkins knows farming so you have to be careful; make it clear Zehlen is stealing from Sexton in a production scam. Hand out a couple of the phony bills. We already have David dead to rights on the

Bergen farm equipment theft. So take advantage of that information. Bring it up only if you have to. I'm worried Bergen might flip on his script under pressure. Some say the father owes Jack fifty grand, so we eliminate Glen as a witness if the case makes it to trial. I assume the bank has probably burned the original loan papers by now; be very careful not to bring up the subject of the MWFSB default. We don't need Bill and St. Bernard sifting through the rubble of *Club Alibi*. David has no proof of a scheme if there is no audit in his defense. I can assure you they will hear only silence from Zehlen, because he still doesn't get it. He still thinks I am on his side, and you–not far from it. All we have to do is argue that it was David's error. It was not your fault Hector; your partner did not provide that information in the April 1992 farming loan application."

No one but Walsh knew Sexton had nothing to worry about as long as he followed orders from headquarters. A dramatic foreclosure on the biggest farm in the county would deflect attention from the promissory fraud. Walsh concentrated on improving his methods, constantly stirring the witch's brew of *confusion* and *accusation* he knew from experience would be good enough to sustain the conspiracy nobody on earth had the wisdom or courage to penetrate. The public defender he had in mind would never allow the subject of the promissory fraud status to enter the court dialogue. Walsh had convinced Nancy a plea bargain to theft and fraud was her husband's only alternative to a stiff prison sentence for federal loan fraud.

CHAPTER 36

According to his family guru, unless he *plea-bargained* in the upcoming trial that David Zehlen was facing in November 1993, he might be looking at spending the next 20 years of his life in prison plus at least a $100,000 dollar fine for the false-witness criminal charges that Robert Walsh, Hector Sexton and County Prosecutor William Watkins had assembled against him.

In the lawsuit's interest, it was Walsh's task to make sure every jot and tittle of the cover up appeared to be legitimate; predictably, a quickie accounting of David's assets proved that he was *paupens* and would need a public defender. Conveniently, the conspiracy had one lined up for him. In the shadows and behind closed doors, it was Walsh who had assembled the scaffold of the conspiracy against a gullible man who kept climbing deeper into the trap set for him every day. It was the intent, cause and evidence content of Walsh's memorandum, accepted as *gospel* by Watkins and Joe Bernard for the same occult reasons it was accepted by his wife–and the community in general–that provided the momentum to propel the fraud through a seamless legal process.

Meanwhile back on the farm, Robbie Walsh kept reminding Nancy that David probably would be helpless to defend himself against the $500,000 "dream team" that Hector Sexton, Ceres, SVO and Lubrizol had assembled against him. Walsh was aware of the caliber of defense David needed, to combat a team of super-lawyers–you needed famous barristers like Ron Meshbesher or Gerry Spence, who enhanced his career and fortune by adopting a Daniel Boone image as his brand.

Under the bleak circumstances of the eminent collapse of the farm, with no money available, Dave was ready to rollover. According to the inept public defender Watkins and Silas *assigned* to the Zehlen defense team, David most likely faced ten years for theft by swindle of over a million dollars from his partner, and extracting a half million dollars from the government on the ASCS fiasco, unless he cut a *deal* for leniency.

Walsh had the criminal insight, based on previous experience with desperate farmers holding far less capital than the Zehlens to lose. With no counsel, they were like Christians thrown to the lions, helpless without proper legal representation Walsh had no intention to provide his clients with.

The whole prosecution's case was based on bearing false witness, one of the oldest sins on the forbidden list, effective after 4000 years and one of the most difficult to detect and understand. Denigration of David's character did the better part of the domestic damage and factored heavily into the assortment of methods the conspiracy used to discredit the victim–all the time remaining hidden, undisclosed, as outside infiltrators.

As power of attorney for Pleasant Valley, Walsh had no intention to divert any remaining cash from the 1992 bank loan *or* the harvest of the other crops assumed on the defaulted mortgage he was administrating–to David's detriment. Since he had become irrelevant, Jack's two hundred-thousand-dollar IRA fund would not be used for his son's benefit; it would be counterproductive to borrow upon, or from the $600,000 Zehlen children's trust fund he had managed since July of 1992, to pay for a legitimate attorney for David. Once he was recruited, John Holbrooke was thoroughly briefed how to augment the state's argument by deflecting, ignoring and excluding any and all interpretations, evidence or ideas that compromised or conflicted with the predetermined design. Walsh monitored security measures, continuously auditing the flow of information the defense was based on, in rigid military-intelligence fashion, after March 1993.

Among themselves, counsel and the prosecutor had a mutual understanding that under no circumstance would David Zehlen be allowed to introduce the information on the pending *Sully* civil case Wilber and Myers were carefully pacing, according to the design that had worked in other foreclosures; that evidence included generated files, sealed folders and secret court filings that indicated attorneys working for the bank–were about to convert the Sexton Zehlen contract to a loan.

Though the prosecution claimed that 25,000 pages of legal documents were involved in the litigation and initiated by Walsh, among the handful of documents the case against him was built upon–no loan papers relative to the Sexton Zehlen contract were ever required by or provided to the court–nor, was an accounting even presented to the court to substantiate the Sexton claims of loss through theft of actual dollars or property, cash or credit supposedly stolen from him by David Zehlen. Under such principles, excluding all exculpatory evidence–the fact Sexton owed Zehlen a million five on promissory fraud would never be acknowledged–the prosecution proceeded. In denying the audit, the guaranty value of the contract was nullified, simply brushed aside by sleight of hand; in so doing, the public defender and the prosecutor served the purposes of Robert Walsh and Hector Sexton, to indict Zehlen on false charges for which he had no defense.

Under the draconian conditions, his defense counsel informed David he would not be able to use material and information related to the South Dakota civil case to defend him; any *Sully* court-related evidence was out of the question. In pretrial discussions, Holbrooke indicated that the default on the ASCS funding was the main issue of concern in Granite County court; assumptions of the county committee that David's actions were penalty worthy, were irrelevant and impartial. Because of the seriousness of the violations, and the evident loss of millions of dollars of government money, the general USDA decision was the *only* audit Zehlen was entitled to. Holbrooke warned him judgment could be harsher, aggravated upward by the judge if he didn't show a more penitent attitude in court than he exhibited in private discussions.

According to Holbrooke, the Sully issues didn't make any difference in his defense in Granite County. He was wondering if there was any evidence that would condemn Zehlen on domestic charges. In the meantime, Watkins locked the strange-looking double sided invoicing files in his safe, and waited for just the right moment to reveal them to Judge Silas.

Following Walsh's chain of intention, Watkins' strategy was simply to extend Walsh's theory of a crime–in effect to create a crime where one never existed–and was the true skill involved. He was intervening to stop a practice that could lead to physical violence. As a footnote, Walsh claimed it was his duty to disclose to the County Attorney there were more examples of situations, where David continued to write unauthorized checks on the Pleasant Valley account, and after his presidency was terminated.

"I did not want to cause any more grief for Nancy. I'm not sure where he got all those blank checks Bill. I am equally puzzled why some of his customers honored them. That account was closed; but that's where Spriegl comes into play."

By March 1993, Walsh was more than insinuating that David was stealing from Pleasant Valley, extracting cash on returns of merchandise, paying by check–basically spending tight Pleasant Valley cash when he was not authorized to do so. Walsh produced documentation to prove David had performed the same artifice at least 26 times, since he took over as power of attorney. In consideration of the family ties already strained to the limit, Walsh claimed that his final allegations would not be pressed with unusual vigor. The crumbling farm had enough problems. Walsh let his new associate Bill know he wanted this particular series of charges handled with *kid* gloves relative to domestic abuse charges, off the record; though he hated to do it, it was against his principles–unfortunately for the Zehlen family, Walsh had discovered more evidence in the course of his work that the prodigal son who never left town, was *still* writing checks on a closed PVC account when he was no longer a partner in the corporation.

* * * * *

With the hearsay evidence piling up against him, David knew he had no chance to defend himself without the audit he was entitled to. Walsh understood that in many cases, judges like Judge Silas in Granite County Court could be manipulated into not reviewing the Zehlen case on its merits–when it had so few to begin with. If his argument was long and confusing enough, the judge would never notice there was no audit; there would be no mention of the Sully lawsuit if David obeyed his gag order never to mention the civil case before the judge.

By November 1993, Walsh had been confusing the court with fictitious arguments and claims in probate court relative to his Queen Latifa Borbon Borbon administration of the Spanish inheritance for nearly three years. The aging judge, sitting on the bench as long as he could to increase his pension, was gullible; in his dotage, Judge Silas could be easily buffaloed by the make-believe scenario created by Watkins in which genuine matters of material interest were suppressed by illegal arguments.

When David's character was completely sabotaged within the family, Walsh's work was accomplished, sparing Jack–the only person with any remaining resources–the *additional* cost of a legitimate attorney from outside the county. Walsh knew from talking domestic economics with Nancy, as a group they could talk David out of a public trial for fear of greater embarrassment. Walsh knew from his courtroom experience in the demise of other farmers, a summary judgment attached to a *plea* bargain would be issued by the court–that would be enough to accomplish his personal objectives.

As the trial date approached, David began to take Ferguson's idea more seriously, combing the library for books and articles about agricultural law. One thing in his favor was that David had always been a records manager. In his research, David learned that, in general, plea-bargaining had replaced the standard trial; that event eliminated any and *all* adversarial debate, as in the comparable *US vs. Morgan* case where the same problems existed, the direction his case was headed.

Why was he the only person on the planet who noticed the obvious he wondered? If the "trial" record indicates the audit has been neglected by the court and suppressed by the conspiracy, the court cannot know the "facts" –unable to validate Zehlen's statements and records–when they had been *tampered* with by his partners. No legal scholar, David knew his account was not *barren of reasons* that brought about an uninformed plea bargain deal without adequate legal representation. As it turned out, without any defense, and the refusal of his public defender–who had become the prosecutor's right hand man–to supply the information and defense argument he needed *at least* relative to a professional audit of the debt Hector Sexton owed; in these circumstances David Zehlen, under duress, had been forced to capitulate to the plea bargain the conspiracy had pre-paid for him.

He accepted the consequences; but was it his fault Watkins had it *completely backwards* when he pressured him to *plea-bargain* to the inflated charge of "obtaining for himself the property of others, intentionally deceiving a Bank with a false representation which he knew to be false, made with intent to defraud and which did defraud the persons to whom it was made." As those claims were, Watkins added, David would be facing twenty-six *more* charges relative to an intelligence report "he was stealing from the business he worked for" –the severity of, related to his many checks written on the Pleasant Valley account while Walsh was owner–and multiples times before, when he was not authorized to spend that money. David rationalized he had been *brainwashed* by Walsh and his wife there was no money in the PVC treasury for a lawyer.

"In my opinion, considering the gravity of the loss involved, the state was giving him the best deal they could." In defending his action on appeal Holbrooke stated, "We went through Zehlen's case in detail and discussed the pros and cons of the case, and what he was at risk of and so on. No different than the usual pre–sentencing dialogue." Holbrooke claimed before the appeal panel.

"In my opinion, the best David could hope for in sentencing would be twelve months in state prison with five years' probation and a fine of $20,000 dollars; and then there was that detail to be determined, the restitution amount he owed Hector

Sexton believed to be in the range of a quarter million dollars, with the exact amount to be determined in a later hearing."

While he was accepting his three plea bargains, David was never counseled that in taking the plea he was proscribed, he would not be able to appeal the sentence of the court under "*Rule 11*" principles. To that effect Holbrooke stated,

"Before a sentencing hearing, it is standard operating procedure to explain to clients, making sure they understand what they are getting is the best deal they can hope for. Be aware the judge cannot accept a plea from a defendant who claims he's innocent, like you continue to claim you are David." John was finding he had problems nudging David beyond that strategic *coordinates* implanted at the Gestalt border of sanity, in David's adamant refusal to admit he was guilty of charges he believed were false.

Holbrooke was aware it was Judge Silas's responsibility to ask those troubling questions about due process; it was the public defender's responsibility to deflect inquiry and finesse a confusing response past a tone-deaf judge. John had years of practice using just the right combination of vagueness and uncertainty to accomplish his client's defeat *hundreds* of times to save the court the trouble of a trial. Attorney for the state Holbrooke knew the methods to overcome any man's resistance, going another country mile beyond Watkins, finally forcing Dave to admit his guilt, and accept a plea bargain to three false charges in Granite County Court.

Demonstrating his philosophy learned through thirty years of hard bargaining for slices of people's lives since the new rules relative to expediency, less devoted to civil rights, emerged–when routine denial of a client's requests and needs became a normal part of the process–Holbrooke comforted his client,

"Just be thankful David. The prosecutor is cutting you a deal, or you might be doing 20 years in Leavenworth on the federal bank fraud charges." John Holbrooke was serious. He *only* intended to place before the judge a plea his client was forced to accept whether or not it was agreed upon.

"We do not want this case going to trial David. You will be in prison unless you fully cooperate with the court and the judge, seeing justice be served due to the severity of the crimes. To give you some sense of a time-frame David, Judge Silas wants to get this damn case off the docket by the end of November–that means before Thanksgiving–because he takes that week off for some big game hunting in Montana."

* * * * *

Following Ferguson's counsel, David researched an article in *Philosophy of Law Summary* that inferred he was entitled to a second explanation. He developed an attitude of defiance in the face of faltering legal and public support–to keep his slim hopes alive. David would admit he didn't understand a lot of the analysis; in the end he agreed with the theory, that by the 1990's prosecutors and judges had agreed with scholars–plea bargaining had become the primary means used by prosecutors to secure convictions. That method was found to be more efficacious as a *tool of enforcement* in Granite County–as violence against women and lawlessness increased in the country.

CHAPTER 37

After his November 1993 plea bargain to three felonies, the most severe of which was swindling his partner Hector Sexton out of an undetermined amount of money somewhere close to a third of a million dollars, David Zehlen served nine months of a two-year sentence in various men's correctional institutions in North Dakota and Minnesota. When his sentence was completed, minus six weeks early release for good behavior, David Zehlen, who in 1992 was one of farming's top producers in the country, by post-conviction 1994 learned in a hurry he was facing *more* problems–the same *stigma* as any other "ex-con" released into the community faced–in finding employment.

There were few jobs in Rockland or Granite County David was suited for; with no income, David was facing paying child support for his three sons and a handicapped daughter with no visible means of support. After three years, David was handed a bill from Granite County social services for over $50K due immediately for back child support, and counseling services for his estranged wife. He was desperate; but acting on a personal reference from Neil Jorgenson who had once owned his father's grain transporting business before going to work for David's father Jack, David found temporary employment taking over-the-road hauling jobs with Milbank based Dakota Valley Trucking. The owner Glen Richards had known Jack since high school days and as he expressed it, offered to *take a chance* on David who needed a fresh start after doing some hard time for agricultural crime.

Dakota Transport ran twenty hopper trucks out of a terminal close to US 12 west of Trevett's Café, shipping grain to markets in Minneapolis and Milwaukee. Richards noticed immediately that David could back an 18-wheeler into a 12-foot loading dock like no other driver on the staff, which ensured him of at least a seasonal position and some distance from his creditors. To relieve some of the palpable alienation David felt after his divorce, he indicated he preferred the long haul, two weeks on the road was fine with him, driving regularly to the market outside of Philadelphia. Richards was a prospering and generous man, never embittered by rough times many of his customers had survived, while a few had not, in the Milbank area. He was a second generation owner of the Roadway Transport franchise, when credit was scarce and a Kenworth 18-wheeler on the road was worth its weight in gold around harvest time. Glen had a sense of when to give a guy a break. David fared considerably better on the highway than in his hometown where suddenly he had no friends; the peace of the cab with the radio humming low, cleared his head of grief, allowing him to think objectively about the past few years of tragedy. With Waylon on the Oldies channel, he celebrated the good times he had back in the day his woman was good-hearted, and his boys were playing sports.

It felt surprisingly good to pick up a paycheck. Richards paid generous subsistence, and mileage. His new employer never asked if there was any change leftover from the trip as he handed David his two week check for eighty hours on the road at teamster wages. After the Walsh experience counting every nickel as if it were his last, it felt good to work for an honest owner and organization in the aftermath of the 3-year tribulation he had survived, but was unable to forget.

CHAPTER 38

According to Ferguson, who volunteered at the Rockland Learning Center two nights a week and Saturday mornings, his assessment of a GED candidate was based on his six required courses for a double minor in psychology and counseling that he had accumulated in the pursuit of a teaching license. Ferguson's evaluation determined his client had *cracked* under pressure as any normal small town farmer would have in the unusual and unexpected circumstances. He and Antonelli determined David needed "brush-up" only, not the full-scale GED training program, to communicate with attorneys and judges about his predicament. David had a diploma, but needed a job-skills course focused on literacy and job interviews.

"From the perspective of adult education Jim, the research question we are developing at this time is whether or not the literacy level of the student had an effect on his business? As educators we test the research hypotheses, 'training in literacy skills leads to effectiveness in business; or such training has no effect at all.'" George used a heuristic approach similar to Rogers, adding a personal touch to the educational research angle; commenting often, the compression element of higher education was missing and along with it the compulsion–but the student must complete the learning element to succeed in business. George would recite how the short envelope of training must imitate the actual work experience– because the livelihood of the person depended on it–training must be intense.

"We certainly cannot underestimate the importance of professional development in a learner's life where there are limited opportunities, and a great deal of competition for them. At the same time Jim, you need not factor in any personal loss of self-esteem in teaching; that sacrifice is unnecessary in the ultimate dismissal, because the person must graduate to a higher level of consciousness, relinquishing the *old* and accomplish for himself the destiny you can *only* guide him toward. And you must not be annoyed at normal complaints about your methods. In post-modern education, you will find your world view routinely rejected."

Although in fundamentalist terms, David had failed to withstand the devil's test of his spirit, just as *Job* had in the Bible according to some; nonetheless, David's supporters in the church faded away as the sense of Zehlen invulnerability–attached to unusual family virtues of generosity and its required attendance that had not protected him from his nemesis–grew in the congregation. In the interview process, David depended upon his experiential knowledge gained in farming and counseling at Anothene,

"Remember George–it's not on the assessment, but I just want you to know I operated a 20-bed inpatient treatment center for nearly eight years. As part of our services, we also offered to local companies and the county an EAP-Employee Assistance Program. One part of this service was to assist the employees, providing financial and personal counseling including chemical abuse and referral services. I found one of the primary issues facing people is their addictive behaviors caused by deeper problems and how those conditions caused drug and alcohol abuse, negatively affecting their occupations."

Through the course of his initial interview, David continued to acquaint George with the parts of his life that did not immediately appear on the application. During a discussion of the assessment process, Antonelli asked Ferguson if he was familiar with *Flowers for Algernon*, the film with Cliff Robertson. Ferguson replied he had not read the book, but he had seen the movie *Benji* based on it, when it was apparent there was some relevance to the analogy as their conversation approached their usual conclusion; the client's mood improved, but the learning process was encountering personality issues in the areas of emotionality and intellect that interfered with the transfer of knowledge, as David insisted on his will as the *final* say, on top of a *semi*-belligerent attitude toward authorities in education he clashed with historically. And here they were again, imposing an opaque rubric upon him, that clashed with his personal bodyguards–anger and resistance–stationed at the borderline of the *denial* ground.

In his sanctuary, David thought of the Control Data program as his intellectual property although he was not drawing royalties. He counted the actual real estate value of the farm as an arm of his personality. His rivals had succeeded in defacing that image on the cover of *Farm Futures* that had served David Zehlen since kindergarten, as a veritable staff of power supporting his activities in the church and society of his peers in the tiny town of Rockland.

His mentors suspected David's trauma was closely associated with loss of his roots, the true source of endless grief that had to be suppressed if he was going to function in society. David never completely adjusted to the power-shift as his successful life declined at its apex, in spite of his expertise beyond his associates in the increasingly narrow and specialized field known as agriculture which had served the Zehlens for generations. David confided that the loss of prestige and esteem, accompanying a sense of alienation from family tradition followed by depression, was so overwhelming at times he would curl up in a fetal position until he passed out.

It took several sessions before David broke down, admitting to his counselors the most stressful dimension of his life, that interfered with his concentration, was his inability to find meaningful employment. The pressure was overwhelming with no solution in sight as his defaulted child support kept piling up, that eventually mounted to $48,000 within two years of losing his livelihood. After the hearing, his nemeses managed to screw down his checking account another notch, placing it under direct-withdrawal authority of the court; a computerized process automatically subtracted county welfare fees from his checking account, at an $800-a-month clip that was administrated on a bi-monthly basis by the Granite County child protection services.

Ferguson and Antonelli recognized David *was* the special case he thought he was; like no other, David was an unusually successful person at a young age who because of that status, basically never received correction of personality issues that would affect him in later life. He was not exactly spoiled–but after toilet training David was *used* to getting his own way and hearing about it later. His father Jack had always been a reticent observer, not interfering with his only son's learning development, when his destiny was already determined.

To complete his EdD, George Antonelli conducted a research project on corrections education based on the case study of a Lino Lakes inmate and his return to civilian life. The subject of David's post-conviction appeal and reemergence in society were among the issues he found relevant in his discovery and development of a learning plan for new students. The criminal record showed that David never had a discipline problem of any kind, debunking the theory Ansel Walsh based his judgment on. George believed other factors were involved. From his youth his father Jack was aware that his only son was his most valuable hand on deck, very competent at every farm task. His father sensed early the only trouble would be keeping his son's mind and interest on the farm–it could be a boring job on rainy days.

Always focused on the task of learning as if it were nirvana itself, Ferguson convinced David he needed to improve his writing, reminding him that Walsh had done most of the damage to Pleasant Valley through his office and writing "skills"–outside of his typed memorandum and the phony bills, Walsh presented no evidence David had actually committed a crime. As his friend urged him to press forward in the search for knowledge, David reminded himself the only educated person he knew well enough to discuss it with, was his sister Kris, who could be blunt and unflattering in her assessment of his learning and writing skills; he knew he had to improve in those areas that were interfering with professional development and humiliating to a person of his intelligence, when he had been failing in reading and writing since elementary school. After three decades he was finally addressing the envelope of the problem.

Ferguson hinted there was another possibility to consider if the relief petition made it to the higher court. There was little doubt Walsh had pressured Zehlen into vaguely illegal acts while he was suffering under untreated depression; the pressure warped his judgment. At the next stage, browbeating by the opposing attorney was a common method of prosecutorial misconduct; those tactics might have caused David's predicament. Pleading guilty to false charges carried with it many resulting problems without solutions. Instinctively, Ferguson knew Dave had been set-up. He didn't know how, he intended to find out.

The English teacher who had read most of King and Vonnegut, promised one day he would write a novel about the predicament David found himself in the summer of 1992, to make sure another version of the tragedy of Pleasant Valley was preserved within the perspective of the landscape it emerged from. In their discussions, Ferguson spent many hours explaining to David how he would write the book; and why his early interest in history and fiction had been replaced by an interest in psychology as a contributing factor of literature.

Ferguson believed findings of research such as those of Perles, Goodman, and the dream analysis of Jung were useful instruments in heuristic therapy relative to issues that were interfering with a person's satisfaction and success dealing with life changing events. He preferred an informal setting, over a cup of coffee, a jasmine candle burning, the alto tones of Cleo Laine wafting through his chilly basement studio–her soothing voice pulsating softly through a Pioneer attached to four ancient Advent stereo speakers, nestled at the corners of a 12x14 blue-toned Persian carpet with cream colored borders.

With David, he found himself relying on aesthetics, mix and matched with various quotations from specific psychologists relating to validity, analytic methods such as dream interpretation, and traumatic experience insight, that allowed the therapist and his patient to engage on a comfortable plane of congruence, in a shared experience–dealing with and identifying problems related to personality.

It was difficult to accept the analysis of his mentor. Each concession he made to his instructors was another indication of

David's sequence of irresponsible decisions that as far as he was concerned, were forgivable under duress. To a sympathetic jury, his irrational actions could be viewed as a side-effect of *pressure* that caused him to allocate the USDA funds to Hector. Ferguson believed that predicament was created by the conspiracy; and David's unknowing attitude toward it, is an irreducible element of David Zehlen's argument in the appeal process. However, Ferguson did not believe that reasoning alone was enough to acquit David of the theft by swindle charges assembled against him by Sexton and Walsh. To gain anybody's attention after so many years, first his attorney would have to unravel the incredibly convoluted plot of the conspiracy that placed Dave in dire straits.

*　*　*　*　*

Rockland, a town of 2000 people in 1990, could only afford one full-time licensed adult education instructor trained in assessment of adult learning and development problems. Head man at the counseling center was the librarian and senior GED teacher Mr. George Antonelli–who like Jim Ferguson, had considerable training in psychological evaluation as part of his licensing and certification program. He and Ferguson were a generation apart, and shared few interests, although they did golf occasionally together on a Saturday morning. As football season approached in view of the many gopher holes on the course, the conditions of local fairways always led to a conversation about the mounting Golden Gopher losses to Michigan, and the coaching situation at the University, between the two duffers.

"I tell you one thing Jim, the last decent coach they had at Minnesota was Cal Stoll, but I don't want to bring that up again as a disgruntled alumnus. In David's situation, I believe we are witnessing a borderline condition that requires a psychological evaluation of the *root* causes. I admit this cocktail might be affecting my judgment, but it might be better to describe Dave's personality in show business terms like, burlesque, contortionism, vaudeville quackery–more like a performer than a farmer." Antonelli reflected deeper than expected as the two hackers discussed athletics and the case at the 19th-Hole Bar on the 4th of July, deferring to *Rogers'* unconditional *positive regard* stipulation, believing that such unusual traits when blended with a farmer's sense of humor, could be confusing to the observer, but not life threatening. In the clubhouse, they agreed that David Zehlen needed some spiritual uplifting, and a review on the scaffold of learning the program had to offer.

"I have never met a character like David," Antonelli conceded. "So I may be handicapped in my game with him."

There was no use comparing him to some of the displaced Sudanese farmers he met at Hubbs. As senior teacher in the Rockland Learning Center located in the basement of the remodeled Andrew Carnegie library, Mr. Antonelli was more accustomed to tutoring high school girls who dropped out their junior and senior year because of pregnancies. There were a few young men who had just plain dropped out because they hated school, finding themselves in need of a diploma to join the National Guard.

"His attitude and his interest tests prove Mr. Zehlen will never be able to hold a competitive job at the cheese factory, or the quarry for that matter, with a *chip* on the shoulder. In terms of literature, like Oedipus, David consciously wants the truth, but unconsciously wants to *suppress it* because it is so awful to him," Antonelli's voice trailed off as he confided to Ferguson. "But I don't suspect he would be interested in starting over there either–wrong skill set." By then his instructors understood why David was reluctant to leave town with little hope of finding work in a city with his criminal record, and no work experience except farming and driving truck. Without a job, he could never pay rent in the city; he could live in his mom's basement for free.

In his initial essays and writing assignment, David wrote of his successes as if they were happening in the present, as though the dimensions of time were fused into a virtual world, continuing success in his imagination that could be depended upon as surely as reality. The Smith-Corona word processor in the education lab allowed him to spell out his dreams as the "World Wide Web" was just coming to life.

Writing proved to be therapeutic for Dave. Hours at a time, negative thoughts of the conspiracy were replaced with a utopian global expansion program he imagined he could partner with Cargill on the Internet; before long, the narrative David created for his instructors began to reflect the *far* side of David's version of what happened in the demise of the farm. The way David spun the drama verbally and on paper–he made it appear as though his actions were the *salvation* of the farm–that might someday lead to a RICO complaint. The better he learned how to write about what happened, his critics would learn he had a contract with Sexton that was never canceled–then there would be no question of guilt or innocence. He would eventually be doing his own pro se discovery that would prove he had been right all along; he would experience even greater achievements in the future, and so on.

Before he went too far with his ideas about exonerating himself on paper, Ferguson suggested David should concentrate exclusively on dates and facts of his trials and hearings, as much as possible leaving out his attitudes, opinions and interpretations of the laws Walsh and Sexton had broken, appended with comments, and endless lists of violations the state committed for lack of investigation. In response, David defended his writing saying it was *necessary* to add as many layers and extensions as possible to draw attention to the conspiracy he had discovered against Pleasant Valley. Though he provided few specific examples, David believed his version went far deeper than even Ferguson and Antonelli imagined; he needed to bring that information into the light of justice before the United States Supreme Court.

In his undefined mission to clear his name–along with the Zehlen name in the community where they had been defamed by Walsh–compiling the *huge* loss of wealth kept David busy on his word processor creating an inventory of due diligence violations by the state, which he then presented to his teachers as if they were attorneys. His instructors immediately recognized the source of David's troubles beyond the lab, trying to explain to judges and attorneys who were calling his ideas *"incomprehensible gibberish."* Under the tutelage of the GED program, David was attempting to change the impression his literacy problems were creating with attorneys and judges, but every paragraph he composed presented a unique set of problems that could never be resolved by short-term lexical rehab.

Under Antonelli's system of scoring, David's early writing samples showed deficiencies in content, organization, and style along with shortcomings in mechanics, grammar, spelling, punctuation and formatting. David's instructor felt that low scores across all domains of writing were also an indication of reading disability, a consistent problem that over time renders an executive in *any* organization dysfunctional.

Ferguson began to wonder if he had done the right thing, encouraging David to improve his writing when David's written communications, if he ever sent them, would only make matters *worse* with his attorneys and judges. In his writing, David accused state and federal courts that they were liable for not protecting him from false charges. He believed the state was negligent in its failures of investigative obligations and protections due to him. Those individuals he continuously named in the "fraud lawsuit" he was assembling had cost him a multi-million-dollar family farming business, 17 years of his life, and a fortune in cash and equity. And they were going to *hear* about it.

While at times it was frustrating to his teachers to observe his unusual approach to lost territory, denial of responsibility, and never actually admitting he had any serious problems; even so, David Zehlen was confirming standard corrections learning theory, that writing about personal struggles during rehab is the best therapy. Writing about the details of his demise, describing his feelings, and what he thought about during his time of tribulation–was a healing process in itself. Ferguson coached him to keep up with his diary and start writing a journal, encouraging David he was off to a good start clearly describing the situation, and creating a filing system to preserve his correspondence and court records in the event the case ever found its way to trial.

David's deficiency in reading ability was easily recognizable in his writing and contributed to it; both his instructors believed the source was a basic literacy deficit combined with a refractory attitude and emotions that interfered with comprehension and explanation of legal arguments that had prevailed against him. David admitted to Ferguson he could not understand what George meant as he stressed that sequence and logic could be carried from paragraph to paragraph, from page to page by creating an outline. The concept of organizing a series of complex issues in his mind, or on a couple pages of word processing was beyond his ability as he was nearing his 60th year on earth.

It took him two days to type a two-page letter. In most of his compositions it was the whining tone, blaming state and federal officials, along with his wife for his entire assortment of problems, in a caustic tone and attitude that stuck out like a sore thumb in his writing. There was little evident content and organization besides emotionalism at his losses, with enough elements of chaos that would relegate his work to the irrelevant file, or the shred bin at the sorting stage, as he soon discovered in sharp rebuttals of his reports in personal letter form, claiming he was innocent to Judge Silas, who steadfastly refused to open *sealed* files for David's benefit.

In his writing, David wobbled between objective reporting, and complaining about his terrible predicament caused by the state and its incompetent, ineffective legal system stacked up against him; again and again, Dave wrote of failures of due process, while the state failed to recognize and protect him from the multiple frauds hatched upon him by a criminal conspiracy. He was reluctant to explore the mystery of what happened to his fortune too deeply, because it might incriminate him even more after ten years.

After many hours of counseling and family therapy sessions, punctuated with endless descriptions and diatribes against Walsh, Sexton, the bank—and, most passionately his by now ex-wife Nancy–Ferguson was able to convince David that one way out of the box he was in was to write about his traumatic experiences with his great nemesis, Robert Walsh, the man responsible for his downfall.

"I was not a natural born writer David. Nobody is," Ferguson reassured him. "English was always my best subject in grade and high school. That was probably because I loved to read. But when I got to Augsburg, when it came to writing, I found out I was a novice in a hurry. It was the competition I imagine. These city kids have much more advanced English and math courses. My first English instructor in college told me he thought I would fail in composition. My first few papers were D's and F's. I mean it. I was shocked. Thinking I could just whip out college assignments without applying the rubric."

"In those days I was distracted, thinking about women and sports. I still recall my instructors lecturing about appreciative, judicial and aesthetic criticism that he wanted applied to the texts we were reading about, writing about select topics, and staying focused on the assignment. You need to reach that level of composition if you expect your attorneys to understand what you are saying. In my college case after nearly failing Freshman English, I got a B+ on my research paper assignment on the Jesuits. Without that grade I would not have retained my scholarship."

"I have a handout for you to read David, about Matthew Arnold and his idea, seeing the object as it really is; an article about what I like to see in my own and other author's writing dealing with substantial themes. Like we see a relevant theme in *Great Gatsby* was about corruption in White Bear Lake, MN. Like Gatsby, you were not prepared to deconstruct a Wall Street swindle in our small town lives. I'm exaggerating to make my point. You know Walsh's thoughts were with his *stakeholders* in organized crime from the letter. We need some analysis in these papers instead of a rude display of raw emotional attitude and voice; you need to study the examples and learn. I am not asking for reports, you need analysis. If I didn't learn that lesson, I would never have understood the sheer vagueness of *Sound and the*

Fury. He learned his lessons about prejudice in the deep south, but between the lines Faulkner tells the story of corruption in these tiny towns on the edge of Frontier Hall," realizing he was losing his student's interest, he concluded.

"Fortunately I had a good understanding of mechanics, grammar, punctuation and spelling. I won a spelling bee in parochial school. Communication is my strong suit. English and French were the only courses that kept me floating my first quarter in college. After that trauma I decided English would be my major; it would be helpful for pre-law if I wanted to convert my love of literacy in general, using the power of language in the legal profession. Now I'm glad I didn't continue with that thought, after witnessing the way the attorneys you have encountered use their skills."

"You need to realize I heard this lecture before from your colleague Jim," Dave responded as he rarely did. "George handed me this book and told me to sit down on the couch and read *The Count of Monte Cristo* if I wanted to learn about swindles. For once I saw the relationship of my case when there was nothing else like it in the *Modern Farming* magazine. From that story I can relate to what happened to Dantes, branded as a criminal by a false witness, like Walsh. But I could never write like that. The best grade I ever got in English was a 'C+' from Leo on a group project when I didn't have to write the paper by myself."

"You don't have to be an author like Dumas David. Imagine writing like Hugo, describing this *phantom* of the farm character creating so much mayhem, in your journal. Remember you are composing a rural *soap opera* featuring Robbie Walsh, about the weird drama behind the conspiracy you have been reporting to me. At this stage your explanation doesn't have to be perfect. I have read over some of Walsh's writing; and it is composed of errors. But he gets his points across effectively, that counted against you. That letter you showed me written to Hector is full of typos. There is no organization to it. As you see David, in his next piece of legal writing, when he has his attorney in Watertown composing the PVC countersuit, his previous vague and ambiguous style serves a purpose. Basically only the insiders–his partners in the conspiracy–can understand what he is writing about. Then he pushes his motions through court by retaining attorneys and bullying the judge," Ferguson theorized.

"I hope you're not suggesting I can write up these legal petitions and motions you are always mentioning. Just the thought of it scares me."

"Theoretically speaking Dave, you should be able to contribute content to a civil lawsuit. You have a general feel for what the legal cites are driving at; but you miss the fine points of argumentation. I can always edit your work. For the remainder of the time I'm in Rockland I will be your guide. Remember creating your huge farm was a combination of mechanical and intellectual effort. A load of logistics was involved in a smooth presentation for the *Farm Futures* article," Ferguson concluded on a positive note.

"In the days before the *tsunami* hit Pleasant Valley, you had the ability to manage the organization. You have shown us your ability to create at least an informal record that reflects your desire to fix the memory of the court with the aid of the evidence you have provided verbally in our sessions in the library and in our phone conversations. If you translate all that information into written evidence of the contract fraud and the actions of Walsh, Hector–then you finalize your complaint explaining the impact of the illegal counsel our incompetent public defender Mr. Holbrooke *framed* you with. From the psychological angle it appears you are trying to restore the previous order these *hoods* have disrupted. Your fate is not in your own hands apparently; if you keep working at it, you never know Dave–something might happen."

"John was beyond incompetent Jim. That fool was culpable!"

"There you go again preaching *law* without a license. See what I mean? Now you are throwing out these legal terms you don't understand all that well in an emotional fashion, scolding the authorities from a powerless position. From now on you should be investing your insight into events and improving your language skills to control your hostile attitude toward the legal system. I believe you have potential to do it yourself. I will try to mold your input into some kind of legal memorandum-format based on a few night classes at William Mitchell–before I settled on teaching."

"Alright Jim, maybe *naïve* is a better word for Holbrooke. Is that what you're saying? Gullible like I was when Walsh suddenly appeared on the scene, looking like a knight in shining armor to my wife, to Phyllis–and then to Watkins," David summarized the plot in a romantic sounding metaphor that applied his media-tuned imagination to the subject of agriculture.

"Pure and simple it looks like he buffaloed Hector with his phony stylistics, just the same; but we will use models of other legal writing like *Harno* and *Sutherland* for our examples. Then move on to creating your own memorandums using evidence of that breach of contract with Hector and how Walsh piggy-backed that crime on his takeover scheme. You have the same pro se rights Walsh bragged of–and used in your demise. These pieces, our protocols so to speak, need not contain every term. They will be the informal records and notes, surgical instruments like Nancy used as a dental technician to get at the *roots* of the decay. A decent attorney should be able to use them to get you in front of a legitimate court."

"That's really what it's all about these days, with the court docket so clogged with misdemeanors; a case like yours with the class-action implications and ramifications, gets *buried* under a pile of frivolous cases. Of course the *psychic* implications–those roots of corruption–can easily be overlooked especially with some super-lawyers shuffling irrelevant motions through the courthouse to dismiss the case before it reaches trial. In your case, there are at least three jurisdictional errors that should be examined by a higher court. Besides that, Hector has never produced a copy of the loan papers; and the conspiracy parties have never produced a cancellation of the contract," Ferguson explained as if he were running out of ideas.

"Instead of speculation Dave, we need hard evidence instead of attitude, and more analysis of exactly what illegal measures Watkins, Walsh and Wilber used to accomplish your four *bogus* plea bargains, under a series of summary judgments that stymied the appeal process under Rule 11. Now that we know where we are at, we will get to that later, once you start writing up what happened to you. There must be at least one idea *minus attitude* you can write about in the three jurisdictions that have put you down. Concentrate on specific events and actions in those areas. If that doesn't work we will have to move on to circuit court that supposedly takes the jurisdiction confusion into consideration in *its* judgments," Counselor Ferguson pressed his points, intentionally practicing law without a license.

"Essentially you become your own judicial critic, interpolating your case details with the violated statutes as they appear in *Strickland and Morgan* for whatever it's worth. Think of it like you are tracking a wounded animal deep into the '*Harno*' never-never-land hunting ground to drag the carcass out of the woods. At best you are creating supporting documentation and an 'informal pro se memorandum' like Walsh did that places your case beyond the various statutes of limitation if we can prove you had incompetent counsel, which is the most *striking* feature of your quarrels with judgment."

"Like I quoted you many times Jim, the only thing I ever read was *Readers Digest* and *Modern Farming*. I never thought a lot about what went into writing those articles. But I did appreciate that magazine article Colleen Nelson wrote about me in *Farm Futures Magazine*."

"That was a fine piece of journalism David. She reported like a physician examining the heartbeat of your operations, with an ear to the political backlash. Like hers, your writing can explain the mystery of why that paradise was lost–so mysteriously, so completely, in an apparently *underworld* fashion, for what originally appeared as minor violations and misunderstandings, within a month after the article appeared. We see some irony there that we can relate vaguely to the drama that George was trying to show you in *Monte Cristo*."

* * * * *

In Adlerian psychological terms, the downfall of Pleasant Valley Farms had placed David in a state of post-traumatic stress at the interruption of his *great upward drive.* Notwithstanding, within three years David was pulling out of a *nose dive* into a deep depression with the help of his instructors at the learning center.

Gradually, as his communications skills improved, he eliminated the constant and predictable whining and moaning about his plight, which was completely understandable. For the time being, the dedicated staff of the learning center appeared to have succeeded in detecting the kernel of the student's distraction, and resulting lack of focus. His instructors concentrated on what they actually believed could be corrected in the legal process, before David's writing drifted into some unconvincing irrelevancy in an unending effort to connect his fall to an exterior source.

Along with the improvement of his learning skills, David's depression receded as his mental state slowly returned to normal. He eventually adjusted to life as a *released-offender* on probation living in his handicapped mother's unfinished basement in Rockland; in such accommodations as spotty work provided—the onetime millionaire now penniless with no income or job—scraped out a living. As fate would have it, David had become the *derelict in the gutter* his best friend Del, by then deceased ten years, had dreamed he would become in the re-telling of his shocking nightmare.

Years later, David credited Ferguson's guidance and mentoring as the only friendship he had left in Rockland after that fateful summer 1992 that spurred him on to rebuilding his life after Cold War III had wiped him off the map. David later credited their weekly meetings at the adult learning center from saving him from despair and maybe worse. During those bleak times it was learning, gaining knowledge of legal recourse available to him, and the potential to overturn judgment through appeal, that sparked his hope of ever bringing the conspiracy to its knees.

ANTHONY FALLS JR.

CHAPTER 39

With the scope of losses to Zehlen in the swindle *smothered* under 25,000 pages of irrelevant documentation, the staggering power of the conspiracy was manifest against its crippled victim. In a formal gesture, Walsh as administrative bursar completed the physical part of the deal by *not making the final payment* on the June 1992 operating loan by January 15th 1993–when the operating loan was declared officially delinquent–as another *illegal* formality of the foreclosure process came to fruition. To no one but Walsh, it was apparent the conspiracy went the distance to ensure every miniscule detail of the turnover appeared legal.

To their credit, it was apparent that Robert Walsh and Brent Wilber had created a confusing and corrupt argument characterized by high degrees of sophistication, design, and planning–the type "Sutherland" warned the courts about–using a series of corrupt, interpretations of the law with the power of a *lightning bolt*, to knock Zehlen to the ground with such force he had no chance to recover from the million-volt shock. Robert Walsh would have probably preferred to work alone but he needed to use Sexton and the First Omaha to achieve his objective.

In an ironic twist of fate, he delivered all the evidence that would ever be needed to prove he engineered the conspiracy, and *hold harmlessly* to the bureau that final spring of infamy. No one will ever know if Robbie left six pages describing the strategy in detail behind *deliberately* in Phyllis's faxes. In 1997, Brent Wilber stepped out of the closet, boldly addressing the confusion in an article on the World Wide Web entitled *"What a Tangled Web We Weave When First We Practice to Deceive"* that announced the Sully *conversion scheme* had been successful on the Internet. In his chef d'oeuvre, Wilber summarized the South Dakota case in a confusing riddle intended to reinforce the

Westlaw heresy, and further muddle the court record, at the same time demonstrating his writing prowess to the globe.

Walsh and the bank attorney relied on the same method of warping irrelevant issues into the court dialogue. Wilber's key analogue–the *Schaum* case example–was lifted from an article on a stolen cattle case that appeared in the 1983 S.D Journal of Law; this and other irrelevant information floated through his writing where his standard "apples to oranges" comparisons sounded logical situated at the heart of the confusing argument the conspiracy depended on in the courtroom. As he acknowledged his letter to his partner Hector Sexton, the Wilber faction was aware of the Sexton leases in South Dakota; it was Walsh's job to manage those leases. The Sully transcript states Attorney Wilber inquired,

"All that time you were putting the leases together for…?"

"David Zehlen who was my employer," Walsh answered mechanically.

"At that time were you able to determine that Mr. Sexton would have some clear claim to any of the 1992 crops you managed in South Dakota Mr. Walsh?"

"No I did not," he replied irascibly. There was no doubt that in Sully civil court Robert Walsh revealed he knew of Sexton's clandestine deal with Zehlen in 1991. He retracted the statement eight months later in June 1992. Wilber effectively created a confusing scenario in which he was able to pursue his *erroneous* intention. Rather than confront Walsh over the evident error Wilber continued,

"It just became clear to you Mr. Walsh, that Hector Sexton had some relationship with David Zehlen, is that a fair statement?"

"No it is not," Walsh barked in reply.

"You just discovered his name then, by chance?"

"I discovered Hector Sexton's name on Zehlen invoices in the office sometime that summer. I never heard his name before that time," Walsh stated unconvincingly.

Closer observation of the transcript indicates Wilber was referring to the summer of 1992. Walsh, acting power of attorney for the lost farm of Pleasant Valley was equivocal, following the legal beagle along *wherever* he led–in a practiced exchange that allowed Robbie to spin his yarn one more time in the courtroom.

* * * * *

At the northern apex of the logistics triangle, the Sully hearing itself would be largely buried under mounds of paper. No one from David's world was at the hearing; no one heard the *crash* as a White Pine was felled *deep in the forest*; no one was at the closed-door hearing that settled the bank's suit, but Walsh, Hector, Nancy, Wilber and Mr. Freeman–Hector's attorneys.

After the Sully judgment, Walsh tightened his control on the organization knowing the question of liability and chain-of-title, as a result of tampering with court processes, was never raised in Sully–it could be if the *cover up* was not successful. In a legitimate hearing those questions would have been raised based on a TILA audit: simple queries into the path of the cash flow, such as–where did the money go? Where did it disappear to? Who stole it from the Zehlens? –were proscribed in the process.

The Walsh administration had measures in place to deflect inquiry; critical questions were never raised and never answered– controversial issues never would be if Walsh or Hector had anything to do with it–controlling inquiry, and with disseminating information that might someday disclose the corrupt roots of the conspiracy. If it ever came down to a court battle between Walsh and Sexton for control, he would be able to raise critical issues for leverage,

"Let me remind you Hector, at that time Jack and David entrusted you to hedge and market their production. In what a white collar law firm might consider embezzlement, you somehow convinced David to deflect $160K of government money into your bank account Hector. You probably know by now, in the Sully depositions there are twenty more pages of error to be deconstructed that amounts to a mixture of lies and truth designed to lead and confuse the court; Freeman is your best example with his list of false ideas–the irrelevant cite from a 1909 case is the extent of Wilber's discovery–plus the threat of witnesses you and Freeman have put together is designed to avoid an audit. That allows Wilber's hypothesis to go untested by a defense in the confusion. When I am the only defense David has for his actions, we don't need an ambitious bureau attorney ever reading the ridiculous arguments in those depositions either. They are pure bunk and you know it, evidence of legal fraud. I can show you the transcript anytime." Walsh had the edge on Sexton long before Sully.

In his future discovery, David found Nancy Zehlen's deposition useful in decoding Brent Wilber's involvement in the conspiracy as he led her through argumentation that indicates Hector Sexton and David Zehlen were in constant communication.

"Would you say David and Hector had frequent contact Nancy?"

"Yes they talked every day to my knowledge Mr. Wilber."

"Alright Nancy, what would they visit about in their discussions?"

"As I recall, I would answer the phone. I would chat with Hector about the weather a while if David was out in the barn or something. I had the impression from both of them they considered each other good friends, and trusted business associates." Nancy responded.

"Did the loans go into the South Dakota crops?" Wilber pressed the issue of ownership.

"Yes"

"Okay Nancy would it be fair to say to the best of your knowledge you don't know of any money from Hector Sexton/Ceres that went into the South Dakota crops?"

"No. I mean yes. Sorry Brent."

As he studied the transcript, David was not amused that his wife had been repeatedly coerced into uncertainty–just as *he* was by his partner–finding that her statement contradicted itself when she said in the deposition the contract existed *but that it was a loan.* In her husband's opinion she didn't know the difference. The depositions never made it clear which way Mr. Wilber was directing his wife through the lines of a prepared script much like her high school drama coach Mr. Nelson had done,

"And who were the parties to that contract if you can recall Nancy?" Attorney Wilber inquired purposefully.

"I... I don't know," Nancy stammered.

"Was that contract presented to Mr. Sexton Nancy?"

"Yes I was told it was," she responded.

"Now then Nancy, do you know if a final contract for 1992 was ever reached with Hector Sexton?" Wilber approached the angle cautiously.

"There never was one," Nancy reacted coldly.

"Have you ever seen a final signed contract for 1992?"

"No."

"And do you know if the contract was signed by Hector Sexton?"

"I was told it was not signed by him."

"Alright, who informed you of this?"

"My husband–David."

CHAPTER 40

After the Granite County judgment, David's probation officer Karen White became designated enforcer of child support judgments against him. Counting his days and weeks spent on the road, David in his nightmares, imagined Ms. White crouching at the door of his mother's house with her calculator enforcing his delinquent child support payments upon his return. A professional at her job, Ms. White had no compassion for his hapless position, and less understanding of the plot David Zehlen was trying to explain to various authorities, including her, who were involved in enforcement of judgment that he had been, and *still was* the victim of an undiscovered swindle. As chief welfare enforcement officer, Karen was in no mood in her position to tolerate an ex-con being late on the seven hundred and fifty dollar a month alimony and child support payments he was required by law to make.

"How much longer do you think the county can afford to support special services to your handicapped daughter, and your three sons David? That is in addition to rising health care costs the county is paying for a PCA for your mother?" White asked bluntly, scolding him further.

"Are you aware Mr. Zehlen those services cost the taxpayers of Granite County over a thousand dollars a month." As far as the county was concerned the strain on David's back driving truck twelve hours a day was an excuse; she repeated her only concern was for his ever dwindling money supply the county could dip into any moment for back payments of alimony and child support.

Three years after his divorce, David was thirty thousand dollars arrears in child support. Ms. White would remind David harshly, instead of complaining about his payments, he should be thankful his wife had a job as a dental technician, or he would be paying higher spousal support. She noted on the budget he submitted, he was running a monthly TV cable, considered a luxury in most households–that money could be allocated to child welfare services. She overlooked that expense for his mother who watched *All My Children* religiously; but his social worker informed David if he missed another child support payment, she had the immediate authority to revoke his probation–he would be back in Lino Lakes in an instant–reminding him that in her work, she thought only of the welfare of the children, as she lectured,

"If you quit smoking cigarettes and went on a vegetarian diet you wouldn't be forced to live on such a tight budget all the time David." White seemed to demand more sacrifice every paycheck.

"You can't squeeze blood out of a rutabaga can you?" David felt like yelling at his new assailant, auditing his budget and monitoring his behavior; he resented her authority, driving around Rockland in a county Taurus, no doubt making a nice salary herself. In his quest for social acceptance, he dismissed her as prejudiced, just another misinformed woman offended by his extroverted personality–probably influenced by stories Nancy told her. Now she was dissecting his behavior like a psychologist. David could only imagine all the sordid details behind White's miserable attitude toward him. Yet he feared the county welfare enforcer was capable of more mischief. He bit his lip, heeding her warning,

"I remind you David, one more late payment without a reasonable excuse and I have the authority to revoke your probation."

It was an unfamiliar situation he never would have dreamed of in his worst nightmares; another morning commute negotiating traffic on ice covered I-90 and turnpikes beyond, jockeying his big Mack through the congestion, just like millions of morning commuters in dense traffic like he had never seen in Granite County. Always on the lookout for rare wayside rests, he attempted to revive himself from the drowsiness that plagued him; he found it was near impossible climbing into the sleeper cabin, for a large man weighing over 200 lbs., with a sore back.

His back injury was aggravated by the constant sitting in the cab of the truck; but his low dose morphine medications made him drowsy, so he lived on aspirin and coffee until he was resting comfortably in a motel along the highway. He was especially grateful at those times that his boss was very understanding and generous with his subsistence; he never questioned David's many overnights in Express Inns with a heated whirlpool sauna where he could stretch his back muscles and relieve the pain.

For what it was worth in monetary terms, David took himself off the unemployment line driving truck full time in the mid '90s. Those were the days when Whitney Houston had already *risen* to fame on the arms of Kevin Costner, and the wings of the Dolly Parton smash hit *"I Will Always Love You."* Houston's voice brought back memories of the nights he and Nancy–it was one of her favorite songs–had slow danced to the soft music after the kids were off to bed, during the best days of his marriage in Rockland.

Every time he heard that particular song, he thought of the synchronicity of the story and events of the *Bodyguard*–the theme of trust, so absent in his marriage, and the correlation of music to his life journey as he navigated the road less traveled Ferguson suggested he was on. His position as an ex-con and his attitude toward his wife happened because he had lost the farm on the lone prairie where Costner played an academy award-winning role as a soldier in *Dances with Wolves*. He had a story better than that to tell a certain Hollywood producer he knew, some day, he might be interested in. Like in *Needful Things* his next task would be about restoring the previous order, when the house of *Job* had taken a beating, with producer Stephen Rivkin focusing the camera squarely on him as the essential character.

As often as he listened to Whitney's voice, he was reminded of his wife's talent before the crash of Pleasant Valley. Those memories that brought stinging tears to his eyes, left the hairs standing up at the back of his neck as a highway patrol cruiser, lights flashing, siren blaring, was suddenly trailing his truck, not more than a car length away. In an instant the sporty Ford, fitted out like a Formula One, flashed by him chasing another suspect into the darkness. The black princess with the golden voice brought back poignant memories of the tragic drama he played a lead role in–that never seemed to end.

The pop rock and rhythmic soul that permeated the airwaves at night made David drowsy as he was trying to put the sentiments of that era behind him. It was country music over the airwaves that kept him awake after dark; he could finally appreciate Nashville for bringing the declining images of Americana back through his senses. After what he had experienced, Waylon and the cheating hearts club composed of jaded lovers, made it a lot more relevant and added a little spice to his life, as one of the few benefits that made over-the-road trips bearable, amidst the variety of physical and psychological pain he struggled with.

During his road trips to Pittsburg and Scranton, David dwelled on the spark his friend Ferguson had rekindled–the hope there was in litigation beginning with PCR. He attended the wedding as Jim married Susan Stegman, valedictorian of the Rockland High School class of 1964. She was the oldest daughter of Vince Stegman who was one of Jack Zehlen's best friends. After the debacle of the early 1990's, David remained friends with the Fergusons who he numbered among the few people in the community that believed, along with his mother–David was innocent of all charges.

The friends stayed in contact while Jim was teaching English in Wisconsin. At the beginning of the 1998 school year, Jim proposed that David should send letters every week from his various locations, truck stops and Super Eight motels he stayed in as he traveled down the many roads back and forth across the country hauling commodities. Jim requested that David please send some of his journal entries about his travel experiences to him and Susan; so Jim could read the reports to his class of fifth graders.

The assignment turned out to be a huge success. On a Friday morning in late April 1999, David took a detour north off I-94 and drove his Mack truck up to the front of the Racine South Elementary School and parked it. Susan had already arrived with a van load of punch and cookies for the class. Within moments of his arrival, Jim's kids came streaming out of the school building onto the parking lot. After introductions, David conducted a tour of his truck inside and out. Some of the more daring boys were offered the opportunity to sit in the cab and honk the horn. He described it later as a day to remember and the undisputed *highlight* of David's over the road driving career.

* * * * *

As a result of his petition for post-conviction relief in 2000, the state assigned him a new public defender. After reviewing the case as it unfolded in Granite County, Richard Schmidt informed David that not all was lost when his first pro se attempt at post-conviction relief was remanded to Minnesota Appeals court; at least it would alert the media the Lindberg baby case was still alive: David Zehlen was continuing to pursue litigation relative to the 1993 judgment in which he believed he was wrongfully convicted.

Schmidt began the appeal process by appending David's pro se argument attacking Bill Watkins' prejudice and less than due diligent investigative work in Granite County. Although the original Zehlen pro se memorandum was rebutted in a weak argument by Bill Watkins who claimed David's appeal was hard to follow, especially the section on abuse of process, nonetheless on the legal side, retired Minnesota Judges Harten and Larken noted that the case was "entitled to review" by the State Supreme Court based on Zehlen's allegations of ineffective assistance of counsel, prosecutorial misconduct and abuse of process.

After his initial failure in litigation, David maintained correspondence with attorney Rich Schmidt of St. Paul, MN, who was the first defense attorney to notice significant problems and obvious defects in his initial plea bargain with the state. Soon after Mr. Schmidt submitted his unsuccessful petition for post-conviction relief to the State of Minnesota Court of Appeals, he received the following letter from David Zehlen;

Dear Richard,

I cannot express my gratitude enough that you have finally begun to understand the scope of the legal problem before us. We need a review to show through our cross examination of Prosecutor William Watkins that these funds were owed to me and that the charge-backs are legitimate rather than the 'phony bills' Hector claimed they were. Through breach of the 1991 and 1992 contracts Hector Sexton and his parent company Ceres, it was Sexton not me who created the absolute need for these refunds, to repay the $160K due to MinGo as the ASCS rules.

I believe you will need this interpretation as evidence of the correct forensics construction of our agreement because this knowledge is necessary to understand the payment connection between Sexton and me; and that we agreed upon this structure so the payback arrangement of the ASCS funds he embezzled does not appear to be his fault to Sexton's stakeholders, when he was ineligible to receive ASCS funds outright. Between us we agreed on the back charges system of compensation. He used that trust against me when he became untruthful about our true arrangement. After following his instructions, I was charged with sending Hector phony bills.

I am writing today to confirm the Zehlen responsibilities for the Sexton contract which is not in evidence yet; I am thinking of the second year extension here, spoken of in the ASCS letter; and that the defendant acted correctly, invoicing Sexton for fertilizer and land as an offset to the ASCS penalty, and clearly received no unjust benefit from the invoicing to Sexton in August of 1992. Over the course of the next year my well-intentioned actions evolved into the trumped up charges by Watkins and Sexton of the theft by swindle charge–that the defendant Zehlen did obtain the property of Hector Sexton, in that he prepared and submitted double billings for cash rent to both a private individual, and farm lender. The indictment reads–as a result of the same scheme David Zehlen obtained money from both sources in the sum of $160,000.

Under duress of the pressure from Walsh and Sexton and the uncertainty of the times was placing on me, with the walls crumbling around me I have explained to you before, this billing adjustment was based on a charge back arrangement I made with Sexton that was approved by

Robert Walsh and carried out on his photocopier. Naively I thought I was obeying legitimate orders from the office boss who I trusted. Unbeknownst to me, my nemesis had by then become power of attorney for Pleasant Valley Farms. I believed my actions were those aligned and discussed with my partners and my interests before the event happened.

The unusual billing arrangement was designed to relieve some of the debt load Sexton had with me for the breach of contract and the repayment of the ASCS funds that he had appropriated. That was all I was trying to accomplish that day in Walsh's Brookings office as I copied the back-charged billings on the other side of the old invoices Walsh gave me to work with. I am referring to the back charge billings for past due bills that would allow Sexton to satisfy his company Ceres that he owed me a large unpaid debt he was liable for relative to the government funds. At that time, I was only the manager of these duties for Sexton and not responsible for these debts–regrettably I did him a favor by taking out another operating capital loan with First Omaha that I have explained the purpose of to you in the past also.

Apparently under so much duress I was not thinking straight; or it would have occurred to me the printing process was illegal. All I could think of was getting that debt settled. At the time my mind wasn't right; my wife was totally alienated. I didn't know it but my crooked partners were calling the shots. I was intimidated into believing I had no other choice. I'm explaining all this to you now so you know exactly what happened when I went in to discuss the circumstances with Bill Watkins. I tried to explain it; but, he wasn't buying my story. So they were all in it together against me by then. How was I supposed to know my associates were swindling me?

I ask you Richard, why didn't the court subpoena Ray Rylance who was my ASCS counsel at the time of the ASCS application? The answer is because the conspiracy had already been hatched by then. Ray would have been able to give the court an expert opinion on the correct construction of ASCS rulings and the Sexton Zehlen contract, as well as the flawed construction of state's claims that 'to provide financial updates to a bank is considered billing a bank'–as Westlaw reported in 1995.

You tell me what a ridiculous statement like that means Rich, and what do a string of words like that cost me? Ask yourself, do they have anything to do with the psychology of the conspiracy in general? It's like the logic of Brent Wilber's article on the Internet–the ruling is as absurd as the 'tangled web we weave' phrase itself the conspiracy strategy is based on, using logic and words, totally irrelevant to what really happened in the takeover operation, when at the bottom line the conspiracy rewrote the laws of our fathers to conform with their own version–more closely associated with lawlessness."

CHAPTER 41

Mentor Ferguson believed that in dealing with troubled adults, the particular trauma that was interfering with learning was a contributing symptom to the disorder that was also interfering with thinking, and could be isolated and treated; he believed pursuing Dewey's logic would lead to a solution in the complex conspiracy his friend had succumbed to. Over the years he compiled an archive of video tape interviews of students and friends, including a half dozen with Dave narrating the saga of Pleasant Valley. Like George, who followed the flexible Adult Education model of therapy based on learning progress, Jim's videos discussed his personality evaluation system, organized into major categories such as extroversion, attitude, conscientiousness, IQ, and emotions, and minor traits such as religiosity, manipulation, sexuality, frugality, risk-taking and sense of humor, measurable in normal children and adults he encountered in his profession.

Ferguson found that the minor categories were applicable across a more complex spectrum of adult personality characteristics, while they did not apply across the same spectrum of traits observable in ten year old males. To his surprise, in his first experience dealing with adult intellect, he observed an incredible range of data. Discipline in class, and next to it, establishing the distinction between teacher and learner, ranked highest on his list of effective teacher behaviors when dealing with parents; that would determine whether or not defective behavior could be dealt with in an academic fashion before learning could proceed in the classroom.

To validate his counseling with Zehlen, Ferguson would occasionally read paragraphs directly out of his college texts, to assure David he was using reliable sources in classical and modern psychology in his lessons. At those sessions, David would often quote of his experiences at Anothene lecturing alcoholics on the "12 Steps to Sobriety" as they suffered withdrawals–equal to some commensurate psychological knowledge of his mentor–and after a treaty at the borderline over quarrelsome interludes, discussions over disputed territory and delivery could proceed.

"I am not sure you will take this seriously, but some psychologists claim therapy consists of absorbing the evil that surrounds us David. I'm not suggesting exorcism is an answer to your prayers. Let's hope counseling turns out to be the blessing guys like Jung and Peck claim it is when I attempt to empathize with these traits in your behavior." In his counseling Ferguson practiced the theory of Carl Rogers who believed a relationship of therapist and client should have congruence at the core their reality experience. David claimed geometry was one of his best subjects. Theoretically speaking, Ferguson hoped David could relate to symbolism, visualizing, and accepting an indirect relationship with his mentor, who loomed over his life like a transparent triangle, expanding and contracting with the trials of his client.

"I hope you're right Jim. I skimmed over the first chapter of *People of the Lie* on top of your recommended reading list over the Halloween holiday. The distinction I noticed in the characters is–Devlen didn't sell his soul to the devil, while Robbie is on the board of directors of true believers."

* * * * *

Two weeks after Dave's voluntary statement in March 1993, Walsh reported to the FBI, "[He] had investigated a number of frauds which resulted in bankruptcies and the general demise of farmers in the Midwest." The individuals he identified had been behind the scenes in all these cases. He was certain that Pete Werner–the same individual he had identified in the Woods Elevator swindle in an earlier interview with the bureau–was continuing the scheme, selling commodities in Iowa. Dave's partner Werner would be involved in putting the same scheme together in Sioux City if *somebody* didn't put a stop to it.

Walsh took the *bull* by the horns when he contacted Hector's lawyer Freeman in Fargo, December 1992, about the legal work to clear up the debt owed Pleasant Valley Corporation, because Ceres had been withholding on the contract. Walsh was making the same deal he had proposed with Hector to his attorney–just before Thanksgiving time when Walsh was talking turkey with Freeman–indicating he was willing to finesse the MN Go debt under certain conditions.

As power of attorney for Pleasant Valley, he had a scheme arranged and *pre-paid* to accomplish his liquidation mission after scarcely a year on job. By then there was nothing of any real estate value to fret over if Hector was willing to re-allocate funds gone with the *wind*–when capital was available within the parent organization he had made billions for in his career–that could be funneled into Walsh's completely *new* entity Interwest.

In the new configuration of power, Walsh as commander and chief had the means to create systems and measures to absorb the debt like major corporations do, rearranging their assets. Pleasant Valley was going under in bankruptcy one way or another–what was the sense squandering stakeholder money on the Zehlens at a time when it is not necessary? There was always the *threat* if his attorney did not agree with Walsh's finesse of the promissory fraud issue–he would introduce the ASCS embezzlement issue into the litigation.

During the 34 months leading up to the Granite County hearing, Walsh composed a series of letters later introduced as evidence, dovetailing various fragments of his intervention, with the takeover strategy in general. As he pecked away intrepidly for hours on his ancient Royal typewriter, usually, by the third page single-spaced Robbie rehashing his life in the process, managed to reach the part about merging his company Marketing International with Pleasant Valley Corporation, notifying Hector that as power of attorney his company would own 100% of the stock and be seeking investors.

The new Interwest would cooperate with the bank in managing the 7500 acres of Pleasant Valley the creditors, Resolution Trust and First Omaha, had claimed as collateral. In his reorganization strategy Walsh claimed credit for completely rewriting the charter of Pleasant Valley Corporation under a new title that solidified ownership. He had every legal right to ensure solidarity, and do whatever he pleased in the best interests of the Zehlen family under his authority which gave him complete liberty to dispose of real or personal property for his own benefit, and others as well–if he chose to, as he swore he would many times–to the best of his ability.

With the signatures of David and Jack completely redacted from the ownership documentation, Walsh completed his *coup* by offering both Nancy and Phyllis Zehlen $10,000 cash apiece, for their fifty percent shares or 100% of Pleasant Valley corporation. Walsh convinced the girls he cared so much about them, he was being generous in paying them as much as he did, going way out on a limb paying $20K up front, when he would be able to buy the farm for a dollar down once it went bankrupt–an estimated fifteen million dollars' worth of Pleasant Valley real estate and machinery was sacrificed as collateral on the deal because of the First Omaha loan default, as part of the bargain between the bank, Sexton and Walsh. To avoid suspicion of fraud Sexton and his partners agreed to take a complete loss on the $350K crop *los lobos* dropped the insurance on–resorting to every unthinkable measure to ensure Zehlen would be held in default on the First Omaha loan underwriting the process since February, 1991.

Though his correspondence had little effect other than irritating the recipient, Walsh became more and more obsessed with putting his thoughts to paper, as the 1994 restitution hearing approached.

> *Dear Hector, Unfortunately I find it necessary to inform you I have been named in the South Dakota lawsuit and I expect that First Omaha will be paid in full so I have no alternative other than to review all of the trades made in and out of certain brokerage houses you supposedly made as a marketing consultant for David Zehlen during the 1991-92 season, to make sure there were absolutely no trades made in the name of Pleasant Valley corporation with regard to certain crops in the past three years; knowing full well that if*

*in fact Ceres did own the crops as you claim; you have no
legal ground to stand on Hector.*

Walsh's memoranda producing apparatus was proven
effective at covering the *wolf's* tracks, avoiding any possibility of
inquiry. By the early 1990's, Mandatory Victim's Restitution had
been on the books at least ten years. It was becoming a part of
the court vocabulary in other parts of the country. The Walsh
takeover coincided with the highly publicized Milken and Boesky
trial publicity. But revelations of corporate fraud in America
made little difference in Granite County which Walsh & Co had
pegged–at least a generation behind the curve of justice–ready
to take on his crime theory out of sheer boredom rather than
concerns for law and order. Walsh staged his crimes in the
outback for good reason, well aware of the new paradigm of
restitution, or triple damages. There was no need to worry over
that detail; a judge as nearsighted as Silas would not see the
conspiracy if it was *staring* him in the face.

> *If a millionaire steals a hundred dollars from a poor person
> Hector, the victim is entitled to compensation at a
> commensurate level; in other words, the poor person is
> entitled to 100 million dollars. We don't want that to happen
> to you, do we?*

Of course not, it would ruin Walsh's plan and expose
Sexton's cover-up on the promissory fraud of nearly $2 million
dollars. Blackmailing the colored man into submission, he would
blow the whistle on him if he made one false move. Walsh moved
ahead with his inexorable purpose. In his Christmas letter to
Sexton, Walsh revealed his incredible insight into white-collar
analysis,

> *In the event there was a 1992 safflower contract offered to
> Pleasant Valley Corporation, or any agreement of that
> nature, it would certainly be a devastating situation if the
> judge called for three times the money. I ask you Hector to
> read over the Minnesota ASCS decision that went against
> David Zehlen. Then look at what will happen to him and all
> his associates, when you are the guy among your investors
> who ended up with all the money. Then look at what the
> intent was in 1992. Needless to say, that decision letter from*

the ASCS that has your signature all over it would be enough to scare me half to death.

I am pressing this issue of embezzlement with you before I report it to the police because it is obvious to me that act against the government was ordered by you, an indirect instruction through me that manager David Zehlen should take advantage of the United States government payment program for the requirement of your stakeholders Ceres, Lubrizol, and SVO. Based on the testimony of Adelman and the two Zehlen women before the USDA committee in St. Paul–everybody knows Zehlen and his associates did not receive the money directly. We know now don't we Hector that David and his partners were being used as a front to deceive the U.S. Government. But one thing I am certain of Hector, you do not want some zealous investigating agent from the justice department researching fraud, investigating predatory lending allegations my associates are already suspicious of, would you Hector? I am offering you the choice to sign on with Interwest before it turns out like the McDonald-Douglas case in Atlanta.

CHAPTER 42

While serving his sentence on related bank fraud charges in Nebraska, David contacted an organization called "Legalbeagle.org", a nonprofit legal defense fund that specialized in white collar crime, hoping to contribute as much knowledge and information as he could toward the restoration project he faced. He spent hours writing emails and letters to similar groups with no response, trying to muster interest in his case as he learned more about what he didn't understand of white collar crime conspiracy theory through research, using the new Windows computers in the library of the Lincoln correctional facility. After spending over a hundred thousand dollars in legal fees, distributed to at least eight attorneys and their prestigious legal firms, David was ready to try a different strategy than verbal jousting with a disinterested representative.

The documents he composed explained the confusing outcome, when for one reason or another each of his attorneys failed to recognize the *hydra*-like conspiracy that Robert Walsh, Hector Sexton and First Omaha Bank attorney Brent Wilber had assembled against him at a staggering price of $500,000 the "dream team" needed to accomplish its dreadful mission according to the much discussed Walsh to Sexton letter of December 1992–in evidence for a defense.

With time on his hands, David spent his lonesome hours combing through sample filing forms and legal documents, writing emails and letters to Beagle and similar groups, including Jerry Spence, with no response. He could handle the double billing explanation; all he needed were the invoices locked away in the Rockland courthouse. The ASCS issues and bank fraud were more serious matters that would require more analytics than he could muster with his limited experience in applying agricultural law.

As time went on, David's many hours in the prison library reaffirmed what he learned from Ferguson who stressed that improving his reading and writing skills were the keys to turn the tide of legal battle which had already cost him a fortune–closing in on a *decade* of his freedom. No one but Ferguson, and Antonelli in his lighter moments, understood what David was being dragged through–the writing his teachers agonized over to decode and analyze would eventually pay dividends; for the first time in his life David felt a certain power of the pen. Each discovery transcript he presented to counsel led to another suppressed argument handled by a sequence of incompetent, ineffective defense attorneys who failed to comprehend the chain links of the conspiracy. Someday he believed he would find the right attorney to represent his mounting claim for a referendum on his sentence based on violations of his civil rights.

David's most successful work during his ten-year probation and incarceration period, was in accumulating and storing records, as he adjusted his argument from one violation after another. Though it has its flaws, the structure of recovery in his mind is a testament of his ceaseless effort to restore his lost homestead–which was taking 10 years longer than it took the allies to recover Poland from the Nazis. David's accumulating batch of pro se drafts would eventually lead to a post-conviction relief motion, and his pro se memorandum State Attorney Richard Schmidt assembled for the Minnesota Appeals Court. As the narrative unfolded chapter by chapter out of the cold case files, exposing the inscrutable conspiracy in his imagination, it was as if Mr. Schmidt by some kind of miracle–*related* to David's new found literacy skills–suddenly appeared, becoming the first of a baker's dozen lawyers to suspect a conspiracy was involved in the Granite County judgment.

Eventually it became possible to detect Ferguson's influence on David's writing if not his attitude toward his situation; his psychological condition was improving as student and mentor exchanged files over the Internet–the combined work merged into a general memorandum of *failures* of the legal justice system. Foremost among the arguments was examining the abuse of process of prosecutor Watkins, who became obsessed with convicting David Zehlen of the vague crimes Walsh was accusing him of, after the personality clash in his office March 1993.

In retrospect, it was apparent defender John Holbrooke was selected by Judge Silas, and the Granite County State prosecutor and Walsh himself because he knew he could finesse the *Brady* issue with him. The defendant argues he is being denied access to exculpatory material; unfortunately, his public defender sides with the state's opinion that David never provided valid paperwork for the ASCS default; that reason was enough evidence to elevate the August 1992 penalty to felony latitude, when connected in Walsh theory with two other felonies in court. Zehlen became even more vulnerable in Granite County Court when a package containing a dozen duplicate invoices appeared on the prosecutor's desk a few days before the plea bargain hearing.

In Dave's words, "People I thought were friends my whole life suddenly turned against me." One of those supposed friends, Bill Watkins, was responsible for buying into Walsh's theory, preventing any other assumptions except those of David's guilt from emerging from the confusion. At the same time, the *scintilla* of evidence that a conspiracy existed in the 1992 Wilber conversion letter, that could have precluded summary judgment, was never introduced to the court by his public defender.

In his draft memorandum, David relied upon the 1985 *Hart and Honore* opinion arguing previously existing evidence that was not evaluated or used effectively, can be introduced as evidence for a new trial–in consequence of this finding David wrote his opinions to Rich Schmidt,

> The State Prosecutor Watkins appropriated information out of the Plaintiff's Voluntary Statement of March 3, 1993 that he then fabricated into a criminal complaint against the Plaintiff David Zehlen; and by such means and ends the prosecutor violated his constitutional rights. Instead of conducting a legitimate investigation of genuine material issues, Watkins constructed a deliberate and false indictment against Zehlen that was predicated on prejudice and twisting information extracted from the "Voluntary Statement" to suit the purposes of the conspiracy.

His document made more sense after Ferguson edited a few paragraphs, warning his friend, the counter-argument based on hard-copy evidence of the phony bills, aligned with the ASCS violation Walsh and Watkins detected in their version of the application for illegal personage, regardless of Ray Rylance counsel–was solid, when that money was intended to be distributed to seven MinGo partners, and six corporate partners, amounting to five hundred fifty thousand dollars or more–and the only second-signature on canceled checks relative to the government allocation was for $160K to Hector Sexton, *who was ineligible.*

"I don't know how you explain those issues, versus the facts you are up against David," Ferguson warned. "Although the conspiracy argument has its weaknesses unless you convince a law firm with major resources like Kaplan, willing to discover and investigate, building a case based on defining the invisible white collar crime, describing the actual strategy and methods of the conspiracy–it appears the conspiracy has a stronger case."

* * * * *

In the future David would have an explanation for his sons and grandsons similar to the explanations of *Job*, in the rehash of the events that had befallen him David responded, imitating Rich Schmidt's courageous stance at the Granite County appeal hearing,

"Your Honor if it pleases the court, the prosecutor in this case Attorney Watkins has revealed to you what little actual physical evidence he has that David Zehlen committed the felonies he plea bargained to, unwittingly, unknowingly. As you can tell there is no evidence on the exhibits table this time. I am here representing the State Attorney General's office in exposing to the court that Attorney Watkins has presented no evidence, but hearsay–in his prosecution of Mr. Zehlen," Schmidt was confident in his opening argument.

"What I am deconstructing for the court today are the series of false accusations presented in prosecutor Watkins' complaint, which is based on the same lack of evidence, and no investigation whatsoever, while avoiding issues of genuine material interest– the theft of David Zehlen's property for unproven reasons validates the false charges the conspiracy Robert Walsh, Hector Sexton and First Omaha Bank have assembled; these are the matters of genuine material we are dealing with here today, ten years after," Schmidt paused for ten seconds to review his notes.

"In the midst of twenty-six unverified Spriegl accusations and un-investigated allegations against my client, I am asking the court to reconsider its unfounded judgment of Mr. Zehlen, realizing there is something seriously missing in his defense. That would be the audit of his partner's accounting he requested many times, to Granite County attorney Bill Watkins and his public defender John Holbrooke. He was entitled to that audit; and his life depended on it. The conspiracy depended on *preventing* the audit," Schmidt cleared his throat and continued.

"What Mr. Watkins has not presented to the court is evidence of the conspiracy in action: the prosecutor realizes the information Mr. Zehlen does not have is crucial to his defense; that would be the forensic audit that Mr. Zehlen is entitled to and had asked for many times, which would prove the losses Mr. Sexton *claims to have suffered* are *fictitious* losses, created to cover up promissory fraud. On the other hand, and more importantly, I ask as the defense attorney David never had, why was it that the zealous prosecutor has never been required to provide those documents that indicate Sexton had made any kind of loan to Zehlen; nor has he presented any that indicate Mr. Sexton cancelled the contract?" Scanning the court Schmidt remained cool despite the controversy he intended to expose.

"And another question I ask you, where *are* the mysterious loan papers? If you will look up on the screen projector you will see, my office assistant has scanned Mr. Zehlen's contract for the court. As you can see, the agreement clearly exists, while no document canceling the contract has ever been entered in exhibits. Neither Mr. Sexton nor his lawyers can show the court those loan papers from 1991 and 1992–because they do not exist! Instead of due diligence that would have served David Zehlen, the interpretation forced upon this court ignores the indemnifying properties of the 1991 'guaranteed contract' between Zehlen and Sexton, just as David Zehlen's foremost false accuser Robert Walsh has indicated he would, in the letter in evidence I am presenting to the appeal panel at this time as exhibit A. If the court will observe the image on the screen please," Schmidt was more animated than usual, gesturing at the screen.

"Ladies and gentlemen of the court, you will see another letter that indicates the '*conversion of the contract to a loan*' thread of the conspiracy was in progress at that time; as early as spring 1991, the predatory loan strategy was in place in the conspiracy landscape. When the bank was informed the time was ripe, it was necessary to bring the half-million dollar '*dream team*' on board, using the same strategy it had relied on in similar cases; this maneuver was probably the most necessary, to extend the bottom line of the scheme, that financed the three hundred dollars an hour fees of the Wilber legal team. In ignoring the contract that existed between Sexton and Zehlen, Prosecutor Watkins confirmed his acceptance of the *nudum pactum* strategy the conspiracy designed," Schmidt was nearing the climax of his introduction. Appearing before the panel was nothing like court TV, closer to the reality of the law school practice arguments attorney Schmidt had learned to succeed from,

"If the panel will consult the evidence file before them defense has prepared; you will notice they correspond to the PowerPoint we have created for you on the screen. This same criminal sequence is indicated in the paragraph we refer to from the Pleasant Valley countersuit in January 1993–that would be the Sully lawsuit documentation Walsh initiated in his position as power of attorney." Hearing no objections Schmidt checked his Bulova, looking forward to an adjournment.

"We know Robert Walsh was still under contract with David Zehlen when he filed false charges against his employer. I ask you–is this not in direct conflict of interest to his employer? Walsh personally arranged the Brookings crop seizure stalemate–Walsh, the bank, and Hector allowed 15,000 acres of flowers to *wilt* in the field–to *succeed* in the illegal South Dakota lawsuit that preceded the case in November 1993; that event led to the Sexton/Ceres default judgment. I affirm before you today, that Mr. Walsh acted criminally and deliberately in not informing his manager of his intent to appropriate the Zehlen farming operations unto himself as a fake trustee. David Zehlen himself was so baffled by the Walsh dialogue and the equivocation about the contract by Sexton, he was unaware of what was happening to his farm except for a feeling something was haywire about the arrangement with the parties until November 1993–when the county unexpectedly filed charges against him. By then it had been two years since the conspiracy hatched against him shifted into battle mode. It would be another six months before David Zehlen reported that Hector Sexton was in breach of their business contract and marketing agreement to Granite County Attorney Bill Watkins, who was already on a five-thousand-dollar retainer from conspiracy central."

"*Brady* requires a prosecutor to disclose exculpatory evidence before the plaintiff waives trial and pleads guilty. With presumably all the exculpatory evidence he needed to clear himself in the South Dakota lawsuit unavailable to him, David Zehlen had no chance to defend himself against the Granite County prosecution process. His defense has recovered sufficient evidence of incompetence and undue prejudice demonstrated in the actions of Granite County Attorney William Watkins that amount to prosecutor misconduct in not bringing critical matters of genuine material interest to a jury trial of his peers; instead offering Zehlen no other choice than to plea-bargain to false and irrelevant charges, while the conspiracy proceeded through four jurisdictions unimpeded, manipulating court volition processes it controlled," Schmidt glanced at his notes for a few moments before continuing with his interpretation.

"Under the authority of the State Attorney General and his investigative staff, we intend to provide evidence of criminal intention and causation on the part of prosecutor Watkins. In order to accomplish the defense of Mr. Zehlen, we will review five counts of negligence and conspiracy that have not entered the dialogue, believing there is sufficient doubt of the effectiveness of the prosecutor's methods to raise the question of whether or not Zehlen's lack of adversarial counsel completely failed him in not validating the contract issues that predicated the fraud leading up to the bank's foreclosure behind false pretenses, he raised at the time of the voluntary statement." Attorney Schmidt wiped his brow with a tissue before continuing.

"David Zehlen claims that if the evidence had been evaluated through related-party transactions in and of secured contracts, the forensics would have exculpated him. This same audit would have inferred that Zehlen had no reason or motive in any but legitimate purposes; while he was falsely accused, he received no benefit whatsoever from criminal transactions he was accused of. He felt no need to further enrich himself when his farm was at the height of prosperity as the *Farm Future* article indicates," He thought he heard the word *amen* coming out of the Zehlen section, echo through the courtroom as Schmidt cleared his throat.

"According to plan, elements for a criminal conviction were fabricated and do not, nor ever did exist; there was never enough evidence to force David Zehlen into a defective plea except under the duress of threats by Watkins and Walsh as power of attorney for the farm who had tricked David's wife into believing that David Zehlen could not afford a private attorney, when there were adequate funds in the Pleasant Valley (now *Interwest*) treasury to afford an effective lawyer. Both Watkins and Walsh threatened Zehlen he was facing as many as twenty-six more *Spriegl* charges that could be filed immediately against him if he did not capitulate to the plea bargain already prepared for him. David Zehlen merely succumbed to human weakness, terror at the prospect of incarceration, and intimidation at the hands of his public defender he couldn't trust. We will mention RICO statutes violated in concluding remarks." Schmidt thumbed through his files searching for some persuasive idea, as the panel appeared opaque and unmoved, apparently annoyed that such an old case had not been settled in two decades. Schmidt used every minute, and, every tactic he could think of, including mystery to influence the appeal judges.

"The absence of a legitimate audit or attempt on the part of Watkins and Holbrooke to *require* one–is evidence for acquittal, for actions of the County Attorney's and the Granite County Court's neglect of due diligence that can be used in civil and criminal court–because lack of due diligence for a plaintiff's rights, allowed the false claims of the bank to succeed. Therefore, the Plaintiff asserts the Granite County court failed procedurally to fulfill its responsibility to investigate or verify the basis of the plea bargain before imposing a death penalty on Zehlen's business. A conviction cannot stand based on charges proved to be false. Mr. Zehlen was denied an audit when it would have provided evidence of loan personality, and collaterally-secured transactions that were never fully investigated by the FBI or the Secret Service." There was a pause in the hearing as defense attorney Schmidt fished his Rexall 2x magnifying glasses from his coat pocket to assist in reading the fine print on a document in the dimly lighted courtroom.

"My closing point today relates to the total failure of due diligence for David Zehlen's civil rights as demonstrated in the application of *contrived* summary judgment to suppress exculpatory information. As I conclude my appeal for justice today before you, Your Honors of the Appeal Court, we must conclude with Mr. Zehlen that in the design of the conspiracy, it has been absolutely necessary as part of the plan that predicated the plea bargain, to prevent the civil case in Sully and its connection to the Granite County swindle from ever being revealed. My shorthand–I remind you there could be a book written about this subject–and its implications as the foundation of class action, understates what is the defective product of lack of due diligence and failures of investigative responsibility by officers of the court such as those of Attorney Watkins and the deputy. Their combined errors of due diligence, each in his own fashion completely disregarding the civil rights of the victim–

instead of responding to a crime against the man's civil rights leading to quantum loss of property–David Zehlen's statement to the county attorney that he thought was his friend, became the *instrument* of prosecution, the exact opposite reaction intended, and devastating results for him and his family-owned business. Investigation of David's complaints that would have provided support for Mr. Zehlen, were effectively *suppressed* in the assumptions of Attorney Watkins, and outsider attorneys Wilber and Myers; in each of those situations affecting the bank's interests, summary judgment was used to suppress evidence vital to Zehlen which was *not its intended use*–and therefore that lawful power of the court to direct the 'flow of justice' has been misused and abused by Mr. Watkins," Schmidt paused, reading another paragraph, to match his thoughts with the paper trail he was unpacking.

"If you look at the screen in front of the court, you will understand why we are gathered here today; what you see is a crucial paragraph in the Zehlen PCR memorandum. On the basis of that argument, Granite County Attorney Bill Watkins is guilty of abuse of process for using his authority for a purpose it was not intended for; the county attorney's actions ranging from ineffective to indifferent and finally to culpable because of the retainer he accepted from the conspiracy–are proven to be acts that ultimately reinforced the organizational structure of the conspiracy that was legitimized through corrupt court process initiated in Granite County Court. As a consequence of catastrophic failures of due diligence, David Zehlen suffered irreparable damage from a plot that was intentionally designed to deceive the legal justice system. Because it was deliberately and cleverly concealed, it was sustained by prejudicial court processes managed by Robert Walsh and Prosecutor William Watkins to conceal the breach of contract, conflict of interest, and violations of confidentiality that led to the degradation of public defense counsel, and deprivation of all the victim's rights; and ultimately would lead to the conversion of millions of dollars of Plaintiff's property into the accounts of Robert Walsh, '*agent provocateur*' of the swindle." Schmidt displayed little emotion for his case he believed was based somewhat on circumstantial, but largely direct evidence, satisfied with details he interpolated to his scant audience, from voice, and screen, as he sifted through various papers in his file.

"Next Your Honors if it pleases the court, in deference to the non-linear design of the conspiracy I have just begun to describe for the appeal court, the defense of Mr. Zehlen will address the issue of ineffective assistance of counsel; and how that sequence contributed to an illegal plea bargain agreement that originated with and favored the conspiracy." Schmidt stepped aside from the microphone to suppress a cough. "Excuse me. I caught a chill staying at the Colombian." The sound of laughter rippled through the courtroom.

"Gentlemen this is a serious matter. Let me remind you. The most relevant evidence to the restitution appeal is the 1999 Jeff Thompson to Mayer letter in evidence in the federal bank fraud case; that paragraph refers to the missing information Zehlen needs, being withheld by the accusing parties, indicating the unwillingness of federal prosecutors to release that information to Zehlen. The Granite County appeal argument of the prosecutor indicates the same pattern of repression and negation of any and all exculpatory evidence existing today, as the guiding principle of obstruction at the heart of the prosecutorial method." State's Attorney Schmidt continued to pursue his argument in the wilderness.

"The plea bargain itself has been found to be contrary to legitimate judicial principles and procedures. This error cited, is evidence in itself of ineffectiveness of counsel. In fact, we believe the defective strategy of his public defender was the direct *cause* of his illegal convictions. If the mountain of evidence Sully amounted to is discounted in the calculus, it is evident the prosecutor made errors so serious as to deprive the accused of effective and competent legal counsel guaranteed the defendant by the Sixth Amendment as it has been applied under *Strickland* and *Morgan*. Conclusions that can be drawn from evidence withheld from Mr. Zehlen by his public defender, indicate that the deficient performance of David Zehlen's defense coupled with general prosecutorial misconduct of Attorney William Watkins 'severely prejudiced' *any* chance Zehlen had." Schmidt was visibly enervated as he approached the end of his argument, as if the prevailing attitude of indifference had sucked the volume of his voice into the void.

"Specifically counsel's errors in advocating summary judgment and plea bargain rather than a fair trial of the issues of genuine interest, relative to the complex and disputed contract involving millions of dollars–is unpardonable." State's Attorney Schmidt continued to pursue his tapestry of an argument.

"These actions led to forfeited collateral appropriations in a distant county in South Dakota; the remote location in a dysfunctional court room enabled the conspiracy to succeed without attracting attention of the media. In all justice to David Zehlen, failure to consider the value of the material of genuine interest under summary judgment rules amounts to *'errors of counsel'* that were so serious as to deprive the defendant of a fair trial. With respect to defense counsel's performance, Zehlen must show that counsel's representation fell below an objective standard of reasonableness which has been done. Until this time, however, his proofs have been obstructed by the ineffective counsel process described on the video, and in the course of my oral argument." With eyes on his notes the public defender continued. "Furthermore, David Zehlen asserts that a valid *contract* exists–he has documentation to prove that if it were examined and evaluated for its substantial 'weight and significance'–it would *prove* his argument. Finally, he has never received a cancellation notice on the original contract and therefore it is still valid." Schmidt continued his argument before the appeal board focusing on the conduct of the prosecutor.

"The next issue the State would like to bring before the court upon appeal, is Mr. Zehlen's assertion that the state failed to carry out its investigative responsibilities. If we examine the first page of the interview that framed the 63-page Voluntary Statement made by the Plaintiff David Zehlen to Granite County Attorney William Watkins, March 1, 1993, Watkins stated,

'Whatever you tell us can be put into a report, then we will review your information and conduct an investigation; charges may or may not be filed, depending upon what you may have to say to us.'"

"Under the intent clause of *Fed R. Crim. P. 11(f)–first*, as you see, the statute illustrated on the screen, the Prosecutor's statements indicate Mr. Watkins is aware of his responsibility to the Plaintiff in conducting an investigation. *Second*, the Prosecutor is aware that the Plaintiff is in circumstances that are reasonably likely to harm the Plaintiff. *Third*, the Prosecutor has indicated that he has an option to take such actions as may be expected to fulfill his investigative responsibilities to effectively protect the civil rights of the Plaintiff," Schmidt adjusted the focus for a few moments.

"The Prosecutor claims he was engaged in enforcement of a purpose, clearly stating he was *investigating* the charges *State of Minnesota v. David Zehlen, 06-11-8-000805*. However, William Watkins did not perform the necessary evaluation, analysis and discovery required under the circumstances, to understand matters of genuine material interest that would have established the Plaintiff's position as a person involved in a complex contractual arrangement–*beyond* the scope of summary judgment in terms of the millions of dollars riding on the contract. Therefore, the substance and complexity of the dispute indicates its resolution is beyond the borders of summary judgment. As you will notice in reference to the statute, in his actions Prosecutor Watkins sustained the will of the conspiracy because summary judgment is not intended to be used for interpreting contracts whose terms are not clear, straight forward and agreed on by all parties–and are clear and unambiguous despite the parties having divergent views on what the judgment provides, as in *Clemons*," Schmidt clicked ahead to the next image on the screen.

"Granite County Prosecutor William Watkins violated the Hippocratic oath of his profession, acting like a doctor taking the insurance but ignoring the injury–deliberately ignoring the prosecutor's duty to seek justice. With all due respect to the people of Granite County who have been deceived, and the long-standing reputation of Mr. Zehlen and his fourth generation family, attorney Watkins was aware of the people involved, and their untarnished reputation in the community; the prosecuting attorney indicated he was aware of his responsibility to conduct an investigation. Attorney Watkins should have known the consequences of error; and that he had an *obligation* to David Zehlen to conduct an inquiry due to the severity of crimes being discussed, the substantial monetary losses involved, and the number of people affected."

"Second. Mr. Watkins should have been aware these are *fatal* career-ending charges if proven; and that under the circumstances, Plaintiff David Zehlen could suffer substantial harm as a result of the situation being discussed on a voluntary basis. On the basis of the information Zehlen was delivering in the voluntary statement, he did not realize the risk he was taking, when he could be sent to prison and the *farm* could be lost. Similarly, Attorney Watkins' statement indicates that the circumstances could reasonably *harm* the Plaintiff," Schmidt clicked ahead to the next slide.

"Third. Attorney Watkins chose to take actions that could not be expected to effectively protect the interests of the Plaintiff Mr. Zehlen. Instead–Attorney Watkins chose to initiate the course of action the *conspiracy* prompted, when he stated– charges 'could be filed' against Mr. Zehlen."

"Fourth. Prosecutor Watkins' statement predicated his actions to fulfill his intention to accomplish a purpose *not intended by the law* which we will argue as abuse of process. In his actions, Mr. Watkins was commencing a prejudicial course of action against the Plaintiff rather than fulfill his investigative responsibilities. In this fallible and prejudiced aspect of misapplied due-diligence, prosecuting Attorney William Watkins erred significantly and grievously in his duties to the Plaintiff. You will notice the green highlighted paragraph where it says,

'Notwithstanding the acceptance of a plea of guilty, the court should not enter a judgment upon such plea without making such inquiry as shall satisfy it that there is a factual basis for the plea.'"

With these remarks Schmidt concluded the introductory portion of his opening argument stating,

"With the element of intent satisfied through proof-account logic, the rest of the elements of a criminal investigation also must be considered in the prosecutor's conduct. If there are no questions we will proceed with an examination of causation factors in the indictment of Mr. Zehlen, because in that aspect of his duty Attorney Watkins proceeded without empathy, concern, or due regard for the fact that Plaintiff was making a voluntary statement in his own words to,

> 'get this confusion about who owes who what cleared up and straightened around, I thought you could understand and help me get out of this mess my partners got me into Bill.'"

"If you glance at the overhead screen, you will notice these words highlighted in pink on the screen." State's attorney Schmidt argued that in not pursuing his rights, Watkins endangered the welfare of David Zehlen who was about to be foreclosed upon–and was in the process of being framed by his corrupt partners. In not investigating other interpretations of a complaint issued basically by Walsh, and rewritten by the Granite County Prosecutor, Watkins violated his responsibility and obligations to the victim of a conspiracy that was proceeding like clockwork on his watch. At 11:30, Appeal Court Judge James Morris called for a recess, with instructions court would resume at 10 a.m. the next morning.

CHAPTER 43

Appeal Court resumed the next morning with Richard Schmidt attacking the incompetence of the Granite County public defender's conduct.

"Yesterday we reviewed the intent portion of my memorandum argument if you will; thank you for your attention. On that basis Your Honors, *causation* is the second major category being reviewed before you today in the Watkins abuse of process issue. We are all aware that under normal probable-cause circumstances, an alleged criminal act is committed and a complaint is issued. In this situation–the opposite occurred. The Plaintiff David Zehlen came to the office of the county attorney for a discussion of genuine issues of material fact concerning a business contract with all the right intentions described above, to get matters cleared up," Schmidt adjusted the projector and cleared his throat.

"Excuse me, we are having some technical difficulties at the moment," Schmidt fiddled with the light control knob. "Instead of getting matters cleared up, the expressed intentions of the plaintiff caused Attorney William Watkins to fabricate criminal charges against a victim; these charges were then constructed into a basis upon which the plaintiff Zehlen was prosecuted. In the *Shoup* case the *Franklin* Supreme Court ruled that,

> 'the State must provide a direct causal relationship between the defendant's conduct and the alleged fate of the victim.'"

"In the Zehlen case, that chain of causation has been tampered with by a series of *false* accusations Granite County law enforcement never investigated. Later, *Franklin* clarified its decision stating,

> 'criminal responsibility is properly assessed against one whose conduct was a direct and substantial factor in

producing the result even though other factors may have combined with that conduct and achieved the result.'"

"The court found that a defendant could be *liable* as a direct and *substantial* factor in the victim's fate. Therefore, it is the burden of Plaintiff to prove the prosecutor's conduct–not David Zehlen's–was a direct and substantial factor in determining the fatal judgment in Granite County that Zehlen is appealing for relief from at this time." Schmidt took a sip of his water.

"Under first cause, the plaintiff in his walk-in conference stated multiple times that he was having difficulties collecting a legitimate contractual debt from one of his business partners, Hector Sexton. Each time David Zehlen mentioned this particular set of circumstances, Attorney Watkins failed to ask pertinent investigative questions–either *deliberately* or *for lack* of pertinent interest that would have established Mr. Zehlen's just claims for payment on a legal contract. Instead, Mr. Watkins created an inquiry that was designed to question the *credibility* of Plaintiff's claims. This *bias* was demonstrated continuously throughout the March 1993, 63-page voluntary statement." Schmidt remained unemotional as he defined various aspects of the conspiracy.

"Under second cause, Defendant was aware a contract violation existed that Plaintiff believed was caused directly by Ceres failure to properly capitalize the seven MN Go partners in 1991. Appearing on the screen, I refer to *David Zehlen v. State of Minnesota,* Court File No: 06-K9-93-44; first page on the overhead, it is clear from the prosecutor's *'Answer to the Petition of the Plaintiff'* signed by William Watkins September 2003, the Defendant meets the first element of the test of culpability–awareness of his duty–to at the very least understand the Plaintiff's concerns 'for the genuine material issues of the contract' comes to mind," Schmidt adjusted the focus on some irrelevant handwriting in the margins interrupting the flow of his speech for a few seconds.

"Finally we have come to a third cause. Despite the fact Prosecutor Watkins was repeatedly informed by Mr. Zehlen that a contractual matter between himself and Hector Sexton was the information he needed to understand–and was the genuine material interest–that data set before the court proved, 'would constitute a legal defense to the claim of the Plaintiff.' Unfortunately for Mr. Zehlen, the record indicates this course of proper procedure was not followed in Granite County." Attorney Schmidt was not surprised no objections were raised to his version of events as he continued.

"In violation of *Brady*, Prosecutor Watkins failed to pursue the required and correct legal process. In prosecution, he made no clear statement of what the *evidence* incriminating Zehlen was; *that* information remains sealed and concealed from David Zehlen. Furthermore, the information Zehlen delivered to Watkins was never brought to trial in an effective and organized fashion, as the basis of a defense that presented Zehlen's case accurately and understandably."

"Under those auspices, prosecutor Watkins himself became initial judge and jury within a closed system of justice–like the appearance of *Caiaphas* before Herod–in a strategy determined to make *his* and Walsh's theory stick. In legal terms of prejudice, which means to pre-judge, Prosecutor Watkins formed his judgment before Zehlen had a chance to present his case. He has become culpable for prosecutorial misconduct for his failures of due diligence in the process of prejudice for the conspiracy." Schmidt paused for a taste of his ice water before continuing.

"The plaintiff naively believed he had a quarter-share of the market on the new partnership with the Sexton deal to count on–unaware until years later of Walsh and Sexton's criminal activity going on behind his back and *apparently* in judge's chambers. Though he presented general details of the promissory fraud Sexton was engaged in, Zehlen had no idea of the connections and separate motives of *each* of the parties to the conspiracy." Schmidt appeared to be faltering after his previous intensity as he scanned the panel of state attorneys for a reaction.

"If the prosecution had performed its due diligence, making even the slightest effort to investigate the allegations of fraud David Zehlen was making in his office–dealing with complex contract matters that were true issues of genuine material interest to Zehlen–the case would have been different. If Watkins had examined the direct evidence of the contract details: specifications, signatures, loan limits, payments due, and guarantees–there would have been more than enough exculpatory information for the plaintiff to *preclude* summary judgment." Schmidt was beginning to realize more than ever, just how iffy the Zehlen case was, buried much deeper in the *occult* of confusion–going far beyond what he ever imagined when he agreed to represent Zehlen on the PCR sentencing issue.

"In addition, although supported allegations in Plaintiff's petition do not necessarily establish clear evidence, until an investigation is conducted to affirm his claims, at least in their magnitude, Mr. Zehlen's account *proofs* clearly establish sufficient basis on which to oppose the original summary judgment that predicated a '*coerced*' plea-bargain David Zehlen accepted in Granite County–and under extreme duress–in a mental condition that rendered him *incapable* of contributing to his defense. Therefore, if we examine a fourth cause, you will notice up on your screen the *Matthew v. Johnson* ruling citing *Brady* that requires a prosecutor to disclose exculpatory evidence for purposes of ensuring a fair trial–to ensure justice is done to the accused, as well as to the state–that concern and due diligence along with it, often quoted as a basic problem of plea-bargain theory, is *absent* when an innocent defendant waives trial and pleads guilty to fabricated charges. That particular chapter of infamy was openly ignored–along with the December 1992 letter of direct *evidence of intent*–by prosecutor Watkins in his crusade to bring the wrong man to justice. In this case, the Prosecutor William Watkins effectively avoided this requisite for a fair trial; in doing so the prosecutor succeeded in shifting the *substantial weight* of the 'material of genuine interest' to other irrelevant issues–phony bills at that time." Although his words sounded inflammatory at moments, Schmidt remained cool amidst the allegations he was exposing.

"The point I am trying to make–long overdue before the honorable judges of the appeals panel is this: a prosecutor is *required* to disclose *'evidence favorable to the accused, that if suppressed would deprive the accused of a fair trial.'* In this case, it was the prosecutor's illegal actions that determined the outcome of Granite County judgment and the fate of David Zehlen," the public defender hesitated paging through his notes.

"There is probable cause for censure, that Mr. Watkins faces an investigation of misconduct before the LPRB that will be reviewing the matter in the future, as I am. I need not go into further detail. A higher court will explore that as what may be overwhelmingly judgmental upon the conduct of the prosecutor; even at a cursory level observation of behavior–his *culpability* is for other courts to decide. We are here to deal with the damage to Mr. Zehlen's life, the *ruin* of his family and his reputation that has been caused by the county prosecutor's lack of professional conduct befitting an officer of the court in his performance–and *void* of attention to due diligence for the victim of a conspiracy–that he by his actions, unwittingly or otherwise has become a part of." The hush over the court intensified as Schmidt approached his conclusion.

"Our office believes a new interpretation is necessary; counter judgment is appropriate in cases of *'extraordinary failures of justice'* I am describing to the appeals court; that opinion was never more relevant than today, because if the actual subject material of the multiple-counts against the Plaintiff in *State of Minnesota vs. David Jay Zehlen* is examined, and compared relative to reasonable probable cause presented– it is apparent the conspiracy could not even *frame up* a charge that made sense–and yet they would *'convict a man on hearsay'* of a convicted felon–Robert Walsh."

"Furthermore, there is no correlation between the charge that defendant David Zehlen,

'did obtain for himself the possession, custody or title to property of another by intentionally deceiving another with false representations which he knew to be false, and made with intent to defraud the person.'"

"Where the conspiracy against him is *obvious*–no clear evidence has *ever* been produced by prosecutors acknowledging the existence of a viable theory of *loss* as alternative explanation–only a *mystery* about the 'mechanics' of the conspiracy exists," Attorney Schmidt was thinking of a way to end his speech in the impending gloom of the courtroom.

"Applying the *Hart Honore* theory, a new interpretation is appropriate where there is doubt; we base our assumptions on the fact Watkins used accusations of the admitted primary conspirator Robert Walsh to organize a complaint based on false allegations in the memorandum. These allegations were then assembled into the host of false charges Zehlen was *bluffed* into pleading guilty to. In fact, the genuine material issues of the disputed Plaintiff contract have absolutely nothing to do with 'custody or title to property' *or* David Zehlen deceiving another one way or the other." His face had turned a brighter shade of pink in the sweltering court room, as Schmidt lambasted the Granite County Court in his closing argument.

"But ladies and gentlemen of the panel, by now you realize– those issues have *everything* to do with covering up systematic fraud across three jurisdictions using language, and lexical measures to achieve the prize. Prosecutor Watkins' interpretations of vague crimes are nothing more than hearsay issues fabricated by the corroborating state's prosecutor in Granite County. Watkins has fabricated a false case against the most successful private businessman, in terms of gross income per year, this community has ever seen. While we witnessed a man obsessed with envy and greed bolster his bogus FBI resume–adding weight as a false witness, making charges that are aiding and abetting the conspiracy–against an innocent man," Schmidt paused to review a paragraph.

"At this moment, I would ask the panel to observe exhibit D on the overhead. Could you put that screen up for me again please? Thank you. Now then, here we see the actual conversion letter of the Zehlen contract to a loan from the bank. This correspondence between Wilber and Myers, was dated a year before the Granite County 'plea bargain'–evidence the conspiracy existed was *ignored* when David was told he could not use evidence from the civil case in his criminal case by his public defense team headed by prosecutor William Watkins."

"If any more evidence of quantum failure in due diligence is necessary for the State Appeal Board to overrule the biased judgment, I have more samples of the same obstruction of justice process. The best example is evident when Judge Silas lacked meaningful insight and discretion into the plot and story; evidence is rampant in his ridiculously harsh wood-shedding of Zehlen–calling him a public *nuisance*–as the conspiracy stripped the 4th generation heir to the throne of Pleasant Valley to *nothing* for David's supposed 'lack of remorse' for the seriousness of his crimes." Rich Schmidt paused a second, taking a draught of bottled Mission Hills spring water, replacing the previous day's foul tasting local water, and then continued.

"In my closing remarks, I will attempt to have more mercy on Granite County Attorney Watkins than he showed toward David Zehlen. He deserves that much credit for accepting Walsh's word alone.

Demonstrated by the beating he is delivering upon David Zehlen, some might argue the county attorney is saving unnecessary *expense* for the state, believing as in *Franklin*–the Walsh *intent* is outweighed in the assumption the victim was the initial cause–just as the other supposed victims were; and under that interpretation, what could be discovered as a class-action level plot. Walsh was administering the final solution to the expendables–crushing the slim hopes of survivors of the savings and loan crisis–offering those farmers the only chance they had of a fresh start through a *no-risk* deal like Dave had with the bank, Sexton, Ceres arrangement; in assumption of original sin, the manipulation of Robert Walsh becomes a secondary factor." As he adjusted his reading glasses Schmidt took a deep breath and glanced at the image on the screen, steadying himself for the final assault on the beachhead.

"Assuming the court knows beyond vague doubt–judgment was based upon a corrupt process to convict David Zehlen of false charges. We now know one man is the mastermind of the miscarriage of justice this appeal is based on, because Mr. Watkins has alleged that the historically-based business practices of Mr. Zehlen are criminal. Mr. Watkins has presented no evidence beyond the biased opinions he was indoctrinated with by Robert Walsh, Hector Sexton and the bank who are the main conspirators." Schmidt hesitated remembering his speech coach's advice.

"Today I stand before you and deliver the evidence that must be exposed once and for all to the people who suffered through it in the original Minnesota jurisdiction in which the versions emerged. And by that I mean, envy mixed with greed–personal enrichment–is at the heart of this strategy we have been uncovering. That content along with the physical evidence of property lost will be dissected under forensic science guidelines. Your Honors I submit to you, the multiple units of the Zehlen appeal itself is united under one banner," Rich looked up at the screen as the bold title "White-Collar Corruption in Granite County" appeared. The court was silent as the panel stared at the black and white image for several minutes.

"Before I discuss the third count of causation Mr. Zehlen is placing before the judges of the appeal panel this morning, I would like to make one more point of what counsel for Mr. Zehlen has determined to be evidence of 'abuse of process' in the prosecutor's conduct, instead of *due diligence* for rights of Mr. Zehlen. If you look up at the screen you will observe that on March 1, 1993, David Zehlen made a 'Voluntary Statement' before Granite County Attorney, William Watkins with the intention to, 'get this stuff, cleared up, straightened around' on page 10 of the 63-page statement. Ladies and gentlemen if you observe the document on the screen we can clearly see Mr. Zehlen's intent and honest responses; his words are highlighted in yellow. At that time, Mr. Zehlen firmly believed that the information he was disclosing to the county prosecutor was not evidence of intention. In his opinion David Zehlen felt that he was describing a business situation that required some discussion involving legal details of a contract between him and his partner Hector Sexton. Therefore, it is for this purpose we review the memorandum paragraphs on the screen, which were those submitted to the State Attorney General's office. I am referring to Exhibit B, the Zehlen pro se memorandum to the Appeals court:"

1. [Intent] that the Defendant made an illegal, improper, perverted use of the process, a use neither warranted nor authorized by the courts, and,

2. [Intent] that the Defendant had an ulterior motive or purpose in exercising such illegal, perverted, or improper use of the process, and,

3. [Intent] caused catastrophic damage to the plaintiff from the illegal direction of the prosecution's case leading to abuse of process.

"Even a superficial reading of the voluntary statement indicates that Prosecuting Attorney William Watkins had no interest in the material of fact that was being presented in the interview–other than applying his biased judgment. Mr. Watkins had no interest whatsoever in the issues of genuine material interest, the breach of contract and promissory fraud David Zehlen believed he was experiencing with Hector Sexton his partner. We have provided evidence Mr. Watkins was on the offensive by March 1993, after he accepted a retainer from Robert Walsh."

"In response to these matters, Mr. Watkins was aware a contract violation existed that plaintiff Zehlen believed was 'caused directly by Ceres failure to properly capitalize his South Dakota partners.' David Zehlen v. State of Minnesota Court File No: 06-K9-93-44, that was predicated by Zehlen's 'Voluntary Statement' of March 1, 1993, and was converted to three false charges–instead of the intervention Zehlen sought on the part of law enforcement–State's Attorney Watkins created a voluntary statement event into evidence of mens rea. He had no reason, but the hearsay of Walsh at the time, to ignore Zehlen's complaint except the previous indoctrination by Robert Walsh. Mr. Watkins turned the occasion into an opportunity to administrate his own version of justice–in kangaroo court I have heard some say–that amounts to evidence of prosecutorial misconduct." Pausing for several minutes, Schmidt wiped his brow with a fresh white handkerchief.

"Now then, with the intent element of the second count of 'Abuse of Process' satisfied, we move on to causation; other evidence will prove beyond reasonable doubt that the defendant's actions endangered the liberty and property of the plaintiff. Therefore, causation directly or indirectly related to Abuse of Process is a major issue concerning Mr. Watkins' prosecutorial method. In previous decisions, courts have determined that in abuse of process the basis of the tort is not commencing an action or causing a prosecution without justification, but rather–*misusing* or *misapplying* processes–for an end *other than that which it was designed to accomplish.*" Schmidt pointed at the screen.

"And that ladies and gentlemen of the appeal board, is exactly what Mr. Watkins did–as he turned David Zehlen's well intentioned voluntary statement into a plea bargain to false charges," Schmidt recalled his cross-country races trailing by a quarter mile at the finish line. "It should be apparent by now, Mr. Watkins conducted himself in a fashion contrary to his responsibility in the legal process, ignoring his obligations to the accused under the circumstances, as he transformed what David Zehlen thought was supposed to be a routine day at the prosecutor's office–into a post-modern day version of the Spanish Inquisition."

CHAPTER 44

In the aftermath of an unsuccessful Granite County post-conviction relief appeal, and continuing his string of successes after the Sully pro se lawsuit, Walsh subsequently appeared in Granite County probate court a number of times introducing motions relative to the distribution of the fortune of Queen Latifa Borbon Borbon, mysterious heir to the Spanish throne in dispersion, inheritor of a billion dollar Euro-African fortune in gold, silver, and priceless art that Walsh was supposedly an administrator of in *this* country–those wonders would one day appear in the Granite County Museum of History he promised to support; that *gift*, among others presumably, amounted to nothing more than adding layers and extensions to the money-laundering schemes Walsh managed, associated with his Marketing International business. Probating the vague Borbon Borbon entities and properties from the Mediterranean gulf through Granite County Court, Walsh maintained relative anonymity as he disposed of, and distributed Pleasant Valley farms property–along with the queen's assets–well into the new millennia. In an unexpected turn of events, a notice appeared in *The Independent* paper a week after the man passed away October 29, 2010:

> In memory of a beloved husband and father his family honors Robert Walsh who maintained strong and deep roots in farming, livestock and hunting even when his professional journeys led him in other directions. He was an award winning automobile and truck salesman at Christiansen Cadillac in Brookings, SD where he eventually served as an award winning Regional Sales Manager. Robert operated the Brookings Livestock Auction in the mid-1970's; his close friends knew him as a model Christian always ready to lend a helping hand, he sparked renewed enthusiasm in the Crystal Springs Rodeo as its owner for several years in the 1980's. In his dedicated and spiritual journey through the farming industry, livestock and grain marketing and buffalo

ranching near Sturgis, SD in endeavors and achievements that ranged from the Nundas, Rutland, Wentworth, and Madison area to other locales in the Midwest, and Texas. Robert worked with various global organizations exploring new horizons and opportunities. He spent his career dedicated to the benefit of the customers he serviced through his business Marketing International located in Brookings. SD. Robert was a committed and undying advocate for farmers and livestock producers in South Dakota and the United States, serving as Director of Agricultural Marketing for the State of South Dakota by appointment of Governor Bill Janklow. He achieved honor and recognition truly deserved for his contributions to child nutrition and health research as a member of the National Nutrition Committee at the request of President Jimmy Carter. Robert was selected by his peers as both President of the South Dakota Livestock Breeder's Association and as National Director for the National Cattleman's Association.

A true believer Robert desired no earthly reward for his contributions to humanity, or his countless kind deeds; we honor the undying Good Samaritan principles he adopted and expected other people to live by. His family is so thankful to be able to celebrate the life of faith he led–for that virtue above all Robbie (as he was called by his many friends and associates) would like to be remembered, for his many contributions to humanism which his deep faith in both the Catholic and Lutheran religion centered around; of even greater significance to Robert and the people he served, was his undying devotion to the Blessed Virgin.

CHAPTER 45

In the month before Walsh passed on to his final reward, Ferguson had a dream slash nightmare as he called them.

"I usually rank my dreams in importance David, according to how relevant they are to events. I wasn't ready to discuss this one with you because I wasn't sure what it symbolized. The night of the dream, Susan and I had just been to her niece's wedding in Hastings, Minnesota. We had a good time chatting with all the relatives and such. I tipped a few too many wine coolers, so Susan who doesn't drink drove back from the evening reception. It was the weekend of teacher's conferences so I was home early that Friday. I had spent the remainder of the day scanning and printing your voluntary confession. Good thing I had a new cartridge; those things are as expensive as the printer. That task alone took over an hour at 63 pages. I barely made it to the post office in time to send it off to you."

"I know I pressured you on that Jim; but I needed the research information for my attorneys. Then they never even looked at it; we will see if my new attorney can read plain English, unlike Majers, Boulton, and Orlando–attorneys who did nothing for me. Holbrooke forked me for free, literally. Thanks again for setting me on the straight and narrow."

"Don't thank me alone David. Susan helped. We English majors are project oriented. Sometimes I swear she knows more about your case than I do."

"I hope so. I put that woman on a pedestal in my younger days. But she was ten years older than me Jim; or I would have proposed, right there and then. Look what I wound up with instead?"

"Changing the subject, you mentioned how much revenue hunting brings to the county–my nightmare gives a little more of the psychic perspective. When I was in graduate classes at state college back in the day, I was lodging with my soon to be sister in law. You probably knew her as Cindy White. I used to take her son Brian Rustad out to the mall now and then, handing him a pocket full of quarters to play the video gallery while I checked out *Barnes and Nobel* on a quiet winter night. That kid could have spent another hour on his favorite video game–*Wolf Hunter*. I observed his shooting skill closely; he would drop in a quarter, first this dark shadow appeared stretching out across an open field in the moonlight; then a close-up of his yellow eyes, a red mouth dripping blood, his tongue licking pearly white teeth in a close-up appears, red tracers followed the path of this huge black wolf loping across an open field. In the dream, I was tracking him through Brian's red paint ball gun scope. I tried it a few times, never actually hitting the beast on the screen–but my nephew could bring it down every time. You had to hit the beast exactly in the heart or lungs; or the bullets bounced off."

"So what does that tell you about my case Jim?" David asked as if he was bored with the details.

"I'm coming to that part. So then the dream went on like this; in the scene now, it is me standing at the video game controller device. Across the video screen there comes this huge beast about ready to charge out of the scene into my face, unless I can bring him down, this time is for keeps as the spectacle was on the big movie screen; just like I'm in the old 'Orpheum' in Rockland; the red dots were following the wolf, slowly gaining ground."

"That theater's not there anymore Jim. Old man Wellendorf tore it down and made a brick house on the lake out of it. I used to fish with him and your Uncle Jiggs."

"I heard that. Finally, I laid a shot into his shoulder blade area. I could tell because it staggered a bit like a whitetail buck hit in the lungs with a twelve-gauge slug."

"I saw that happen once on opening day of deer hunting when I was with my dad and Uncle Monte. We had to track that deer in the snow for at least an hour before it toppled over in the corn. They say the lungs fill up with blood, the deer suffocates."

"That's right, and then you know what happens next. This is a nightmare mind you. Apparently the slug hit the lungs, not the heart; or it would have dropped like an anvil–the beast kept running, slowly, winding down. Finally, the wolf dropped to its knees."

"That was it? But what does that have to do with my dilemma Jim?"

"Nothing yet Dave, like I said the dream had two parts. The first one was very vivid, like a cartoon. I had to analyze that nightmare a while until I released my autopsy. The scenario shifted–like I was standing at my scanner, like the day you were copying the phony bills in Walsh's office. As I was going about my task, you think about where the light from the scanning bar moves along the bed when you press the green button. You see these thousand points of light moving along the edges of a document. In the next scene these tiny flashes of light became a host of mini angels surrounding the scanner bed. When I lifted the cover–like a small shapeless object appeared on the bed of the scanner that materialized into a tiny 'Rodin' sculpture of a man reduced to his knees. In a split second, the figure disappeared in a puff of white smoke. Can you can think of any relevance in part two David?"

"Yes, a situation comes to mind when I imagine that sequence is relevant, because it means something to me personally" –then it all went up in smoke, Dave reflected on the musical phrases that added sense to his life. "Walsh would joke about death when he was being sociable, being cynical like a mean clown you might say. Once I heard Walsh talking with Phyllis about modern cremation technology when his wife wasn't recovering well after some serious female surgery in Sioux Falls. On the dark side, Walsh was associated with the occult as much as his religion–if you want my opinion."

"In his own crude way, Walsh was reminding Phyllis all the time what a practical man he was. Robbie was prepared in case Shirley didn't make it. A modern funeral he said can cost fifteen thousand, while the alternative is much cheaper than a standard plan. Not all the fuss either; they incinerate the whole shebang, coffin and all. He had it all arranged. My guess was at that time Shirley didn't know what Robbie was up to on his midnight runs from Nundas to nowhere. She owns Anothene now. Rumor has it the area health services bought it from somebody–or appropriated it, and are remodeling it into a downtown clinic and counseling center. They rent the presidential suite for $1500.00 month to an H.M.O," Dave laughed in an affected tone of grief as he completed the sentence.

"And the best news of all Dave–is that Walsh saved us all the trouble of hunting him down–finally, we have Robbie in a box where he can do no more harm." Ferguson was satisfied that some kind of resolution was imminent, as he handed Dave a tiny jump drive. "I squeezed all the drama I could get out of it David. Take a look at this last piece of work I have been chipping away at for the record; no sense talking MVR when you can't find a lawyer to take the case. The subject is predatory lending–and how that motive segues into the promissory fraud."

"I certainly will from now on Jim. I don't know what I would have done if you hadn't taken your psychic interest in the case seriously when I have no training in that area, in dealing with my sisters, and my sons–apparently away from your main interest in my case that always seems to be about these moral and ethical issues I seldom think about–I don't know how to explain it. I hope somebody can understand the psychology input, because Ansel Walsh had a huge impact with his reports in the Granite County judgment."

"As Samaritans we do our best work. Researching the case fulfilled my latent needs as a research assistant, my preferred work in forensics of the text–focusing on a case where they never found the body, the murder weapon or any evidence of a *homicide*–and *you* David fit the suspect's description. And now I believe I have found a worthy subject documenting the damage Walsh caused–to channel my English author personality into. I never was much of a non-fiction writer you know. My goal will be to transform your continuous memorandum into a novel."

The End (Part I)

"I shall no longer be called a ravening *wolf* on account of your ravages but a worker of the Lord distributing food to them that work what is good."

– Lost Books of Eden

Made in the USA
Lexington, KY
14 July 2017